Investigating
High-Tech Crime

Investigating
High-Tech Crime

Michael Knetzger
Jeremy Muraski

PEARSON
Prentice
Hall

ISBN 0-13-188683-5

Upper Saddle River, New Jersey 07458

Library of Congress Cataloging-in-Publication Data

Knetzger, Michael R.
  Investigating high-tech crime / Michael R. Knetzger, Jeremy A. Muraski.
   p. cm.
  Includes index.
  ISBN 0-13-188683-5
  1. Computer crimes—Investigation—United States.   2. Computer crimes—United States.
  3. Computer crimes—United States—Prevention.   4. Computer security—United
States—Evaluation.
  1. Muraski, Jeremy A. II. Title.

  HV8079..C65K54 2008
  363.25'9680973—dc22   2006051565

Editor-in-Chief: Vernon R. Anthony
Senior Acquisitions Editor: Tim Peyton
Assistant Editor: Mayda Bosco
Editorial Assistant: Jillian Allison
Marketing Manager: Adam Kloza
Managing Editor: Mary Carnis
Production Liaison: Barbara Marttine
  Cappuccio
Production Editor: Linda Zuk, WordCraft, LLC

Manufacturing Manager: Ilene Sanford
Manufacturing Buyer: Cathleen Petersen
Senior Design Coordinator: Christopher
  Weigand
Cover Designer: Allen Gold
Cover Image: Nice Rowe/Getty Images
Formatting: Carlisle Publishing Services
Printing and Binding: R. R. Donnelley & Sons

Pearson Education Ltd.
Pearson Education Singapore, Pte. Ltd.
Pearson Education Canada, Ltd.
Pearson Education—Japan

Pearson Education Australia PTY, Limited
Pearson Education North Asia Ltd.
Pearson Educacion de Mexico, S.A. de C.V.
Pearson Education Malaysia, Pte. Ltd.

13
ISBN 0-13-188683-5

To my wife Lisa,
whose patience, love, and dedication made this possible ~
I love you.

To my children, Ashley, Madeline, and Noah ~
less time typing, more time with you.
I love you too.

—Mike Knetzger

To Sarah and Brooke,
whose endless patience, support, and encouragement
make anything seem possible.

—Jeremy Muraski

Contents

chapter four

chapter five

chapter six
TRACKING AND TRACING INTERNET CRIMES   147

chapter seven
PEDOPHILES, ONLINE CHILD ENTICEMENT, AND CHILD PORNOGRAPHY   183

chapter eight

chapter nine

chapter ten

chapter eleven

Preface

This is a book about the continuing evolution of criminal behavior and criminals' adaptation to the technological world we live in. Although traditional crimes continue to be a problem, law enforcement is now faced with the additional challenge of combating a new criminal element. Instead of wearing masks and carrying guns, some criminals now sit behind keyboards and mask their identities electronically. Whereas a traditional bank robbery might yield $10,000, the skilled computer criminal can potentially make millions.

Law enforcement is constantly adapting to the latest criminal trends, and in past generations the adaptation usually involved adjusting to a new technology. The inventions of gunpowder and the automobile drastically changed law enforcement and those inventions can be perceived as the boundaries of different eras. The invention of the automobile heralded the end of horseback marshals and introduced the era of high-speed chases. Similarly, the computer age marks the beginning of a new era in law enforcement, and those of us in the field must adapt to fight these new criminals, while also continuing our traditional policing.

The realm of high-technology crime unfortunately presents many great challenges to law enforcement. Previous inventions had a pervasive effect on society, and there is no reason to think that computers and technology will be any different. People rely more and more on technology to perform even mundane tasks such as retrieving money from an automatic teller machine (ATM). We are, like a gangly teenager, in that awkward time between the beginning of a change and its total effusion into society. Until such time as all law enforcement officials have grown up with computers, using them for their entire lives, there will be many in the field who do not possess the requisite skills to understand or investigate the crimes based on this technology. In fact, many perceive computing as a "foreign language." Other challenges to law enforcement include the ongoing battle of the budget, straining to keep a sufficient number of well qualified officers employed, and adding the additional responsibilities of homeland security to our duty list. Because training and equipping a high-tech computer crime team are both expensive and time-consuming, they are perceived by some as the last straws that can break the budget's back. However, failing to prepare and take action will be far more expensive for society as a whole in the long run.

Recognizing the problems inherent in being in the early and middle stages of this dynamic shift, we began creating classroom materials to teach the concepts in this book to law enforcement officers. Officers discovered, as their development progressed, that there was no one source of information on this topic. It was this desire to create a teaching textbook as well as a field reference guide that led us to create a proposal for writing this text. Because of its dual role, the material presented has to be easy to learn and comprehend, and the text must be well organized for easy reference in the future. The experience gained from teaching hundreds of law enforcement officials, from police officers to probation agents, has shaped our teaching style and subsequently the style presented in this book.

Because we recognize that the book will be used to teach a wide variety of people from the absolute beginner to the seasoned computer user, we use a building-block approach, starting with broad base-level knowledge chapters and working steadily toward explaining the complex rules and methodologies associated with a full computer seizure and forensic examination. The preliminary building-block chapters enable the "newbies" to learn at their own pace and learn the language of computers. This text hopefully also demystifies the notion of computers as "magic boxes" that seems to intimidate many people, including our brave men and women in uniform.

Acknowledgments

This textbook would not have been possible without the loving support of my wife Lisa. Her willingness to stand by me and take care of the many day-to-day activities involved in raising a family allowed me to spend countless hours researching and writing the manuscript. I love you. To my children—Ashley, Madeline, and Noah—who have not seen enough of their daddy lately, this book is that light at the end of the tunnel. I love you all. To my parents, Thomas and Llani Knetzger, who have supported me in all my endeavors and without whom this text would have never been written, I love you, too.

A special thank-you is due Elizabeth Paape, a fantastic associate dean in the NWTC Criminal Justice Division who has opened up countless educational and teaching opportunities for me. You supported our vision of a high-tech crimes course for first responders, and here is the ideal text for that course and many others throughout the country. Thank you to the entire NWTC criminal justice team: Associate Dean Ed Jahnke; Instructors Robert Willis, Mike Albertson, Kevin Rathburn, Ian Nishimoto, Randy Revling, Dave Allen, Dawn VanBuren, and Gail Mandli; support staff members Annette Halverson, Lou Damiano, Tom Martin (who yells because he cares), and Sara Deuchert. To CTU*online* Dean of Academic Affairs Lauren Woods, who introduced me to the dynamic world of online learning, and Associate Dean Eric Jankovic, whose progressive thinking keeps the CTU*online* Criminal Justice Division on the cutting edge of virtual learning.

Thank you to ITT Tech Associate Dean Scott Borley and Criminal Justice Chair Mike Schneider for the creative criminal justice teaching opportunities. Finally, to all of my current and future students, a criminal justice career is a noble one that requires unmatched dedication to the values of liberty, freedom, and equality of justice for all. Embrace those concepts and continue to make America great. And to all those who wear the uniform: together we walk the thin blue line between order and chaos.

I credit my very good friend, colleague, and coauthor Jeremy Muraski with introducing me to the world of computers. Thank you for sharing your vast knowledge of everything high tech and putting up with my workaholic qualities. Our vision has become a reality! I would be remiss if I didn't mention Sarah Muraski—thanks for providing us with the best brain food of all: homemade chocolate chip cookies.

Mike Knetzger

Numerous people in my life provide me with the best support network a man could ask for. To my wife, Sarah, I cannot hope to adequately express my love and gratitude for all of your additional work and support over the last year and a half. From helping with editing drafts to providing "healthy" snacks, you have definitely been there for me throughout this process. Your ability to juggle tasks while teaching our daughter so much was a source of inspiration during the late nights. To my daughter Brooke, literate 4-year-old computer nerd, I give my love and thanks for helping Daddy with "editing" the text with your scribbles, drawings, and finally writing your name on the manuscript. You make me so very proud, and I can't wait to see you published. Grandma Brooke would be so proud!

My father John has given me so many things, including the gifts needed to succeed and the discipline to use them. You have always been a source of great support and inspiration to me, and it has been very exciting to support you in your endeavors this past year.

I would also be remiss if I did not mention my father- and mother-in-law, Jim and Lee Anne Scovell, and my brothers- and sisters-in-law, who helped keep Brooke entertained and excused my absences from gatherings so I could complete this text. To Maureen and Robin, thank you for suggesting all of this in the first place and giving the vote of confidence that got us started. I too thank the staff of NWTC for "giving me my shot"—my first teaching job. Without the help, inspiration, confidence, and support of everyone listed above, I could not have done this.

I credit my esteemed friend, colleague, coconspirator, and "big brother" Mike Knetzger with being my law enforcement mentor and guide. Where you find the patience for my occasional crusades and tirades, I do not know.

Last, but not least, I would like to acknowledge the brave men and women in uniform, civilian and military, who give of themselves to help all of us. To the police at home, thank you for making our streets safer. To the troops stationed worldwide and our retired veterans, thank you for serving.

Jeremy Muraski

We are both indebted to the following reviewers, who spent their valuable time providing us with honest and constructive criticism: Robert Garofalo, Monmouth University, Long Branch, New Jersey; Jennifer Gossett, Indiana University of Pennsylvania, Indiana, Pennsylvania; Dave Pettinari, Colorado State University, Pueblo, Colorado; and Chris Harding, Canyon College Inc. Your responses and those of our students over the years really shaped this work. It is your feedback that has helped us make this manuscript great. Thank you!

Finally, to the awesome staff at Prentice Hall. Mayda Bosco, you're wonderful to work with and your dedication to our project is greatly appreciated. Thank you for guiding us through this process with a great deal of patience and a sense of humor. To all of those employees, especially the editors and graphic designers who work behind the scenes who we have not personally met, thank you for your countless hours and adding the countless finishing touches.

About the Authors

Jeremy A. Muraski is an eighty-year law enforcement veteran and a vanced patrol officer, Webmaster, and field training officer with the Green Bay (Wisconsin) Police Department. Prior to serving and protecting in Packer City, USA, he worked as a network administrator for Kimberly Clark Corporation at a paper and help desk specialist supporting online investors for Fidelity Investments. A proud graduate of the University of Wisconsin-Madison, Mr. Muraski is also certified to teach for the Wisconsin Technical College System and teaches criminal justice courses at Northeast Wisconsin Technical College (NWTC), including Investigating High-Tech Crimes and Juvenile Law. He has successfully completed AccessData's Forensic Toolkit Course, the National White Collar Crime Center's Basic Data Recovery and Analysis (BDRA) course and several other courses and seminars on investigating Internet crimes. Mr. Muraski has written and developed college course curricula and cowrote the Investigating High-Tech Crimes course at NWTC. In addition to computer forensics certifications, Mr. Muraski also holds numerous computer certifications, including Microsoft Access Database Design and Administration and Website Design and Computer Network Administration. Mr. Muraski holds a bachelor's degree in Behavioral Science and Law from the University of Wisconsin-Madison, with a Criminal Justice Certificate. Mr. Muraski lives in the Green Bay area with his wife and daughter.

Michael R. Knetzger is a fourteen-year law enforcement veteran and currently a lieutenant and field training supervisor with the Green Bay (Wisconsin) Police Department. Prior to policing in Titletown, USA, he served as a patrol officer and detective for the town of Brookfield (Wisconsin) Police Department. Mr. Knetzger is also a certified State of Wisconsin Technical College Instructor and teaches criminal justice courses at Northeast Wisconsin Technical College (NWTC), Colorado Technical University Online (CTU*online*), and ITT Technical Institute. He has successfully completed the International Association of Computer Investigative Specialists (IACIS) forensic examiner program, Basic Data Recovery and Analysis (BDRA) course, and several other courses and seminars on investigating Internet crimes. Mr. Knetzger has written and developed college course curricula and cowrote the Investigating High-Tech Crimes course at NWTC. He is also a certified tactical instructor and teaches defensive and arrest tactics (DAAT), firearms, and professional communications skills courses to new law enforcement recruits.

Mr. Knetzger holds a master's degree in Public Administration from the University of Wisconsin–Oshkosh, a bachelor's degree in Justice and Public Policy from Concordia University (Wisconsin), and an associate degree in Police Science from Waukesha County Technical College.

Mr. Knetzger has also coauthored the book *True Crime in Titletown, USA— Cold Cases,* released in 2006. He lives in Green Bay with his wife and three children.

Jeremy A. Muraski is an eight-year law enforcement veteran and currently an advanced patrol officer, Webmaster, and field training officer with the Green Bay (Wisconsin) Police Department. Prior to serving and protecting in Packer City, USA, he worked as a network administrator for Kimberly Clark Corporation at a paper mill in Neenah, Wisconsin. Prior to that he worked as a computer support engineer and help desk specialist supporting online investors for Fidelity Investments. A proud graduate of the University of Wisconsin–Madison, Mr. Muraski is also certified to teach for the Wisconsin Technical College System and teaches criminal justice courses at Northeast Wisconsin Technical College (NWTC), including Investigating High-Tech Crimes and Juvenile Law. He has successfully completed AccessData's Forensic Toolkit Course, the National White Collar Crime Center's Basic Data Recovery and Analysis (BDRA) course, and several other courses and seminars on investigating Internet crimes. Mr. Muraski has written and developed college course curricula and cowrote the Investigating High-Tech Crimes course at NWTC. In addition to computer forensics certifications, Mr. Muraski also holds numerous computer certifications, including Microsoft Access Database Design and Administration and Website Design and Computer Network Administration. Mr. Muraski holds a bachelor's degree in Behavioral Science and Law from the University of Wisconsin–Madison, with a Criminal Justice Certificate. Mr. Muraski lives in the Green Bay area with his wife and daughter.

chapter one

Computer Hardware, Software, and the Internet

■ **LEARNING OBJECTIVES**

1. Learn the basic structure of computer data, data size measurements, data transfer rates, how data is stored, and how it is manipulated within a computer system.
2. Explain the standard types of basic computer hardware and how each component interacts with the other component parts.
3. Learn the difference in technical specifications measurements, including the use of mathematical powers of 10 in regard to computer data capacities, bandwidths, and speeds.
4. Examine the history and structure of the Internet, including its data routing protocols, how an investigator is able to trace data paths, and what potential investigative uses the Internet has.

In almost every workplace, there are employees who do not think of themselves as computer savvy and in some cases even "hate" computers. This book is intended to help bridge the gap and bring every criminal justice student, law enforcement officer, or other investigator up to a baseline knowledge level regarding computer technology and crime. In this day and age, every frontline investigator should be able to identify the major components of a home computer and know how to properly seize them, should the need arise. After all, many of today's criminals are men in the 18 to 35 age range, and they grew up using computers. It is only natural that the criminally inclined would find a way to use computer technology to further their criminal enterprises. Criminals throughout history have continually endeavored to advance their trade and innovate new ways to avoid detection and prosecution. This chapter jump-starts a reader's baseline knowledge of computer components, the role of software, and the functionality of the Internet to help students catch up to the latest trends in high-tech criminal activity.

In later chapters, this text details exactly how computers and the Internet are used in the commission of high-tech crimes or even aid those committing run-of-the-mill crimes, but before any discussion of high-tech crime can begin, you must first have a baseline understanding of the technology to be discussed.

1.1 UNDERSTANDING DATA

To understand high-tech crime, or computers for that matter, you have to first understand the nature of information. Computers are, after all, nothing more than machines that process raw information called data. That data is structured on a very basic electrical level. The smallest piece of data is called a **bit (b). Binary language** is so named because there are two possible electrical states for each bit of data, on and off. On is represented by the number one, off is represented as a zero. Think of a light switch in the on or off position. A bit by itself doesn't really mean much; it just means essentially whether an electrical circuit has power or doesn't.

A group of bits together can mean different things. One circuit on or off is pretty meaningless, but when eight circuits are grouped together there are numerous possible combinations. Each potential combination can be assigned a different value, and a character such as a letter or number is made of eight binary bits. For example, the capital letter *A* is represented by eight bits, 01000001, or in electrical terms off-on-off-off-off-off-off-off-on. These eight bits that make up one character are more commonly called a **byte (B)** of data (Mims 1991). There are, therefore, eight bits in a byte and one byte per character. Examining a simple sentence such as, "I am Sam." you see 7 characters, including the period. In addition, there are 2 spaces, which are also counted as characters. There are, therefore, a total of 9 characters, or 9 bytes of data in that sentence.

The preceding paragraph consists of approximately 843 characters, including spaces. It contains 843 bytes of data. A full written page of text can have anywhere from 2,000 to 3,000 characters. An entire book would contain millions of bytes. As data structures have become larger, it is common to quantify data capacity sizes using standards for larger measurements such as **kilobytes (KB), megabytes (MB), gigabytes (GB),** and **terabytes (TB).** Because data is binary in nature, the size of a piece of data can be determined mathematically. To find

Table 1–1 Data Capacity Measurements and Powers of 10

1 bit (b)	= 1/8 of a byte	
1 byte (B)	= 8 bits (one alphanumeric character)	= 2^0 bytes
1 kilobyte (KB)	= 1,024 bytes	= 2^{10} bytes
1 megabyte (MB)	= 1,024 kilobytes = 1,048,576 bytes	= 2^{20} bytes
1 gigabyte (GB)	= 1,024 megabytes = 1,073,741,824 bytes	= 2^{30} bytes
1 terabyte (TB)	= 1,024 gigabytes = 1,099,511,627,776 bytes	= 2^{40} bytes

comparative sizes of data, 2 (the base of binary systems) is multiplied by 2 a set number of times. For example 2 to the zero power (2^0) is equal to 1. The result of 2^{10} ($2 \times 2 \times 2 \times 2 \times 2 \times 2 \times 2 \times 2 \times 2 \times 2$) is 1,024, which is why there are 1,024 bytes of data in a kilobyte and 1,024 kilobytes in a megabyte. A kilobyte is a factor of 10 greater than a byte, and a megabyte is a factor of 10 greater than a kilobyte, and so forth (Glover and Young 2001). Table 1–1 shows a size comparison using the different capacity terms.

In abbreviations, bits are always represented as a lowercase *b* to differentiate them from bytes, which are abbreviated as a capital *B*.

Learner Activity

Go to a computer store or Web site for computer hardware sales. Locate three items that store data (such as hard drives, USB keys, CD-ROMs, etc.). Document what each item is and its data capacity. For each item, convert its capacity to bits, bytes, and kilobytes. The item will most likely be listed as having a capacity of megabytes or gigabytes. Once you have mathematically converted each item into its size in bits, bytes, and kilobytes, examine the price of the item. Last, calculate the price per megabyte of storage. Example: A 40-gigabyte hard drive priced at $57.00: $40 \times 1024 = 40,960$ megabytes

$40,960 \times 1024 = 41,943,040$ kilobytes
$41,943,040 \times 1024 = 42,949,672,960$ bytes
$42,949,672,960 \times 1024 = 43,980,465,111,040$ bits
$57.00/40,960 = 0.0014 per megabyte

Now that we have discussed measuring the size of a given chunk of data, we need to discuss how fast we can move that data from place to place. Data flows along electrical circuits in many places on a computer system, and each data pathway, called a **bus**, can move only a certain amount of data at a time. **Bandwidth** is the

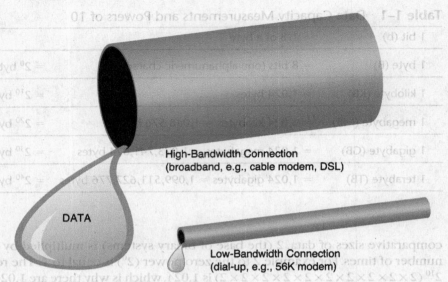

Figure 1–1 Bandwidth comparison.

High-Bandwidth Connection
(broadband, e.g., cable modem, DSL)

DATA

Low-Bandwidth Connection
(dial-up, e.g., 56K modem)

term used to measure the capacity of how much data can travel in a given data path at any given time. A data pathway is often compared to a water pipe, and we measure the pipe's diameter (bandwidth) to determine how much water (data) can flow through it at one time. (see Figure 1–1.)

Bandwidth—A rate of data transmission; the maximum amount of information that can be transmitted along a data channel. It is commonly measured in units of bits per second (bps), kilobits per second (kbps), or megabits per second (mbps).

With this understanding of data structures, you can now begin to examine how data is handled by computer hardware components. The discussion of computer hardware components is typically rife with technical jargon, and practical instruction in this area must begin on the basic component level.

1.2 COMPUTER HARDWARE

Tower and Mainboard

The main and most important component of any computer is its mainboard, also known as the **motherboard.** Figure 1–2 shows a simplified view of the basic structure of a computer motherboard, with major components labeled for clarity.

Every computer has a case, or a tower, that physically contains the main components of the computer system. Mounted inside the case are the motherboard, a power supply to power the mainboard, case cooling fans, and the other installed devices such as hard disk drives, CD-ROM drives, sound cards, video cards, modems, and so forth. The power supply (Figure 1–3) has a capacity that is rated in watts;

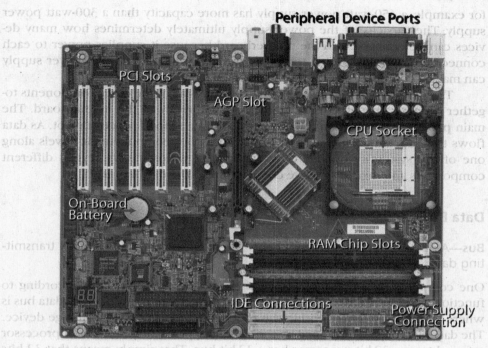

Figure 1–2 Motherboard components.

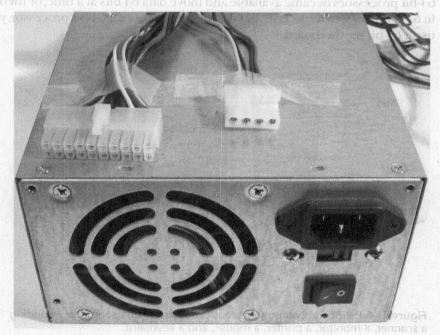

Figure 1–3 Computer power supply unit.

for example, a 450-watt power supply has more capacity than a 300-watt power supply. The capacity of the power supply ultimately determines how many devices can be connected to the motherboard because it supplies power to each connected device. Mounting too many devices and straining the power supply can make a computer system unstable and prone to crashing.

The motherboard is the component that ties all of the other components together because they all connect directly or indirectly to the motherboard. The main **processor** resides on the motherboard in a snap-in processor slot. As data flows to and from the main processor to the other components it travels along one of the system's buses. Review Figure 1–4, which shows several different components and their respective connections to the motherboard.

Data Bus

Bus—A path between two components where electrical impulses travel transmitting data.

One computer system contains several buses, and the buses vary according to function and bandwidth. The first bus is the processor's *data bus*. The data bus is where information moves within the processor and to or from a storage device. The data bus size is determined by the age and type of the processor. A processor referred to as a 32-bit processor has a 32-bit bus. That simply means that 32 bits of data can be traveling along that processor's data bus at any one time. As of 2004, 64-bit processors became available and move data 64 bits at a time, or theoretically in 64-bit pieces, twice as fast. To take full advantage of a 64-bit processor, you must use a 64-bit motherboard.

Figure 1–4 Peripheral components that can connect to a computer, including a scanner, a monitor, a printer, a mouse, and a keyboard.

Comparison of Bus Speeds for Various Components

PCI Bus = 33 MHz (sound cards, modems, network card, etc.)
AGP Bus = 66 MHz (graphics cards, CD-ROM drives)
IDE Bus = 100 MHz or in ATA-133 systems 133 MHz (hard drives)
Serial ATA = 150 MB/s (high-speed hard drives)
Universal Serial Bus (USB) 2.0 = 480 Mbps

Central Processor or Microprocessor

The motherboard is home to the central processor chip (Figure 1–5), which sits in a socket or slot. There are various types of processor sockets standardized by manufacturer and model. The microprocessor computes all commands executed by the computer. The rate at which it performs these calculations is determined by the speed of the processor.

Processors are rated by their relative speed using **hertz (Hz)** Hertz, also known as cycles per second, measures the number of calculations a central processor can make within a given time period. When personal computers first hit the mainstream in the mid- to late 1980s, processor speeds ranged from 4 to 7 **megahertz (MHz).**

Later, in the early to mid-1990s, computers became faster as new generations of processors (286, 386, and 486) yielding speeds of 33 to 133 MHz became available. The processors of the late 1990s and turn of the twenty-first century commonly had speeds in the 400- to 900-MHz speed range. Retail personal computers have processor speeds in the billions of hertz, measured as **gigahertz,** or **GHz.** It is not uncommon to see computers running in the 2.5- to 4.0-GHz range, although the speeds are constantly increasing.

Figure 1–5 Processor chip.

Processor Speeds and Powers of 10

1 Hz	= 1 hertz or	2^0 hertz
1 KHz	= 1,024 hertz or	2^{10} hertz
1 MHz	= 1,048,576 hertz or	2^{20} hertz
1 GHz	= 1,073,741,824 hertz or	2^{30} hertz

Each level increases by a power of 10, or by multiplying the previous level by 2^{10}, which is the same as saying multiply it by 1,024. Example: 1,024 * 1,024 = 1,048,576

In addition to their specification relating to calculation speeds, processors are also rated on the basis of their **front-side bus (FSB)** speed, which is also measured in megahertz. The front side bus carries data back and forth between the processor and other devices such as video cards, system random access memory, and hard drives. The higher the front-side bus speed, the faster the computer. Most processors also have built-in memory storage, commonly referred to as the level 2 memory cache, or L2 cache for short. These can range in size from 128 MB to 1 GB and provide very efficient short-term memory to assist the processor. Because the cache is on the same board and directly accessed by the processor, the size of the level 2 cache can have a significant impact on the speed of the processor.

Other Device Buses

Other devices on the computer's motherboard also have buses. For example, the Accelerated Graphics Port (AGP) card shown in Figure 1–6 is on the **AGP bus,** which is a 32-bit bus. AGP cards are commonly used for sending data to and from video graphics cards. The newest bus specifically devoted to graphics cards is the

Figure 1–6 Accelerated Graphics Port (AGP) video card.

Figure 1–7 USB (a) cable; (b) symbol; (c) ports.

PCI Express bus. This is an updated version of the longstanding Peripheral Component Interconnect bus (**PCI bus**), which is used to connect expansion cards to the motherboard. These expansion cards can be sound cards, modems, network interface cards, on additional ports such as universal serial bus (USB) ports.

Another increasingly common bus is the **universal serial bus,** commonly called **USB.** (see Figure 1–7.) Because there were so many different and divergent bus and connection standards, industry professionals decided to try to create a standard connection for all brands and a wide variety of devices. A conglomerate of many top vendors created this standard. Thus, USB was born. As bandwidth needs increased, the developers of the USB standard decided that USB still wasn't fast enough, and so created USB 2.0 with a much higher bandwidth. USB 1.0 could move data at 12 megabits per second (Mbps). The capacity of USB 2.0 jumped much higher to move up to 480 Mbps (Koon 2005).

These buses move data to and from many different types of components. Knowing the difference between PCI Express (commonly used bus for high-end graphics cards) and Universal Serial Bus (USB connections used for a myriad of devices) is considered common knowledge among entry- to midlevel computer users. A general knowledge of bus types, memory capacities, and processor speeds gives an investigator credibility in court. A lack of this baseline knowledge can be devastating when an investigator is cross-examined by a dedicated defense attorney. When defense attorneys have no other case, they attack an investigator's credibility.

But what of the components themselves? What they are, what they do, and how they are classified are discussed in the following sections. Anyone who has ever shopped for computers has seen a dazzling array of numbers and measurements associated with computer specifications. These specifications determine the computer's speed and performance much like an engine's horsepower, torque, and volume classify an automobile. The following subsections explain the units of measure most commonly used with computer hardware specifications.

Random Access Memory (RAM) or System Memory

Also connected to the motherboard is the system's **random access memory (RAM),** which enables the computer to store information temporarily in its short-term memory (see Figure 1–8). RAM is very fast and efficient, relying on electrical impulses to read and write small pieces of data. It does not have any moving parts. RAM stores data only temporarily and is cleared whenever a computer is powered down. RAM is measured in terms of how much data it can store (megabytes of RAM) and how fast it can find that data (seek time). RAM also functions at a certain rate of speed, measured in megahertz. For example, Double Data Rate (DDR) 400 functions at 400 MHz or roughly twice as fast at DDR 200.

Memory chips are also available in a number of physical layouts or formats. The most common format is the dual inline memory module (DIMM). It is not uncommon for computer systems to have 512 MB or 1 GB of RAM or more. High-end systems used for memory-dependent applications such as digital video editing can have several gigabytes of RAM.

From an investigative standpoint, the important thing to remember about RAM is that whatever is stored in RAM is lost when the computer is powered down. In the case of a system with 1 GB of RAM, that is a significant amount of data to lose, which is why investigators attempt to document what is on the screen and what programs are running before shutting down a suspect computer for transport.

Hard Disk Drives and Other Mass Storage Devices

Whereas RAM stores information only while the computer is on, the computer will read from and write to a **hard disk drive (or hard drives)** for long-term or permanent data storage. (see Figure 1–9 for an image of a hard disk drive and other storage devices.) This can be compared to the functioning of the human mind. RAM contains the equivalent of what you are actively concentrating on at a given moment, whereas

Figure 1–8 Example of a RAM chip.

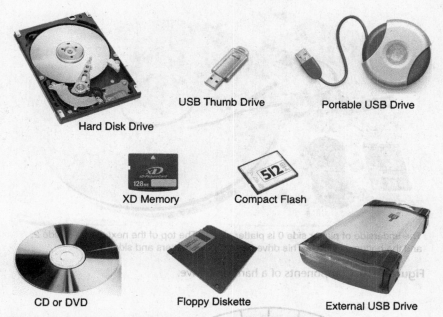

Figure 1–9 Examples of different types of storage media.

the hard disk drive storage is the equivalent of all of the knowledge you have obtained during your lifetime. Obviously, then, hard disk drive capacity must be greatly larger than the RAM capacity, but like the human mind, access to long-term memories is slower, similar to having to concentrate to remember something from your past.

Hard disk drives, like RAM, are measured in terms of capacity and seek time. Unlike RAM, however, hard disk drives do not lose data when they are powered down. Further, they have moving component parts and are therefore necessarily slower than RAM, which relies only on electrical impulses. Hard disk drives have magnetic disks called **platters.** The platters spin around a central axis, not unlike a record player, while a read and write arm moves back and forth across the surface of the disk. At the end of the read or write arm there is a read/write head that finds the correct area of the disk and reads or writes information there. The presence of the read and write arm makes the record player analogy very appropriate, although a hard disk drive is much more complex. Figure 1–10 is a picture of the inside of a hard disk drive showing the components just described.

Each platter or disk within the hard disk drive can be used on both sides. The top side is side 0 and the bottom side is side 1. There are also read and write heads for each side, head 0 and head 1, respectively. The circular drive is divided into concentric circles that are very large at the outside edge of the platter and become progressively smaller as you move toward the center (see Figure 1–11). Each ring is called a *track*. Generally, a standard hard disk drive has 1,024 tracks, starting with track 0 on the outside edge and ending with track 1,023 closest to the center of the drive.

The underside of platter side 0 is platter side 1. The top of the next platter is side 2, and the bottom is side 3. This drive has only two platters and sides 0–3.

Figure 1–10 Components of a hard disk drive.

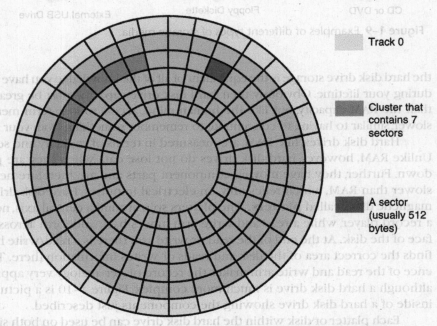

Track 0

Cluster that contains 7 sectors

A sector (usually 512 bytes)

Figure 1–11 A simplified view of the layout of a hard disk drive platter.

Tracks are divided into smaller segments called *sectors*. A line from the center of the platter to the outside divides one sector from another. Sector size is determined when the drive is first formatted by the operating system (e.g., Windows or Linux), but sectors are almost always 512 bytes in capacity. Once the sectors are established, sector identification data is placed at the very beginning of the sector before any data is written there. If a piece of data is larger than 512 bytes, it will occupy multiple sectors. For example, an 800-KB file will be assigned to two sectors. Sectors that are grouped together are called *clusters*. In an ideal situation, data is stored in sectors that are contiguous, or adjacent to each other.

In some cases, there is not enough space available in any one place, so multiple sectors in different locations are used to store the data. This is called *fragmentation* and slows down the process of reading, writing, and finding the data because the read and write heads have to move across more places to access the data. If you have ever heard the term *defragging* a hard disk drive, this refers to the process of defragmenting a drive. Most operating systems have utilities that enable users to clean up and reorganize their hard disk drive to place all parts of a file close together on the drive instead of having it scattered or fragmented. Midlevel computer users often defrag their drives monthly.

Although individual sectors can generally contain up to 512 bytes of data, files do not come in nice round 512-byte packages, however; so wasted space within a sector is quite common. For example, a 300-byte file will leave 212 bytes of wasted space within that sector. This is sometimes referred to as the *file slack*, or *slack space* (Figure 1–12). Slack space can be important to the investigator because the 300-byte file will not overwrite that 212-byte space, leaving any old data there. Investigators can recover those data fragments left behind in the slack space and examine them.

When a hard disk drive is initially configured, there are a number of ways it can be set up. A drive can be used whole as one drive and not subdivided into mul-

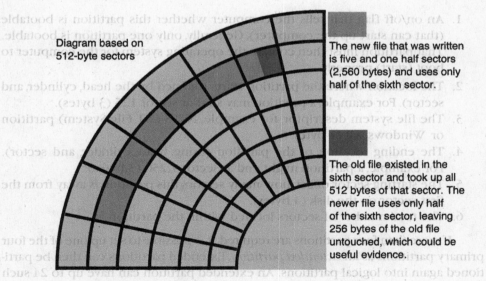

Diagram based on 512-byte sectors

The new file that was written is five and one half sectors (2,560 bytes) and uses only half of the sixth sector.

The old file existed in the sixth sector and took up all 512 bytes of that sector. The newer file uses only half of the sixth sector, leaving 256 bytes of the old file untouched, which could be useful evidence.

Figure 1–12 Diagram of slack space.

tiple partitions. For example, the computer's primary hard disk drive, the C drive, generally is set up as one whole drive and is not partitioned. It is possible, however, to break a drive into sections and make one physical drive behave like it is actually two or more separate hard drives. This is called *partitioning a disk*. A disk with two partitions can appear to the computer to be the C drive and the D drive, although there is only one physical hard drive installed.

Hard drives use a table of contents to tell the computer how the hard drive is laid out and formatted. The very first sector of the hard drive is called the **Master Boot Record (MBR).** The MBR is created when the first partition is made on the disk. Even if the drive is just one whole partition, it will still have a Master Boot Record. The location of the MBR is always cylinder 0, head 0, sector 1, which is also listed as (0,0,1). This can also be described as track 0, side 0, sector 1. The MBR is the beginning of the table of contents for that particular hard drive. It contains a partition table that details the structure of the hard drive, how many partitions it has, and where each partition starts and ends. The MBR generally occupies the first 446 of 512 bytes available in sector 1. There are four partition table entries (each of which has the 6 elements listed below), which each take up 16 bytes (64 bytes total). The MBR and partition table, therefore, use up 510 bytes of the 512 bytes available in the first sector. The last two bytes are used as an MBR signature, which puts an end cap on the MBR. The MBR is important to the investigator because the partition tables can indicate the number of volumes into which a hard drive is divided. A single hard drive could be partitioned to appear as drives C, D, and E if it were divided into three partitions. All three drives, or volumes, exist on one physical hard drive, but appear as three separate virtual drives (Kozierok 2001b).

Each of the four partition table entries includes certain standardized data, as follows:

1. An on/off flag that tells the computer whether this partition is bootable (that can start up the computer). Generally, only one partition is bootable. That partition must then contain the operating system for the computer to boot (start) properly.
2. The location where the partition starts (defined by the head, cylinder, and sector). For example, a partition may start at sector 125 (3 bytes).
3. The file system descriptor, for example, NTFS (NT File System) partition or Windows XP (1 byte).
4. The ending location of the partition (using head, cylinder, and sector). For example, a partition might end at sector 1,250 (3 bytes).
5. The starting sector offset: how many sectors this partition is away from the first sector on the disk (4 bytes).
6. The total number of sectors located within the partition.

If more than four partitions are required, it is possible to set up one of the four primary partitions as an *extended partition*. Extended partitions can then be partitioned again into logical partitions. An extended partition can have up to 24 such logical partitions. The extended partition also has its own table of contents in the form of a nested partition table detailing each of the logical partitions. This is sometimes referred to as the *extended Master Boot Record*, or EMBR (Kozierok 2001a).

A number of factors determine the speed of a hard drive. One factor is the revolutions per minute (RPMs) of the spinning platters. Common drive speeds range from 5,400 to 10,000 RPMs, with 7,200 RPMs being very common for home systems. Another factor is whether the hard drive has a small onboard electrical impulse memory cache to assist with storing small bursts of data. This is called a **drive cache** and generally ranges from 2 MB to 16 MB in size. Another major factor in drive speed performance is its bus speed to the rest of the system. Generally, hard drives are connected by an **ATA-133** connection, meaning that they can transfer 133 MB per second (MB/sec). (*ATA* stands for Advanced Technology Attachment.) Older hard drives and most CD-ROM drives are connected at **ATA-66,** which means they transfer up to 66 MB per second. The up-and-coming standards are **Serial ATA** with a bandwidth of 150 MB/sec and Serial ATA II with speeds of 300 MB/sec (Serial ATA International Organization 2006). The final factor is, of course, drive capacity, which like most data is measured in bytes. Because of the extremely large size of modern hard drives, drive capacity is classified in gigabytes.

Knowledge of hard drive structure and function is absolutely fundamental to the investigation of high-tech crime because most computer forensic evidence is obtained from suspect hard drives. The way in which investigators handle these drives and investigators' baseline knowledge of hard drives are two areas that are commonly challenged by defense attorneys. Chapter 10 discusses the process of seizing, cloning, and analyzing a suspect hard drive to gather evidence, so an investigators's baseline knowledge will be put to practical use.

CD-ROM/DVD-ROM Drives and Burners

Another place to store data is by writing it to optical discs such as CDs and DVDs. Optical drives are named by their functions. A DVD-ROM is a DVD reader only, because ROM stands for *read-only memory*. A DVD-RW is a reader and a writer. This also applies to CD-ROMs and CD-RW drives. CDs hold approximately 650 to 700 MB of information, whereas single-layer DVDs hold up to 4.7 GB. Newer dual-layer DVDs can hold up to 9.4 GB of data. A writer such as a **CD writer** (see Figure 1–13) or **DVD writer** is often called a **CD burner** or **DVD burner,** respectively, because of it etches data onto the surface of the optical disc using a small laser beam.

As mentioned earlier, **optical drives** are connected to the motherboard by an ATA-66 connection. CD-ROMs, CD writers, **DVD-ROMs,** and DVD writers also measure their speeds using a multiplier. A drive that is a reader only, whether for CDs or DVDs, has only a one-number multiplier. CD readers commonly read at 52×. DVD readers commonly read at 8×. When the drive is a writer, it generally has three numbers in the multiplier: the first is the write speed, for a rewriteable or reusable disk; the second number is the rewrite speed; and the third number is the read speed. A common CD writer might have a multiplier of 52×/10×/52× (write/rewrite/read). What do these multipliers really mean? When optical drives were first created, they

Figure 1–13 A CD drive.

wrote at 1×, which is equivalent to writing 150 KB per second for a CD burner. For a DVD burner, the default 1× speed was 1.385 MB/sec. CD burners are currently rated at up to 52×, which is equivalent to approximately 7.6 MB/sec (52 × 150 KB/sec = 7,800 KB/sec 1,024 = 7.6 MB/sec). Because DVDs have so much more capacity, DVD writers are offered at multipliers up to 16×. An 8× DVD burner can write approximately 11 MB/sec (8 × 1.385 MB/sec = 11.08 MB/sec), whereas a 16× model writes at just over 22 MB/sec (16 × 1.385 MB/sec = 22.16 MB/sec). It is easy to see why someone burning a movie to a DVD or backing up the system would choose the 16× model because it cuts the burn time in half (Marianna 2003).

External Peripheral Devices

There are almost as many external peripheral devices as there are uses for computers. Most commonly, however, the devices can be broken down into general categories including: human input devices, scanners, printers, external storage, modems, cameras (digital still and digital video), and scientific instruments. Peripherals such as these connect to the computer by ports on the motherboard. Examples include PS/2 ports for human input devices such as mice and keyboards, parallel ports for older printers (see Figure 1–14), and USB ports for most modern devices. One up-and-coming trend is the use of external flash memory to store data. These *thumb drives* or *USB keys* connect to the computer by a USB port and can store data indefinitely (see Figure 1–15). They contain small flash memory chips. External hard drives and cameras may also be connected by another interface, an **IEEE 1394 port,** which is commonly referred to as a **FireWire.** See Figure 1–16.

Computer hardware cannot move or otherwise manipulate data in a vacuum. Hardware relies on instructions that tell one piece of hardware what to do in relation to another piece. Without any installed software, computer hardware is nothing more than a stack of electrified components with no known tasks and no instructions to carry out tasks. In other words, a computer needs software

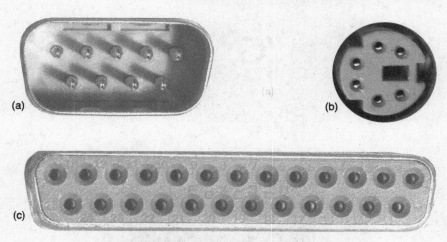

Figure 1–14 (a) Serial port, (b) PS/2 port, (c) parallel port.

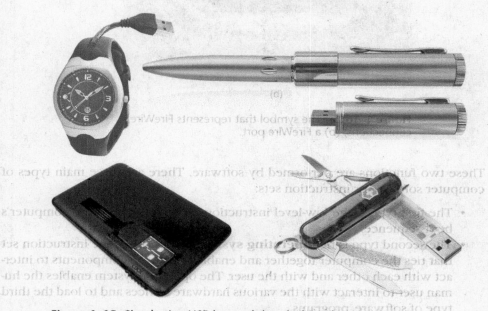

Figure 1–15 Clandestine USB key and thumb drive devices.

instructions to function and manipulate data. The next section focuses on the role of software in the basic computer system.

1.3 THE ROLE OF SOFTWARE

All of the physical components of a given computer system are useless without instructions to tell the components how to interact, and without a user interface.

Figure 1–16 (a) The symbol that represents FireWire connections; (b) a FireWire port.

These two functions are performed by software. There are three main types of computer software or instruction sets:

- The first type is the low-level instructions accessed during the computer's boot sequence.
- The second type is the **operating system (OS).** This is the instruction set that ties the computer together and enables hardware components to interact with each other and with the user. The operating system enables the human user to interact with the various hardware devices and to load the third type of software, programs.
- The third type of instruction sets is the executable programs that carry out specific tasks in concert with the operating system. An example of an executable program is a word processing program. The program is specifically set up to create documents. The executable file interacts with the operating system to create and then output the document to the computer's printer.

It is important for the investigator to know that all three types of instruction sets interact with the computer's hard drives, memory, and some of its data.

The mere act of powering on a computer can modify data files (digital evidence), which calls into question the integrity of the digital evidence seized. The following paragraphs examine each type of these instruction sets individually.

Boot Sequence

The boot sequence is what occurs when someone turns on a computer. The computer must go through several steps after it is powered on before it is usable. This process is called the *boot sequence* because the computer is "pulling itself up by its bootstraps." The low-level data first accessed during this process is contained in the computer's CMOS, a small memory chip on the motherboard. A tiny battery located on the motherboard also allows the computer to store the current date and time on the system. This data tells the computer which drives to access and in which order, and also contains basic hardware information such as which processor speed to run at, how much memory is in the system, and so forth.

The first phase of the boot sequence is the power-on self test, commonly referred to as the POST. This process checks the hardware to ensure everything is functioning at full efficiency. It usually includes a memory count (you can watch the tally on the screen) to verify all of the system's RAM is present and accessible. Often, the POST is followed by a short beep if everything passes the test. From there, the computer loads the operating system, including the user interface, and any other programs set up to launch upon startup. Once this process is complete, the hard drive light stops flashing and the computer is ready to use and waits for user input. Typically, the POST takes less than a minute for a modern, well-configured system, but loading a variety of start-up programs, such as an antivirus program, increases the time of the boot process.

Operating Systems

Operating systems have been around as long as personal computers have. Computers have always required something to be the go-between for humans and computers. One of the first operating systems was DOS, the Disk Operating System (see Figure 1-17). It predated the first hard drives. A user would have to place a large, flimsy diskette (nicknamed floppy) into a disk drive and load the instructions manually from the disk, hence the name DOS. There were no graphics associated with DOS, only text-based instructions. When typing commands into a DOS prompt, you had to be very careful to type everything correctly. This was called *using the proper syntax*. Failing to type each and every letter perfectly resulted in the much-dreaded syntax error.

DOS spawned a variety of newer operating systems that finally started to make it easier for users to interact with computers. Several different vendors strove to make the best system, and several came out with the first graphical user interface

```
C:\>dir/p
 Volume in drive C has no label.
 Volume Serial Number is 985E-B5DF

 Directory of C:\

08/16/2005  04:43 AM                    0 AUTOEXEC.BAT
04/21/2006  12:25 AM           12,175,055 AVG7QT.DAT
08/24/2006  05:28 PM        <DIR>          col3927
08/16/2005  04:43 AM                    0 CONFIG.SYS
08/09/2006  08:25 PM        <DIR>          dell
04/20/2006  03:18 PM        <DIR>          Documents and Settings
04/14/2006  12:16 PM        <DIR>          drivers
04/26/2006  03:35 AM        <DIR>          i386
04/20/2006  04:15 PM                4,128 INFCACHE.1
04/20/2006  09:02 PM        <DIR>          My Music
08/11/2006  02:25 PM                  166 myinstall.log
04/14/2006  12:46 PM        <DIR>          Netscape
10/18/2006  04:42 PM        <DIR>          Program Files
04/14/2006  12:46 PM                   87 SystemInfo.ini
08/11/2006  02:25 PM                   90 temp.log
09/29/2006  10:30 PM               29,696 test.doc
09/29/2006  10:30 PM               29,696 testcopy.doc
08/15/2006  06:05 PM        <DIR>          Wallpaper
10/12/2006  11:18 AM        <DIR>          WINDOWS
               9 File(s)       12,238,918 bytes
              10 Dir(s)    67,701,764,096 bytes free

C:\>_
```

Figure 1–17 A sequence of DOS commands.

(GUI) to enable a more user-friendly approach. This caused the need for some kind of visual interface pointer or controller, and the mouse became a mainstream input device. This enabled the user to point and click graphical representations of data files or software programs. The user could run many different commands on the files without having to worry about entering the exact command syntax. The user-friendly GUIs also made it much easier to organize files into directories to better organize the data. The GUI continues to evolve in the operating systems available today (Windows, Linux, Mac OSX, and others).

Program Software

The third and final category of software encompasses executable program files, commonly called executables. Programs are nothing more than sets of instructions for a computer that enable it to perform certain tasks. Examples of executables are word processing programs, Internet browsers, and antivirus programs. Users generally install the program files into their operating system. The operating system enables the programs to talk to the hardware components to instruct the hardware to perform the programs' designed functions. These days, a wide variety of computer programs perform almost any imaginable task.

Unfortunately, some malicious or bored programmers have taken it upon themselves to see what kind of havoc they can wreak on a computer system by writing programs specifically to perform bad deeds. This type of program is generally called **malware** (or malicious software), based on its malicious intent. There are many different categories of malware, including viruses, browser hijackers, Trojan horses, and spyware. The one thing they all have in common, however, is that they are intended to delete data, damage system software, or allow unauthorized access to a computer for the purposes of stealing data. Essentially, there is an ongoing arms race between software developers and antivirus software developers on the good side, and hackers trying to exploit every single security flaw for their own purposes or enjoyment on the other side. Investigators should take special care to ensure their forensic systems are virus free, and they should also document any viruses found on suspect systems. A defense team might try to blame illegal content on viruses and argue the viruses are at fault instead of the defendant.

After this brief examination of the basics of data structures, computer hardware, and software, you can now begin to study the more common functions of computers and how they are used in the commission of crimes. One of the most popular mainstream uses of the personal computer is accessing the Internet to surf Web pages, view e-mail, or download data files such as music, pictures, or video. The history and structure of the Internet are the primary focus of the next section.

1.4 STRUCTURE AND FUNCTION OF THE INTERNET

The explosion of the online community and its associated millions of users has created a new environment or "virtual community," rich in opportunities to commit traditional crimes. It has also given rise to many new types of online crimes based on the same technologies that make the Internet such a powerful communications tool. Because millions of citizens are online interacting in that community, law enforcement must also establish a presence online.

A Brief History of the Internet

The Internet is nothing more than a large interconnected computer network made up of thousands of smaller computer networks or computers. It is not uncommon for the terms *Internet* and *World Wide Web* to be used interchangeably. This is actually incorrect. The Internet is the communication backbone that enables the sharing of many kinds of data across the network of networks. The World Wide Web, however, refers specifically only to that portion of Internet communications that actually have to do with Web sites and Web pages. The term *World Wide Web* does not include other forms of communication such as e-mail, newsgroups, or **File Transfer Protocol (FTP).**

The Internet enables users worldwide to share data and files literally at the speed of light, or the speed of the electrical impulses traveling across wire, or in some cases by using wireless networks. The Internet was originally created in the

United States for the Department of Defense to be used as a secure network for communications. Its use was expanded into the realm of higher education, and finally, in the beginning of the 1990s to general, personal, business, and commercial use.

Connecting to the Internet and Internet Bandwidth

During the Internet's popular infancy, the general public had to connect to the Internet using a telephone line and a modem. This is commonly referred to as a *dial-up connection*. The word *modem*, which is made up of abbreviations for the words *modulate* and *demodulate*, describes the physical hardware that connects the computer to the telephone line. A modem takes binary data signals (0s and 1s) and modulates them into sounds. A companion modem on the other end demodulates the sounds back into data. Anyone who has ever used a dial-up modem can remember the distinctive metallic screeching sound of the two modems connecting. When first introduced, modems were very slow, having very little bandwidth. A data transfer rate of 300 baud was not uncommon. **Baud** is an older measure of bandwidth used in the infancy of Internet connectivity, when data transfer speeds were very slow. Baud measured how many bits per second a modem could send or receive.

As technology evolved, modems of 1200, 2400, 4800, 9600 baud and so forth came into existence. As modem bandwidth speeds increased, a new speed designation was used, called bits per second (bps), and for higher speeds Kbps and Mbps. Kbps stands for **kilobits per second,** Mbps for **megabits per second.** Remember, a bit is one-eighth of a byte. When dealing with Internet bandwidth, we will generally see them in bits per second (bps), but in dealing with hard drive or other types of bandwidths, we generally talk about bytes per second (Bps), with the uppercase *B* designating bytes. Therefore, 1 kilobit is actually approximately 128 bytes, or 128 alphanumeric characters; 1 megabit, therefore, is approximately 131,000 characters.

The final evolution of the dial-up modem is known as 56K, which is shorthand for a transfer rate of 56 Kbps or the equivalent of 7,168 characters (bytes) per second. This is the theoretical bandwidth limitation of a standard telephone wire using a standard dial-up, or analog, modem. In other words, under perfect conditions, no analog modem can transmit more than 7,168 bytes per second.

As data became more complex, users wanted more efficient ways to transfer larger data files such as sound and music files, high-resolution images, and even

---

Data Bandwidth Measurement Comparisons

1 bit = $\frac{1}{8}$ of a byte

8 bits = 1 byte = 1 alphanumeric character

1 kilobit (Kb) = 1,024 bits = 128 bytes = 128 alphanumeric characters

1 megabit (Mb) = 1,024 kilobits = 1,048,576 bits = 131,072 bytes = 131,072 characters

video files. These files can range from several megabytes to several gigabytes in size, so a much faster transport mode was needed. This was the dawn of the broadband age.

Broadband Internet connections generally fall into one of three types, Digital Subscriber Line (DSL), cable modems, or dedicated lines. Corporate or government networks commonly have a high-bandwidth connection such as a 1.5-megabit T-1 dedicated line. Broadband lines can have varying bandwidths, but generally range in bandwidth from 384 Kbps to 3.0 Mbps. A 3-megabit connection can download 393,216 bytes per second, roughly one-third of a megabyte. A 3-megabyte song file, for example, could conceivably be received in roughly 9 seconds under ideal conditions. That same song file on a dial-up 56K modem would take at least 7 minutes to download. A brief table comparing download speeds under ideal conditions is shown here.

	56K Dial-Up	768 Kbps	1.5 Mbps	3.0 Mbps
500-KB file	71 seconds	5.2 seconds	2.6 seconds	1.3 seconds
1-MB file	146 seconds	10.7 seconds	5.3 seconds	2.65 seconds
5-MB file	12.2 minutes	53.3 seconds	26.7 seconds	13.35 seconds
100-MB file	243.8 minutes	17.75 minutes	8.9 minutes	4.45 minutes

Internet Communication Standards

Now that connection to the Internet has been described, we can examine the ways the Internet enables data to be transferred. The Internet has several standard protocols for handling data transfers. In this sense, a **protocol** is nothing more than an agreed-upon language that standardizes the way a given type of data is handled. This universality is what enables users around the world to send and receive data on the network.

The first protocol, **Hypertext Transfer Protocol (HTTP)**, is the standard protocol for downloading Web pages on the World Wide Web, one of the most common uses of the Internet. To navigate the World Wide Web, users launch a software program called a Web browser. The Hypertext Transfer Protocol is prominently listed when looking at the browser's address bar or **Uniform Resource Locater (URL)** for a Web page. For example, http://www.prenhall.com is the URL you type in to browse to the Prentice Hall Web site. The *http* at the beginning of the address indicates the *HyperText Transfer Protocol*. Web pages are written in a language called **Hypertext Markup Language**, or **HTML** for short. It stands to reason that we use the Hypertext Transfer Protocol to handle **hypertext** documents. This is also where the term **hyperlink** comes from. A hyperlink in a hypertext document simply links one hypertext document to another.

Another very common use of the Internet is for sending and receiving e-mail (electronic mail), which uses two protocols. It can use **SMTP**, which stands for the **Simple Mail Transfer Protocol** and which is used in handling the addressing and sending of e-mail messages. E-mail transfer also, in many cases, uses **POP**, or

Post Office Protocol, to retrieve messages from an e-mail server. In other words, an outgoing e-mail message uses SMTP and incoming e-mail messages use POP. Most Internet service providers have one SMTP server and one POP server, and the names of these servers are configured in the user's default e-mail program. E-mail can also be accessed by using a Web page link. For example, you might find the following line on a Web page: mailto:johnsmith@smith.com. In this case, the "mailto" is an instruction to the browser to load an e-mail application to send an e-mail message to the address specified in the link. This is another form of a hyperlink, but it links to an e-mail address instead of another hypertext document. This is very common on Web pages where the page author is seeking feedback.

A third very popular protocol is the standard method used to upload or download complete data files. It is simply called FTP, which stands for File Transfer Protocol. When people create Web pages, they generally create the HTML documents that make up the Web pages on their home computers. To place the Web page on the Internet, that is, upload the pages to their Web server, they will generally use an FTP client. They can therefore create 10 Web pages, and then open the FTP client and upload all 10 to their Web server at one time. FTP clients can also be used to download multiple files from one Web site or FTP server at a time as well. Many technology companies have their users' manuals or technical support materials on FTP servers, making it easier for users to gain access to the material.

Learner Activity

Go to the Internet on your PC or school library PC. Write down what type of Web browser the PC lab uses. You may find the lab uses Microsoft Internet Explorer, Mozilla Firefox, or a third-party browser. Once you have opened the browser, locate the address bar, and type in www.google.com. Your screen should show the Google Web page. Print out the Web page and circle the address bar where you typed in the URL. Then circle a hyperlink on the page. Click the hyperlink and note what Web page you navigated to by printing out that page as well. Next, pick out a Web site and type the Web site address in the address bar to navigate there. Print out that page and circle the address bar and any hyperlinks you see. Finally, do a Google search or Internet search using another search engine to find a freely available FTP client. You might use search terms such as "freeware FTP" or similar phrases. Select one and print out the Web page for that FTP software. Free software applications are available on the Internet to perform almost every imaginable task. Conduct another Internet search, again using Google or your favorite search engine, for a free software item of your choice, such as freeware drawing/graphics or freeware games. Print out the Web page for the free software you find.

Internet Data Transfer Standards

The Internet has very precise ways of routing data, similar to a large international version of the post office. For a data packet to get where it is going, logically it has a starting point and a destination point. It also passes through a variety of servers along the way that route it in the right direction. The best analogy is the mailing of a letter. The letter has a destination address of the recipient and a return address of the sender. It is then stamped at the post office in the sender's city. From there, it travels to another city and is stamped at that post office. Finally, it arrives at its intended destination address.

The post office uses a physical street address, whereas for data to travel across the Internet, it has to have an address for each and every computer connected to the Internet that is routes through. Every computer that is online has an assigned **Internet Protocol address**, called an **IP address** for short. An IP address consists of 12 digits that are separated by periods (dots) into groups of three digits. The digits must be the numbers 0 through 255. For example, 192.168.0.1 is an example of an IP address. Notice, however, that the last two sections do not contain three digits. In this case, there really are three digits, but the two zeros preceding the 1 in the fourth section and the 0 in the third section are simply not shown, but rather are implied. The address would read 192.168.<u>00</u>0.<u>00</u>1 with the underlined zeros visible instead of implied.

Data on the Internet also has a return IP address, which routes through Internet servers, is stamped with each server's IP address(es), and then finally ends up at its destination IP address. *This addressing scheme enables trained investigators to trace data from its source to its destination and vice versa.* This is discussed in further detail in the e-mail tracing section of Chapter 6.

One other important difference between post office mailing addresses and IP addresses is that IP addresses change. One computer can have multiple IP addresses at different times of the day or week. The address is called a **dynamically allocated IP address.** Most Internet service providers (ISPs) have more subscribers than they have IP addresses. Each ISP has a pool of IP addresses assigned or registered to it. When a user goes online, the user's computer talks to a computer at the Internet service provider, which assigns the user's computer a temporary IP address from the pool of available addresses. This is similar to going to a bowling alley and renting a pair of bowling shoes. Each time you go to the alley, you get bowling shoes, but perhaps a different pair every time. However, like bowling shoes, where only one person can wear a pair at a time, only one computer at a time can use a particular IP address. Chapter 6, Tracking and Tracing Internet Crimes, contains more in-depth information on IP addresses.

Web Page Addressing

Just as data sent over the Internet has source and destination addresses, and "snail mail" uses physical addresses, locations on the Internet that visitors might want to see must be named and tracked by address. You would be hard pressed to find someone who has not heard the phrase "dot com." The most commonly recognized Internet Web site addresses end in *.com*. So how does an Internet browser know where to go when you type in an address such as www.google.com?

Most Web servers on the Internet have a **static IP address.** In other words, unlike the computers of Internet users who might be assigned a different, dynamic address for each Internet session, a Web server has an IP address that doesn't change. IP addresses (e.g., 64.233.187.99) are great for computers, but human beings do not want to have to remember and type in a 12-digit number to visit a Web site. Most people are much more word oriented and prefer to type in words or a Web site's name to access a specific Web page. Therefore, computers called **domain name servers** act as the go-betweens or translators between Web site domain names and their corresponding IP addresses. For example, you can type in the URL www.google.com to visit that Web site, and the domain name server will automatically locate the IP address for the domain you've requested and route you there. You could also get the same result by typing in the exact static IP address associated with www.google.com, such as 64.233.187.99. Manually typing the IP address instead of the domain name circumvents the task the domain name server normally performs in translating domains names into IP addresses.

Investigative Uses for the Internet

Although Chapter 8 contains a thorough discussion related to the use of the Internet for intelligence gathering, it is worth introducing the concept here. There are countless uses for Internet technology. It can be used for the greater good or to commit crimes. Because of the Internet's inherent functionality that enables detailed information, including text, pictures, sound files, video files, and so forth, to be shared among users in various geographic locations, it is of great assistance to investigators. Some of its many uses are intelligence gathering, information sharing, telephone directory assistance/reverse lookup, transmittal of photos and information for AMBER or Crime Alerts, instant access to case law and statutes, and even processing of forms and other case paperwork. Many areas of the country have online interactive maps with embedded geographic information systems that show prior police calls for service, parcel numbers and tax information, property owner information, and in some cases street-level photographs of residences. You can literally see what a house looks like from the street, or from an overhead satellite photo of a neighborhood, without ever leaving your desk.

The Internet can also be a tremendous training tool. In addition to posting training and interactive video content for widespread viewing online, the Internet can also be used to establish private password-protected chat rooms or Web sharing spaces. In these private sites, law enforcement professionals can share tips and observations on the latest trends they see, enabling individuals, even in smaller organizations, to benefit from a collective pool of knowledge. In short, the Internet is the best and fastest mass information sharing medium in history.

■ SUMMARY

This chapter studies the nature of computer data and how it relates to a computer's hardware and software components. The chapter also discusses the Internet, one of the most common uses for computers today. If first responders are not knowledgeable in these basic areas, the information given in rest of the text might be hard to apply. A law enforcement officer's baseline knowledge in this area will be tested by every defense attorney the investigating officer encounters as they probe for weaknesses in the prosecution's case.

■ REVIEW QUESTIONS

1. Why is computer language referred to as binary?
2. What is the significance of the number 1,024 in relation to data storage capacity and data transmission speeds?
3. List five major components of a computer system and describe their function and relationship to each other.
4. What are the three main types of computer software?
5. Explain the difference between dynamically allocated IP addresses and static IP addresses.
6. Define the following terms: bandwidth, bus, IP address, and serial ATA.
7. FTP, HTTP, POP, and SMTP are all communications protocols for which communications mechanism?

■ TERMS

AGP bus	File Transfer Protocol	Internet Protocol (IP)
ATA-66	(FTP)	address
ATA-133	front-side bus	kilobits per second
bandwidth	(FSB)	(kbps)
baud	Fire Wire	kilobytes (KB)
binary language	gigabytes (GB)	malware
bits (b)	gigahertz (GHz)	Master Boot Record
bus	hard disk drive	(MBR)
bytes (B)	hertz (Hz)	megabits per second
CD writer or burner	hyperlink	(mbps)
domain name servers	hypertext	megabytes (MB)
drive cache	Hypertext Markup	megahertz (MHz)
DVD-ROM	Language (HTML)	motherboard
DVD writer or burner	Hypertext Transfer	operating system (OS)
dynamically allocated IP	Protocol (HTTP)	optical drive
addresses	IEEE 1394 port	PCI Express bus

platters
post office protocol (POP)
processor
protocol
random access memory (RAM)

serial ATA
simple mail transfer protocol (SMTP)
static IP addresses
terabytes (TB)

uniform resource locator (URL)
universal serial bus (USB)

■ REFERENCES

Glover, Thomas J., and Young, Millie M. 2001. *Pocket PCRef*. Littleton, CO: Sequoia Publishing.

Koon, John. 2005. Breakthrough: USB 2.0 and USB OTG. *Everything USB*, March 25. www.everythingusb.com/breakthrough.html (accessed June 5, 2006).

Kozierok, Charles M. 2001a. Master boot record (MBR). *The PC Guide*, 2.2.0. www.pcguide.com/ref/hdd/file/structMBR-c.html (accessed June 5, 2006).

——— 2001b. Primary, extended, and logical partitions. *The PC Guide*, 2.2.0. www.pcguide.com/ref/hdd/file/structMBR-c.html (accessed June 5, 2006).

Marianna, Roland. 2003. DVD burner test: seven times the capacity. *Tom's Hardware Guide*, February 7. www.tomshardware.com/2003/02/07/dvd_burner_test/ (accessed June 5, 2006).

Mims, Forrest M., III. 1991. *Getting started in electronics*. Fort Worth, Tx: Tandy Corporation.

Serial ATA International Organization. 2006, SATA technology: Technical overview. www.sata-io.org/technicaloverview.asp (accessed June 5, 2006).

chapter two

Introduction to Operating Systems

■ LEARNING OBJECTIVES

1. Define the function of a computer's operating system.
2. Describe the features within a computer's operating system that assist in gathering evidence in high-tech crimes.
3. Define the various ways that operating systems organize data with and without a user's input.
4. Examine the various types of information an operating system tracks for every data file.
5. Explore various types of computer file name extensions and how they relate to the actual content of the file.

An **operating system,** or **OS** for short, is the software component of any computer system that enables a user to interact with that computer's hardware and the data that it contains. The OS is also responsible for the organization of data on a storage drive and for enabling all of the hardware components on various system buses to interact in a smooth, efficient manner. The operating system also enables programs or other executable files to access the computer's hardware devices. For example, it enables an after-market word processing program to print out a document on the computer's default printer or save a word processing document to the computer's C drive. One other important function of an operating system is allocation of system resources. One of the system's resources is its random access memory (RAM). The operating system can configure the system's RAM to maximize efficiency, and it can also allocate a portion of the system's hard drive as virtual memory to help out when the RAM is overtaxed. Essentially, the operating system determines how data are created, modified, stored, accessed, or deleted. Knowledge of operating systems is vital for those responding to or investigating high-tech crimes.

2.1 A BRIEF HISTORY OF OPERATING SYSTEMS

Prior to the 1980s, computers were massive machines, in many cases taking up entire rooms in academic or military facilities. These monsters often relied on input in the form of cardboard cards with a pattern of holes cut out of them. These were called punch cards and allowed for rudimentary calculations that often took the computer a while to compute. The term *hacker* actually was first used to denote someone who spent time hacking holes in the punch cards. As you can imagine, these first, rudimentary, card-based systems were not user-friendly and were generally only used by engineers and scientists. As technology became more sophisticated, cheaper, and able to produce smaller machines, the size of computers, like many other devices, was reduced enough so one could fit on a desk. Computers also became easier to use as operating systems evolved.

Following on the heels of the punch card, a text-based user input system was used by the mainstream personal computers in the early 1980s. Instead of cards with holes punched systematically in different areas, users entered information into the system by using a keyboard. This text system was simply called **DOS**, which stood for **Disk Operating System.** DOS was a very basic command language that enabled users to perform tasks from a finite list of functions or commands. To start a DOS system, a user would place a floppy diskette with DOS system files into a floppy diskette drive on the computer. Any disk containing system files was called a *bootable diskette* because the computer could access the DOS files and boot itself up (make itself ready to use).

As discussed in Chapter 1, the term **boot** means that the computer is "pulling itself up by its bootstraps" from a powered-off state. In short, the DOS diskette loaded the most commonly used commands into the computer's temporary random access memory (RAM) to allow users to perform disk tasks. DOS commands were used to organize disks, create directories, rename directories, execute programs, and create, edit, delete, print, or otherwise manipulate files.

In the early PC days, every DOS command was entered after a DOS prompt by using a keyboard. The DOS prompt generally featured the drive letter for that diskette (e.g., A or C followed by a flashing underscore (_) character). (See Figure 2–1.)

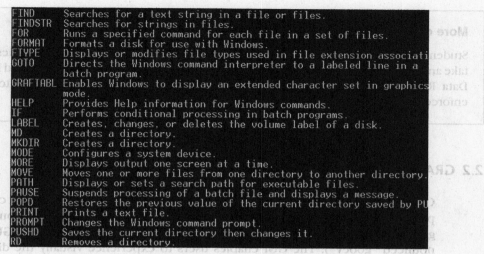

Figure 2–1 What DOS looks like on screen.

The flashing was meant to catch the user's eye and "prompt" the user to input a command. This is sometimes referred to as **command-line** entry. Many early PCs did not have a mouse input device because they did not have any graphics. They were completely text-based, meaning that the only input device that enabled a user to interact with the computer was a keyboard (Tanenbaum 2001).

Entering commands at the DOS prompt was a somewhat cumbersome task because of strict rules regarding the spelling, order, and punctuation of the commands. Using the proper **syntax** was of the utmost importance. Syntax is nothing more than grammatical rules for a given language, and computers had their own specific language for command-line entry. Misspelling a command or entering the commands in the wrong order meant that the computer would either be unable to process the command or would do so in the wrong order, yielding surprising or frustrating results. A baseline knowledge of DOS and entering commands from a DOS prompt is still relevant today, however, as there are many DOS commands that can be run within an operating system such as Microsoft Windows. Further there are several computer forensics software utilities that rely on DOS version 6.22.

Because of this somewhat unintuitive user interface, computers did not achieve quick mainstream popularity in the early 1980s. Some of the initial experiences with this interface left people with such a bad feeling that computers were (and still are) actively mistrusted and hated in many circles. Computers were, at first, popular only in business and the sciences, where people recognized their advantages in performing certain tasks such as word processing and creating mathematical spreadsheets. Although the text-based interface was much more user-friendly than having to punch holes in a card, users still demanded even more user-friendly systems, and not until such systems were developed did computers make the leap from scientific/business use to mainstream use in most homes and businesses.

More on DOS 6.22 and DOS Software Utilities

Students or investigators looking to learn more about DOS-based software utilities can take an introductory course through the National White Collar Crime Center called Basic Data Recovery and Analysis (BDRA). This course is available free of charge to law enforcement officers. See the course Web site at www.nw3c.org.

2.2 GRAPHICAL USER INTERFACES

Computers, like other technology, continue to evolve, and there is a constant push to make computers more user-friendly. As part of that effort, computer programmers developed what is called the **graphical user interface,** or **GUI** (pronounced "gooey"). The GUI enables users to experience visually the directory structure on their disks and to see their files (see Figure 2–2). This enables them to organize the contents of their computer much more easily. Further, the invention of another user input device, the mouse, gave users a much more intuitive way to move, delete, or otherwise manipulate data files. Instead of typing in a complex command to move a file, users could simply click a mouse button, drag the file to

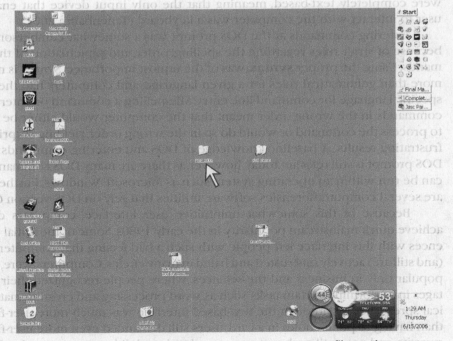

Figure 2–2 Graphical user interfaces use icons to represent files and applications on a computer.

another directory, and drop it there. In addition to being much simpler, interacting with a GUI was also much faster. It also gave users the feeling that data on their computer were tangible because data could essentially be grabbed and moved around. This analogy is so apt, that many cursors actually look like hands grabbing the object the user is interacting with on screen.

As computers entered the graphical age, they started to gain widespread acceptance because they became much easier to use and performed many useful operations. Graphical applications also enabled computer users to perform tasks other than word processing and mathematical computations. The ability to produce graphics quickly on screen enabled people to use computers for publication layout, drawing, computer-aided design (CAD) drafting, and virtual modeling of structures. As anyone who has played computer solitaire knows, the GUI also enables users to play electronic games. Computers also came to be used as powerful research tools because complete dictionaries or encyclopedias could be placed on a computer's hard drive for easy access. For these reasons—and for the fact that computer hardware was becoming cheaper to manufacture—computers started to enter the mainstream.

The implementation of modems that allowed fast two-way data sharing between computer systems further made computers more useful. Instead of mailing information, users were able to share large amounts of text with each other very rapidly. With the birth of the Internet, data sharing became extremely efficient and practical. The Internet explosion of the 1990s demonstrated the extraordinary potential of the personal computer. From a data terminal, users could interact with the world, performing research at the world's libraries and "surfing" millions of Web sites with information on every conceivable topic. Of course, if users can use these tools for good and legitimate purposes, users could also use computers for more nefarious pursuits. For good uses and bad, the Internet cemented computers in the mainstream psyche and the number of households with computers in the U.S. continues to skyrocket.

All of the preceding tasks are made possible by the operating system of the PC. It is, in essence, the go-between that enables users to "go hands-on" with the hardware components of the computer system. The operating system enables users to start a program such as a word processor. For instance, the OS enables the word processor to interact with a printer so the user can generate a hard copy of text. The OS also performs an interfacing role between a word processor and a hard drive, allowing a user to save a data file to the hard disk. In short, the OS directs traffic between software, user commands, and the various input and output devices.

2.3 EVOLUTION OF MODERN OPERATING SYSTEMS

In a continuing endeavor to make the computing experience easier, more useful, and more satisfying for the general user, developers of operating systems have created several generations of OS software. Some of the earliest were OS/2, Windows 3.1, and the Macintosh OS. Windows and the MAC OS have gone through several generational evolutions. Windows has gone through versions Windows 3.11, Windows 95, Windows 98, Windows Me, Windows 2000, and Windows XP. As of this writing, the Macintosh OS is version 10. In addition to these operating systems, there are several others such as Unix and Linux. Each generational upgrade was made to improve upon the last version or to enable more advanced functionality. In some cases, the OS upgrades went along with hardware improvements such as moving from a 16-bit system to a 32-bit system. A 32-bit OS coupled with a 32-bit processor is obviously much more efficient than a 16-bit system is. There are currently 64-bit processors and software on the market, and it is logical to assume that the industry perhaps is only a few years away from deploying 128-bit systems.

Another area that undergoes continuing development and improvement is overall system stability and reliability, which is another function of the operating system. Because the greatest market share of PCs use the Windows operating system, this text focuses predominantly on Windows. Macintosh computer forensics is still in its infancy, which has a lot to do with the much smaller number of Mac users compared to Windows users. More recent versions of the Windows operating system feature a different file system (the mechanism for organizing all of the files on the hard disk). Windows 98 and earlier versions featured the File Allocation Table (FAT) file system. Windows NT and Windows XP use a newer, more stable file system called the NT file system (NTFS), which spreads the organizational data for that given drive across the volume, making it less likely the entire drive could fail. Under FAT32 (the 32-bit version of File Allocation Table), if the file allocation table is damaged, the hard disk drive could be rendered useless and unreadable. This is one of many stability features that was designed into the newer operating systems. Table 2–1 provides a summary of file allocation table comparisons and functions.

Another stability feature the operating system must handle is the relative isolation of programs as they interact with the operating system. Under older

Table 2–1 File Allocation Table Comparisons and Functions

FAT12	Earliest File Allocation Table	Used by DOS, floppy disks, and the very low capacity (under 16 MB), earliest hard disk drives
FAT16	16-bit File Allocation Table	Used by early small and medium-sized (16-MB to 2-GB) hard disk drives under 16-bit operating systems, such as Windows 3.1
FAT32	32-bit File Allocation Table	Used by medium to large modern hard disk drives (2-GB to 120-GB), under 32-bit or higher operating systems, and most USB keys
NTFS	NT file system	Used for very large hard disk drives (40 GB and up) under modern operating systems such as Windows NT or Windows XP

operating systems, a program that "froze" or "locked up" in many cases required that the entire computer be rebooted. Sometimes the user could command a restart by using the Ctrl-Alt-Delete command (pressing the Ctrl, Alt, and Delete keys on the keyboard simultaneously). Other times, the user would have to perform a "hard boot" by manually powering down the computer. In most modern operating systems, the programs are generally isolated from each other. Therefore, if one application freezes or crashes, the user may need to terminate only that specific application. The rest of the operating system and the other programs will continue to operate as usual. To shut down a frozen application, the user presses the "three-finger salute"—Ctrl+Alt+Delete—to access the Windows Task Manager. The user can then select the application that is not responding and click End Task to shut it down. Keeping the system active and not requiring a full reboot can save a great deal of time. In addition, hard boots generally result in the loss of all unsaved data. The evolution to application isolation really took the sting out of the once-dreaded computer crash.

Another unique improvement among newer operating systems is the plug and play capability, which enables the computer to configure new hardware devices added to it even while the computer is powered on and running. The second release of Windows 98 was the first operating system to enable **Plug and Play (PnP)** devices to be added to the computer while running. For instance, this enables a universal serial bus (USB) device, such as a digital camera, to be plugged into the computer, and after a few-seconds delay, the camera can interact with the operating system. No longer was it necessary to restart the computer after installing a new hardware device. Rebooting is often viewed as inconvenient because it takes time to do all of the tasks that must be performed during the boot process, which is discussed in greater detail in the next section.

2.4 THE BOOT PROCESS

Before an operating system is activated, several processes must be completed when a computer is first turned on. As discussed briefly in Chapter 1, the computer pulls itself up by its bootstraps from an off state to an on state. That process involves several steps, starting on a very basic level. The first thing that occurs when a computer is turned on is a rudimentary test of the hardware devices needed to complete the rest of the boot process. The first and most basic test is the power-on self test, or POST for short. The POST runs basic diagnostics to check the functionality of the processor, the system memory (RAM), and the basic input output system (BIOS). If all items pass their diagnostic test, the system is able to move on to the next step in the boot process, which is accessing the BIOS.

BIOS information usually comprises low-level instructions stored on a read-only memory chip, also known as a ROM. The instructions are needed to activate the mass storage devices (hard disk drives) of the system so that the computer can access data stored on the hard disk drive. Once this occurs, the computer can access the Master Boot Record (MBR) on that drive to obtain other information it needs to continue booting. By using the MBR and file allocation table, the computer is able to locate the first part of the operating system installed on the machine, and then begins to execute the instructions in the operating system code.

When the OS loads, it must load several sets of instructions, called *device drivers,* that correspond to hardware devices the operating system will use. For example, the OS will load a graphics device driver so that the user will be able to see icons, the mouse pointer, task bars, and other visual items once the OS is fully loaded. The OS also loads sound card device drivers to enable the OS to play sound effects and music on the computer's speakers. It also loads drivers for the mouse, keyboard, and any other devices currently connected to the computer. When a new device is added to the computer while the computer is running (plug and play), the delay after the device is installed is partially caused by the computer loading that device's driver. Device drivers usually load in a few seconds, allowing for almost instant use.

2.5 TASKS PERFORMED BY THE OPERATING SYSTEM

The OS is responsible for completing many different tasks, and if it improperly performs any of them, the system could crash, lose data, output unexpected or unpredictable results, or fail to function entirely. The tasks that the OS performs fall into six general categories:

- Processor management
- System resources configuration
- Hardware device configuration
- Storage management
- Program interface
- User interface

Processor management specifies how the computer best takes advantage of the computer's processor chip. The OS determines which programs can access the processor, how many can try to access it at any given time (multitasking), and what portion of the processor's power can be used by a particular function. When multiple programs attempt to access the processor at the same time, the OS can also act as a traffic director and send the programs to the processor in a logical, ordered manner to take the best advantage of available processing power. The OS can also monitor what percentage of the processor's available computing power is already in use and what spare capacity is available. In Windows, The Task Manager (see Figure 2–3) enables users to view the processes running on the computer as well as statistics on system performance.

The second task, system resource management, is related to processor management, but deals with system resources other than the available processing power. One of the most important resources is the system memory (RAM). The OS can analyze how much RAM is available, what items are loaded into the system RAM, what items are waiting for available RAM space, and how much hard disk drive

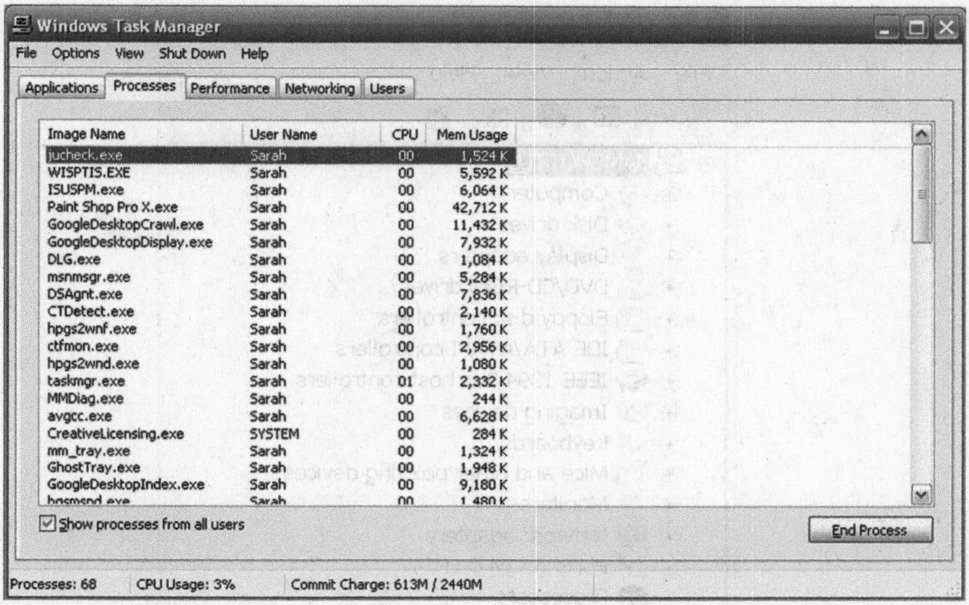

Figure 2–3 Windows Task Manager offers a graphical representation of processor management tasks.

space is allocated as a dumping ground for data that won't fit in available system RAM. This allocated hard disk drive space is sometimes called the *swap file* or *page file*. An OS can set aside virtually any quantity of drive space for use as *virtual RAM*. If a system is constantly using up its available system RAM and needs to access the virtual RAM on the hard disk drive, one way to speed up the system is to increase the size of the RAM by adding RAM memory modules to any available memory slot on the motherboard. The computer can store electromagnetic impulses on memory chips attached to the motherboard far faster than it can read and write data to the hard disk drives on the Integrated Device Electronics (IDE) or serial ATA bus.

The third task, hardware device configuration, enables the programs installed on a system and the user to interact with installed hardware devices. It also enables the computer to be further customized on the fly by allowing users to install new devices. Further, modern operating systems using USB and FireWire devices can customize the system by using Plug and Play devices. For example, a user can plug a digital camera into an available USB port and turn the camera on. The computer, after a short time, recognizes a new device is attached to the computer and after a brief configuration period is able to interact with that device. This is very useful for dumping digital pictures or video off of a camera's memory card and onto the computer for long-term storage. In windows, Device Manager enables user to view and configure installed and attached devices (see Figure 2–4).

In the days before Windows 98SE when Plug and Play technology was not available and devices were not "hot swappable," meaning they had to be installed

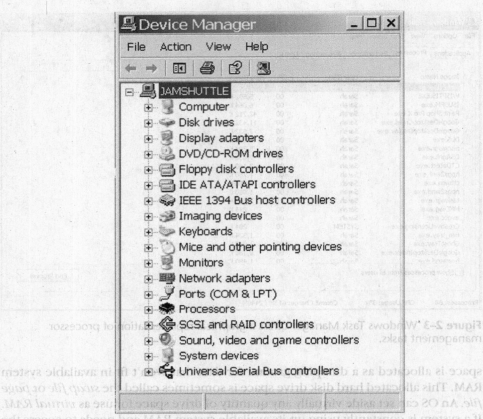

Figure 2–4 Windows Device Manager enables users
to view and configure installed and attached devices.

when the computer was turned off, installing a new device usually meant having to restart the computer and reboot so that the device would be recognized during the initialization of the OS. This resulted in a delay of many minutes. In the days since, operating systems are fully integrated with hot-swappable USB and FireWire standards and allow systems to add and remove multiple hardware devices without having to reboot. This is a virtual "nerdvana" to advanced computer users who have desired this functionality for years. Another great application of Plug and Play capability is the use of USB thumb drives also known as USB keys. A user can simply plug the thumb drive into an available USB port on a running computer and the computer will recognize the drive as another mass storage device. The user can then save data to the drive, remove the drive, and walk away with data in hand. USB drives, with smaller physical size, much faster read and write speeds, and higher storage capacity than floppy disk drives, have made floppy disks practically obsolete.

The ability to add and remove drives by using USB and FireWire is directly related to task 4, storage management. The operating system configures and organizes the various storage devices connected to a computer. One of the main

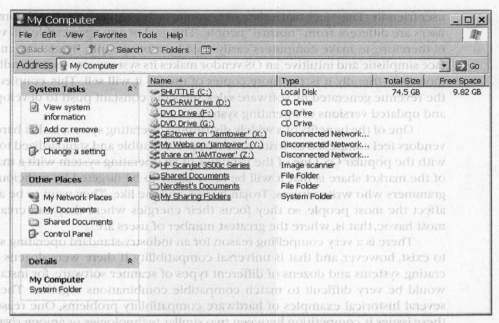

Figure 2–5 An example of the operating system assigning drive letters to multiple devices.

functions is to assign drive letters to the various drives. For example, the standard default hard drive is assigned the letter *C*. The first CD-ROM drive might then be assigned the letter *D*. If a USB thumb drive is added, the OS would likely temporarily designate it as drive E. The OS generally works its way up from *C* to *Z*, assigning new drive letters as needed (see Figure 2–5). The OS can also be used to format and partition newly added drives for increased storage, although the primary drive where the OS is stored must be formatted and partitioned before the OS is installed. For example, Windows installations usually guide the installer through formatting and partitioning the drive before any Windows system files are copied onto the hard disk drive. Last, the OS organizes the drives into a coherent folder and subfolder structure to enable the user to sort data into categories and subcategories. See Section 2.6, "Data Organization," for more specific information on the file structure.

The fifth task the operating system performs is the program or application interfacing. The OS enables executable programs to access hardware devices installed on the system. A bunch of software programs with no central platform in common would generally have problems working together. The OS provides a standard "playing field" and allows software to be written to work on that playing field. For example, a graphics program may need to access a scanner to import a graphics file to be edited. Without the operating system acting as a translator and go-between, the graphics application might not speak the same language as the scanner.

The sixth, and most often complained about, task of the OS is allowing the user to interact with the computer. People often comment that a computer is not user-friendly. They feel that using a computer is highly technical, and computer users are different from "normal" people. The goal of any respectable OS vendor is, therefore, to make computers easily used by more people. By making an interface simplistic and intuitive, an OS vendor makes its system very user-friendly. The more user-friendly it is, the more copies of the OS it will sell. This, coupled with the revenue generated by software sales, fuels the constant push to develop new and updated versions of operating systems.

One of the benefits of a widely distributed operating system is that hardware vendors feel compelled to write code that is compatible and standardized to work with the popular OS. One of the liabilities of an operating system with a majority of the market share is that it will be more likely to be targeted by malicious programmers who write viruses, Trojan horses, and the like. They want to be able to affect the most people, so they focus their energies where they can create the most havoc, that is, where the greatest number of users are.

There is a very compelling reason for an industry-standard operating system to exist, however, and that is universal compatibility. If there were dozens of operating systems and dozens of different types of scanner software, for instance, it would be very difficult to match compatible combinations together. There are several historical examples of hardware compatibility problems. One reason for these issues is competition between two similar technologies or among rival electronics corporations. A famous example from the 1980s was the competing standards of Beta VCRs versus VHS VCRs. Both performed roughly the same task, but each was different enough that they were not interchangeable. Another example is incompatible power connectors in Europe versus the United States: to plug a U.S.-made device into a European power outlet requires an adapter, and vice versa. Another more recent example is the standards battle between DVD optical media manufacturers. DVD+R and DVD+RW formats are supported by Philips, Sony, Hewlett-Packard, Dell, Ricoh, Yamaha, and other manufacturers. The competing standards DVD-R and DVD-RW are promoted by Panasonic, Toshiba, Apple Computer, Hitachi, NEC, Pioneer, Samsung, and Sharp, to name a few. In other words, speaking a common language is very necessary, and the OS is the common language that allows equipment from various manufacturers to work with software from many other vendors. In many ways, it can be called the glue that binds any computer system together.

2.6 DATA ORGANIZATION

Operating systems perform a number of functions, but perhaps the most important is the organization of data on a computer's mass storage devices. The modern-day operating system generally is stored on the computer's primary hard disk drive, which in most cases is called the C drive. One frequently asked question is why the primary drive is named C instead of A. The system starts with the C drive because in the early years when computers were booted from large floppy disks, systems usually had two floppy disk drives designated A and B. The oldest systems had very little random access memory, and often the DOS diskette had to be left in drive A. The "work" or data diskette would have to go in the second drive, drive B, because the computer could not keep all the DOS commands in memory and often had to refer back to the DOS diskette in drive A. Now, many systems do not even include a floppy disk drive because floppy media is slow, inefficient, and has a tiny data storage capacity by today's standards; it is, for all practical purposes, extinct. As such, no devices listed as drive A or B might exist anymore on a system, but the computer still defaults to starting at C during the installation of the OS.

As more disk drives are added to the system, they are assigned driver letters, usually starting with D, then E. For example, a computer with three hard disk drives and a DVD burner may have hard disk drives C, E, and F, and the DVD burner labeled as drive D. The way the drive letters are assigned is usually determined by the order the drivers were installed on the system. In the preceding example, you can conclude that the C drive was installed first, followed by the DVD burner, with the latter two hard disk drives added last. When a portable drive, such as a USB jump drive, is attached to the system, that drive is usually assigned a temporary drive letter by the operating system. In this scenario, it would likely be assigned drive letter G when plugged into a USB port.

Computers organize all of these drives and their directories into a **directory structure.** The top-most organizational level of a hard disk drive is called the **root** of the drive. The root can contain a large number of **directories.** Each directory can contain a large number of **subdirectories.** The only real limitation on the number of directory entries on a hard disk drive is the size of the drive and the number of sectors (individual sections) the drive is divided into. Similar to the branches of a family tree, the subdirectories can also have their own subdirectories. Understanding directory structures is vital to any first responder, especially when he or she must describe where a piece of evidence is found on a computer. Merely saying, "I found the image of child pornography" is not enough, and the first responder must be able to describe the exact **file path** where the evidence resides on the computer. (See Figure 2–6.)

A file path is the exact description of where on the disk drive a file exists. For example, assume a file called Address.txt is located on the C drive. It is located within a folder called Homework. The Homework folder is on the first level, or root, of the C drive. The complete file path for this file is as follows: C:\homework\address.txt. The backslash character (\) indicates a folder level. Documenting the exact file path of an evidence file or contraband file is very important. This is similar to documenting where a baggie of cocaine is located in crime scene. It is not enough to say the baggie was in the bedroom. A much better description is say the baggie is in a red shoebox under the bed in the northeast bedroom on the second floor. That degree of specificity is every bit as important with digital evidence files.

Operating systems enable a user to organize task-specific data on the system's hard disk drive(s). For example, an operating system might have a feature known as an address book for storing street, mailing, or e-mail addresses and phone numbers. It will similarly have a Bookmarks or Favorites folder that stores links or shortcuts to a user's favorite Internet Web sites. Although it may seem at

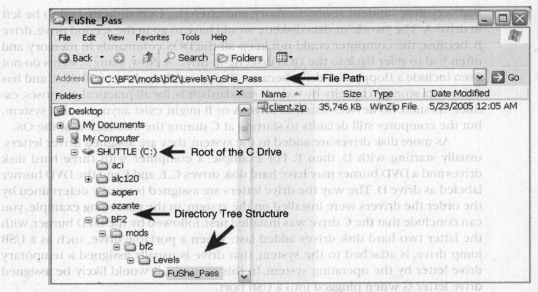

Figure 2–6 Graphical representation of a computer's directory structure.

first glance that a favorites folder or address book might not be part of the operating system, the line between the OS and Internet browsers has become quite blurred, particularly since the same methods are being utilized to search the Internet as to search a computer's hard drive. Using Windows Explorer, for example, a user can view hard drive contents by selecting a drive letter, or just as easily type in a URL to browse to a Web site. It can be argued that an Internet browser, then, is an integrated component of an operating system. Some operating systems have special folders for storing a user's picture collections, movie files, or music library containing songs and audio files.

2.7 OTHER OS UTILITY PROGRAMS

In addition to data organization, most operating systems have a number of other installed software components designed to perform various tasks. Most, if not all, feature a search utility that enables a user to quickly search for a file on the hard disk drives based on a number of different search criteria. For example, a user could search for all word processor documents should the need arise. (See Figure 2–7). In addition, most modern operating systems come with utilities that enable users to open most file types. For example, Windows has graphics viewing utilities that enable users to preview, open, edit, and print graphics files. An OS may also feature a media utility so users can play videos, sound, or other multimedia files.

Another great feature of modern operating systems is the capability of allowing a computer to perform multiple functions simultaneously. This is often

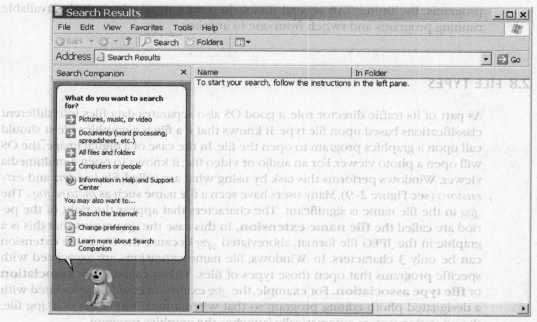

Figure 2–7 A search utility.

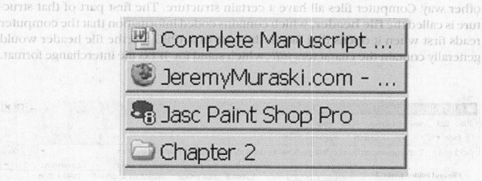

Figure 2–8 Taskbar icons.

referred to as **multitasking.** A textbook author, for example, could listen to music in a media player while typing in a separate word processing program. The earliest computers did not have enough memory to hold more than one application at a time. Further, text-based operating systems did not offer an efficient way to switch between applications, even if the memory capacity was available. Most Windows users are familiar with the taskbar icons, or Alt-Tab command, which enables them to switch easily between open program windows and functions. (See Figure 2–8.) When a user holds down the ALT key on the keyboard and hits TAB, the multitasking window pops up showing the icons for available running programs. By hitting TAB several times, the user can tab through the available running programs and switch from one to another.

2.8 FILE TYPES

As part of its traffic director role, a good OS also separates data files into different classifications based upon file type. It knows that if a file is a graphics file, it should call upon a graphics program to open the file. In the case of a digital image, the OS will open a photo viewer. For an audio or video file, it knows to open a multimedia viewer. Windows performs this task by using what are called *file headers* and *extensions* (see Figure 2–9). Many users have seen a file name such as *picture.jpg* . The *.jpg* in the file name is significant. The characters that appear the right of the period are called the **file name extension.** In this case the .jpg means that this is a graphic in the JPEG file format, abbreviated *.jpg* because the file name extension can be only 3 characters. In Windows, file name extensions are associated with specific programs that open those types of files. This is called a **file association** or **file type association.** For example, the *.jpg* extension could be associated with a designated photo editing program so that when a user double-clicks a .jpg file, the operating system automatically launches the graphics program.

In addition to the file name extension, computers can determine file type another way. Computer files all have a certain structure. The first part of that structure is called the **file header,** which contains coded information that the computer reads first when it opens that file. In the case of a JPEG file, the file header would generally contain the characters *JFIF*, which stand for JPEG file interchange format.

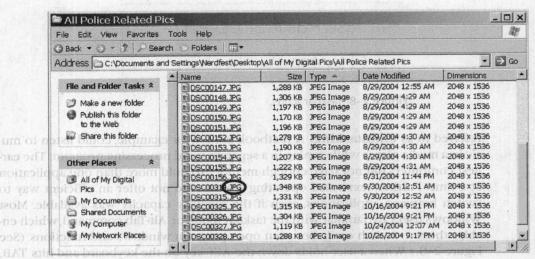

Figure 2–9 Every file has an extension as part of its file name.

Table 2–2   Common File Types

File Type	File Name Extension	Description
ASP	.asp	Active Server Pages (enhanced Web page functions)
AVI	.avi	Audio Video Interleaved (movie files)
Batch	.bat	DOS batch file
Binary	.bin	Binary file type, commonly found on CDs
Bitmap	.bmp	Bitmap graphics (common to paint programs)
Cabinet	.cab	Microsoft installation cabinet file
Checkdisk	.chk	Temporary file that holds data recovered during a ChkDsk operation
DLL	.dll	dynamic-link library (file common to Windows)
Document	.doc	Microsoft Word document file format
Executable	.exe	A self-contained program or executable file
GIF	.gif	Graphics Interchange Format—file that holds low-resolution graphics or an animation
Help	:hlp	File format associated with a program's built-in user's manual or help screen functions
JPEG	.jpg	Very common digital photo or graphics file format. JPEGs are compressed, making file sizes smaller and making this file type popular on the Internet
Movie	.mov	Quicktime or Apple movie file format
MP3	.mp3	Compressed format for audio files such as those ripped from music CDs.
MPEG	.mpg	Common movie file format that features file compression

Any OS or other program that reads the file header instead of the file name extension can still know the file type. Table 2–2 lists common file types that can be found on most modern computers. The list is by no means complete, and there are Web sites that keep updated lists of new file types as they are developed. For example, www.filext.com is a Web site that contains a database of file name extensions and the various programs that can open such file types. It's a great resource for any computer user or investigator who might encounter unfamiliar file name extensions.

Learner Activity

Section 2.7 discusses the Windows Search utility, and Section 2.8 examines the various file types that can be found on a PC. This exercise demonstrates how a user can search a PC for all files of a specific type. Because .jpg files are the most common image format, the first search focuses on these. To access the Windows Search utility, click Start, then click Search. Windows will ask what you want to search for. Click All Files or Folders. The search box will then come up with blanks for entering information. In the blank titled All or part of the file name, type *.**jpg.** The asterisk is a wildcard character that means all files that contain the .jpg extension will be searched for. By typing in *.jpg, you are asking the search utility to find and list all JPEG images it locates. In the search box titled Look in, select the My Computer option. This will search any drive or device connected to that computer. Conduct the search for all JPEG images. Pick three images and document the file locations, size, date created, and date modified. To get this file property information, right-click a file (click with the rightmost mouse button). A menu of possible actions will appear. At or near the bottom of the list, you will see the word *Properties*. Left-click Properties to display file properties for this file, including the File Name, File Location (Path), Size, Size on Disk, and the Dates the file was created, modified, and accessed. Once you have completed the search for all JPEG images and documented three of them, search again, this time using a different file name extension such as *.wmv , *.avi, or *.mpg to search for movie files on the computer. As in the first search, pick three files that you find and document their file location, size, date created, and date modified.

2.9 OPERATING SYSTEM DATA ARCHIVAL

Another function performed by the OS is storing user-customizable settings for later use. User set up their computers in the way they deem to be organized and efficient. For example, a user might place program icons (small pictures that represent a program functions) in certain locations on the screen, such as all work-related icons in the upper-left-hand corner and all video game icons in the lower right. Operating systems also store a lot of data, often without the knowledge or consent of the user. One example is the Internet history archive. If users don't specifically disable this feature, their computer automatically tracks which Web sites the computer has visited. It may even keep small pictures or other small file downloads in a cache or archive folder. These files are generally downloaded to the computer the first time a user goes to a particular Web site. (See Figure 2–10.) The reason the computer saves these is to speed up the Internet Web site browsing experience for the user. The computer can store graphics, such as a company's logo, locally on the computer's hard disk drive. That way, the next time a user visits that Web site, the computer does not have to download the logo image a second time;

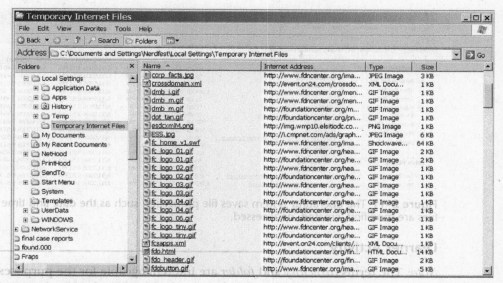

Figure 2–10 Temporary Internet files stored on a hard disk drive.

it just pulls the file from its own local hard disk drive. In this era of broadband connections, caching data is not really a necessary process, but in the previous dial-up era, not having to download a graphics image every time you visited the same site sped up the browsing experience considerably.

The operating system also stores a list of the most recently used files and most recently run programs. These lists are handy to investigators because they likely can reveal the last 10 or 20 operations that were performed on a given suspect computer. Most application programs also remember the most recently used files. A word processing program may, for example, remember the four most recent documents that were opened in it and can keep that information in a recent files list.

2.10 SYSTEM DATE AND TIME, FILE DATE AND TIME

The OS also keeps track of the **file properties,** including date and time (see Figure 2–11). The OS does this for a number of reasons, but one of them is to track when files are created, modified, or deleted. Every file on a computer should have a **file creation date, file modified date,** and generally a **file last accessed date.** Note the important distinction between *accessed* and *modified*. *Accessed* merely means the file was opened or examined, but no changes were made to it (it was not *modified*). This is an important distinction because a forensic investigator, whether at a real-world crime scene or an electronic one, should never make changes to (modify) the crime scene. Accessing the file is necessary to see what it is, but technology crime investigators must never modify a file.

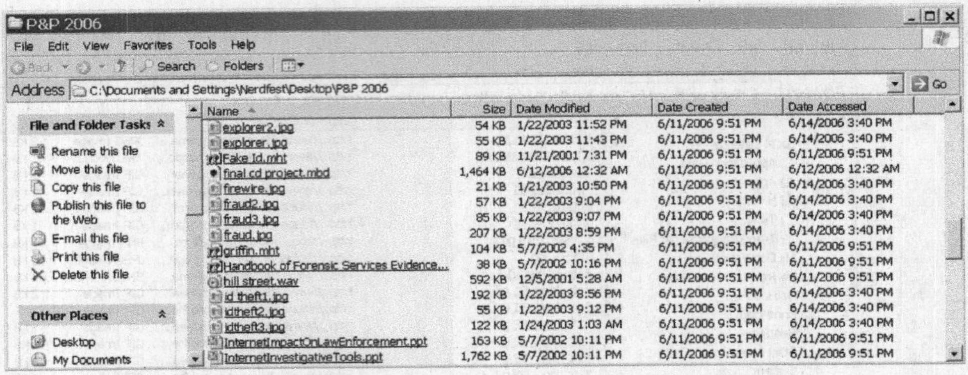

Figure 2–11 The operating system saves file properties, such as the date and time files are modified, created, or accessed.

Learner Activity

Note: The terms *directory* and *folder* are interchangeable for the purposes of this exercise. On a Windows-based computer, double-click the My Computer icon. This should display all drives and devices currently connected to the computer. Record each drive letter and the device it represents. Note that the C drive almost always is the computer's main hard disk drive. Double-click the C drive icon to open the C drive and display all of the folders and files located on the root of the C drive. Record the names of at least three different folders or directories. Choose one of the directories and double-click it. You should see files and possibly other subdirectories listed in that folder. Record three file names in this directory. Next, right-click a file (click with the rightmost mouse button). A menu of possible actions will appear. At or near the bottom of the list you will see the word *Properties*. Left-click Properties to display file properties for this file, including the File Name, File Location (Path), Size, Size on Disk, and the Dates the file was created, modified, and accessed. Document this information for all three files you select. *Hint:* You can easily take a "picture" of the computer screen by pressing the Print Screen (PrtScr) key on the keyboard. If you are typing this assignment in word processing software such as Word or WordPerfect, you can simply paste this screen capture into your document by pressing Ctrl+V or by clicking the Edit menu and choosing Paste. *This is not a forensic technique that is acceptable for a formal court case, but can be a great technique for homework and computer-related assignments.*

A trick often played by computer criminals is to change the date and time of the operating system clock, which is very easy to do (see Figure 2–12). It is easy to see that a system clock set ahead 5 years must necessarily complicate an investigation. For example, if it is really 2007 and the computer believes it is 2010, all of the files created may indicate that they were created in 2010. It is therefore very important to note the system's established date and time when you are examining a suspect's computer so you can account for any such oddities in the time and date stamps associated with files.

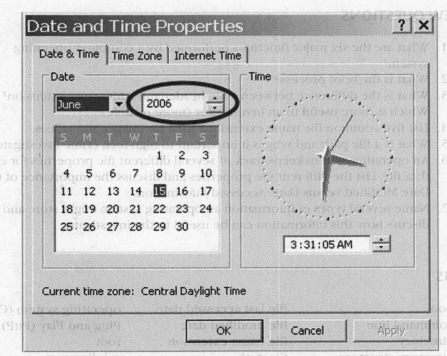

Figure 2–12 The Date and Time Properties feature, which enables users to set the date and time of the computer's system clock.

Because most operating systems keep track of information without any input from the user, users often forget about these functions. Therefore, even a high-level computer criminal may forget to delete or reset one of these archive systems, thus leaving a minute piece of evidence behind. Criminals may forget to delete one incriminating e-mail message, or they may deny ever visiting a child pornography Web site even though the URL of a known child porn site is archived in their Internet history cache. One such oversight on the part of the criminal, and the investigator wins.

■ **SUMMARY**

This chapter examines the history and evolution of operating systems and the graphical user interface. Operating systems have evolved to be more stable and efficient, enabling hardware to be added while the computer is running, and reducing the likelihood of a total system crash or failure. Rebooting the system and all that it entails are no longer required as frequently as earlier. This chapter discusses the boot process, the various tasks performed by modern-day operating systems, and how operating systems organize data on a computer. The focus of the next few chapters is on how criminals put computers to work for them.

■ REVIEW QUESTIONS

1. What are the six major functions performed by a computer operating system?
2. What is the boot process?
3. What is the difference between a file header and a file name extension? Which is more useful to an investigator (more reliable)?
4. List five common file name extensions used for images and videos.
5. What is a file path and why is it important to high-tech crime investigators?
6. An operating system keeps track of several different file properties for each data file. List the different file properties and discuss the importance of the Date Modified versus Date Accessed information.
7. Name several types of information an operating system might store and discuss how this information can be useful to the investigator.

■ TERMS

boot	file last accessed date	operating system (OS)
command line	file modified date	Plug and Play (PnP)
directory	file name extension	root
directory structure	file path	subdirectory
Disk Operating System	file properties	syntax
(DOS)	file type association	
file association	graphical user	
file creation date	interface (GUI)	
file header	multitasking	

■ REFERENCES

Tanenbaum, Andrew S. 2001. *Modern operating systems.* 2nd ed. Upper Saddle River, NJ: Prentice Hall.

High-Tech Criminal Offenses and E-Mail-Based Crimes

LEARNING OBJECTIVES

1. Explain the legitimate uses of high technology.
2. Describe e-mail harassment, threats, and cyberstalking.
3. Explain how violations of restraining orders are being committed with technology.
4. Explain identity theft and how it's committed with technology.
5. Explain the classification of criminality and the hierarchy of proof applied to all criminal investigations.
6. Explain the first responder's proper response to common high-tech crimes committed today.
7. Explain the proper investigative protocols for investigating high-tech criminal offenses and e-mail-based crimes.

As civilizations evolve, so do criminals. There have always been battles between law-abiding citizens, represented by law enforcement officials, and the criminal element. Advancements in law enforcement have often been forced by the unique criminal mind, causing the police to play catch-up.

The digital age has left law enforcement in the dust. A small number of front-line officers or first responders—the backbone of the police department who are first on the scene and ultimately decide which cases are brought into the criminal justice system—do not have the requisite skills to properly respond to and report on the many high-tech crimes that are committed each day. First responders need training, education, and skill development in high-tech crime recognition and evidence collection (Stambaugh et al. 2000). This chapter explores many of the types of high-tech crimes committed by criminals or used in support of unlawful gain. Each type is discussed in great detail and supported by practical examples and investigative protocols.

Computer crime is often a term used synonymously with *child pornography* or *hackers*. However, computers and the World Wide Web (WWW) are being used with increasing frequency to commit more common crimes. What once required criminals to work in disguise, under the cover of darkness, or forcefully take from another can now be done from the comfort of their own homes with little threat to their own personal safety. Why engage in a risky bank robbery where the average take is less than $5,000 (Federal Bureau of Investigation 2002) when you can pull off a high-tech identity theft from your living room and make an average of $10,200 (Federal Trade Commission 2003). High-tech crimes are generally much safer physically than committing a traditional crime against persons is. Furthermore, the low cost of the Internet and its perceived level of anonymity enable it to be used by criminals of all demographics and socioeconomic statuses.

3.1 OVERVIEW OF HIGH-TECH CRIMES

Research, networking, commerce, communication, and entertainment are some of the legitimate uses of the Internet. In contrast, the list of high-tech crimes include is but not limited to e-mail harassment and threats, e-mail and Web site scams, credit card fraud, identity theft, violations of restraining orders, child pornography (creation, possession, and distribution), child enticement, hacking, drug trafficking, cellular/phone fraud, terrorism and organized crime, and manufacturing fake identification. These crimes are all being committed with the use of computers, the Internet and WWW, and by other high-tech means. This list contains only the more common types of offenses that first responders might encounter.

The true number of high-tech crimes committed each year cannot be accurately measured. No agreed-upon national or international definition of terms, such as for *computer crime*, *high-tech crime*, or *information technology crime*, exists (Goodman 2001). Furthermore, the current Uniform Crime Reports do not track, measure, or report on these types of criminal offenses.

High-tech crime is a worldwide, national, and local problem. Successfully combating it begins at the front lines with municipal, county, and state law enforcement officers. However, most law enforcement agencies do not have the funding available to hire dedicated computer crime cops. The responsibility of responding to, reporting on, and investigating high-tech crime in most agencies falls on the shoulders of the first responders. Because of its worldwide nature, oftentimes it appears to be an uphill battle, and in many respects it is.

Many of the crimes discussed in this chapter are misdemeanors, which forbid extradition from one state or country to another. Some of them are serious felonies with full extradition, and others are ordinance violations that carry only a civil forfeiture or fine. The classification of criminality and hierarchy of proof are outlined in Figure 3–1.

If a municipality has adopted a state law as its own ordinance, and it wishes to prosecute a criminal that lives in another state, it could mail the summons to appear in the municipal court to the suspect. If the suspect fails to appear, the municipal judge could issue a warrant and patiently wait for the suspect to travel to the state, city, town, or village, and then make an arrest. If the suspect never leaves his/her home state, then the suspect could never be brought to justice. The same scenario also applies to misdemeanors. However, there is a remedy for this problem. **Vicinage** is a term used to describe parallel jurisdiction over the same offense, and it is not considered double jeopardy. An offender whose cybercrime affects different counties within a state or in other states may be tried in any of those locations that are consistent with constitutional limitations (Brenner 1999). For example, if the suspect resides in Texas and sends a harassing e-mail message to a victim in California, both jurisdictions could prosecute for the same offense. The virtual nature of the Internet often blurs jurisdictional boundaries, forcing some agencies to argue over whose case it is. Consequently, the victim becomes victimized again, like a virtual pinball being sent from one police agency to another until one finally decides to take the complaint. Cases of this nature can be and have been prosecuted in different jurisdictions for the same offense. It isn't considered double jeopardy because the case is being heard in two different court jurisdictions. Convincing a local district attorney of this can be another matter, however.

This chapter discusses high-tech crimes that use e-mail or other Internet-based communications media (e.g., instant messaging) as a vehicle for specific criminal offenses. These offenses include e-mail harassment, threats, and cyberstalking, violations of restraining orders, identity theft, and 4-1-9 scams—advance fee fraud. Fake or fraudulent identification is also discussed because of its relationship to identity theft.

3.2 E-MAIL HARASSMENT, THREATS, AND CYBERSTALKING

Make no mistake: this kind of harassment can be as frightening and as real as being followed and watched in your neighborhood or in your home.

Former Vice President Al Gore

Harassment can be defined as continued communication or interaction with someone with the goal of intimidating, upsetting, or otherwise emotionally

Felony   The most serious level of criminal acts, which carry a minimum of a one-year prison sentence for anyone convicted. Substantial fines may also be levied on convicted felons. Examples of felony crimes include rape, murder, aggravated assault, and many crimes against children.

Misdemeanor   A criminal act of moderate severity that may result in a jail sentence of up to one year and/or a substantial fine. Many states establish maximum fine limits for misdemeanor convictions. For example, the state of Virginia has a maximum misdemeanor fine of $2,500.

Ordinance violation   An ordinance is a law enacted by a city, local, or municipal government. Because these levels of government do not have the same legal authority as state or federal governments, the maximum penalty for an ordinance violation is a civil forfeiture (fine). Ordinance violations result in civil forfeiture because ordinance violations are not criminal acts. Because of this, municipal courts have lower standards of evidence than "beyond a reasonable doubt," and convictions can be made with a "preponderance of evidence."

Proof beyond a reasonable doubt   This is the level of certainty required for a guilty verdict in a criminal case. A juror voting for a guilty verdict must believe that no reasonable person could doubt the guilt of the accused.

Preponderance of evidence   This is the level of certainty required for a guilty verdict in a municipal ordinance violation case. The standard is met when there is more evidence indicating guilt than that indicating innocence. A balancing scales analogy is appropriate in determining preponderance.

Probable cause   The level of certainty required for law enforcement officers to make an arrest. It is generally defined as "that quantum of evidence which would lead a reasonable police officer to believe that the defendant committed a crime. It is more than a hunch or suspicion, but less than the evidence required to convict at trial" (State of Wisconsin 2003).

Reasonable suspicion   Commonly referred to as a "Terry Stop" (*Terry v. Ohio* 1968), this is the level of certainty that allows for a law enforcement official to detain and or frisk a subject, for the official's own safety, based on reasonable belief that the subject is armed or has committed, is committing, or is about to commit a crime.

Figure 3–1 Classification of criminality and hierarchy of proof.

affecting the target. It is unwanted communication or interaction with no other legitimate purpose. **Threats** can be defined as communicated warnings of some imminent negative event, injury, or other harm. Often the person communicating the warning implies that he or she will cause the injury or harm. Harassing or threatening somebody by e-mail or by some other electronic means has also been referred to as cyberstalking. **Cyberstalking** is defined as the repeated use of the Internet, e-mail, or related digital electronic communications devices to annoy, alarm, or threaten a specific individual or group of individuals (Ovidio and Doyle 2003). Cyberstalking has also been defined by the National Center for Victims of Crime (NCVC) "as threatening behavior or unwanted advances directed at another using the Internet and other forms of online and computer communications" (National Center and Victims of Crime 2004). Although spam or unsolicited e-mail can also be rather harassing, it's not the focus of this section.

The virtual Web has made it simple to harass or threaten somebody, and such offenses are happening at an alarming rate. According to a 1999 Department of Justice study on cyberstalking, tens or even hundreds of thousands of people may have been victims of electronic harassments or threats. A lack of sufficient reporting and statistics on this type of criminal activity makes it difficult to arrive at a more accurate number. It is also underreported to police because many victims feel that nothing can be done. Furthermore, many police agencies are reluctant or ill equipped to deal with the problem (Masters 1998).

In 2001, we assisted an e-mail harassment victim who resided in another jurisdiction. When asked why he didn't report the harassment to his local police, he replied, "I don't think the police in my community know what a computer is." Law enforcement needs to change these negative perceptions. Legislatures must draft laws that address these offenses, and many of them have. The state of Wisconsin has taken a proactive approach to combating e-mail harassment and threats. Wisconsin State Statute 947.0125, Unlawful Use of a Computerized Communication System, outlaws threatening and harassing electronic messages. This virtual disorderly conduct law can be found in the Wisconsin State Statute (WSS) book directly below the traditional disorderly conduct law (WSS 947.01) and states, in part,

> Whoever does any of the following is guilty of a Class B misdemeanor: With intent to frighten, intimidate, threaten, abuse or harass another person, sends a message to the person on an electronic mail or other computerized communication system and in that message threatens to inflict injury or physical harm to any person or the property of any person. (WSS 947.0125(2)(a))

The Wisconsin law and many others like it throughout the country clearly outlaw harassment or threats made by e-mail, instant messaging, or any other electronic means. Additionally, Title 18, Section 875, of the U.S. Code criminalizes threatening messages transmitted electronically in interstate or foreign commerce. The use of federal legislation to prosecute cases of cyberstalking, however, is limited, by law, to instances when the harassing messages are transmitted across state lines or outside the United States. Despite the existence of Title 18, Section 875, the federal government historically has limited its involvement in prosecuting cases related to electronically transmitted threatening messages to cases involving special circumstances, such as threats made against the president of the

United States. As with stalking that does not involve the Internet, local authorities investigate and prosecute most cyberstalking cases in either the jurisdiction where the victim resides or in the jurisdiction where the messages originated. However, because these crimes are often classified as misdemeanors, officials lack the power to extradite or arrest offenders across state lines. Some cities, such as Green Bay, Wisconsin, have adopted the state law as their own ordinance violation, which allows for local enforcement. This works well if the victim and offender are within the same locale or state and officers can issue court orders to appear in municipal court. If the offender lives in another state, law enforcement has to rely on the investigative efforts of local police in the offender's jurisdiction, who may not have the necessary skills, resources, the same or similar local laws, or even the desire to warrant the investigation. If the offender lives outside the United States, investigating this type of case can be an exercise in futility.

E-mail harassment and threats are a very real problem that must be addressed by municipal law enforcement. Simply telling victims to change their e-mail address or phone number is insufficient. Federal law enforcement agencies are overwhelmed with similar and more serious complaints and must rely on local law enforcement to take the lead on these investigations. However, federal law enforcement officers may get involved in an e-mail harassment case if it crosses state lines and if there is an explicit mention of bodily harm. The FBI Web site (www.fbi.gov), however, advises anyone receiving threats to notify the local law enforcement agency.

The fact that cyberstalking does not involve physical contact may create the misperception that it is more benign than physical stalking. This is not necessarily true. As the Internet becomes an ever more integral part of our personal and professional lives, stalkers can take advantage of the ease of communications as well as increased access to personal information. In addition, the ease of use and nonconfrontational, impersonal, and sometimes anonymous nature of Internet communications may remove disincentives to cyberstalking. Put another way, whereas a potential stalker may be unwilling or unable to confront a victim in person or on the telephone, he or she may have little hesitation sending harassing or threatening electronic communications to a victim. Finally, as with physical stalking, online harassment and threats may be a prelude to more serious behavior, including physical violence. (U.S. Department of Justice 1999)

Cyberstalking is similar to real-world stalking, including similarities in the profiles of the people who commit such offenses. The profile of typical cyberstalkers is as follows (Ovidio and Doyle 2003):

- 80% Males
- 74% White, 13% Asian, 8% Hispanic, 5% African American
- E-mail used 79% of the time, instant messenging 13%, chat rooms 8%

In comparison, the typical profile of a traditional stalker is as follows (Wood and Wood 2002):

- 87% Male
- 57% White, 37% African American, 6.5% other racial minorities

Learner Activity

Conduct a keyword search on the Internet and locate a practical example of a cyberstalking case. Note the profile of the cyberstalker and describe whether it matches the typical cyberstalker profile. Explain why the cyberstalker matches the typical profile or why not. What are some reasons the person may not meet the typical profile?

The disparities between the cyberstalker and traditional stalker profiles can be partially explained by the access and availability of computer technology. Those in lower socioeconomic groups are less likely to have access to the necessary technology for cyberstalking. (see Figure 3–2 for a description of an actual cyberstalking incident.)

Internet use and ever-growing popularity of technology among young children and teens have also brought about a similar form of cyberstalking called "cyberbullying." **Cyberbullying** always involves a child, preteen, or teenager who is involved in using the Internet, interactive and digital technologies, or mobile phones to torment, threaten, harass, humiliate, embarrass, or otherwise target another minor (WiredKids n.d.). Although very similar to cyberstalking, and able to be prosecuted under similar cyberstalking laws, the main difference is that cyberbullying involves only minors and cyberstalking is usually when adults become involved.

Investigating an e-mail harassment or threats incident is relatively simple, and the chances of identifying the account holder or physical location from which the electronic communication was sent is likely. Unless the sender is using an anonymous remailer that strips off the original Internet Protocol (IP) address and omits it completely or alters it before forwarding a message to the recipient, tracing the

In the first successful prosecution under California's new cyberstalking law, prosecutors in the Los Angeles District Attorney's Office obtained a guilty plea from a 50-year-old former security guard who used the Internet to solicit the rape of a woman who rejected his romantic advances. The defendant terrorized his 28-year-old victim by impersonating her in various Internet chat rooms and online bulletin boards, where he posted, along with her telephone number and address, messages that she fantasized of being raped. On at least six occasions, sometimes in the middle of the night, men knocked on the woman's door saying they wanted to rape her. The former security guard pleaded guilty in April 1999 to one count of stalking and three counts of solicitation of sexual assault. (He was convicted and sentenced to six years in prison.)

Figure 3–2 Actual cyberstalking incident.
Source: U.S. Department of Justice. 1999. 1999 report on cyberstalking: A new challenge for law enforcement and industry. www.usdoj.gov/criminal/cybercrime/cyberstalking.htm (accessed May 31, 2005).

message's origin is very possible. In any case involving e-mail, it is necessary to expand the e-mail header and view the entire header as opposed to the standard brief header. Each e-mail program makes this header information viewable differently, but usually the command to expand the header is in the Options section of the program. The expanded e-mail header contains the IP addresses that the message traveled through to reach its destination, and ultimately this trail of addresses leads back to the computer from which the message was sent. See E-mail tracing in Chapter 6 for additional information on tracing IP addresses.

These crimes can also be committed by cell phone instant messaging (IM) as well. The instant message can be sent from one cell phone to another or from a computer to a cell phone. In the latter case, the cell phone number can be traced back to the sender by the IP address. In the former case, the cell phone number can be traced back to the sender by using the phone number. The sender's subscriber information is available if the person used a credit card or some other valid form of payment to set up a legitimate account. This information is not available if the sender uses a "throw-away" phone that doesn't require a contract and the person buys minutes cards that are activated at the time of purchase.

A search warrant and/or subpoena is required by law enforcement if they wish to obtain any of the previously mentioned subscriber information. However, in many instances, upon request, cell phone and Internet service provider companies will provide the victim with IP addresses and phone numbers. Simply having the victim call his or her service provider at the time of the report can garner valuable leads that would otherwise require a search warrant or subpoena to obtain. For example, in a recent case we investigated, the victim had his car broken into and a firearm and cell phone were taken. At the scene, the victim phoned his cell phone provider and obtained several phone numbers that had been called by the suspects using the victim's phone. (A search warrant and/or subpoena would have been required for law enforcement to get this same information.) These phone numbers were then traced by a reverse directory search to associates of the suspect, who ultimately provided the suspect's name, which resulted in both items being recovered within three hours of the theft. Had these immediate measures not been taken, the firearm and cell phone would have likely been sold or disposed of, never recovered, or used in the commission of another crime.

Additional investigative protocol for investigating cyberstalking can be found at the end of this chapter. First responders should also provide cyberstalking victims with the following tips to assist in the investigation:

- The stalker must be made aware that the behavior is unwelcome. The victim or a law enforcement officer on the victim's behalf could serve notice by telling the stalker to stop.
- One effective intervention technique is to report the cyberstalker to the Internet service provider (ISP). The name of the ISP generally can be determined by reading the last half of the e-mail address, for example, the e-mail address joecool @ aol.com likely indicates the e-mail account is administered by AOL.

- Save copies of all threatening e-mails, messages, Web site text, and the like for use in possible law enforcement prosecution. Such data can make up the bulk of the prosecution's evidence. Try to preserve the material in electronic format whenever possible because computer investigators may need to trace information contained in an e-mail messages header.
- Report the incident(s) to the local law enforcement agency(ies) in the victim's and suspect's location, if different.

3.3 VIOLATIONS OF RESTRAINING ORDERS

Although using high-tech means to violate restraining orders is not an epidemic, it's worth mentioning because of the very real possibility that it could happen and has happened in many regions of the United States. For example, in a 2001 case we investigated, the suspect in a domestic violence arrest had been placed in jail and was released on bail with a temporary restraining order forbidding contact with the victim. The suspect traveled to a neighboring county that same night and began e-mailing the victim who, in turn, notified police. The e-mail messages were viewed and confirmed, and the suspect was rearrested and placed back in jail for violating the temporary restraining order. When asked why he blatantly violated the order, he said, "It [the order] didn't say I couldn't e-mail her." He failed to read the fine print that indicated he was forbidden from contacting her by "any electronic means."

A domestic violence protection order from Indiana contains the appropriate language that forbids defendants (respondents) from contacting victims (petitioners) where it states, "The defendant is ordered to have no contact with (victim) in person, by telephone or letter, through an intermediary, or in any other way, directly or indirectly, except through an attorney of record, while released from custody pending trial. This includes, but is not limited to, acts of harassment, stalking, intimidation, threats, and physical force of any kind." It would be helpful if such orders also included language directly related to e-mail or other electronic communications (e.g., text messaging). The state of Indiana included such language in its injunctions, or orders prohibiting violence or threats against employees (i.e., workplace violence restraining orders; see Figure 3-3): "Specifically, defendant shall not telephone or send correspondence to the employee and other protected persons by *any* means including, but not limited to, the use of the public or private mails, interoffice mail, fax, or computer e-mail."

According to the U.S. Department of Justice, annually 1,131,999 victims of intimate partner rape, physical assault, and stalking obtain restraining orders against their attackers. Approximately 60 percent (646,809) of these orders are violated (Tjaden and Thoennes 2000). It is not known to what extent e-mail or other forms of electronic communications are used when violating these orders.

First responders who receive a report of a violation of a restraining order using e-mail or some other electronic means should follow the appropriate protocols outlined at the end of this chapter.

---

8. _____ ***RESTRAINING ORDERS*** _____ ***To be ordered
   now and effective until the hearing***

   a. ***Defendant shall not engage in unlawful violence or make threats of
   violence against the employee and the following members of
   employee's family or household who reside with the employee:***

   (1) (***Name***): _____

       Sex: _____ Male   _____ Female

       Date of birth: _____

   (2) (***Name***): _____

       Sex: _____ Male   _____ Female

       Date of birth: _____

   (3) (***Name***): _____

       Sex: _____ Male   _____ Female

       Date of birth: _____

       _____ Continued on Attachment 8a.

   b. **Specifically, defendant**

   (1) _____ shall not batter or stalk the employee and other protected
   persons.

   (2) _____ shall not follow or stalk the employee and other protected
   persons to or from the place of work.

   (3) _____ shall not follow the employee and other protected persons
   during hours of employment.

   (4) _____ **shall not telephone or send correspondence to the
   employee and other protected persons by any means including,
   but not limited to, the use of the public or private mails, interoffice
   mail, fax, or computer e-mail.**

   (5) _____ shall not enter the workplace of the employee and other
   protected persons.

   (6) _____ other (*specify*): _____

       _____

Figure 3–3 Excerpt of indiana workplace violence restraining order.

3.4 IDENTITY THEFT

This result suggests that almost 10 million Americans have discovered that they were the victim of some form of ID theft within the last year.
— Federal Trade Commission, Identity Theft Survey Report, 2002

It's difficult today to go more than a couple of days without hearing the term *identity theft*. We are bombarded with ads and real-life examples of this type of crime on a daily basis. Financial institutions take measures to protect their customers from it. People must take measures to protect themselves from it, and law enforcement must take proactive steps to combat it. The personal and financial losses from identify theft are staggering, and significant increases in this crime are seen from year to year. In 2002, the Federal Trade Commission received 161,896 ID theft complaints, and in 2004 it received 246,570 complaints—an increase of nearly 40 percent, at an estimated cost to consumers of more than $547 million (Federal Trade Commission 2005). These figures do not include complaints that were also received by local law enforcement nationwide. (Additional information about nationwide identity theft trends can be viewed at www.consumer.gov/sentinel/pubs/Top10Fraud2003.pdf.)

Identity theft can be defined as the unlawful use of another's personal identifying information without their knowledge, to fraudulently obtain money, goods, services, or anything of value. It can also be defined as "a fraud that is committed or attempted, using a person's identifying information without authority" (Federal Trade Commission 2004).

Most states now have identity theft laws, but many do not refer to them as such. For example, in Arizona identity theft is called "taking identity of another person or entity" (Arizona State Statute 13-2008), and in Wyoming it is referred to as "Unauthorized use of personal identifying information" (Wyoming State Statute 6-3-901). A comprehensive list of state identity theft statutes is shown in Figure 3–4.

Common elements of identity theft statutes, like Wisconsin State Statute 943.201, "Unauthorized use of an individual's personal identifying information or documents," require that a person's personal identifying information or personal identification document be used without the person' consent to obtain money, credit, goods, services, employment, or anything of value. Identifying information includes an individual's name, phone number(s), Social Security number, identification number assigned by an employer, identification number of a depository account, DNA profile, electronic serial numbers, address, driver's license number, employer name, maiden name of individual's mother, taxpayer identification number, and personal identification numbers. Types of personal identification documents include any document containing personal identifying information (e.g., driver's license); an individual's card (e.g., ATM card) or plate if it can be used alone or in conjunction with another device to obtain money, goods, services, or anything of value; or any other device that is unique to, assigned to, or belongs to an individual and that is intended to be used to access services, funds, or benefits.

Alabama	Alabama Code § 13A-8-190 through 201 (search Alabama Code for "Identity Theft")
Alaska	Alaska Stat § 11.46.565 (click Title 11, Chapter 46, Section 565)
Arizona	Ariz. Rev. Stat. § 13-2008
Arkansas	Ark. Code Ann. § 5-37-227
California	Cal. Penal Code § 530.5-8
Colorado	Does not have specific ID theft law
Connecticut	Conn. Stat. § 53a-129a (criminal) Conn. Stat. § 52-571h (civil)
Delaware	Del. Code Ann. tit. II, § 854
District of Columbia	Does not have specific ID theft law
Florida	Fla. Stat. Ann. § 817.568
Georgia	Ga. Code Ann. § 16-9-120, through 128
Hawaii	HI Rev. Stat. § 708-839.6-8 (see Statutes and Documents)
Idaho	Idaho Code § 18-3126 (criminal)
Illinois	720 Ill. Comp. Stat. 5/16 G
Indiana	Ind. Code § 35-43-5-3.5
Iowa	Iowa Code § 715A.8 (criminal) Iowa Code § 714.16.B (civil)
Kansas	Kan. Stat. Ann. § 21-4018
Kentucky	Ky. Rev. Stat. Ann. § 514.160
Louisiana	La. Rev. Stat. Ann. § 14:67.16
Maine	ME Rev. Stat. Ann. tit. 17-A § 905-A
Maryland	Md. Code Ann. art. 27 § 231
Massachusetts	Mass. Gen. Laws ch. 266, § 37E
Michigan	Mich. Comp. Laws § 750.285 (see Michigan Compiled Laws section)
Minnesota	Minn. Stat. Ann. § 609.527
Mississippi	Miss. Code Ann. § 97-19-85

Figure 3–4 Identity theft state statutes.
Source: Federal Trade Commission. (n.d.). Federal and state laws.
www.consumer.gov/idtheft/federallaws.html (accessed June 11, 2005).

Missouri	Mo. Rev. Stat. § 570.223
Montana	Mon. Code Ann. § 45-6-332
Nebraska	NE Rev. Stat. § 28-608 & 620
Nevada	Nev. Rev. State. § 205.463-465
New Hampshire	N.H. Rev. Stat. Ann. § 638:26
New Jersey	N.J. Stat. Ann. § 2C:21-17
New Mexico	N.M. Stat. Ann. § 30-16-24.1 (go to Statutes section, Chapter 30)
New York	NY CLS Penal § 190.77-190.84
North Carolina	N.C. Gen. Stat. § 14-113.20-23
North Dakota	N.D.C.C. § 12.1-23-11 (see Consumer Protection)
Ohio	Ohio Rev. Code Ann. § 2913.49
Oklahoma	Okla. Stat. tit. 21, § 1533.1
Oregon	Or. Rev. Stat. § 165.800
Pennsylvania	18 Pa. Cons. State § 4120
Rhode Island	R.I. Gen. Laws § 11-49.1-1
South Carolina	S.C. Code Ann. § 16-13-500, 501
South Dakota	S.D. Codified Laws § 22-30A-3.1
Tennessee	TCA § 39-14-150 (criminal) TCA § 47-18-2101 (civil)
Texas	Tex. Penal Code § 32.51
Utah	Utah Code Ann. § 76-6-1101-1104
Vermont	Does not have specific ID theft law
Virginia	Va. Code Ann. § 18.2-186.3
Washington	Wash. Rev. Code § 9.35.020 (click Title 9, then Chapter 35)
West Virginia	W. Va. Code § 61-3-54 (scroll down to § 61-3-54)
Wisconsin	Wis. Stat. § 943.201
Wyoming	Wyo. Stat. Ann. § 6-3-901
U.S. Territories	
Guam	9 Guam Code Ann. § 46.80
U.S. Virgin Islands	Does not have specific ID theft law

The national identify theft law is known as the Identity Theft and Assumption Deterrence Act (18 U.S.C. 1028), which also makes identity theft a federal offense. The act makes it a federal crime when someone knowingly transfers or uses, without lawful authority, a means of identification of another person with the intent to commit, or to aid or abet, any unlawful activity that constitutes a violation of federal law, or that constitutes a felony under any applicable state or local law. The penalties include up to 15 years imprisonment and a maximum fine of $250,000. Most identity theft crimes occur by telephone or on the Internet and across jurisdictional boundaries (Dadisho, 2004); once the criminal act crosses state lines, federal statutes apply.

The federal Fair and Accurate Credit Transactions Act (FACT Act) of 2003 (15 U.S.C. 1681) establishes safeguards, processes, and protocols to be followed by credit reporting bureaus to ensure accuracy and fairness of credit reporting. The act requires identity theft victims to provide a copy of a police report to the respective credit reporting bureaus or financial institutions that shows evidence of their victimization. In response, states should make identity theft reporting mandatory. It's not uncommon for a victim to walk into a police department and report an identity theft when the suspect lives in another jurisdiction. It is a disservice to turn away the victim and tell the person to report the crime elsewhere. If victims cannot turn to their local police, then who can they turn to for help? Mandating that first responders take identity theft complaints and properly report them must be the norm. For example, Wisconsin State Statute 943.201(4) mandates that law enforcement officers prepare a report for alleged identity theft violations or refer victims to the appropriate jurisdiction to make the report (Figure 3–5). This proactive Wisconsin statute and many others like it across the country not only allow for timely reporting and appropriate investigation of identify theft incidents, it also helps the industry to gather valuable statistical data to further study the scope of the problem.

There are three primary types of identity theft: true name fraud, account takeover, and criminal identity theft (Benner, Givens, and Mierzwinski 2000). **True**

If an individual reports to a law enforcement agency for the jurisdiction which is the individual's residence that personal identifying information or a personal identifying document belonging to the individual reasonably appears to be in the possession of another in violation of this section or that another has used or has attempted to use it in violation of this section, **the agency shall prepare a report on the alleged violation.** If the law enforcement agency concludes that it appears not to have jurisdiction to investigate the violation, it shall inform the individual which law enforcement agency may have jurisdiction. A copy of a report prepared under this subsection shall be furnished upon request to the individual who made the request, subject to payment of any reasonable fee for the copy.

Figure 3–5 Wisconsin State Statute 943.201(4).

name fraud occurs when the thief uses the victim's information to open up new accounts in the victim's name. **Account takeover** occurs when the thief gains access to the victim's financial accounts and makes unauthorized charges. **Criminal identity theft** happens when the thief is arrested by law enforcement and provides police with the victim's identity, thereby creating a false criminal record for the victim.

People can become the victims of identity theft in a variety of ways, and although certain measures (which will be discussed later) can be taken to prevent it, it's almost impossible to be completely shielded from it. According to the Federal Trade Commission, some of the more common ways thieves steal another person's identity include the following:

- Stealing information from employers
- Bribing, paying, or working in concert with employees who have inside access to desired records
- Hacking into computer systems and stealing the records
- Dumpster diving—one person's garbage is another identity thief's dream
- Stealing mail, especially junk mail (e.g., credit card offers) and completing a change of address form in the victim's name
- Stealing wallets or purses
- Burglarizing a home
- Social engineering—the art of convincing somebody in person, by phone, or by e-mail that the thief is a legitimate person who needs the desired information (e.g., pose as landlords, coworkers, telemarketers, prospective employers, or others who may need the victim's personal information)
- E-mail and Web site scams
- Open source Web sites (www.anywho.com)
- Shoulder surfing—looking over the victim's shoulder as he or she enters personal information into a phone, computer, or ATM
- Skimming—the most prevalent form of counterfeit fraud whereby a card's magnetic stripe details are electronically copied and put onto another card (CardWatch 2005)

Learner Activity

Conduct a keyword search on the Internet and locate an actual identity theft case. Unfortunately, there are many to choose from. Summarize the facts of the case. Identify how the thief obtained the victim's information. Recommend some ways that the victim could have prevented the theft.

Identity theft, in and of itself, is a criminal offense. It is most often used for some sort of financial gain or to conceal a criminal's true identity and evade apprehension by law enforcement. It is also regularly used by illegal immigrants to obtain employment unlawfully. The average victim of immigrant-based identity theft has his or her Social Security number shared about 30 times (Sullivan 2005). Twenty years of unlawful employment of an illegal immigrant can entitle the person to future illegal Social Security benefits. Furthermore, this type of identity theft often is discovered when the victim submits his or her tax return without documenting the income or earnings of the immigrant who is using the victim's name. The IRS promptly notifies the victim of the additional taxes due, and it is the victim's burden to right the wrong. Immigrant-based identify theft doesn't stop at unlawful employment: many times thieves establish credit or obtain loans using the victim's Social Security number and damage or ruin the victim's credit. Figure 3-6 describes an identity theft incident.

The side effects of immigrant identity theft also include false criminal records created when the thief is arrested under the victim's name. For example, if local law enforcement fails to establish a true identity, a criminal record is created under the false (victim's) name. Commonly, this is discovered when the victim has a relatively minor contact with police (e.g., gets a speeding ticket) and is informed that a warrant is out for his or her arrest. Again, the burden of proof falls on the victim to show that he or she did not do the crime to create the record. If an identity thief uses multiple identities, a different one for each subsequent police contact, then multiple false criminal records are created for each name. If such suspects are properly fingerprinted and photographed, eventually the multiple records will be discovered and consolidated into one. Correcting these errors, however, takes considerable time and resources. It must be a primary goal of law enforcement to properly identify all people with whom they have contact.

Undocumented immigrants often have two names, a "working" name and their real name. During a police contact, they often provide the working name, the one established in the United States. Any supporting documents for the working name should be confiscated and destroyed. These documents normally include a false Social Security card, which may be based on a legitimate name and number, or a randomly generated Social Security number in the proper format. Sometimes that same number is used again and again.

In 2005, a female resident of northeast Wisconsin reported to us that she recently applied for an auto loan and, according to her credit report, she owed the Indiana Power and Light Company thousands of dollars in unpaid electric bills. She had never lived in Indiana, she didn't have any relatives there, nor did she ever visit the state. Follow-up investigation revealed that her identity had been stolen by an undocumented illegal immigrant who had used her full name, date of birth, Social Security number, and other personal identifying information to establish residency and an account for electricity at a residence in Indiana. The victim was required to spend considerable time convincing the potential creditor that the debt was not her responsibility. Additional time and effort was spent to have the negative entry removed from the victim's credit report.

Figure 3–6 Actual identity theft incident.

For example, In Schuyler, Nebraska, an illegal immigrant worker can obtain an authentic-looking Social Security card and matching birth certificate for $1,300.00 (Simon 2005). To the trained eye, a fake Social Security card is relatively easy to identify. According to the Report to Congress on Options for Enhancing the Social Security Card (1997), the following publicized security features are present on a legitimate Social Security card:

- The stock is a blue tint marbleized random pattern. Any attempt to erase or remove data is easily detectable because the tint is erasable. The words *Social Security* are printed in white.
- Planchettes (small multicolored disks) are randomly placed on the paper stock and can be seen with the naked eye. These yellow, pink, and blue disks can appear anywhere on the card, including the area on the card that contains the seal and identifying information.
- Intaglio printing of the type used in U.S. currency is used for some areas on the front of the card. Intaglio printing on the card provides a raised effect and abrasiveness that can be felt when examined by touch. This printing technology is not widely available and is difficult to replicate.
- Other security features not obvious to the naked eye are not publicized, but are made available to law enforcement.

To improve future Social Security card security features, this same report discusses the following recommendations:

- *Four-color Printing*   This is a basic card-printing process that is used in the preprinting of blank card stock. The four-color process refers to printing using the subtractive combination of three primary colors, yellow, magenta, and cyan, together with black as a sustaining color, to raise the contrast of the print. The four constituent parts of the image are successively printed on top of one another in exact register. Use of four-color printing makes counterfeiting more difficult because the card production equipment that is needed to produce cards using this process is expensive and complex.
- *Transparent Hologram*   This is a security feature in which a clear holographic image is bonded to the top surface of the plastic card. This feature complicates counterfeiting and makes tampering evident because both the holographic image and how it is registered (i.e., where the image[s] appears on the card surface) create a unique appearance that can be distinguished from copies and, if altered, shows evidence of tampering. If an attempt is made to remove or alter the holographic topcoat, tampering is evident without the need of special equipment.
- *Miniprinting and Microprinting*   This is a printing technology used to produce very small (miniprinting) and microscopic (microprinting) fonts. (Miniprinting can be seen with the naked eye; microprinting can be seen only under magnification.) Miniprinting and microprinting often are combined with other artwork and printing effects on the card surface. Both techniques require sophisticated, expensive printing equipment, making forgery

costly and difficult. Accurate reproduction of miniprinting/microprinting cannot be accomplished today by photocopying or by commercially available color photography or color scanners. Microprinting is used on the current Social Security card and on U.S. currency. The trained eye can recognize the microprinting security features, and cards without it are counterfeit.

- *Ultraviolet Ink* This is a printing technology used to print an image on the card surface that is visible only under ultraviolet light. When properly exposed, the hidden image can be used to verify card authenticity. Forgery is difficult because the special inks used to produce the image in the card surface are difficult to obtain and, in some cases, are available only to government agencies or other secure users.
- *Linking the Number Holder to the Social Security Card* This option displays a unique identifier (e.g., fingerprint or photograph) that would match the Social Security card number. Current cards do not allow for this type of functionality.

Some of these proposed security features have yet to be implemented.

Another proactive step taken by the federal government to help combat identity theft is the new National Crime Information Center (NCIC) Identity Theft File and password program that went into effect in April 2005. The identity theft file serves as a means for law enforcement to "flag" stolen identities and identify the imposter when he or she is encountered. When an individual becomes a victim of identity theft and reports the incident to law enforcement, first responders should collect pertinent information from the victim (discussed further later). This information is used to create a victim profile, which is entered into the NCIC Identity Theft File. The profile includes information such as victim name, date of birth, Social Security number, and type of identity theft the person is the victim of. In addition, the victim chooses a password that will be used to identity him or her as the victim in any subsequent police encounters. The password is also entered into the profile listed with NCIC. If the person (suspect) who stole the identity is later stopped by police and he or she provides the stolen name, the officer will receive an NCIC "hit" indicating that the particular identity has been stolen. The officer would then ask the person for the password. Presumably, he or she will not know it and the thief will be discovered.

Although identity theft is a criminal offense, it's also considered a "gateway crime" that leads to other criminal offenses, including credit card fraud, forgery/check fraud, mortgage fraud/account takeover, theft of phone service, and satellite and cable theft, just to name a few. Credit card fraud and forgery/check fraud are discussed separately in Chapter 4.

Mortgage fraud or account takeover is gaining in popularity for identity thieves and organized gang members. The potential reward is high with little personal risk to the offender. Many of the mortgage fraud schemes are elaborate and require multiple actors. Mortgage fraud often involves a "customer," real estate broker, straw sellers, and straw buyers who funnel the money into accounts that have been established with false or stolen identities. The following excerpt from a May 13, 2004, U.S. Department of Justice press release highlights this scheme:

> The indictment charges that the DEFENDANTS, along with others made purchases of residential properties primarily in the Mountain Oaks, North Shore, Southland and Waters Edge Subdivisions located in Lithonia and Stone Mountain, Georgia, and other residential properties in the Douglasville, Elberton, Fairburn, Griffin and Atlanta, Georgia, area for resale at artificially inflated prices, often using the proceeds of the resale to pay for the initial purchase, a practice commonly referred to as "flipping." The defendants would recruit, pay or otherwise induce co-conspirators, commonly referred to as "straw sellers," or locate identities to use as "straw sellers," to falsely claim current ownership of the properties which were sold to straw borrowers at amounts fraudulently inflated by as much as $100,000. Thereafter, the property just sold would be purchased at a much less amount, with the artificially inflated loan amount being shared by co-conspirators through disbursements to themselves and their shell companies. The DEFENDANTS would recruit, pay or induce other co-conspirators, commonly referred to as "straw borrowers," to sign and submit documents containing false qualifying information to banks and mortgage companies to obtain mortgage loans. They would also use the stolen identity of other people as straw sellers and straw borrowers for the purpose of fraudulently obtaining mortgage loan proceeds, falsely represent that required down payment amounts were paid from borrower funds and that the property would be the primary residence of the straw borrowers. (www.usdoj. gov/usao/gan/press/05-13-04.html)

The stolen identities in the preceding case were obtained from another accomplice who had access to student names and Social Security numbers at the Pharmacy School of Florida A&M University. The names were used as "borrowers" on the mortgage loans.

In 2004, members of the Vice Lords street gang in Chicago were arrested for their involvement in a $70 million drug money laundering scheme. Gang members tried to conceal the funds by filing more than 100 fraudulent mortgage applications (Spielman and Main 2004). Committing mortgage fraud can be lucrative and, for the gang member, it is much safer than drug deals gone awry, plus the potential return is much greater (www.mortgagefraud.squarespace.com/illinois/). Currently, the states identified as the top 10 "hot spots" for mortgage fraud are Georgia, South Carolina, Florida, Michigan, Illinois, Missouri, California, Nevada, Utah, and Colorado (Frieden 2004).

Organized crime groups also use boilerroom operations to further capitalize on the stolen identities. To establish credit it is necessary for creditors to able to verify a credit applicant's employment or references. This hypothetical case shows how this type of scheme works. With stolen identity in hand, one gang member completes a credit application with all fictitious information and leaves a cell phone number where he can be reached. All of the references, both professional and personal, are actually the names and cell phone numbers of fellow gang members who will "confirm" the information. With all information verified, the credit is then granted.

Experts agree that the unauthorized opening of a phone account is the second most common type of identity theft—criminals know that credit card companies and banks often demand documentation of a utility account to prove identification and residency (AT & T 2006; Federal Trade Commission 2005). Not only is it used for these purposes, but identity thieves set up phone accounts for their personal use, rack up significant charges in long-distance calls in a short period of time, and then discontinue use of the phone without paying and move on to a different location where another fraudulent phone service is established.

In a 2000 case we investigated, an identity theft victim reported discovering $3,000 in fraudulent long-distance phone calls against an account in his name that he never authorized or created. Investigation revealed that the victim had lived with a friend for a short period of time a few months prior. The suspect had taken the victim's wallet and photocopied his driver's license and Social Security card. The suspect then established a phone account in the victim's name and used it to call relatives in Guatemala. The bills were mailed directly to the suspect and were never paid. The scheme went on for about three months, at which time the victim moved out and established his own residency. The victim called the phone company to set up his account, which was denied until he paid the outstanding long-distance phone bill. A subsequent interview and search of the suspect's apartment revealed the documents that he had copied to establish the account.

With such a focus on high-tech means of stealing identities, we often forget the rather simplistic and low-tech ways that offenders use to steal another's identity. From photocopying a victim's driver's license and Social Security card to Dumpster diving, offenders take advantage of victims' carelessness. The public paper recycle bin at the base of apartment complex mailboxes is an identity thief's dream. Victims become unwitting accomplices when they drop their junk mail (e.g., credit card offers) in the bin and walk away. The thief scavenges the bin and walks away with an array of identities from which to choose.

One of the more alarming and potentially deadly types of identity theft is known as *medical records identity theft*. Imagine arriving at the hospital for a routine procedure and being asked questions about a medical condition that you do not have, but that the hospital has documented on their charts. Even worse, consider what might happen if a criminal with a different blood type from yours stole your identity to receive medical treatment and altered your chart to reflect his blood type. According to a 2003 federal report, there have been at least 200,000 instances of medical identity theft nationwide (Menn, 2006).

Medical identity theft appears to be an uncomplicated crime to commit, and the presentation of the victim's stolen medical insurance card can enable the criminal to receive treatment. Unfortunately it is not a common procedure for medical treatment facilities to request a photo identification card to confirm the name on the insurance card. The health care centers and hospitals that do require photo identification as well as insurance cards for nonemergency treatment appear to be weeding out the impersonators (Alexander 2006). It can be particularly difficult for victims to correct the imposter's changes in records because of the privacy rights and regulations that control the release and altering of medical records. Although law enforcement is becoming more experienced in investigating identity theft complaints, the medical industry typically is much less experienced in handling identity theft cases. Police might incorrectly consider it a civil matter and turn the victim away, suggesting they contact their insurance company. State statutes across the country support prosecution for medical identity theft because the suspects are using the stole identity to obtain a service and receive something of value (Alexander, 2006; Menn, 2006).

The Internet also serves as a store of personal information for the identity thief. With just a couple clicks a thief can obtain enough information to establish a bogus full name, date of birth, address, and phone number. For example, the former www.anybirthday.com Web site contained the birth dates of more than 135 million people in the United States. Identity thieves could obtain the full name, date of birth, and zip code on potential victims. For a fee, they could also obtain the person's address. Or a thief could visit one of the many open source name and phone number directories and obtain a current address and phone number, confirming the personal data with the zip code. Similar resources can also be used by the cyberstalker to locate victims. If your name and date of birth exists on any of these sites, take advantage of the "opt-out" options and have your name removed. Anybirthday.com has since gone offline, but other similar open source sites and databases still allow for such information gathering.

Other "breeder crimes" that are committed by identity thieves include loan fraud, bank fraud, employment fraud, and government documents and benefits fraud (Federal Trade Commission 2005).

A well-done and thorough preliminary investigation can increase the chances of apprehending the identity thief. The responding officer must gather the necessary information that will reveal the most leads. Because most police agencies across the United States are small, the responding officer will also play the role of lead investigator and work the case from beginning to end. In medium- to large-sized agencies, detectives will likely be assigned to follow up on the case utilizing the preliminary information obtained by the first responder. Not only is it critical to obtain the necessary information from the victim to conduct a thorough investigation, much of the information is digital in nature and time-sensitive.

Most victims discover that they have become the victim of an identity theft when fraudulent charges are discovered on their credit card (Federal Trade Commission 2005). First responders should recommend that the victim obtain a complete copy of their credit report from all three credit reporting bureaus: TransUnion, Equifax, and Experian. The credit reports can reveal, among other things, the number of unauthorized accounts that have been opened under the victim's name. If the accounts are active, the victim can phone each company to find out when and where purchases have been made, including the amount of each transaction. The transactions could involve shipment of items to a physical location that can be checked or monitored for the suspect(s). The accounts may also contain other possible addresses for the suspect(s). If an active account is being used at a physical location, it is critical to determine where and when purchases have been made. Retail locations or convenience stores may have surveillance cameras that captured the suspect using the victim's credit card or account information.

After obtaining the victim's full name, date of birth, address, employer name, home and work phone numbers, first responders must consider a whole host of other questions that are critical to a successful identity theft investigation. The ultimate goal is to apprehend the offender(s) or uncover other crimes committed by the same offender(s) (i.e., link other incidents together). The following list was created based upon investigations we conducted and from the U.S. Secret Service *Identity Crime Resources for Law Enforcement* guide. Not all questions apply to each type of identity theft case, and it is recommended that a document be created that can be handed to the victim to fill out. The questionnaire can then become a permanent part of the case file.

1. What is your Social Security number?
2. What is your cell phone and/or pager number?
3. What is your e-mail address?
4. How did you become aware of the identity theft?
5. When did you first become aware of the identity theft?
6. Do you know when the identity theft first began?
7. What fraudulent activity has been committed in your name?
8. If a purse or wallet was stolen, what documents were kept in your wallet or purse? Include Social Security numbers, driver's license numbers, credit card numbers, and so forth.
9. To your knowledge, has your mail ever been stolen in the past?
10. Do you have a post office box?
11. What do you normally do with junk mail (e.g., credit card offers)? Shred them or just throw them away?
12. Do you put outgoing mail in your mailbox or deliver it to a stand-alone mail receptacle or the post office?
13. What other crimes have you been the victim of (e.g., burglary, theft)?
14. Have you recently misplaced any financial documents (e.g., debit/credit cards)?
15. Have you recently viewed a copy of your credit history?
16. Do you have a personal Web site or have you posted your personal information to any Web site (e.g., genealogy sites, blogs) or is it listed in any open source directories (e.g., white pages, birthday sites)?
17. Have you recently used your credit card to purchase services over the phone or online?
18. Have you recently filled out any online forms that included your personal information?
19. Do you use your Social Security number as a unique identifier for medical records, mortgage records, and so forth?
20. What schools or colleges have you attended? Dates of attendance?
21. Is your Social Security number or driver's license number printed on your checks?

22. What financial institutions do you do business with?
23. Do you use online banking, bill pay services, or purchase items on online auction sites?
24. What utility companies provide your power, light, phone, and Internet services?
25. What credit cards, including merchant credit cards, do you have in your name?
26. Do you know who may have stolen your identity?
27. Have you recently received and replied to any e-mail messages that requested personal information from you?

Time is of the essence and not only must law enforcement begin to follow up on leads as quickly as possible, victims can also begin to take proactive steps to repair the damage. Depending on the type of identity theft, the average victim spends anywhere from $500.00 to $1,200.00 along with 30 to 60 hours of time resolving and repairing the damage (Federal Trade Commission, 2003).

Many of the victims that first responders encounter will be distraught and not know what to do next. The most frequent complaint the Federal Trade Commission (FTC) Identity Theft Resource Center receives is that the "police just don't care" (Newman 2004). First responders can avoid this perception and help begin the healing process by providing victims with positive and proactive steps toward recovery. Victims can be directed to the FTC Web site (www.ftc.gov/bcp/conline/pubs/credit/idtheft.pdf) where they can obtain a copy of "Take Charge: Fighting Back Against Identity Theft," which provides written step-by-step directions for repairing their good name. Copies of this document can also be ordered by law enforcement agencies and can be provided to all identity theft victims.

All victims should also be provided with an identity theft affidavit, which can be downloaded from the FTC site at www.ftc.gov/bcp/conline/pubs/credit/affidavit.pdf. The affidavit can be used by victims to send to credit card companies and other financial institutions to prove that they were the victim of identity theft and are not liable for the charges or damages incurred by the thief. Finally, first responders should direct the victims to contact all three credit reporting bureaus and have fraud alerts placed on their accounts:

Equifax: 1-800-525-6285   Experian: 1-888-EXPERIAN   TransUnion: 1-800-680-7289
www.equifax.com   www.experian.com   www.transunion.com

Another proactive step that first responders and local law enforcement agencies can take is to provide victims with a packet or "identity theft handbook for victims" that contains information specific to the state in which the crime occurred. The handbook could be created by the law enforcement agency and should include the following information:

• All pertinent contact information for the law enforcement agency investigating the case
• Name and address of the state criminal investigative division or attorney general's office

- Credit bureau names, phone numbers, addresses, e-mail addresses, and fax numbers
- Contact information for federal agencies in their state (e.g., Social Security Administration, FBI, Secret Service)
- Contact information for state motor vehicle records
- Contact information for local post office or postal inspectors
- Contact information and directions on how to obtain a new birth certificate, especially if it was stolen
- Contact information to remove their name from junk mail lists (www.dmaconsumers.org/offmailinglist.html#how)
- Contact information to remove their name from telemarketing lists (www.dmaconsumers.org/offtelephonelist.html#register) or to have their name added to statewide Do Not Call lists

Identity theft victims should also be provided with proactive steps they can take to prevent becoming a victim again. The previously referenced guide, "Take Charge: Fighting Back Against Identity Theft," discusses how victims can remain vigilant, and some of the tips are summarized here:

- Do not give out personal information over the phone, through the mail, or over the Internet unless you have initiated the contact and know whom you're dealing with.
- Treat your mail and trash carefully—if you're living without a shredder, you're living dangerously. Place outgoing mail in a U.S. Post receptacle and not in your mailbox with the "steal me" flag up that notifies thieves there is mail waiting to be taken. If you're planning to be away from home, request a "vacation hold" on all mail.
- Photocopy all the personal identifying contents in your wallet or purse and keep them in a secure place.
- Do not carry your Social Security card with you.
- Only provide your Social Security number when absolutely necessary and ask for an alternative number citing that you have been the victim of an identity theft.
- Carry only identification and credit cards that you actually need.
- Keep your purse or wallet in a safe place at work.
- When ordering new (blank) checks, pick them up at the bank instead of having them mailed to you.

Last, advise victims that they should also file a complaint directly with the FTC by visiting www.consumer.gov/idtheft/. First responders should also enter the victim's information into the FTC Identity Theft Data Clearinghouse at www.consumer.gov/sentinel/idtchart.htm.

Identity theft will continue to be a national problem that can be effectively addressed through appropriate response and follow-up investigation by first responders and investigators alike. Awareness is a powerful defense against identity theft, and first responders can arm local consumers, victims, and businesses with the information they need to help protect themselves from it.

Summary of Identity Theft Investigative Protocols

- Confirm jurisdiction and either initiate a report and/or refer the victim to the appropriate law enforcement agency.
- Gather all pertinent victim information along with potential suspect information and recommend that victims obtain a copy of their credit report, seeking evidence of any other victimization (e.g., unauthorized accounts).
- Complete the identity theft questionnaire with the victim.
- Provide victims with resources to help them repair the harm, such as the FTC's guide, "Take Charge: Fighting Back Against Identity Theft."
- Provide the victims with recommendations to prevent repeat victimization.
- Follow up on all potential leads as soon as possible.

3.5 FALSE IDENTIFICATION DOCUMENTS

While there he had been put to work in the Bertillion room where the measurements, fingerprints, and photographs and records of the inmates were kept . . . with raw materials in hand to fabricate passes for them . . . they presented their passes at the gate and slipped off into some brush.

Description of 1930 Leavenworth prison escape
of bank robbers Tommie Holden and Francis Keating
in J. Evett Haley, Robbing Banks was My Business

From the common criminal to the violent terrorist, each has one thing in common: the need to conceal their identity from law enforcement to evade apprehension. Some offenders hide their identity by not carrying forms of identification and by providing an alias name and date of birth when stopped by law enforcement. Others carry false identification documents with them, such as a forged birth certificate, state identification card, or Social Security card. As discussed earlier, those seeking unlawful employment often carry a fake Social Security card and/or identification card, such as a Resident Alien identification card (see Figure 3–7), to prove employment eligibility.

When these same people commit law violations and establish a criminal record under the false identity, this presents an entirely different problem for law enforcement. When the criminal fails to appear in court and ceases using the false identity, it's that much more difficult to apprehend the person later. However, fingerprint technology allows for quick identification at the time of apprehension, but first responders on the street have to go through the extra effort to make that happen. For example, the offender might be stopped for a minor speeding infraction and provide different false identification documents. Because of high call

Note the uneven lamination, ragged, and nonparallel edges of the cardboard
background, and poor cutting and insertion of the photographs of the subjects.
Note also the poor or incomplete (not fully rolled) fingerprints. Also of interest
on the first card is the incorrect use of AO in place of the A-Zero alien number.
These documents and other forms of fraudulent identification documents, such
as fake Social Security cards, are often used to seek unlawful employment in
the United States.

Figure 3–7 Resident alien card.

volumes and other priorities, the first responder might accept these documents at
face value, issue the offender a traffic citation, and send the person on his or her
way, thus creating another false identity, and the vicious cycle continues.

However, if the first responder takes the time to use fingerprints or some
other sort of biometrics, it likely results in "positively" identifying the offender.
Positively appears in quotes because offenders who do not have the prerequisite
legitimate documents (e.g., birth certificate, Social Security card) obtained in the
United States or some other modern nation may never really be "positively" identified. For example, in many third-world countries individuals do not know their
birth date, nor do they have a birth certificate because such documents are not issued by their governments.

Fake identification cards can be purchased, manufactured, created by
altering an existing legitimate identification card, or obtained by using other false
identification. Purchasing a fake identification card is the simplest way to obtain

one. Fake identification cards can be purchased on the Internet, at flea markets, at storefronts, on street corners, or from concealed manufacturing operations anywhere from suburbia to the inner city. Underage students oftentimes seek out fake identification cards so they can then purchase alcohol. In 2002, 11 Edgewood High School students in Hamilton, Ohio, were arrested for selling fake identification cards for $20.00 to $50.00 apiece (Morse and Kiesewetter 2002). A keyword search for "buy fake drivers license" reveals several Web sites, one of which contains 10 links to "FAKE ID SITES." Many of these sites sell templates for any state and advertise them as "novelty" identification cards or driver's licenses. The templates often contain superimposed text that reads "For Entertainment Only" or something to that effect, which is printed when the card is created. However, over-the-counter photo imaging software can easily remove that text and print legitimate-looking identification cards. Ordering an entire template can help a person set up a manufacturing operation. Those who need just one "novelty" identification card can order it for about $99.00, and it will include their photograph and signature. It's a given that anybody ordering a template would remove the "Novelty I.D." or "For Entertainment Only" print from created identification cards. However, assuming this gives the common criminal too much credit. For example, in one recent incident we investigated, the suspect was asked for identification and he produced a seemingly legitimate-looking identification card from the State of Texas Department of Public Safety. The back side of the card, however, stated, "For Entertainment Only." The card was promptly confiscated and destroyed.

More technically advanced criminals can manufacture their own fake identification cards or make them for others. By using an average color printer, digital scanner, one of the previously mentioned templates, a digital camera, and basic photo editing software, fraudsters can create fake identification cards in mass quantities. Normally, these cards are of average quality because it's more difficult to create the holograms, watermarks, and magnetic striping that is present today on many legitimate identification cards. However, enterprising fraudsters who want to create high-end fake identification cards can purchase a dye sublimation printer for about $1,500.00 that will encode magnetic striping and create holograms and watermarks. To further conceal their activities, fraudsters could purchase the necessary equipment using an established false identity (e.g., by identity theft).

Another relatively simple way criminals falsify identification cards is by altering certain features, such as the date of birth, to make the card holder look older than the person is actually. Laminated cards, that contained the paper document between the two sides of laminate, were more susceptible to these types of techniques, such as erasing one number and inserting another or adding ink to one numeral to make it appear like another (e.g., changing the numeral 6 to the numeral 8 by adding a small curved line on the right-hand upper edge). The more advanced dye sublimated identification cards that are imprinted on plastic and that include holographic and watermark security features along with magnetic coding have largely eliminated these types of frauds.

Last, people can obtain legitimate identification cards for a false identity by using other false identification documents (e.g., false birth certificates, false Social Security cards, utility bills established in the false name) for support. For example, according to a 2005 Americans for Legal Immigration online article "N.C. a destination for fake ID seekers," the state of North Carolina has the reputation for being "easy" for those seeking fake identification cards. In response, the North Carolina Department of Motor Vehicles and others across the United States have begun teaching their examiners and front counter personnel how to better spot supporting fake identification documents. The state of Connecticut has addressed this problem by issuing temporary licenses and cards that remain valid for 60 days until applicants' Social Security numbers can be verified (Wireback 2005). It's troubling when department of motor vehicle employees are involved in the fraudulent identification card business. For example, according to a U.S. Department of Justice News Release (2004), a New Jersey Division of Motor Vehicle employee pled guilty to conspiring to unlawfully produce driver's licenses. She received from customers between $100 and $200 per bogus license.

The real problem with verifying supporting identification documents is that there are no nationwide standards for identification cards and driver's license security features vary from state to state. In response, the federal government has proposed the "Real ID Act of 2005," which will require the following minimum document requirements for all states:

- The person's full legal name
- The person's date of birth
- The person's gender
- The person's driver's license or identification card number
- A digital photograph of the person
- The person's address of principal residence
- The person's signature
- Physical security features designed to prevent tampering, counterfeiting, or duplication of the document for fraudulent purposes
- A common machine-readable technology, with defined minimum data elements

Many of these features exist on current state identification cards, but not all states have the same machine-readable technology that would enable law enforcement officers nationwide to use the same technology to digitally read the identification cards. At the time of this writing, the "Real ID Act of 2005" is still making its way through the congressional approval process.

First responders must be diligent in their efforts to positively identify all persons with whom they come in contact. Identification cards cannot be accepted at face value, and they must be scrutinized for authenticity. The following checklist, which appeared in a February 1997 FBI *Law Enforcement Bulletin* article written by Roger Johnson, is still useful today when examining for fake, altered, or borrowed identification cards.

Fake IDs

- Check the size, thickness, and color of the card.
- Check the placement, size, and typeface of the letters and numbers.
- Check the photograph for shading, glare, or "red-eye."
- Check the state seal for accuracy.
- Check the back for blurred or dark images.
- Check for such phrases as "for personal use," "office use only," or "not a government document."
- Request backup documentation.
- Reject and confiscate questionable cards.

Altered IDs

- Check for numbers that have been scratched or bleached out and inked over or cut out and reinserted.
- Check for overlapping numbers; the laminate may have been peeled back and replaced.
- Check for cloudy images; a new laminate may cover the old one.
- Compare the birth date to the driver's license number because in some states these numbers match.
- Check for rough spots, especially around the edges and over the photograph.
- Check the state seal for accuracy and completeness; an inserted photograph may cover part of it.
- Request backup documentation.
- Reject and confiscate questionable cards.

Borrowed IDs

- Compare the photograph and physical identifiers to the cardholder and question discrepancies.
- Ask the presenter to verify personal data on the card.
- Obtain a signature and compare it to the one on the card.
- Be wary of expired and duplicate cards.
- Request backup documentation.
- Reject and confiscate questionable cards.

When encountering a false, altered, or borrowed identification card, in addition to rejecting and confiscating questionable cards, first responders should also place the individual under arrest for violating applicable local or state laws. Then, proceed with fingerprinting or other available biometrics to establish positive identity. If all attempts to positively identify the individual fail, it's not uncommon to book the individual in jail as "John Doe" or "Jane Doe" until additional identifying documents can be obtained from family members or other sources. It's also important to keep in mind that offenders possessing fraudulent identification documents are often involved in other criminal acts and follow-up investigation into their background should be commenced immediately.

Local law enforcement agencies can also take a proactive community policing approach to educating the public about fake identification documents and how to detect them. For example, the Brewer, Maine, Police Department has an informative Web page titled "Detecting Fake, Altered or Borrowed IDs," which can be viewed at www.brewerpolice.org/cprevguide/detfakeids.htm.

3.6 4-1-9 SCAM (AKA NIGERIA SCAM OR ADVANCE FEE FRAUD)

This is a five billion US$ worldwide scam which has run since at least 1989 under successive Governments of Nigeria. It is also referred to as "Advance Fee Fraud" and "419 Fraud" after the relevant section of the Criminal Code of Nigeria.
—Les Henderson, Crimes of Persuasion, 2000

Advanced fee scams may take the form of disbursement from wills, contract fraud, purchase of real estate, conversion of hard currency, transfer of funds, the clearinghouse, or sale of crude oil at below-market values. Of these, according to the Secret Service and U.S. Department of State, the most prevalent and successful cases, about 90 percent of advance fee fraud is in the form of **fund transfer scam.** In this scheme, a company or individual receives an unsolicited letter by mail from a Nigerian claiming to be a senior civil servant. In the letter, the Nigerian informs the recipient that he is seeking a reputable foreign company or individual into whose account he can deposit funds ranging from $10 million to $60 million that the Nigerian government overpaid on some procurement contract.

Messages that were once mailed or faxed to attract willing participants interested in easy money are now e-mailed in mass numbers thousands of times a day. Some consumers have told the Federal Trade Commission that they receive dozens of offers a day from supposed Nigerians politely promising to share big profits in exchange for help moving large sums of money out of their country. It's likely that many readers have received a 4-1-9 scam message and never identified it as such.

Although these scams come from other parts of the globe as well, Nigeria is considered the "419 capital of the world" (Oyesanya 2004). Named after the Nigerian Penal Law that deals with this type of fraud, 4-1-9 scams first surfaced in the mid-1980s around the time of the collapse of world oil prices (U.S. Department of State 1997), which decimated that country, which relies so heavily upon petroleum profits. Unstable and corrupt governments that have been accused of participating and profiting from these scams have helped sustain this type of fraud.

Also known as advance fee fraud, the 4-1-9 scam has historically targeted business-persons or even church clergy, tempting them with the opportunity to fall into big money. This correspondence, on official-looking letterhead, oftentimes contains text similar to "The Nigerian National Petroleum Corporation has entrusted me a $79,000,000.00 overpayment that we must move off shore and overseas. We are looking for a reputable business partner to assist in this transfer and in exchange receive 20% for your assistance." Basic math reveals that one could benefit $15,800,000 from this simple and seemingly harmless transaction. Unfortunately, a common perception is that no one would be persuaded to enter into such an obviously suspicious relationship. However, a large number of victims are enticed into believing they have been singled out from the masses to share in multi-million-dollar windfall profits for doing absolutely nothing (Public Awareness Advisory Regarding "4-1-9" or "Advance Fee Fraud" Schemes, United States Secret Service 2006). Victims lose money by paying fraudulent "application" or official "transaction" fees necessary to complete the funds transfer. The longer the fraudsters can carry out the scam, the more money they stand to make from their willing victim. Without a cooperative victim, the scam will not work. It is hard to pinpoint how much has been lost to these scams because many victims fear reporting their unlawful partnership gone awry or are too embarrassed to report it, but it is estimated that hundreds of millions are lost annually by those who succumb to the scam (U.S. Secret Service 2006).

The advent of e-mail no longer requires the sender to be target-specific because sending e-mail messages out in mass costs next to nothing. Like basic marketing, such fraudsters' success comes by getting the word out. Reaching large numbers of people increases the chances of finding willing participants or "customers"—the more, the better. No longer are these offenders required to create fraudulent postage or thumb through international business directories to find potential targets. A simple click of a mouse button in a "boiler room" operation or at the corner café can reach thousands of potential victims in very short order. Even if the success rate is 1 percent or less, the scam can make the offenders substantial amounts of money with cooperative victims.

A typical 4-1-9 e-mail scam message may look something like the message shown in Figure 3–8, which we received. The spelling errors and formatting have been left in the original form.

It is interesting to note the significant number of spelling and grammatical errors present in this sample and the many others like it. In addition to seeking empathy by using uneducated parlay, this is also done to avoid detection by e-mail spam or junk mail filters (which work using keywords) and permits successful delivery. It appears obvious that the intent of this scheme is to clean out the account of the bank account number provided. Although this is possible, it's often not the case, and if a victim provides the bank information, it is merely a signal that the scammers have hooked another victim. According to the U.S. Secret Service and by studying several 4-1-9 scams, we suggest they tend to have the following characteristics:

- In almost every case there is a sense of urgency; messages are marked "urgent" or "confidential."
- The victim is eventually enticed to travel to Nigeria or a border country.
- There are many forged official-looking documents.
- An offer is made to transfer millions of dollars in "over invoiced contract" funds into the victim's personal bank account.

NIGERIAN PETROLEUM CORPORATION

FALOMO OFFICE COMPLEX,

IKOYI,

LAGOS,NIGERIA.

Dear friend,

first I must solicit your confidence in this transaction for this is by virtue of its nature as being confidential. And I will also asssure you that all will be well at the end of the day.We have decided to contact you by email due to the urgency of this transaction. I want to start by introducing myself properly to you. I am Mr Robert Tont Isu the chief accountant of the NIGERIAN NATIONAL PETROLEUM CORPORATION (NNPC). I came to know of you in my private search for a realiable and reputable person to handle this confidential transaction which involves the transfer of the sum of FORTY EIGHT MILLION EIGHT HUNDRED THOUSAND UNITED STATES DOLLARS to a foreign account. This amount was secured from excess oil sales from Nigeria crude oil. The sum of $48.8 Billion oil windfall was realized by the Nigerian National Petroleum Corporation for the month of August 2001 . Organistion of Peroleum Exporting countries (OPEC) crude oil price was peg at $22.00 per barrell and fortunately for oil producing countries like Nigeria, there was rises in oil price to about $27.00 and $28.00 per barrell and as a result there was excess oil sales and I believe you would be aware of this rise in oil price . Out of this $48.8 BILLION excess oil funds, myself and my colleage because of our position in the Account Department of the Nigerian National Petroleum Corporation divertd the sum of FORTY EIGHT MILLION EIGHT HUNDRED THOUSAND UNITED STATES DOLLARS we want to transfer into your Account which is the excess CRUDE OIL sales Account.Please note the reason for the transfer of this fund into your account will be for a mobilisation fee for a contract that is awarded to you by my ministry NIGERIAN NATIONAL PETROLEUM CORPORATION. All the necessary documentation for the approval of this fund into your account will be taken good care of and this business is 100% risk free as all the modalities for the smooth transfer of this fund has been concluded already. My colleages and I have agreed on the following as soon as you agree to assist.

1) That thirty percent (30%) will be for you for helping us recieve the fund.

2) That ten percent (10%) will be mapped out for reimburesment of any expenses incured by the two parties (your party and my party) during the tranfer of this fund into your account.3) that the rest will be left for us in your account for sometime before any of us will be able to get to you for withdrawal.You are urgently required to send me your opinion on this and Your reply will enable me give you my private telephone line and for security reasons I will not give you my office telephone line. yours sincerely,

Mr Robert Tont Isu.

ACCOUNTS DEPT.

NNPCLAGOS DISTRICT.

NIGERIAN.

Figure 3–8 Actual 4-1-9 e-mail scam message.

- Most of the correspondence is handled by fax or through the mail, which has evolved to also include e-mail.
- Blank letterheads and invoices are requested from the victim along with the victim's banking particulars, name, phone number, and e-mail address.
- Any number of Nigerian fees, various taxes, attorney's fees, transactions fees, and so forth are requested for processing the transaction; each fee is purported to be the last required.
- The confidential and secretive nature of the transaction is emphasized.
- There are usually claims of strong ties to Nigerian officials.
- A Nigerian residing in the United States, London, or other area may claim to be a clearinghouse bank for the Central Bank of Nigeria.

Figure 3–9 lists the various themes and variations on themes of the advance fee fraud.

In a new twist, fraudsters have sent e-mail victims a cashier's check for thousands of dollars to be deposited in the person's bank account. These checks appear to clear instantly and, as agreed, victims then wire their foreign correspondent a large portion of the funds and keep their commission. A day or two later, the victim is informed that the check was fraudulent, and the victim is held liable for the transfer amount (Barrett 2004). A similar lottery scam out of Canada helps to highlight how this scam works. An actual letter received by a potential victim is re-created in Figure 3–10.

It is the goal of the scammer to have the victim cash the enclosed check and wire the money before the bank or check cashing entity realizes that it's a bad check. If successful, the victim is out the money wired to the scammer and might be held responsible for the amount of the bad check.

Once scammers have a cooperative victim, they next must have the victim literally buy into the rest of the scam. According to the U.S. Department of State (1997), the typical Nigerian scam progresses through several steps. Although the publication on which these steps are based is about eight years old, the techniques used by criminals are basically unchanged, except today they use technology more to their advantage. The 4-1-9 fraud proceeds as follows:

- For several days, the fraudsters continue to establish a level of trust with the victim by sending the victim more "official" documentation verifying the bona fides of the deal and the people involved.
- Correspondence may continue via e-mail, standard mail, or fax (we add emphasis to e-mail correspondence).
- At some point, the victim is advised that the deal is near completion; however, an emergency has arisen and money is needed to pay for an unforeseen government fee or tax before the victim's money can be released. If the victim pays the fee, the criminals devise another "problem" that requires immediate payment by the victim. Each problem is supported by official documentation.
- The criminals can run this ruse for months or even years, depending on the gullibility of the victim or how desparate the victim is to recoup the losses.

Disbursement from Wills   Normally aimed at charities, religious groups, universities, or nonprofit organizations. The organization receives a letter, fax, or e-mail from a mysterious benefactor interested in the group's cause and wishing to make a sizable contribution. Before the contribution can be released, the recipient must first pay inheritance tax or various government fees and taxes. The victim may also be requested to travel to Nigeria and/or a bordering country to collect the gift. The "gift" doesn't exist, and once the fees are paid the benefactor disappears.

Contract Fraud (COD of Goods and Services)   Sometimes referred to as "trade default," this scheme normally targets small companies with little export experience. The targeted company receives an order from a Nigerian company and a bank draft for items to be shipped via air freight. The Nigerian company is attempting to obtain a sample of the product at an introductory price under the guise of planning to introduce the product to Nigeria. The Nigerian company also tries to convince the target company that registration, import, and other fees are required to bring the product to Nigeria by sending the target company documentation from real or fictitious law firms. The fraudsters then normally place a number of small orders (less than $10,000) and pay with legitimate bank drafts. Once they have established trust with the target company, an urgent and larger order is placed and paid for with a fraudulent bank draft. By the time the victim realizes the bank draft is false, the items have already been shipped, the Nigerian company doesn't exist, and the products are not recoverable.

Purchase of Real Estate   This fraud involves an offer to purchase real estate using the services of a real estate broker or "well-established" business executive. Once a home is located, the broker or person acting on behalf of the home "buyer" is required to pay certain fees to close the deal. Once the fees are paid, the "broker" disappears.

Conversion of Hard Currency (Black Money)   A letter, fax, or e-mail message entices the victim with a "chance of a lifetime" offer. Once the victim agrees to allow the criminal to obtain a visa for him/her and to meet the offender in Nigeria or a neutral country, the following occurs: the victim is shown a suitcase allegedly full of U.S. currency in $100.00 denominations that have been temporarily defaced by using a black, waxy material (petroleum jelly and iodine) to mask their origin. To remove the material and restore the notes the victim must purchase a special cleaning solution (a commercial cleaning fluid), which is very expensive—$50,000 to $200,000. The victim will receive 40 percent of the money as his/her commission. In front of the victim, the scammers wash one of the bills with the special solution, restoring a $100 to its original condition. To further show good

Figure 3–9 Advance fee fraud: Themes and variations.

faith, the victim is sometimes allowed to keep the briefcase a short time, but is told not to open it because exposure to air will cause the black substance to ruin the money. The criminals walk away with the victim's money for the "solution," and the victim ends up with a suitcase filled with blank paper.

Sale of Crude Oil at Below-Market Values The victim is offered special crude oil allocations at lower-than-market rates. Consistent with similar frauds, the victim is required to pay special registration and licensing fees to acquire the crude oil. The victim soon discovers that the "sellers" have disappeared once the fees have been paid.

Figure 3–9 (*Continued*)

Source: Summarized from U.S. Department of State. 1997. "Nigerian Advance Fee Fraud."

Delta Financial Trust Inc Tel...1-647-999-9999

Notice of Winning

We are please to inform you that you are one of the second category winner of the lottery draw held on November 23rd, 2005.

So many attempts were made to locate you regarding this winning.

Your ticket with serial number 76992762 drew the lucky winning number 89287383.

You are approved of lump sum payment of (US $200,000.00) payable to you either by banks draft or certified check. Payable after confirming if you are the rightful owner.

Your claim number is RF-876352427-UA

We enclose this check US $2450.00 which was deducted from the winnings. The purpose of this check is for the payment of **TAXES and SERVICE CHARGES** on you're big winnings.

The TAX amount is 0.75% of the winning amount ($1500.00) will be paid through WESTERN UNION OR MONEYGRAM MONEY TRANSFER.

You are required to contact your assigned agent, **John Smith or Lillian Duke,** for further instruction on how you can claim your big winnings.

CALL JOHN SMITH OR LILLIAN DUKE AT 1647-999-9999

Congratulations!

Yours, Truly,

Edward Dave (Promotion Manager)

Figure 3–10 Letter received by potential fraud victim.

- At some point in the fraud, the criminals attempt to entice the victim to travel to Nigeria or a bordering country to "finalize" the contract, money transfer, or other transaction.
- The criminals tell the victim that a visa is not necessary, which is untrue—travel to Nigeria requires one. In some cases, criminals pay off airport security personnel to allow the victim entry.
- Once in country, the victim will attend "meetings" with criminals who pose as government officials. If the victim is sufficiently duped and makes the payments, he or she returns home unharmed and the scam continues. However, if the victim decides not to pay additional payments and/or sign a contract, the victim is subjected to threats and physical abuse until he or she arranges for more payments to be made.

Travel to Nigeria is the most dangerous part of the scam. In many cases, people have been kidnapped, held for ransom, tortured, or even killed. Since 1992, 17 people have been killed in Nigeria attempting to recover their funds, and the U.S. State Department has documented more than 100 cases in which U.S. citizens have been rescued from Nigeria (Smith, Holmes, and Kaufmann 1999). Since September 1995, at least 8 Americans have been held against their will by these criminals in Lagos (U.S. Department of State 1997). On May 20, 1995, the U.S. Embassy in Lagos reported that James Breaux, a U.S. businessman, was shot and killed in Surulere, Lagos. There were strong indications that Mr. Breaux was lured to Nigeria by advance fee criminals (U.S. Department of State 1997).

To avoid requiring victims to travel to Nigeria and to increase cooperation, criminals also use accomplices in Canada to complete these frauds. The case study in Figure 3–11 is taken from a March 11, 2005, U.S. Department of Justice press release and exemplifies how the scam is pulled off currently.

The international nature of these scams makes prosecuting them difficult. Local and state law enforcement agencies do not have jurisdiction over international crimes, and the lead investigative agency in these scams in the United States is the Secret Service. In 1995, the Secret Service launched Operation 4-1-9 to combat these schemes. Since then, agents have been assigned to the Lagos, Nigeria, U.S. Embassy on observer status to assist with investigating these schemes. On July 2, 1996, officials of the Federal Investigation Bureau (FIIB) of the Nigerian National Police, accompanied by Secret Service agents in an observer/advisor role, executed search warrants on 16 locations in Lagos that resulted in the arrests of 43 Nigerian nationals. Evidence seized included telephones and fax machines, government and Central Bank of Nigeria letterhead, international business directories, scam letters, addressed envelopes, and files containing correspondence with victims from around the world.

Ongoing efforts continue to combat these scammers, and in May 1998, Massachusetts Congressman Edward Markey proposed the Nigerian Advance Fee Fraud Prevention Bill, which would specifically outlaw this type of scam in the United States (Combating International crime in Africa, 1997). Although the bill didn't pass, it highlighted the nature of the problem and brought it to the forefront.

SACRAMENTO MAN SENTENCED TO 8 YEARS IMPRISONMENT FOR ROLE IN MULTI-MILLION DOLLAR NIGERIAN ADVANCE FEE FRAUD SCHEME

SACRAMENTO—United States Attorney McGregor W. Scott announced today that ROLAND ADAMS, 38, of Sacramento, the owner of Adams Business Services, was sentenced today by United States District Judge Edward J. Garcia to 97 months imprisonment for conspiring to commit mail and wire fraud, and conspiring to launder money in connection with an international fraud scheme that resulted in losses to victims exceeding $1 million. The defendant pleaded guilty on August 18, 2003. This case was the product of an extensive investigation by the United States Secret Service, with the assistance of the Royal Canadian Mounted Police. At sentencing, Judge Garcia noted the sophistication of the scheme that lost many victims their life savings and commented upon ADAMS' unsuccessful attempts to minimize his role in the international fraud scheme. Parole has been abolished in the federal system, and ADAMS will be required to serve at least 85% of the prison time imposed.

U.S. Attorney McGregor W. Scott said: "Nigerian advance fee schemes are a pernicious form of fraud. Although they are merely annoying to many people who receive solicitations by mail, fax, or e-mail, they can be financially devastating for those who are duped. The sentence imposed on Roland Adams today should serve both as a warning to perpetrators that they will be brought to justice, and as an alert to the public to avoid responding to suspicious entreaties involving get-rich-quick schemes."

According to Assistant United States Attorney Camil Skipper, who prosecuted the case, at the time of his guilty plea, ADAMS admitted that between February 2001 and June 2002, he conspired with others in Nigeria, South Africa, and Canada to operate a Nigerian advance fee fraud scheme (also known as "4-1-9" fraud after the section of the Nigerian penal code that addresses fraud schemes). As part of the scheme, ADAMS and international co-conspirators mailed solicitation letters, purportedly from officials of African governments or government agencies, to hundreds of potential victims around the world. The solicitation letters sought assistance in diverting to private use millions of dollars purportedly held in investment accounts or trusts. In exchange for the victims' agreement to receive the diverted funds and return the substantial majority to the purported official, the victims were promised a portion of the diverted funds. In fact, there were no such funds.

Victims, who often communicated with ADAMS and his co-conspirators using e-mail, were assessed "fees" to facilitate the diversion of the fictitious funds. Those fees typically amounted to 1% of the total fund transfer amount, totaling anywhere from several thousand to several hundred

(continued)

Figure 3–11 4-1-9 Case study.
Source: U.S. Department of Justice, March 11, 2005.

thousand dollars. Some victims were required to send the fees to specified individuals in South Africa and Canada; other victims were instructed to wire fees to other accounts around the world. A portion of the funds collected by his international co-conspirators was forwarded to ADAMS in Sacramento. As part of the scheme, ADAMS posed as a banker in his communications with victims. ADAMS registered the Internet domain names Afribankcorp.com, Bancofafrica.com, and Bancofeasterncarribean.com [sic] and had web sites created for the fictitious banks. (These banks supposedly held the diverted funds.) Victims were directed to these web sites, which were used to track the progress of the transactions and give the fraud scheme the illusion of legitimacy.

In addition to a sentence of imprisonment, Judge Garcia ordered ADAMS to pay $1,201,092.90 in restitution to victims of the scheme. It is anticipated that ADAMS's Elk Grove home and over $87,000 seized from various bank and investment accounts, which were forfeited to the government following a non-jury trial before Judge Garcia on September 22, 2003, will be used to partially satisfy ADAMS's restitution obligation. A laptop computer and Internet domain names used in the scheme were also forfeited to the government.

ADAMS also was found guilty on April 14, 2004, following a jury trial, of unlawful procurement of citizenship or naturalization and making a false statement. The jury found that ADAMS, a naturalized United States citizen originally from Nigeria, made false statements during his naturalization interview. Judge Garcia sentenced ADAMS to 97 months and 60 months imprisonment for those offenses, to be served concurrently with his 97-month sentence on the fraud and money laundering convictions. Pursuant to his conviction, Judge Garcia today ordered that ADAMS be stripped of his U.S. citizenship. It is anticipated that ADAMS will be deported following service of his sentence.

Figure 3–11 (*Continued*)

In August 2000, the U.S. Secret Service opened an office in Lagos to share information, technical expertise, and some resources to help Nigerian authorities battle advance fee fraud and other Nigerian criminal activity, such as money laundering and counterfeiting. Since 2002, an FBI agent has been assigned to work exclusively with Nigeria's Economic and Financial Crime Commission to root out advance free fraud schemes (Ashcroft 2004). In 2004, the U.S. Justice Department launched Operation Web Snare partly aimed at combating these frauds (Ashcroft 2004).

Although Nigeria is considered the birthplace of these frauds, they now occur throughout the world, including within the United States. According to the FBI, African criminal enterprises that participate in advance fee fraud, among other things, have been identified in several major metropolitan areas from coast to coast, but are most prevalent in Atlanta; Baltimore; Washington, D.C.; Chicago; Milwaukee; Dallas; Houston; New York; and Newark, N.J.

Advance fee fraud historically is a transnational crime involving scammers who reside in places around the globe, and thousands of 4-1-9 e-mail messages are sent and received every day; at some time or another, the first responder will be exposed to one of these complaints. Although the U.S. Secret Service is the lead agency in these matters, many citizens turn to local law enforcement for assistance. Even the International Criminal Police Organization recommends that victims contact local police and "follow their advice" (Interpol, 2005).

A preliminary step in the investigation of a 4-1-9 e-mail complaint includes tracing the origin of the e-mail message (see e-mail tracing, Chapter 6). Keep in mind that many of these e-mail messages are probably sent through anonymizers or several mail servers before they arrive at their destination, which can make tracing them difficult. However, a trace could lead to a U.S. location and provide valuable leads for federal investigators to follow up on. If nothing else, tracing messages helps the first responder become more familiar with the origins and tracing of these types of messages.

Any recipient of a 4-1-9 letter, fax, or e-mail message who has not sustained a loss should be directed to send the correspondence to the U.S. Secret Service using the following contact information:

E-mail: 419.fcd@usss.treas.gov
Fax: (202) 406-5031
Mail: United States Secret Service
Financial Crimes Division
Attn:419
950 J. Street, NW, Suite 5300
Washington, DC 20223

If a victim sustains a financial loss from this type of fraud, he or she should be referred to the nearest U.S. Secret Service Field Office, which can be found at www.secretservice.gov/field_offices.shtml. First responders can assist by gathering the preliminary data, such as when the first letters were received, how the scam progressed, how much money has been taken, which types of correspondence were sent and how (e.g., e-mail, fax, mail), and by gathering any copies of documents related to the scam. If communications were sent via e-mail, the victim must be directed to save all e-mail messages. The first responder can also notify the victim's e-mail service provider and direct it to preserve all communications to and from the victim's e-mail address pursuant to the official investigation. Once all of the preliminary information and evidence is collected, the first responder can forward a report and all supporting documentation to the Secret Service for any follow-up investigation.

The best way for first responders to help citizens avoid becoming victims of these types of scams is through public awareness. The U.S. Secret Service has created a Web site called "Public Awareness Advisory Regarding "4-1-9" or "Advanced Fee Fraud" Schemes, at www.secretservice.gov/alert419.shtml. This advisory information can be added to existing law enforcement Web sites, and first responders can direct victims to an agency's site for additional information.

Proactive efforts by federal law enforcement agencies in cooperation with Nigerian authorities appear to be reducing the frequency of 4-1-9 scams originating from Nigeria. As a result, the FBI's Operation Cybersweep has now identified Ghana, Latvia, and Romania as the most common sources of fraud after Nigeria (U.S. Department of Justice, 2003).

A relatively new form of the 4-1-9 scam is called the Your E-mail Address Won the Lottery, which appears to be primarily coming from European countries. One example that was sent to us came out of Spain. The e-mail message informs the recipient that he or she has won a lottery, such as the "Euromillion," and also lists the matching/winning numbers. The recipient is instructed to keep this completely confidential and to reply by providing his or her full name, home and office telephone and fax numbers, mobile telephone numbers, and the winning ticket reference number for processing of the winning funds. Once the "winner" provides this information, the victim is requested to pay endless "administration fees" to complete the transaction. Once the fees are paid, the fraudsters keep the victim's money and may even request additional fees, and the "winner" soon realizes he or she is a "loser" and will never receive the supposed winnings.

Some people have little sympathy for those who fall victim to such scams, citing that victims should have known better. However, the lure of easy money that can cure all ills or sustain that nonprofit organization or church is why such scams still work. In 2002, a pastor in Milwaukee, Wisconsin, who was considering "investing" in an offer that he had received via e-mail contacted us. We educated this near-victim about the scam and promptly deleted the e-mail message.

The global nature of high-tech crime continues to create legal hurdles and challenges for first responders. Some law enforcers take a proactive approach, while others continue to pawn off high-tech crime on other agencies, citing the fact that they don't have jurisdiction or, more likely, do not have the skills to respond properly to and/or investigate such crimes. "It's a civil matter" is an all-too-common and unacceptable response.

Identity theft and other scams will continue to grow, and first responders cannot stand idly by hoping that things will get better. False identification documents are not merely used for financial gain, but also are used by terrorists to facilitate terrorist acts. Private citizens, local law enforcement, and federal agents all need to take a proactive approach to combating high-tech criminals.

Summary of Investigative Protocols for E-mail-Based Crimes

- Preserve the unlawful e-mail communication by printing a copy and/or making a digital copy.
- Expand the e-mail to view the full header and identify Internet Protocol addresses that need to be traced.
- Conduct an IP lookup and determine the Internet service provider (ISP) that was used by the suspect to send the unlawful e-mail message.
- Draft a subpoena for the ISP and obtain the subscriber records associated with the e-mail address that was used for the unlawful communication.
- Utilizing the information obtained with the subpoena, such as a physical address, establish contact with the suspect or take additional/appropriate investigative or enforcement action.

■ SUMMARY

Criminals, like law abiding citizens, take advantage of the Internet. Law enforcement and legislators must take proactive steps to combat these high-tech criminals. Thorough investigations must be conducted, followed by prosecution. Labeling these criminal acts as "civil matters" is unacceptable. Serious consideration also needs to be given to increasing the penalties for many high-tech crimes—those currently classified as misdemeanor or forfeitures, lack the enforcement "teeth" they should have.

Using the Internet and other technologies to harass or threaten an individual, including one's spouse in cases of domestic violence, is no less serious than Internet crimes committed in the business world. Law enforcement agents must familiarize themselves with the methods of operation, properly collect the digital evidence, and preserve it for prosecution. Working cooperatively with victims can enhance investigative efforts, as can knowing how to create and submit the appropriate legal paperwork to compel, when necessary, cooperation of Internet Service Providers and others who possess evidence. All of these actions must take place in a timely fashion because the digital evidence is perishable.

Identity theft will continue to plague consumers in the United States and abroad. It is committed by gang members, terrorists, and common criminals. It is a "gateway crime" that leads to other criminal offenses, including credit card fraud, forgery and check fraud, mortgage fraud and account takeover, theft of phone service, medical records theft, and satellite and cable theft, among others. Identity theft complaints must be taken seriously, with prompt reporting and victim assistance. Frequently victims are seeking resources and personal guidance. If they are bounced from one police agency to the next because the crime is not in that agency's jurisdiction, they are victimized again. Immediate investigation is required to increase the chances of apprehension. Unfortunately many police departments cannot and do not dedicate the resources necessary to address this ongoing problem. Efforts must also be made to continually educate consumers in order to help them avoid becoming victims of identity theft, a serious criminal offense.

Advance fee fraud (4-1-9 scams) are alive and well today. What began with the fax machine has moved to the Internet. With the click of a mouse, fraudsters can reach out to thousands of potential victims at once. Willing and cooperative victims continue to be lured into the scam with promises of easy money, and new forms of the scam are constantly evolving. A current scam is lotteries that mail victims fraudulent checks. The victims are instructed to wire a percentage of the money to the lottery company to cover necessary "fees," and to keep the rest. Winners soon become losers when they discover later that the check was fraudulent and they are responsible for the full amount.

■ REVIEW QUESTIONS

1. What are the three classifications of criminality discussed in this chapter? Define each one of them.
2. What is the level of certainty/proof required for a guilty verdict in a criminal case?
3. What is the level of certainty/proof required in a municipal ordinance violation case?
4. What is the level of certainty/proof required for law enforcement officers to make an arrest?
5. What is the difference between "harassment," "threats," and "cyberstalking"?
6. What is the difference between "cyberstalking" and "cyberbullying"?
7. What is an acceptable definition of *identity theft*?
8. What are the three primary types of identify theft discussed in this chapter?
9. List and explain at least five common ways thieves can steal a person's identity.
10. In relation to identity theft, what is a "breeder crime"? Provide an example.
11. What are the three major credit reporting bureaus to which first responders should direct identity theft victims?
12. What are the overreaching impacts of the Real ID Act of 2005 proposed by the federal government?
13. Explain what is meant by the term *4-1-9 scam* and provide an example.

■ TERMS

account takeover	cyberbullying	felony
criminal identity theft	cyberstalking	fund transfer scam

harassment	ordinance violation	reasonable suspicion
identity theft	preponderance of evidence	threats
misdemeanor	probable cause	true name fraud
mortgage fraud	proof beyond a reasonable doubt	vicinage

■ REFERENCES

Ashcroft, J. 2004. Justice department targets online fraud, attorney general says. U.S. Department of State. www.usinfo.state.gov/gi/Archive/2004/Aug/ 27-422714.html (accessed June 20, 2005).

AT&T. 2006. Consumer information: Identity theft. www.sbc.com/gen/general? pid=1419 (accessed September 25, 2006).

Barrett, R. 2004. The check's in the mail, "419" e-mail schemes change with the times. Consumer Reports WebWatch. www.consumerwebwatch.org/ dynamic/fraud-investigation-checks-in-mail.cfm (accessed June 21, 2005).

Benner, J., Givens, B., and Mierzwinski, E. 2000. Nowhere to turn: victims speak out on identity theft. Privacy Rights Clearing House. www.privacyrights.org/ar/ idtheft2000.htm (accessed June 28, 2005).

Brenner, S. 1999. Model state computer crimes code. Cybercrimes. www.cybercrimes. net/98MSCCC/Article1/commentarysection109.html (accessed July 1, 2005).

CardWatch. 2005. All about skimming. www.cardwatch.org.uk/cardholders.asp? sectionID=3&pageid+97 (accessed September 25, 2006).

Combating International Crime in Africa. 1997. Hearing before the subcommittee on Africa of the Committee on International Relations, House of Representatives, 105th Congress, July 15, 1998. http://commdocs.house.gov/ committees/intlrel/hfa50884.000/hfa50884_0.HTM (accessed October 14, 2006).

Dadisho, E. 2005. Identity theft and the police response: The problem www. policechiefmagazine.org/magazine/index.cfm?fuseaction=display_arch& article_id=493&issue_id=12005 (accessed October 14, 2006).

Federal Bureau of Investigation. 2003. Crime in the United States 2002. www.fbi.gov/ucr/cius_02/pdf/02crime.pdf (accessed June 23, 2005).

———. Bank robbery in the United States. www.fbi.gov/ucr/cius_02/html/web/ specialreport/05-SRbankrobbery.html (accessed July 1, 2005).

Federal Trade Commission. 2003. Identity theft survey report. www.ftc.gov/os/ 2003/09/synovatereport.pdf (accessed July 1, 2005).

———. 2004, October 29. FTC issues final rules on FACTA identity theft definitions, active duty alert duration, and appropriate proof of identity. http:// ftc.gov.opa.2004/10/facataidtheft.html (accessed September 25, 2006).

———. 2005. National and state trends in fraud and identity theft, January–December 2004. www.consumer.gov/sentinel/pubs/Top10Fraud2004.pdf (accessed June 22, 2005).

———. (n.d.). Federal and state laws. www.consumer.gov/idtheft/federallaws.html (accessed June 11, 2005).

Frieden, T. 2004. FBI warns of mortgage fraud "epidemic". Seeks to head off next "S and L crisis." CNN. www.cnn.com/2004/LAW/09/17/ mortgage.fraud/index.html (accessed June 6, 2005).

Goodman, M. 2001. Making computer crime count. *FBI Law Enforcement Bulletin*, 70. www.fbi.gov/publications/leb/2001/aug01leb.pdf (accessed June 22, 2005).

Gore, Albert A, Jr. 1999. Report on cyberstalking: A new challenge for law enforcement and industry. www.usdoj.gov/criminal/cybercrime/cyberstalking.htm (accessed June 11, 2005).

Haley, J. E. 1973. *Robbing Banks Was My Business: The Story of J. Harvey Bailey*. Canyon, TX: Palo Duro Press.

Interpol. 2005. Advanced fee fraud: 4-1-9 letters (Nigerian letters). www.interpol.int/Public/FinancialCrime/FinancialFraud/NigerianLetter.asp (accessed June 17, 2005).

Masters, B. A. 1998. Cracking down on e-mail harassment. *Washington Post*, November 1, 1998. www.washingtonpost.com/wp-srv/local/frompost/nov98/email01.htm (accessed May 31, 2005).

Morse, J., and Kiesewetter, S. 2002. 11 students charged in fake id case. *Cincinnati Enquirer*, March 1, 2002. www.enquirer.com/editions/2002/03/01/loc_11_students_charged.html (accessed June 25, 2005)

National Center for Victims of Crime. 2004. Cyberstalking. www.ncvc.org/ncvc/main.aspx?dbName=DocumentViewer&DocumentAction=ViewProperties&DocumentID=32458&UrlToReturn=http%3a%2f%2fwww.ncvc.org%2fncvc%2fmain.aspx%3fdbName%3dAdvancedSearch (accessed July 8, 2006).

Newman, G. R. 2004. Identity theft. *Problem-Oriented Guides for Police, Problem-Specific Guide Series*, 25. www.cops.usdoj.gov/mime/open.pdf?Item=1271 (accessed June 24, 2005).

Ovidio, R., and Doyle, J. 2003. A study on cyberstalking. *FBI Law Enforcement Bulletin* 72, no. 3.

Oyesanya, F. 2004. Review of draft Nigerian cybercrime act. www.nigeriavillagesquare1.com/Articles/femi_oyesanya6.html (accessed June 20, 2005).

Simon, B. 2005. IDs sold to illegal immigrants. CBS News. www.cbsnews.com/stories/2005/04/18/60ll/main688900.shtml (accessed June 23, 2005).

Smith, R. G., Holmes, M. N., and Kaufmann P. 1999. Nigerian advance fee fraud. *Australian Institute of Criminology: Trends and issues in crime and criminal justice*, July, 21. www.aic.gov.au/publications/tandi/ti121.pdf (accessed June 17, 2005)

Spielman, F., and Main, F. 2004. Cline says gang laundered $70 mil. through mortgage fraud. *Chicago Sun-Times*, October 1, 2004. www.suntimes.com/output/news/cst-nws-gangs01.html (accessed June 6, 2005).

Stambaugh, H., Beaupre, D., Icove, D., and Baker, R. 2000. State and local law enforcement needs to combat electronic crime. National Institute of Justice. www.ncjrs.org/txtfiles1/nij/183451.txt.

State of Wisconsin. 2003, *State of Wisconsin Criminal Law Handbook.* www.wilenet.org/secure/html/trainstand/instructcntr/basicle/legal/ constitutional/ Handbook%20Large%20Complete2.pdf (accessed June 29, 2006).

Sullivan, B. 2005. The secret list of ID theft victims. MSNBC. www.msnbc.msn. com/id/6814673/ (accessed June 6, 2005).

Terry v. Ohio, 392 U.S. 1 (1968), caselaw.lp.findlaw.com/scripts/getcase.pl? court=US&vol=392&invol=1 (accessed June 29, 2006).

Tjaden, P., and Thoennes, N. 2000. Extent, nature, and consequences of intimate partner violence. National Institute of Justice. www.ncjrs.org/pdffiles1/ nij/181867.pdf (accessed June 21, 2005).

U.S. Department of Justice. 1999. 1999 report on cyberstalking: A new challenge for law enforcement and industry. www.usdoj.gov/criminal/cybercrime/ cyberstalking.htm (accessed May 31, 2005).

———. 2003. Operation Cybersweep. www.fbi.gov/cyber/cysweep/cysweep1. htm (accessed June 21, 2005).

———. 2004. Another DMV employee admits taking cash to fraudulently produce drivers licenses. www.usdoj.gov/usao/nj/press/files/moor0116_r.htm (accessed October 14, 2006).

U.S. Department of State. 1997. Nigerian advance fee fraud. www.state.gov/www/ regions/africa/naffpub.pdf (accessed June 16, 2005).

U.S. Department of State. 2003. Patterns of global terrorism 2003. www.state.gov/documents/organization/31912.pdf (accessed June 30, 2005).

U.S. Secret Service. (2006). Public awareness advisory regarding "4-1-9" or "advance fee fraud" schemes. www.secretservice.gov/alert419.shtml (accessed July 8, 2006).

WiredKids,Inc.(n.d.) What is cyberbullying? www.stopcyberbullying.org/ what_is_ cyberbullying_exactly.html (accessed July 8, 2006).

Wireback, T. 2005. N.C. a destination for fake ID seekers. Americans for Legal Immigration. www.alipac.us/article147.html (accessed June 28, 2005).

Wood, R. A., and Wood, N. L. 2002. Stalking the stalker. *FBI Law Enforcement Bulletin* 71. www.fbi.gov/publications/leb/2002/dec02leb.pdf (accessed June 11, 2005).

chapter four
High-Tech Frauds

■ LEARNING OBJECTIVES

1. Explain the various types of high-tech fraud.
2. Explain the various ways high-tech fraud is committed today.
3. Describe the techniques used by law enforcement to combat high-tech fraud.
4. Describe the techniques used by private industry to combat high-tech fraud.
5. Explain the current and emerging technologies used to prevent and combat high-tech fraud.
6. Explain how fraudsters exploit technology and human nature to commit fraud.

From phony businesses and miracle cures, to deception and trickery, fraud is nothing new. Economies of scale require people to earn money to survive. Some choose to do it legally, while others use deception and trickery to make a quick buck. What previously required clever schemes today can be done with a few keystrokes and the click of a mouse. The tools used to pull off a fraud still include using fake identities, setting up false businesses and virtual storefronts, funneling money through entities, placing funds in mail drops and accounts, and most important, the right person. Creating these false documents and locating sources for ill-gotten gain used to take considerable time and effort. Fraudsters often had to have access to the right people to perpetrate fraud. Today, technology makes it much simpler, and fraudsters can create all the tools needed on a desktop computer. Templates to make fake identification documents are available on the Internet. Stolen credit card numbers are shared in chat rooms. E-mail takes the place of the fax machine, and legitimate-looking documents are just a click away.

Technology has not only changed the way we do legitimate business, but it has forced law enforcement and industry to learn new ways to combat and investigate the modern high-tech fraudster. This chapter discusses some of the many high-tech frauds committed today, specifically credit card fraud, auction fraud, and cellular/phone fraud. How these frauds are committed also is discussed as well as technologies and techniques that law enforcement and industry use to combat them.

4.1 CREDIT CARD FRAUD

At number 1 on the Federal Trade Commission list of "How Victims' Information Is Misused" (2006), credit card fraud is an epidemic with no signs of a real cure. There is one very good vaccine for the problem, and that is biometrics, especially for in-person purchases. **Biometrics,** which means "life measurement," is the science of using biological properties to identify individuals; for example, fingerprints, retina scans, and voice recognitions (Lexias n.d.) (www.lexias.com/html/glossary1.html). There are three types of biometrics: **high biometrics, low biometrics,** and **esoteric biometrics** (Joseph and Simlot 2005). High biometrics are most reliable and measure physical characteristics with high accuracy (e.g., retina, iris, and fingerprints). Low biometrics measure distinct features that have a reasonable level of accuracy (e.g., hand geometry, face recognition, voice recognition, and signature recognition). Last, esoteric biometrics, which are still in early development, include vein measurement or analysis of body odor. See Figure 4–1 for a picture of a handprint scanner.

Some credit card companies, such as Citibank, allow the option for cardholders to have their photograph imprinted on the front of their credit cards. Although this technique is not technically considered a form of biometrics, it's a good first step toward decreasing fraud. A digital fingerprint recognition system could replace the personal identification number (PIN) for use at retail locations or automatic teller machines (ATMs). In the future, the fingerprint could replace the credit card completely, and all transactions would be done using the pad of your index finger (Bruce 2001). Industry experts believe that the use of a smart card that incorporates fingerprint identification could eliminate 80 percent of fraudulent charges (O'Sullivan 1997). To combat credit card fraud over the phone some banks are experimenting with voice recognition software to authenticate their customers and ensure they are indeed the cardholder they say they are

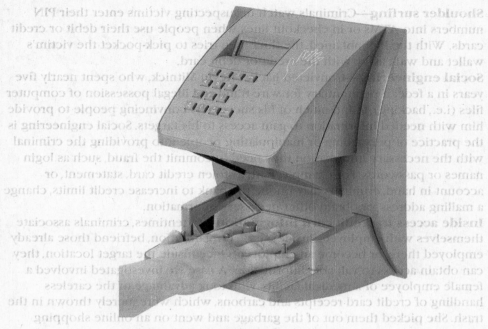

Figure 4–1 Biometric handprint scanner.

(Kharif 2005). Although 56 percent to 91 percent of the U.S. public supports the private sector use of biometrics (Privacy and American Business 2003), citizens also need to be assured that biometric information will not be abused, especially by Big Brother, the government. The appropriate safeguards must be in place to avoid misuse and any perceptions of misuse. However, until fingerprint transactions and other biometrics are in place, fraudsters could still steal credit card numbers simply by taking a cardholder's statement out of that person's mailbox and using it for an Internet shopping spree. With that in mind, the credit card is here to stay, and first responders need to combat credit card fraud effectively.

According to the Federal Trade Commission (1997), a U.S. Department of Justice COPS guide to check and card fraud (Newman 2003), and cases we have investigated, thieves obtain credit card information in the following ways:

Dumpster diving—Criminals sift through garbage cans, garbage placed at the curb, and Dumpsters, all of which are all significant sources of credit card information. Garbage placed at the curb, in common areas, or inside a Dumpster within an apartment parking lot have a lower level of privacy—it is even legal for law enforcement officials to take or sort through this garbage without a warrant (see *State v. Sigarro* 2004 WI App 16, *State v. Stevens*, 123 Wi 2d 303 1985, or *California v. Greenwood*, No. 86-864, 486 U.S. 35 1988). As a result of consumer carelessness, such as when people throw away credit card offers or statements, criminals can simply reach in and take advantage of the situation.

Shoulder surfing—Criminals watch unsuspecting victims enter their PIN numbers into ATMs or in checkout lines when people use their debit or credit cards. With the PIN obtained, the thief then tries to pick-pocket the victim's wallet and walk away with the credit or debit card.

Social engineering—Convicted hacker Kevin Mitnick, who spent nearly five years in a federal penitentiary for wire fraud and illegal possession of computer files (i.e., hacking), found much of his success by convincing people to provide him with needed information to gain access to his targets. Social engineering is the practice of persuading or manipulating people into providing the criminal with the necessary information they need to commit the fraud, such as login names or passwords. For example, with a stolen credit card, statement, or account in hand, criminals may phone the bank to increase credit limits, change a mailing address, or obtain other necessary information.

Inside access to credit card information—Oftentimes, criminals associate themselves with employees inside a target organization, befriend those already employed there, or become an employee. Once inside the target location, they can obtain access to valuable information. A case we investigated involved a female employee of a medical facility who took advantage of the careless handling of credit card receipts and carbons, which were merely thrown in the trash. She picked them out of the garbage and went on an online shopping spree using the victims' credit card numbers.

Credit card number–generating software—Criminals have used software programs that randomly generate valid credit card numbers. A few examples of these programs are Credit Master 2, Credit Wizard, and Credit Probe, which are all available on the Internet. The programs use the bank algorithm to generate legitimate credit card numbers. The generated numbers are not necessarily valid for use, but rather the string of characters that the programs randomly create is valid to each type of common credit card (e.g., Visa, MasterCard). In the 1990s, such software programs were commonly used to generate credit card numbers to obtain instant services, such as a phone sex or online pornography. Criminal groups have also used these software programs to obtain real credit card numbers and produce forged credit cards with identical bank identification numbers (Upadhyay et al. 2000). Today, credit card company security features have advanced to defeat this type of scheme. However, criminals are always finding ways to thwart new security technologies.

Skimming—This is the most prevalent form of counterfeit fraud whereby a card's magnetic stripe details, including the account number and PIN, are electronically copied by a small handheld device known as a skimmer, which is used to make a counterfeit card or for online purchases (American Express 2005; CardWatch 2005). It is currently estimated that skimming now accounts for 20 percent of all credit card fraud (International Card Manufacturers Association, n.d.). This statistic has remained steady throughout the first half of this decade. The technology behind credit card skimmers is similar to the common magnetic stripe encoders and decoders that are used in hotels to

Figure 4–2 Credit card embosser.

encode and decode the plastic room keys. A simple Internet keyword search for "magnetic stripe card reader/writer" reveals that a thief can purchase a small handheld skimmer online, along with the blank magnetic strip cards onto which the skimmed data can be programmed, a hologram applicator, a card printing machine, and a card embossing machine (Figure 4-2) to make fraudulent or counterfeit credit cards. Embossers are used to imprint numbers and letters on blank credit card stock. The average skimmer, as shown in Figure 4-3, fits in the palm of a hand, and the act of skimming takes only a second or two. Recently, a keyword search at eBay for "credit card reader" revealed 57 items (readers) for sale. Skimming often takes place in businesses with high turnover, such as restaurants, hotels, and retail stores. A more complex skimming scheme was discovered on an ATM machine where a skimmer was attached over the legitimate card slot and a hidden camera was used to capture PIN numbers. Until the credit card industry rolls out the encrypted "smart card" that eliminates magnetic coding and will make credit cards "skim proof," skimming will continue to be a problem.

Internet chat rooms—The Internet is a great way for criminals to meet online and discuss their activities or share their ill-gotten gain. The anonymity and ability to communicate with thousands of like-minded individuals make it the perfect gathering place. Whether through common instant messaging programs, where users choose with whom they wish to communicate by using a buddy list, or Internet Relay Chat (IRC), where users can communicate with people throughout the world to discuss and explore the good, bad, and the ugly—credit card numbers obtained or the techniques used to get them are openly shared online. With a few simple keystrokes a victim's credit card number can be

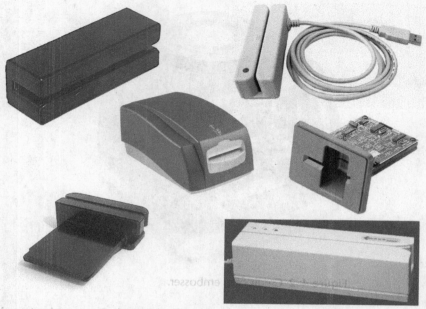

Figure 4–3 Magnetic card readers (skimmers).

shared with hundreds of others. The IRC network can be searched at www.searchirc.com. A keyword search for "credit card" reveals several chat rooms where users share stolen credit card numbers with each other.

E-mail and Web site scams—These scams are commonly referred to as **phishing,** whereby thieves use false e-mail return addresses, stolen Web page graphics, stylistic imitation, misleading or disguised hyperlinks, social engineering, and other artifices to trick users into revealing personally identifiable information. After obtaining this information, the "phisher" then uses the information to create unlawful identification documents and/or to unlawfully obtain money (credit cards/numbers) or property (Antiphishing Act 2005). More simply put, e-mail messages are constructed in such a way to look identical to common and recognizable company e-mail communications, and personal and credit card information is requested from the victim that the victim believes must be entered to update the account records and/or to remain a customer, client, or user.

E-mail phishing often involves some sort of financial communication requesting that the user update personal information to ensure continued service or to authenticate the customer or account status by providing a user name, credit card number, or password (Figure 4–4). Web site scams can involve fake storefronts where thieves create an authentic-looking retail site that purportedly sells merchandise, such as computer supplies or other items, at bargain prices. Popular Web building software programs that thieves can illegally obtain for free through file-sharing Web sites make it simple for thieves to create their own

Dear South Trust Bank Customer,

Technical services at the SouthTrust bank are carrying out a planned software upgrade. We earnestly ask you to visit the following link to start the procedure of confirmation of customers data.

www.southtrust.com/st/PersonalBanking/custdetailsconfirmation

Please do not answer this e-mail—follow the instructions given above.

We present our apologies and thank you for co-operating.

Copyright © 2005 South Trust All Rights Reserved

South Trust Bank, Member FDIC

Figure 4–4 Actual e-mail phishing example. We received this e-mail phishing message. Clicking the link provided would lead the unsuspecting victim to a legitimate-looking customer details information page that requests personal identifying information.

sites. Images of "items" to sell can be obtained from any other site, including the Secure Socket Layer (SSL) icon, which looks like a padlock and which usually indicates that a transaction is secure at time of checkout. Customers are duped into providing their credit card numbers, addresses, and other personal information to complete a purchase of items that will never be delivered. Their stolen credit card numbers are then used by thieves for other illegal gain. These Web sites disappear as fast as they go up to avoid detection.

The Uniform Resource Locater (URL) or Web site address that the scammers provide often appears legitimate. But close inspection of the URL used in many phishing incidents can reveal deception. For example, a phishing e-mail that appears to come from www.paypal.com could look like www.paypa1.com . The 1 is inserted in place of the lowercase *l*, and unless the unsuspecting victim looks closely, this deception would likely be overlooked. Add a legitimate-looking Web site as the link's destination, and the phisher will have the victim hooked.

Through public awareness campaigns, citizens are becoming more cognizant of these scams. For example, Antiphishing.org is an online organization dedicated to combating and wiping out this type of Internet fraud. Its campaign, and others like it, has made successful phishing scams more difficult to pull off. This forces the phishers to try a new twist, and instead of asking potential victims to click a link and supply personal information, some are now providing a phone number that leads to an automated answering machine where victims can willingly leave their personal information. It is believed that some consumers might be less suspicious of this because providing the information over the phone is more typical of the way some legitimate organizations do business. Phishers also use a technique known as *caller identity spoofing*, a program that displays a false number from which the scammer is calling on the receiver's caller identification unit. An Internet keyword search for "caller ID spoofing" can reveal several services and software programs for this potentially nefarious activity. Currently (in 2006), the Truth in Caller ID Act of 2006 is pending in Congress to help curb this activity.

Learner Activity

Visit Antiphishing.org (Anti-Phishing Working Group) and examine the Web site. What resources and information does it offer for first responders and consumers alike? Then, visit the Federal Trade Commission (FTC) Web page titled How Not to Get Hooked by a "Phishing" Scam at www.ftc.gov/bcp/conline/pubs/alerts/phishingalrt.htm. Read and, in your own words, report on what the FTC recommends consumers do to avoid becoming a victim of a phishing scam.

Steal it—Outside of the many high-tech means of obtaining credit card information, some thieves just steal it by breaking into cars, committing burglaries of homes or businesses, or watching for the residential mailbox "steal me" flag to appear and taking the outgoing mail. The credit card statement reveals the victim's credit card number, name, mailing address, and other personal information. The thief then fills out the change of address form to have the statements sent to another location, might make a few minimum payments to keep the card valid for a time, and then uses it to make significant purchases. Once the items are received and to avoid detection, the thief stops using the card or number, stops making payments, and disappears. A popular forwarding address used by thieves is a private box number that may have been set up with false identifying information. Thieves might also have the merchandise shipped to another location, such as a vacant house, and allow for drop off at the site. Knowing when the item(s) is likely to arrive, the thief will wait in the vicinity and retrieve it after it is delivered. Figure 4–5 describes an incident of identity-related fraud.

Until other high-tech credit cards are created or credit cards are eliminated altogether and replaced with digital smart cards, the theft of credit card numbers and accounts will continue. Credit card companies have gone to great lengths to secure the plastic cards themselves. However, this still allows for the credit card number to be stolen. Many of the specific credit card security features on common cards are law enforcement–sensitive and cannot be shared specifically within this text. Some of the common, more general, standard security features that appear on most credit cards include the following:

- Holographic industry or trade emblems
- Clear, uniform, evenly spaced, and raised credit card number embossing
- Standard three-digit validation numbers

On October 3, 2003, a 32-year-old "Brooklyn busboy," Abraham Abdallah, pleaded guilty to a 12-count indictment alleging wire fraud, mail and credit card fraud, identity theft, and conspiracy. He attempted to transfer more than $80 million from the country's richest people, including Steven Spielberg, Martha Stewart, and George Lucas, just to name a few. Using a library computer, Abdallah tricked the big three credit reporting agencies and obtained confidential information on his victims, which he used to access their credit card account information. His crimes were discovered when an alert bank employee contacted one of the victims to confirm a suspicious request to move $10 million from one of his accounts. Upon his arrest police found personal identifying information and photographs of more than 200 victims and more than 400 credit card numbers with matching addresses on his computer.

Figure 4–5 Credit card fraud case study.
Source: Smith, R. G. 2003. Addressing identity-related fraud. Australian Institute of Criminology. www.aic.gov.au/conferences/other/smith_russell/2003-09-identity.pdf (accessed July 1, 2005).

- Tamperproof/resistant signature panels
- Microprinting

Learner Activity

Using your text, the Internet, and other academic resources, research the life of Kevin Mitnick. What crimes did he commit? How much time did he spend in federal prison? How did he use social engineering to help facilitate his crimes? What is Kevin Mitnick doing today?

4.2 AUCTION FRAUD

According to the Federal Trade Commission (FTC) report *National and State Trends in Fraud and Identity Theft* (2004), Internet auction fraud is the second most common form of fraud, accounting for 16 percent of all complaints. (Identity theft is still ranked number 1, accounting for 39 percent of all complaints.) **Internet auction fraud** is defined as the use of the Internet in an online transaction between buyer and seller to defraud the buyer through deceptive means, including but not limited to failure to deliver merchandise, intentionally delivering defective merchandise, or delivering merchandise other than what was promised or purchased (of a lesser quality). Some of the common fraud schemes are described in Figure 4–6.

Easy money is the primary motive for auction fraud. Many fraudsters prey on unsuspecting victims and even believe that they can outsmart authorities. In the

- **Bid siphoning** When con artists lure bidders off legitimate auction sites by offering to sell the "same" item at a lower price. Their intent is to trick consumers into sending money without proffering the item. By going off-site, buyers lose any protections the original site may provide, such as insurance, feedback forms, or guarantees.

- **Shill bidding** When fraudulent buyers or their "shills" bid on sellers' items to drive up the price. This is also sometimes referred to as "phantom bidding."

- **Bid shielding** When fraudulent buyers submit very high bids to discourage other bidders from competing for the same item and then retract those bids so that people they know can get the item at a lower price.

Figure 4–6 Common forms of auction fraud.
Source: Federal Trade Commission. 2004, June. Internet auctions: A guide for buyers and sellers. www.ftc.gov/bcp/conline/pubs/online/auctions.htm (accessed November 18, 2005).

beginning, fraudsters may create a semblance of trustworthiness by establishing a positive profile. For example, a fraudster might create an account on an auction site and sell low-cost goods for months to build up a positive feedback score. These scores are used by potential buyers to gauge the trustworthiness of the seller. The higher the feedback score, the better. Once established as a "legitimate" seller, the fraudster might then begin selling big-ticket items, such as laptop computers, but upon receiving payment, the fraudster fails to deliver the products.

Buyers also sometimes commit auction fraud in an attempt to obtain free merchandise. This type of fraud normally involves the buyer purchasing the item using a bad check or fraudulent money order. The buyer hopes the seller will ship the merchandise before the check or money order clears the bank and is discovered to be false. The buyer may also have the item shipped to a private box that has been established under a false identity, which makes recovering the item or funds difficult. In a 2003 case we investigated, a buyer purchased auctioned merchandise under one name and paid for it with an online account established under a different name. The account had been under investigation, but had not yet been determined to be fraudulent. Upon receiving what appeared to be a legitimate electronic payment, the seller shipped the merchandise, only to be informed 72 hours later that the electronic payment was fraudulent. Follow-up investigation led to a physical address in another state where authorities obtained a confession from the suspect, who ultimately reimbursed the victim with a legitimate money order.

Law enforcement agencies that do not have the requisite training, skills, or resources to investigate these complaints may sometimes pass them off as "civil matters" or tell the victim that there is nothing they can do. Victims may also be referred to the law enforcement agency in the location where the suspect lives.

Upon calling this other agency in an attempt to file a complaint, the victim might be referred back to his or her hometown agency to make an in-person report. The victim becomes a victim of the system, a virtual pinball, until an agency finally agrees to accept the complaint.

Auction fraud is a criminal offense in all states. It is synonymous with Theft by Fraud statutes that already exist. For example, the state of Arizona defines a Fraudulent Scheme as "a scheme or artifice to defraud, knowingly obtain any benefit by means of false or fraudulent pretenses, representations, promises or material omissions is guilty of a class 2 felony" (Arizona State Statute 13-2310). In comparison, Ohio State Statute 2913.421 (illegally transmitting multiple commercial electronic mail messages; unauthorized access of computer) contains numerous definitions related to computers and the Internet. In relation to online fraud, Ohio defines a "transactional or relationship message" as an electronic mail message whose primary purpose to "facilitate, complete, or confirm a commercial transaction that the recipient has previously agreed to enter into with the sender." An auction fraud transaction is a transaction within this definition. Therefore, it is clear that it was the intent of this Ohio State statute to outlaw auction fraud and other electronic schemes.

United States (federal) Criminal Code 18 U.S.C. §1343 (wire fraud) and 18 U.S.C. §1341 (mail fraud) outlaw auction fraud. The wire fraud statute has been used successfully to prosecute auction fraud cases because the communications between buyer and seller take place over a wire (i.e., telephone lines connected to the Internet). The mail fraud statute has also been used in these cases because the transaction of funds and/or items often takes place through the mail. Figure 4–7 contains a practical example of a recent auction fraud case that was prosecuted by the U.S. Department of Justice.

According to the Internet Fraud Complaint Center (2006), of typical suspects committing Internet auction fraud, 75.4 percent are male and 24.6 percent are female. The suspects most likely reside in one of the following states: California, New York, Florida, Texas, Illinois, Pennsylvania, or Ohio. Suspects also have been identified as residing in Nigeria, the United Kingdom, Canada, Italy, and China. The vast majority of suspects were in contact with the complainant through either e-mail or via the Web.

The Internet Fraud Complaint Center (2006) also offers a profile of auction fraud victims. The victims' average age is 40.2 years, and the majority (64 percent) were male, between 30 and 50 years of age, and a resident of one of the four most populated states: California, New York, Texas, or Florida. The average loss per victim ranged from $401.00 to $543.00.

Consumers can help avoid becoming victims of auction fraud by familiarizing themselves with the auction site, knowing what recourse the site offers in the event they become a victim, examining the feedback that other buyers/sellers have provided about the seller, noting whether the seller provides more than just an e-mail address for contact information and is within the country, paying particular attention to any warranties and/or return policies offered, and noting whether the

Gregory A. White, United States Attorney for the Northern District of Ohio, announced today that on Monday, March 28, 2005, Timothy L. Deceuster, age 33, of 3800 Rosemont Blvd, Apt. 103F, Fairlawn, Ohio, was sentenced in connection with his recent wire fraud conviction in connection with an e-Bay Internet auction scam conducted in 2000 and 2001. U.S. District Judge James Gwin sentenced Deceuster to 5 months in prison, to be followed by 3 years of supervised release, the first 5 months of which will be served in home confinement with electronic monitoring. Deceuster was also ordered to pay restitution in the amount of $60,139.00 to the victims of the offense, and a $200 special assessment to the Crime Victims' Fund.

On November 23, 2004, a federal grand jury in Cleveland, Ohio, returned a nineteen-count indictment charging Deceuster with twelve counts of wire fraud, in violation of 18 U.S.C. § 1343, and seven counts of mail fraud, in violation of Title 18, U.S.C., § 1341. On January 3, 2005, Deceuster pleaded guilty to two counts of wire fraud.

The indictment charged that between, on, or about November 9, 2000, and on or about September 4, 2001, Deceuster knowingly devised and intended to devise a scheme to defraud victims, and obtain money by means of false and fraudulent pretenses, representations and promises, in connection with various items, including Sony laptop computers, Sony Playstation 2 games, and a plasma screen television which Deceuster advertised for sale on the Internet auction site e-Bay using the seller name "TM72900." Deceuster advertised said items for sale, instructed the victims to send payment via the U.S. Mail or via PayPal, an Internet payment system. Despite receiving payments from the victims totaling $60,139.00 for said items, Deceuster failed to send any merchandise to the bidders.

This case was prosecuted by Assistant U.S. Attorney Robert W. Kern, following an investigation by the Canton Office of the Federal Bureau of Investigation.

Figure 4–7 Case of a Fairlawn, Ohio, man sentenced in e-Bay auction scam (March 28, 2005). *Source:* White, G., and Kern, R. 2005. Fairlawn, Ohio man sentenced in e-Bay auction scam (March 28, 2005). www.cybercrime.gov/deceusterSent.htm (accessed November 18, 2005).

auction price includes reasonable shipping prices. Oftentimes, fraudsters auction off an item at a significantly lower price only to charge exorbitant shipping fees and make their profit from them.

When investigating an auction fraud case, first responders should pay particular attention to important digital evidence likely available to them. The first responder should ask the victim the following questions:

- What is the name of the Web site and/or what is the Web address (URL) of the site on which the purchase was made?

- Did you save a copy of the screen that documented the transaction?
- Did you save any e-mail messages in connection with the transaction?
- Did you save any electronic payment receipts in connection with the transaction?

All available information and documentation should be collected and made part of the case file.

Auction fraud is not a civil matter and deserves law enforcement attention when it is reported and/or discovered. In many cases, victims are satisfied if they get their property back and/or receive payment for what they sold. These frauds can be even more challenging to investigate when the suspect resides overseas. A "friendly" nation may assist in, at the very least, seeing that the victim is paid, even if it means forgoing any prosecution. Other nations may not cooperate with U.S. authorities, and then there is little to no chance for recovery. Auction fraud is here to stay, and recent trends indicate that its frequency will continue to increase. According to the FTC (2004), the number of Internet fraud complaints, including auction fraud, has risen from 241,792 in 2002 to 388,603 in 2004, an increase of more than 60 percent.

Learner Activity ————————————————————————————————

Visit a local Internet auction store and/or Web site and examine and report on the measures it has in place to prevent auction fraud. What protocols does it have in place for victims of auction fraud? With this information, create a one-page flyer that can serve as a community service announcement for citizens in your community with the goal of helping them avoid becoming victims of auction fraud.

4.3 CELLULAR PHONE FRAUD

On the way home from work, a woman dashes into a convenience store to pick up a gallon of milk. When she returns, the phone is gone. Across town, another cellular phone owner opens his mail and discovers, to his dismay, that his monthly phone bill includes over $800 in calls he never made. Both of these people have become victims of cellular phone fraud.

——P. Beseler, "Operation Cellmate"

Before the infamous computer hacker or cracker there was the phone phreaker. **Phone phreaking** is the art and science of cracking the phone network (Digital Guards 2005). Some phreakers phreak to discover and explore the phone system, while others phreak to make free phone calls. John T. Draper (AKA Captain Crunch) was one of the most well known phreakers. In 1972, he was approached by a blind neighbor who introduced him to a Capt'n Crunch cereal whistle that produced a perfect 2,600-hertz tone. This whistle and a "blue box" (a special tone-generating device) allowed the phreaker to take control of long-distance phone switching equipment and place free phone calls (Webcrunchers International 2005). The phone companies didn't take his experimenting lightly, tracked him down, arrested him, and he was sentenced to prison for violating Title 18, Section 1343: Fraud by wire. Phone companies have since improved technology that has rendered these tone-dialing devices useless.

Public cellular telephone service was inaugurated in the United States in 1983 (Clarke, Kemper, and Wycoff 2001). The number of cell phone users has skyrocketed from 340,213 in 1985 to 182,140,362 in 2004 (CTIA 2004), and continues to increase. It is not uncommon today for a cell phone to replace the traditional home telephone landline. Phreakers, like their hacker counterparts, take great interest in knowing how cellular technology works for their personal knowledge or illegal gain.

First responders must understand how cellular phone calls travel through the airwaves. Each cellular phone has a unique pair of identifying numbers: the **electronic serial number (ESN)** and the **mobile identification number (MIN)** (Biderman et al. 2000)—both of which are emitted when the phone is turned on. The assigned ESN and/or MIN can be viewed on most cell phones by removing the battery cover and battery.

With a cellular signal scanning device, such as a modified police scanner or altered cell phone set to capture ESNs and MINs, a phreaker can capture these number combinations and load them onto another cell phone, thus creating a cloned phone. At the time of this writing, a keyword search on eBay for "ESN" revealed a Curtis Cell Phone ESN Reader for sale (item 5784343065) for only $9.95. This device could be used to capture ESNs to enable phone cloning. To make cloning more difficult, many cell service carriers offered PINs, similar to the PIN used for ATM withdrawals, that users were required to enter to complete a call (O'Brien 1998). Phreakers soon learned how to hack PINs, and PIN use is not very common today (Clarke, Kemper, and Wycoff 2001).

Newton's Telecom Dictionary, 17th edition (2001), defines and discusses three types of cellular phone cloning: **cloning fraud, clone fraud,** and **cloned phone.** Descriptions of all three types are summarized here:

Cloning fraud—It occurs when criminals use scanners to obtain legitimate MIN/ESN/PIN combinations and then program these numbers into illegitimate phones. (Recall, PINs are not used very often today.)

Clone fraud—A legitimate serial number is programmed into an imposter's cell phone. Crooks get the numbers because they are broadcast with every cellular call and can be picked up by ordinary radio scanners.

Cloned phone—A cell phone has two basic ways it identifies itself to the cell phone service it wants to use—its telephone number, which can be changed, and a special secret number embedded into the silicon chip inside the phone called the ESN. When the phone makes a call, it sends out these numbers, and the cell carrier uses them to check whether the call is authentic.

According to a 2000 United States Sentencing Commission Report (Biderman et al., 2000), four major types of cellular fraud have been identified: counterfeit fraud, subscription fraud, network fraud, and call selling operations.

- *Counterfeit Fraud (cloning):* Involves the use of illegally altered cellular phones. Offenders gain access to legitimate account number combinations and reprogram them into other handsets to gain unauthorized access to those accounts.
- *Subscription Fraud:* Includes schemes related to fraudulently obtaining cellular telephone accounts. These schemes may involve employees of the cellular carrier, forgery of application information, or theft of subscriber information.
- *Network Fraud:* This advanced type of fraud includes efforts to exploit weaknesses in phone switch equipment and billing systems. Manipulation of current systems can result in third-party billing, use of nonexistent account numbers, or use of multiple phones on single accounts.
- *Call Selling Operations:* This type of fraud involves using stolen calling card numbers and/or cellular account numbers to sell less expensive cellular long distance (often international) service to others.

Cell phone cloning may seem somewhat complex, but with the necessary equipment and requisite knowledge, an experienced phreaker can program a cloned phone in 10 to 15 minutes (Biderman et al. 2000). The necessary scanners or cloning devices can be purchased on the Internet. A keyword search at www.groups.google.com for **"clone phone"** revealed the responses shown in Figure 4-8 from 1998.

Cell phone cloning might be simple for some and more difficult for others to perform, and criminals go to great lengths to pull it off. Of all the cell phone frauds discussed, **subscriber fraud** is the simplest. Subscription fraud and identity theft go hand in hand and are the most common types of telecom fraud today (CFCA 2003). The cellular industry estimates that carriers lose more than $150 million per year because of subscriber fraud (FCC 2003).

Another type of cellular fraud is **roaming fraud,** which is often committed by the subscriber fraud criminal. With the fraudulently obtained phone in hand, the phreaker takes it to another cell area outside of the provider's network. The phone then enters the roaming mode, utilizing cell towers from another provider. By the time the other provider bills the original provider for the roaming fees, the thief has racked up significant charges. Because the phone was obtained using false information, locating the criminal is extremely difficult.

It's also important to realize that many thieves obtain free phone service simply by stealing a cell phone. Unlocked cars, convertibles, and open windows make it simple for a thief to reach in and grab an unattended phone. By the time the theft is discovered and reported to police or the cellular provider, hundreds, even thousands, of dollars in charges might have been incurred.

According to Clarke, Kemper, and Wycoff (2001), in 1995 alone, the cell phone industry in the United States lost more than $800 million to cell **tumbling**

CLONE PHONE MACHINES FOR SALE

SThom84584 Apr 9 1998, 3:00 am

Newsgroups: **alt.cellular**

From: **sthom84...@aol.com (SThom84584)** – <u>Find messages by this author</u>

Date: **1998/04/09**

Subject: **CLONE PHONE MACHINES FOR SALE**

<u>Reply to Author</u> | <u>Forward</u> | <u>Print</u> | <u>Individual Message</u> | <u>Show original</u> | <u>Report Abuse</u>.

We have the 7-way Startac ESN Copycat for sale, If interested call 313-705-8998

CLONE PHONE PROGRAMMER BLOW OUT SALE

SThom84584 Apr 8 1998, 3:00 am

Newsgroups: **alt.cellular**

From: **sthom84...@aol.com (Sthom84584)** – <u>Find messages by this author</u>

Date: **1998/04/08**

Subject: **CLONE PHONE PROGRAMMER BLOW OUT SALE**

<u>Replay to Author</u> | <u>Forward</u> | <u>Print</u> | <u>Individual Message</u> | <u>Show original</u> | <u>Report Abuse</u>

If u want a **clone phone** programmer machine call 313-705-8998. Leave a message and your call will be promptly returned.

Figure 4–8 Responses to keyword search at www.groups.google.com for "clone phone."

and cloning, which prompted implementation of security measures, some of which are summarized here, that have virtually eliminated this type of fraud today:

Roamer verification/reinstatement (RVR)—When a visited server (provider) does not recognize a number pair (EIN/MIN), RVR "hotlines" the caller to an operator who can verify his or her identity. Once the caller is authenticated, the caller's ability to roam in that market is reinstated.

Radio frequency fingerprinting (RFF)—Every phone has a unique radio wave pattern that is recorded by the phone company when it is first used. Whenever a mobile phone purporting to be that phone attempts to access the network, its emissions are tested to see whether they match the characteristics previously recorded. If the match is close, the call is completed.

Data mining—Data mining is another way that cellular companies have been detecting and preventing fraud. Data mining, also known as knowledge discovery in databases (KDD), is the practice of automatically searching large stores of data for patterns. The cellular industry uses data-mining programs to monitor and detect fraud by creating customer profiles that track average call duration, percentage of no-answer calls, percentage of calls to/from a different area code, percentage of weekday calls (Monday–Friday), percentage of daytime calls (9 A.M.–5 P.M.), average number of calls received per day, and the average number of calls originated per day (Weiss 2005). Deviation from the profile may indicate fraud, and if subscriber records are updated in real time, it can increase the chances of detecting fraud sooner and minimizing loss.

What does all this mean for law enforcement? Organized crime groups and street gangs have been and are committing cellular fraud throughout the country. To avoid law enforcement monitoring calls or tracing them back to a particular gang member, members of these groups seek out cloned or throw-away phones. Other criminals step forward to meet the demand, offering cloned or fraudulently obtained phones for sale. These groups may also have an insider connection at a cell phone company, a fellow gang member or associate who has secured employment and funnels free phone service to the group. Law enforcement personnel must remain alert for source information (i.e., intelligence) provided by informants or gained through other investigations of cell phone fraud. Because of the mobility of these offenders, follow-up investigation should begin immediately, and soliciting the help of local or national cellular providers can help generate digital leads.

First responders can also use cellular technology immediately during criminal investigations. For example, in a recent case we investigated, a victim's car was broken into and a firearm and cellular phone were stolen. On scene, the victim phoned his cellular provider and obtained a list of phone numbers that the suspects had called since stealing the phone. Cellular providers will not provide this information to law enforcement without a warrant or subpoena, but in most cases will give it to directly to victims over the phone. Follow-up on these phone numbers led to the arrest and apprehension of the thieves and the recovery of the firearm and the victim's cell phone.

One of the most significant law enforcement operations combating cell phone fraud was called Operation Cellmate, which occurred in 1996 and combined the efforts of the Florida state attorney's office, U.S. Secret Service, and the Naval Criminal Investigative Service. An April 1997 *FBI Law Enforcement Bulletin* article written by P. R. Beseler, titled "Operation Cellmate" chronicled the success of the operation, but also highlighted the nature of other crimes associated with cell phone fraud. Investigators set up a storefront location in Jacksonville, Florida, and opened up "Cellmate Communications, Inc.," where they specialized in cloning cell phones for the criminal community. They operated strictly on a referral basis and handed out business cards to informants to distribute to drug dealers, prostitutes, burglars, and others engaged in criminal activity. Within days, customers began calling, and over the course of 36 business days, investigators conducted 172 separate transactions with 98 different suspects. "Customers" were also involved in a host of other criminal activities, and investigators were offered a variety of different drugs, stolen property, weapons, and even illegal cable television descrambling devices in exchange for the cloned phones.

Today, because advances in cellular technology have greatly reduced cloning, the phreaker or identity thief focuses on subscriber fraud. When investigating identity theft complaints, first responders should also inquire about whether the victim has a cellular phone and, if so, look for any suspicious calling activity. When apprehending an identity theft suspect, first responders should determine whether the person has a cell phone(s) and establish the name of the provider with the ultimate goal of determining in whose name the account is registered. Chances are the identity thief established the account under a false name. All of these account records must be obtained by filing a subpoena or search warrant upon the provider of the documents. Most cellular providers have a law enforcement point of contact or corporate investigator available to assist in many aspects of the investigation. They also have technology, such as a Doppler directional finder, which can be used to pinpoint the location of a cell phone with extreme accuracy (Films for the Humanities and Sciences 1997).

When working with victims of cellular fraud, whether they have become the victim of the less common cloned phone or more common subscriber fraud, first responders can provide some helpful preventive advice to reduce the chances of them being victimized again. Law enforcement agencies can also reach out via the Internet and provide the community with cellular fraud prevention and detections tips. The CTIA's Web site (www.ctia.org/content/index.cfm/AID/310) offers the following fraud prevention and detection tips for consumers:

Consumers can help prevent fraud by:

1. Locking phones or removing handsets and wireless antennas (to avoid drawing attention to the vehicle) every time a vehicle is left with someone, such as a parking lot attendant or mechanic
2. Protecting sensitive documents such as subscriber agreements, which include electronic serial numbers
3. Immediately reporting a stolen phone to the wireless phone carrier
4. Not leaving the phone in an unattended car in an isolated or questionable area or parking lot for an extended period of time; locking the phone out of sight; and using the lock code

Consumers can help detect fraud by:

1. Looking for unusual call activity on their monthly wireless phone bill
2. Reporting frequent receipt of wrong numbers or hangups on the wireless phone, which may indicate someone else is using their mobile number

3. Asking the wireless provider to eliminate overseas toll or North American toll (long-distance) dialing capabilities if the customer does not intend to call long distance

4. Immediately contacting the wireless phone company if a wireless subscriber suspects fraud

Finally, establishing a cooperative relationship and points of contact with local cellular providers can help prepare first responders to address this type of fraud by providing baseline technical knowledge and skills needed to properly investigate cellular fraud. First responders will also become familiar with what types of information local providers will provide with and without search warrants and/or subpoenas.

High-tech fraud is here to stay. The information contained in this chapter clearly highlights the need to educate current and future law enforcement officers in the techniques and strategies to investigate these types of crimes. As technology advances, so will the skills of the fraudster. Proactive measures must be taken to combat the high-tech fraudster effectively. Failing to stay abreast of the latest technological advancements and failing to work cooperatively with other law enforcement entities at all levels can result in ineffective enforcement and ultimately ineffective prosecution. Establishing relationships with private investigators and industry experts is also necessary to dismantle fraudulent organizations and to bring digital thieves to justice. Between January and December 2004, fraud cost U.S. consumers more than $547 million (Federal Trade Commission 2005). Failing to combat fraud effectively could result in the collapse of an economy.

■ SUMMARY

The technology available today makes practical elimination of credit card fraud possible. Using a combination of biometrics and computer technology, the magnetic-striped credit card will became a thing of the past and will be replaced with the digital "smart card." No signature will be needed, and the cardholder's identity will be verified with a fingerprint. Online purchases will be protected with private personal identification numbers.

Proactive efforts must be made to convince consumers and civil libertarians that the biometrics information will not be abused or used for any other reason. In order for biometrics to work, the population must be willing to submit fingerprints into a database for comparison and identification. Protection of consumer credit must be balanced with the freedom and liberty of individuals. Unfortunately, the more secure a nation becomes, the less freedom and liberty its citizens have. Until these more proactive steps are taken, credit card fraud will continue to be the most common criminal act committed by identity thieves.

Fencing stolen property, stealing credit card numbers, outright theft, and auction fraud are all-too-common occurrences in the online world. Proactive investigative and enforcement actions are necessary to combat these criminal offenses: law enforcement agencies cannot brush them off as "civil matters." The sooner the investigation is started, the greater the chance of a successful resolution. Consumers can avoid becoming victims by bidding only at reputable sites they are familiar with, examining seller feedback, noting the sellers' e-mail addresses and locations, and noting any return policies. Furthermore, first responders must familiarize themselves with the basic protocol for investigating auction fraud.

Advances in technology have greatly reduced the incidence of traditional phone phreaking. However, cell phone theft is still common, and thieves can rack up significant dollars on the victim's bill in a very short time. Identity thieves can also establish cell phone accounts in the victim's name, with considerable financial losses incurred before the crime is discovered. Finally, law enforcement can use cell phone technologies to help track wanted criminals or even to locate victims who leave their cell phone on, allowing the signal to be detected.

■ REVIEW QUESTIONS

1. List and discuss the three types of biometrics discussed in this chapter.
2. Who is Kevin Mitnick and how did he use "social engineering" to his advantage?
3. According to the Internet Fraud Complaint Center, what is the typical profile of a suspect committing Internet auction fraud?
4. Explain the difference between *cloning fraud, clone fraud,* and *cloned phone*.
5. List and discuss at least five ways criminals obtain credit card information.
6. What is *phishing* and what are some ways that consumers can avoid becoming a victim of phishing?
7. When investigating an Internet auction fraud case, what are the four questions the first responder should ask the victim?

■ TERMS

biometrics	counterfeit "lifetime"	electronic serial number
clone fraud	phone	(ESN)
cloning fraud	counterfeit "tumbler"	esoteric biometrics
cloned phone	phone	high biometrics
counterfeit "clone"	data mining	internet auction fraud
phone	dumpster diving	low biometrics

mobile identification number (MIN)
phishing
phone phreaking
radio frequency fingerprinting (RFF)

roamer verification/ reinstatement (RVR)
roaming fraud
shoulder surfing

skimming
social engineering
subscriber fraud

■ REFERENCES

American Express. 2005. Fraud protection center: What is fraud? www.124. americanexpress.com/cards/loyalty.do?page=FraudCenter.whatisfraud (accessed June 14, 2005).

Beseler, P. R. 1997. Operation cellmate. *FBI Law Enforcement Bulletin*, April. www.fbi.gov/publications/leb/1997/apr971.htm (accessed May 31, 2005).

Biderman, P., Blanchard, A., Brown, T., Desio, P., Gabriel, J., Gilmore, G., Kitchens, C., et al. 2000. Cellular telephone cloning. United States Sentencing Commission. www.ussc.gov/publicat/cloning.PDF (accessed June 26, 2005).

Bruce, L. 2001. Face scanning, fingerprinting ATMs gain ground. www.bankrate. com/brm/news/atm/20010302a.asp (accessed June 11, 2005).

CardWatch. 2005. Useful definitions. www.cardwatch.org.uk/ (accessed June 11, 2005).

Clarke, R. V., Kemper, R., and Wycoff L. 2001. Controlling cell phone fraud in the US—lessons for "foresight." *Security Journal* 14, no. 1. www.admin.foresight. gov.uk/servlet/Controller/ver=3134/userid=2/essay3.doc (accessed June 27, 2005).

CTIA. 2004. Semi-annual wireless industry survey. www.files.ctia.org/pdf/ CTIAYearend2004Survey.pdf (accessed June 26, 2005).

Communications Fraud Control Association (CFCA). 2003. Communications Fraud control Association (CFCA) announces results of worldwide telecom fraud survey. www.cfca.org/pressrelease/FraudLoss%20%20press%20release% 203-03.doc (accessed June 23, 2005).

Digital Guards. 2005. Glossary. www.digitalguards.com/glossary.htm#top (accessed September 26, 2006)

Federal Communications Commission (FCC). 2003. FCC consumer advisory: Cell phone fraud. www.fcc.gov/cgb/consumerfacts/cellphonefraud.html (accessed June 23, 2005).

Federal Trade Commision. (n.d.). Internet auctions: A guide for buyers and sellers. www.ftc. gov/bcp/conline/pubs/online/auctions.htm (accessed November 18, 2005).

———. Avoiding credit and charge card fraud www.ftc.gov/bcp/conline/pubs/credit/ cards.pdf (accessed June 11, 2005).

———. National and state trends in fraud and identity theft. www.consumer.gov/ idtheft/pdf/clearinghouse_2004.pdf (accessed November 19, 2005).

———. Identity theft victim complaint data. www. consumer. gov/idtheft/pdf/clearinghouse_2005.pdf (accessed October 14, 2006).

Films for the Humanities and Sciences. 1997. *Forbidden places,* unauthorized access, [videorecording]. Princeton, NJ: Films for the Humanities and Sciences.

International Card Manufacturers Association. n.d. Hypercom launches attack on credit card skimming. www.icma.com/info/hypercom7801.htm (accessed June 14, 2005).

Internet Fraud Complaint Center. 2006. IC3 2005 Internet Crime Report. www.ic3.gov/media/annualreport/2005_IC3Report.pdf (accessed October 14, 2006).

Joseph, J., and Simlot, R. 2005. Technocorrections: Biometric scanning and corrections. In *Key correctional issues* ed. R. Muraskin, 128–148. Upper Saddle River, NJ: Prentice Hall.

Kharif, O. 2005. May I see your voice, please? *BusinessWeek Online*, April 20. www.businessweek.com/technology/content/apr2005/tc20050420_1036_tc024.htm (accessed June 11, 2005).

Lexias Inc. n.d.. Glossary of terms. www.lexias.com/html/glossary1.html (accessed September 26, 2006).

Newman, Graeme. 2003. *Identity Theft*. Problem-Oriented Guides for Police, Problem-Specific Guides Series. No. 25. Washington, DC: U.S. Department of Justice.

O'Brien, J. 1998. Telecommunications fraud. *FBI Law Enforcement Bulletin* 67 (May). www.fbi.gov/publications/leb/1998/mayleb.pdf (accessed May 31, 2005).

O'Sullivan, O. 1997. Biometrics comes to life. *ABA Banking Journal*, January. www.banking.com/aba/january.htm (accessed June 11, 2005).

Privacy and American Business. 2003. New survey shows public willing to accept biometric identifiers. www.pandab.org/biometricsurvey.html (accessed June 11, 2005).

Smith, Russell G. 2003. Addressing identity-related fraud. Australian Institute of Criminology. www.aic.gov.au/conferences/other/smith_russell/2003-09-identity.pdf (accessed July 1, 2005).

Upadhyay, S., Miyamoto, T., Gondal, Z., Yokokawa, T., NgorNgor, A., King'wai, I., Inada, M., Aizawa, K., Tachi, Y., Nosaka, A. 2000. Current situation of organized crimes in trafficking in stolen vehicles, card fraud, money laundering and major transnational organized criminal groups. www.unafei.or.jp/english/pdf/PDF_rms/no58/58-18.pdf (accessed June 22, 2005).

Webcrunchers International. 2005. The story so far. www.webcrunchers.com/crunch/story.html (accessed September 26, 2006).

Weiss, G. M. 2005. Data mining in telecommunications. Department of Computer and Information Science at Fordham University. http://storm.cis.fordham.edu/~gweiss/papers/kluwer04-telecom.pdf (accessed June 26, 2005).

chapter five

High-Tech Vice Crimes, Hackers, and Terrorists

LEARNING OBJECTIVES

1. Describe the common high-tech vice crimes committed by criminals today.
2. Describe different types of hackers and how they operate.
3. Explain some of the tools and tricks that are used by hackers.
4. Explain how terrorists and other organized crime syndicates use technology to operate and carry out the goals of their organizations.
5. Explain the common protocols for investigating high-tech crimes.

From the hacker to the cracker, to the pedophile and terrorist, the Internet serves as a tool of the trade. The illicit sex trade has been around for centuries. From concubines and houses of ill repute in the early 1900s to the street worker and escort services of today, the sex industry continues to thrive. Third World countries fraught with poverty, illiteracy, and unemployment force women and even children into the sex trade. Many parents are aware that their children work in the industry and use the income for survival. For years, tourists have traveled to these destinations to participate, but the Internet has brought it to the United States and other democracies.

119

Technology has made it much simpler for the pedophile to find like-minded persons who are willing to share photographs of their victims. What used to take place in back alleys or secret rooms now occurs on monitor screens across the nation. A simple copy and paste operation can create numerous photos that are then shared around the globe. Every time a photo is shared, the photographed child is victimized again. It is a tragedy and much too easy.

The term *hacker* has a negative connotation and most believe it defines a person who breaks into computer systems for illegal gain. That is the goal of some hackers, but many hack just to figure out how systems work. Some hackers work for governments, while others work for organized crime syndicates and terrorists. This chapter explores hacking, from the white hat hacker to the black hat hacker.

Terrorists also take advantage of the Internet. Unsecure wireless connections enable them free access where they can do the necessary research to carry out their plans or share plans with operatives. They can do this with little risk of detection because the Internet Protocol (IP) trace will ultimately lead back to the wireless network they were exploiting and not to the specific terrorist. This and other ways that terrorists use the Internet and other technologies is discussed in this chapter.

High-tech vice crimes, such as child pornography and drug trafficking, as well as hackers and terrorists are discussed in this chapter. The focus is on the ways these criminals use the Internet and other technologies to commit their crimes and what first responders can do to combat such vice.

5.1 CHILD PORNOGRAPHY: CREATION, POSSESSION, AND DISTRIBUTION

According to the Federal Bureau of Investigation (FBI) "Computer telecommunications have become one of the most prevalent techniques used by pedophiles to share illegal photographic images of minors and to lure children into illicit sexual relationships. The Internet has dramatically increased the access of sex offenders to the population they seek to victimize" (Lourdeau, 2004).

This topic, including child enticement, is further discussed in Chapter 7. However, first responders must be aware of the proliferation of child pornography that affects communities worldwide. There isn't one standard definition of child pornography. An acceptable definition, based upon an examination of several state laws, is "a photographic, film, or other visual representation made by electronic, mechanical, or other means that depicts a child less than eighteen years old engaged in or depicted to be engaged in explicit sexual activity." Child pornography is also directly related to child sexual exploitation, trafficking, prostitution, and sexual or physical abuse.

What used to be traded in back alleys and secret rooms is now shared by the click of a mouse. In the past, Polaroid photos or 35-millimeter pictures developed in makeshift darkrooms were traded in person or through the mail. A roll of film or Polaroid cartridge was used to photograph one victim, and the number of photos was limited. Today, a simple copy and paste operation on a computer creates an unlimited number of copies of photos, victimizing the same child pictured thousands of times when the image is posted on illicit Internet sites, traded in chat rooms, or shared by e-mail.

Realizing the need to help combat the ever-increasing child pornography problem the Bush administration proposed a virtual child pornography law, the Child Pornography Prevention Act of 1996, which was later struck down in *Ashcroft v. Free Speech Coalition* (American Center for Law and Justice 2001). The bill would have outlawed computer-generated images of minors engaged in sexual situations. Because such images do not victimize real children, the court reasoned, they do not qualify as child pornography. This case alone provides a defense for defendants arrested for possession of child pornography who can argue that any photos they possess are computer-generated images. Whether it is a successful defense is another matter.

In light of the *Ashcroft* decision, which might alarm some law enforcers and make them feel as if they must authenticate every potential child pornography image, there is some comfort in knowing that actually creating images that cannot be detected as digital creations takes serious time, skill, and high-end graphics software. It is, therefore, likely that at least one image of child pornography, which might be encrypted or hidden, will be found on a typical pedophile's computer, and that will be enough to make an arrest (18 U.S.C.S. 2252A(a)(5)(b)). Many child pornography collectors seem to have addictive personalities, and the likelihood that such a personality possesses *only* one computer-generated image is slim.

The actual number of child pornography victims and suspects arrested in the United States for possession, creation, or distribution is difficult to measure because the Uniform Crime Reports (UCR) don't specifically collect data on these types of crimes. The new National Incident-Based Reporting System (NIBRS), designed to replace the UCR, allows for tracking pornography and child exploitation arrests. According to a U.S. Department of Justice study, in 2000 there were 2,900 crime incidents of pornography with child involvement known to state and local police (Finkelhor and Ormrod 2004). This same study also found that, of these offenses, most were committed by an adult male offender, occurred in a residence, and didn't involve a computer. It's important to note that these are cases *known to police*, and the statistics do not include major investigations, such as the 2002 Operation Candyman, conducted by the FBI and other federal agencies, which netted 86 arrests of pedophiles and child pornographers. In contrast, studies estimate that 20,000 images of child pornography are posted on the Internet each week (Hughes 2001).

The United States and countries that have cracked down on the child pornography trade have displaced the problem to other regions of the world. Although child pornography is hardly nonexistent in the United States, the former Soviet Union has become the capital of the child pornography trade. An unstable political climate along with high unemployment rates create perfect conditions in which illicit trade and organized crime can flourish. Child prostitution, child sex tourism, child pornography, and child trafficking have become widespread forms of sexual exploitation in Russia; 20 percent to 30 percent of street children in Moscow are involved in prostitution or in the production of pornographic material (Tjurjukanova, Rusakova, and Sakina 2003). The child pornography industry is international and highly commercialized, with a market worth approximately $2 billion to $3 billion annually (Carr 2001). It is estimated that more than 100,000 child pornography sites exist on the Internet today (CBC News 2003).

Although most child pornography cases that involve computers eventually will be handled by forensic experts, on many occasions first responders are the first to discover cases on the streets. A case could be found while a law enforcement officer is investigating unrelated complaints, such as loud noise or domestic disturbances, or in response to anonymous tips. In any event, if a computer or other high-tech device is involved, first responders must view the images in question to establish probable cause to seize the device for further examination. Consent is always an option, but probable cause is ultimately needed to make an arrest and prosecute the individual(s) in possession of the child pornography. The elements of the offense must also be established, and in smaller agencies that burden may lie with the first responder. Most state statutes contain the following criteria that must be satisfied to prove a child pornography violation:

- Knowingly possesses an undeveloped film, photographic negative, motion picture, videotape, computer image, or other recording
- Of a child (a person under 18 years old)
- Or person he/she should have reasonably known was a person under 18 years old
- Engaged in sexually explicit conduct or a sexually explicit sex act

For a complete list of all U.S. child pornography laws, visit the National District Attorney's Web site at www.ndaa-pri.org/pdf/statute_child_pornography_2004.pdf.

In some instances it can be difficult to prove that a particular image is child pornography. "Lolita images", which are eighteen-year-old "models" that look much younger to satisfy the child porn perversion, are not illegal. In other cases when first responders or investigators are unsure, they can contact the Department of Defense Cyber Crime Center and submit the image(s) for **MD5** message digest comparison of known child pornography images. The MD5 message digest is an algorithm that creates a 128-bit "fingerprint" similar in appearance to an automobile vehicle identification number (VIN), but much longer. Known images of child pornography are kept in this Department of Defense database, which can be searched by the MD5 message digest number that each image creates. The MD5 message digest fingerprint is unique, and the possibility of two images with the same MD5 message digest is 1 in 2^{128} chances (Rivast 1992). It is conjectured that it is computationally infeasible to produce two messages that have the same message digest, or to produce any message that has a given pre-specified target message digest (Rivest 1992).

Once the first responder determines that the computer or other electronic device contains child pornography, he or she must properly seize and transport the device for further examination. See Chapter 10 for guidelines regarding handling digital evidence and for additional information about MD5 values.

5.2 DRUG TRAFFICKING

Drug use, abuse, and sales are significant problems in this country. According to the most recent statistics from the National Office of Drug Control Policy, nearly 35 million persons aged 12 years or older used an illicit drug within the past year, and approximately 3.8 million were dependent on or abusers of illicit drugs in 2003, the latest year for which such data are available (National Drug Intelligence Center 2005).

The War on Drugs policy implemented in the 1980s by the Reagan administration is still alive and well today. As drug laws were toughened to include stricter penalties, three strikes laws were enacted in several states, and innovative investigative techniques to apprehend dealers were used, arrest and imprisonment rates skyrocketed. In response, drug dealers have also become more innovative in their trade, from concealing drugs inside secret compartments in household cleaning containers to hiring juveniles to deliver the drugs to avoid detection. Just like hackers, drug peddlers constantly seek ways to beat the system. They are also using high-tech devices in their illicit trade. A 2001 study titled, "Electronic Crime Needs Assessment for State and Local Law Enforcement" (Stambaugh et al. 2000) reveals that drug dealers make up approximately 6 percent of the Most Frequent Electronic Crime Offenders. As technology becomes even easier to obtain, this percentage is sure to increase.

Throwaway cell phones, for which no contract is required for activation and minutes are purchased at local convenience stores, are drug dealers' communication device of choice. Because no contract is required, their names are not associated with the phone, making a trace rather useless. However, high-end cellular signal sniffing and tracing technology is used by law enforcement to trace and locate the suspected drug dealers while their throwaway phone is in use. Dealers use pagers to stay in contact with customers, making the dealer "digitally wired," always able to be reached. New portable thumb drives or flash memory devices that are 126-megabytes (MB) to 1 GB in size can easily be concealed and contain all of a drug dealer's nefarious information. These devices, along with handheld personal digital assistants (PDAs) and personal computers are used by the drug dealer to keep track of customer names, phone numbers, and even addresses, money owed, quantities purchased or requested, and any other unlawful data. Dealers can protect these data with strong encryption, such as with the program Cryptainer LE 5.0.3, which is freely available on the Internet. This encryption software allows users to encrypt up to 20 MB of files or folders and archive them on hard or removable disks. When used properly, encryption can make the ledgers nearly impossible to access. No longer can first responders and narcotics investigators presume that paper ledgers will be found during the execution of a search warrant, which must be written broad enough to include the search and/or seizure of high-tech devices.

> The advent of new technology affords drug dealers more effective means with which to store their information as well as to conceal their communications by encrypting electronic messages and telephone conversations. They are not necessarily technically skilled; rather, they hire people to keep track of their transactions and handle sophisticated communications equipment. They make use of high-end laptops, cellular phones, and other equipment that is easy to conceal and transport from one drug deal to the next. (Stambaugh et al. 2000)

Surveillance is common during narcotics investigations, and drug dealers also use surveillance to counter law enforcement attempts to apprehend them. It is not uncommon for drug dealers to have their site wired with covert surveillance systems and alarms, both of which we have encountered in the field. A covert pinhole surveillance camera can also be concealed on the outside of automobiles (e.g., inside the license plate frame) so drug dealers can see who might be approaching their car during transactions. Once installed on a rear license plate frame or behind it, the camera projects an image on a screen near the center console, allowing drug dealers to monitor who is approaching them.

If drug dealers wish to diversify, they could also have an online presence, such as a Web site, to peddle their product. Such Web sites do not normally stay up long and are often launched on servers that allow free Web space. For the drug dealer, it is a win-win situation, and in many cases dealers can even fail to deliver goods with little fear of recourse. For example, if a customer in the United States purchases marijuana from the Web site and the dealer fails to deliver, it is unlikely that the "victim" is going to report the fraud to police because he or she was participating in an illegal transaction. Other legal authorities, such as the Better Business Bureau, can offer little to no assistance either. If the dealer does deliver, the package is shipped in a plain brown wrapper or bag and is addressed to the customer. If intercepted by Customs, it is a buy/bust that has just fallen into their lap. Customs will implement a controlled delivery, and once the customer takes control of the unlawful package, that person can be arrested for possession of the controlled substance.

Instant messaging or text messaging using computers or cell phones, respectively, is another common way for drug dealers to communicate with their customer base. Chat rooms, such as Alt.drugs.hard, exist at www.google.groups.com where drug dealers or users can discuss their trade. These same chat rooms can be monitored by law enforcement, which is discussed further in Chapter 8, "Online Intelligence Gathering." For example, a recent keyword search for "buy cocaine" at www.google.groups.com revealed the following post made by a user named "me": "We wanna buy some cocaine . . . but don't want to deal with the street dealers? Any suggestions? Anybody willing to ship?" As silly as it may appear, this user was apparently seeking a way to obtain cocaine through the mail and wasn't afraid to post this message in this public forum. The user's e-mail address is also available along with the date and time of the post. With such information, law enforcement could obtain the IP address used and ultimately trace the post back to the server and owner of the computer that was used to make it.

Another common worldwide chat program is Internet Relay Chat (IRC), which is also free and can be downloaded from www.mirc.com. This small program enables users to gain access to thousands of chat servers worldwide. The chat rooms contain topics on the good, the bad, and the ugly. From discussing the latest fashions, getting gossip on popular entertainers, to sharing drug recipes or bomb-making directions—anything can be found in the IRC system and other chat rooms mentioned earlier. These chat servers also serve as popular environments for child pornographers to trade "pics." Law enforcement officers can also surf these chat rooms undercover to detect and apprehend child predators. See Chapter 7, "Pedophiles, Online Child Enticement, and Child Pornography," for additional information on working undercover online.

Groups at www.groups.yahoo.com are another online meeting place for drug dealers. Some groups are public, while others are "private" and a user must be approved by the administrator before being allowed to join. Pipes_cocaine_nstuff is one Yahoo!group that is for recreational users of any substance, where they can anonymously meet to discuss their substance of choice.

Conducting keyword searches within these online groups can reveal drug information and intelligence that are just waiting to be discovered by law enforcement. Criminals or others posting questionable information believe that law enforcement will not find this information, won't take the time to look, or don't know how to search for it.

First responders encountering drug dealers should be on the lookout for high-tech devices that might be used in the trade. Incident to a lawful arrest, all pagers and cell phones should be seized and warrants (if necessary) sought to search them. The courts have allowed law enforcement to search pagers without a warrant because of the perishable nature of the data they contain. This is discussed further in Chapter 9. The names, including street names and phone numbers, of other drug dealers or "customers" can be found stored on these devices. Records relating to drug sales, amounts purchased, and purchase prices can also be saved in these devices. Any personal computers or other digital devices (e.g., thumb drives) that might be involved should also be seized consistent with the guidelines discussed in Chapter 10. First responders should not search any of these high-tech devices themselves without the necessary legal authority and training to preserve the integrity of the evidence and data contained therein.

5.3 HACKING

Based upon several informal interviews of first responders we surveyed, when asked the first word that comes to mind when they hear the words *computer crime*, a common response is **hacker.** Although many first responders may never investigate a full-fledged hacking case—they often fall under federal jurisdiction—they must familiarize themselves with the hacker mentality and mind-set.

Hacking is nothing new and has theoretically been around since the 1870s when male teenagers first hired to operate telephone switchboards had a predilection for disconnecting and misdirecting calls—"You're not my Cousin Mabel?! Operator! Who's that snickering on the line? Hello?" (Slatalla 2005). The advent of the computer age brought about the traditional hacker, who was first thought of as a harmless user with a curiosity about how things worked. The best way to figure that out is by taking things apart or viewing the internal structure that makes them function, and hackers did just that with electronic devices and systems. Regarding digital systems, a hacker is a person who enjoys exploring the details of programmable systems and how to stretch their capabilities, as opposed to most users, who prefer to learn only the minimum necessary (Outpost 9, n.d.). Over the years, *hacking* has taken on a completely different meaning and is often synonymous with the activity of a computer criminal. Hackers, both good and bad, are here to stay, and they do have their place in society. There are three types of hackers:

White Hat Hackers—A person who identifies weaknesses in a computer system or network but, instead of taking advantage of them, exposes the weaknesses to the system's owners and recommends a fix before such flaws can be taken advantage of by others. Many major corporations employ people with such skills to help keep their systems secure.

Black Hat Hacker—In contrast to a white hat hacker, a black hat hacker breaks into systems (e.g., networks, Web sites) with malicious intent to steal, damage, or deface them. Black hats are sometimes referred to as **crackers,** a term coined by the hacker community to separate themselves from the white hats.

Gray Hat Hacker—A gray hat is one who is on both sides of the hacking fence. A gray hat hacker discovers and supplies information about network security issues and weaknesses to network administrators and also to black hat hackers. Some gray hat hackers may work in conjunction with black hat hackers and benefit monetarily from any illicit gains.

Even with these definitions, the term *hacking* continues to have a negative connotation and implies any illicit activity with or against a computer system or other digital device.

Although hackers can be defined or categorized, there is no one-size-fits-all hacker profile. Attempts have been made to profile hackers, and Kovacich and Boni (1999) propose the following hacker profile:

- White
- Male

- **Young (14 to middle 20s)**
- **Intelligent**
- **Avid computer enthusiast**
- **Introverted**
- **Insecure**
- **From a middle- to upper-middle-income family**

Another study (Stambaugh et al. 2000) profiles hackers as almost always males, 15 to 25 years old, intelligent social outcasts or loners who have had previous problems in school and lack positive outlets for their talents. They are also the technical superiors to criminal offenders and are most difficult for law enforcement to track.

Many hackers, both black and white hat, are sought after by industry, private and sometimes public entities, to help protect computer and network systems with the belief that organizations must hire a crook to catch a crook. For example, in Sneek, Netherlands, because he thought the hacker would make a good expert on computer security the local mayor offered a job interview to a 20-year-old hacker who confessed to spreading a computer virus that offered a photo of tennis star Anna Kournikova and that backed up e-mail systems worldwide (McDonald 2001). Black hat hackers may also try to find employment within an industry that they wish to exploit. They then become insiders within the industry and help the illicit hacker community succeed on the outside. Disgruntled employees can also become primary sources of exploits as a result of their intimate knowledge of an organization's systems, which can enable them to steal data or damage systems. In contrast, many white hat hackers find themselves employed as system administrators or within law enforcement agency computer crime units.

First responders may also encounter self-proclaimed hackers while investigating unrelated incidents. For example, in 2001 we arrested a self-proclaimed hacker for battery (assault) who explained that he had created a program to capture and read all of the police mobile data transmissions (MDT) sent from car to car or from dispatch to squads on the street. The hacker provided sample messages that he had read and also revealed how he did it by slightly altering a Bear Cat police scanner so that it captured the messages and displayed them on a computer screen.

Many hackers like to brag about their exploits. In the previously mentioned arrest, we did little talking and the hacker freely offered much of the information we sought. Silence is unusual among criminal hackers, who seem to have a need to talk about their latest conquest. Web sites have been set up on which hackers brag about their exploits. For example, www.attrition.org is known as the largest mirror (database) of Web site defacements where hackers can post their "work," including the Uniform Resource Locator (URL) that was attacked. Although hackers typically crack into networks for the thrill of the challenge or for bragging rights in the hacker community, recently there are more cases of hacking for illicit financial gain or other malicious purposes (Freeh 2000).

The actual number of hacking attacks against private and public industry is unknown. Many businesses do not want to publicize when their company has become the victim of a hacker attack. Businesses can lose hundreds of millions of dollars of value, brand equity, and corporate reputation when they fall prey to a hacker (Goodman 2001). As a result, most system administrators don't contact law enforcement officers when their computer systems are invaded, preferring instead to fix the damage and take action to keep hackers from gaining access again—with as little public attention as possible (Morris 2005). A national survey conducted by the Bureau of Justice Statistics and reported by Statistician Ramona R. Rantala (2004) of 500 U.S. companies revealed that of the 95 percent using computers, 99 percent reported incidents of cybercrime. Of those incidents, computer viruses, denial of service attacks, and vandalism/sabotage were the most common. A total of 31 percent of these cybercrime incidents were attributed to hacking. However, hackers often use computer viruses, denial of service attacks, and vandalism/sabotage to carry out their illegal activities.

Businesses need to protect their company assets, proprietary data, and customer information from intruders. Hackers have tried to bring some businesses down by extorting money from them or threatening digital harm. Police departments also need to protect intelligence information, arrest records (especially protected juvenile records), police personnel information, and other sensitive data kept on computer networks. Hacker attempts to access these networks can be thwarted by implementing appropriate security measures and early detection. However, many times attempts are discovered too late or the bureaucratic decision-making structure (e.g., chain of command) negates timely action and reporting. By the time the private or public institution takes action, the valuable time-sensitive data, such as the Internet Protocol address, is lost. Timely detection can be improved not only through regular system monitoring and appropriate intrusion response protocol, but also through use of real-time intrusion detection software. For example, Carole Moore (2005) reports in *Law Enforcement Technology*:

> The nonprofit organization Cyber Incident Detection and Data Analysis Center (CIDDAC) is on the cutting edge of cyber-terrorism prevention. . . . CIDDAC prevents attackers from getting inside the target database by employing "real-time cyber attack detection sensors or RCADS." . . . Once an intruder is detected and enters into the RCADS, the incident is immediately noted by the CIDDAC center and analyzed. . . . [the victim] is notified of the attack in real time . . . and is also passed to the appropriate law enforcement agency, but without information that identifies the victim or the victim's clients.

The real-time detection of an attempted intrusion along with the anonymous reporting features of the CIDDAC program and others like it to come should increase the chances of apprehension along with increased reporting of these incidents.

Some of the more common forms of computer sabotage include the following:

- ***Denial of Service (DoS)*** —Hackers attack or flood a server with phony authentication methods to prevent people from accessing the server and ultimately shutting it down.
- ***Viruses*** —A computer program designed to "infect" a program file that may create annoying screen messages to wipe out an entire hard disk drive. Like a biological virus, a computer virus infects a "host" and uses the capabilities of its host to replicate. Once executed, a virus can cause damage by erasing or altering data or files, or by simply replicating until no disk space remains and the computer ceases to function. Viruses can be transmitted from one computer to another by e-mail.
- ***Worms*** —Worms are computer programs designed to make copies of themselves automatically. Unlike viruses, a worm is self-executing, largely invisible to the computer users, and spreads from computer to computer over a network without any user action. For example, the Slammer worm that spread during the weekend of January 25, 2003, attacked a known flaw in the Microsoft SQL Server 2000, shutting down computer systems nationwide, including American Express and the Seattle (WA) police and fire 911 center. Believed to be the fastest-spreading Internet worm on record infecting 90 percent of vulnerable computers nationwide (Wilson 2005), it challenged popular opinions that vital services were largely immune to such attacks.
- ***Trojan Horses*** —A program that appears to be useful or benign but that actually conceals another program designed to be damaging, annoying, or "humorous."
- ***Logic Bomb (AKA "Slag Code")*** —A program designed to execute (or "explode") under certain conditions specified in the coding, for example, on a certain date, after a specific lapse of time, or following some response (or lack of response) by the computer user.
- ***Web/IP Spoofs*** —Hackers create a false or shadow copy of a legitimate Web site that looks just like the real one, with all the same pages and links. All network traffic between the victim's browser and the spoofed site are funneled through the hacker's machine. The hacker can acquire private information, such as passwords, credit card numbers, and account numbers.
- ***Social Engineering*** —As discussed earlier, the use of "wetware" or humans to provide the information needed by the hacker to exploit the system. It is the manipulation of people to coerce them into giving out critical information about a computer, network, or phone system. It works well because people are oftentimes the weakest link in a secured system.
- ***E-mail Bombs*** —When hackers flood an e-mail account server with thousands of messages rendering it unable to accept or send mail.
- ***Dictionary Attacks*** —A technique used by hackers to figure out passwords. Software programs such as Word Password Recovery 1.0j are available on the Internet and can randomly apply all letters of the alphabet to a

targeted password until it figures out the correct password to open the application. Using strong passwords consisting of a combination of numbers, letters, and characters can help prevent a successful dictionary attack.

- *Sniffers*—Programs that detect all data traveling through a network, enabling hackers to search for passwords that will allow for account access.

All of the exploits or techniques discussed are potential obstacles that first responders and investigators might encounter when tracking a hacker.

Once a private or public entity reports a computer intrusion to law enforcement, the report will, sooner or later, become a public record. When called upon, untrained first responders might arrive on the scene unsure about how to proceed properly and work under the temporary guidance of the system administrator or corporate investigator that is reporting the intrusion. An effective overall investigative strategy must include the owners and operators of computer networks (Salgado 2001). The first responder must act as the legal expert, and the system administrator must be the technical expert.

To negate many of the fears that businesses have when reporting the intrusion to law enforcement (listed in the following box), first responders should assure victims that law enforcement investigators will work with them and keep them informed of the ongoing status of the investigation—victims' rights legislation in several states gives victims the right to know. First responders should also assure businesses that all necessary measures will be taken to protect proprietary, customer, and essential data with minimal disruption of the day-to-day business activities. If the responding agency doesn't have the necessary resources to investigate a complex hacker attack, then businesses must be assured that authorities with the capabilities to conduct the investigation will be notified and will assist.

During the preliminary investigation, the system administrator will refer to computer logs, if available, that show the IP address from which the hacker gained access along with the dates and times of the intrusion. The IP address is a unique number that can be traced to a particular computer, and the path data takes through a chain of IP addresses can be traced. (IP addresses are thoroughly discussed in Chapter 6). Unless the hacker alters the victim's logs once he or she gains unauthorized access, the victim's logs should list the precise computer address from which unauthorized access was gained (Morris 2005). A simple IP trace via a standard IP lookup Web site, such as www.arin.net, can reveal the Internet service provider (ISP) or server that the hacker was using at the time of the intrusion. Presuming the incident was reported on time and the log files at the ISP have not been deleted, subscriber information (e.g., full name on the Internet service account, address, phone number) needed to help locate the hacker could be found. At the same time, the investigation could reach a dead-end here if it's discovered that the hacker used an anonymizer or spoofed the IP address to mask the hacking activities. See Chapter 6 on tracing e-mail and IP addresses for additional information on how best to proceed.

Myths and Misunderstandings: Why Businesses Are Reluctant to Report Computer Intrusion

- The victim company does not know which law enforcement entity to call. Surely, the victim reasons, the local or state police will not be able to comprehend the crime and the FBI and Secret Service would have no interest in the system.
- If the victim company does report the intrusion to an appropriate agency, law enforcement will not act. Instead, the fact of the intrusion will become public knowledge, irreparably shaking investor confidence and driving current and potential customers to competitors who elect not to report intrusions.
- If law enforcement does act on the report and conducts an investigation, law enforcement will not find the intruder. In the process, however, the company will lose control of the investigation. Law enforcement agents will seize critical data and perhaps entire computers, damage equipment and files, compromise private information belonging to customers and vendors, and seriously jeopardize the normal operations of the company. Only competitors will benefit as customers flee and stock value drops.
- If law enforcement finds the intruder, the intruder likely will be a juvenile, reside in a foreign country, or both, and the prosecutor will decline or be unable to pursue the case.
- If the intruder is not a minor, the prosecutor will conclude that the amount of damage inflicted by the intruder is too small to justify prosecution.
- If law enforcement successfully prosecutes the intruder, the intruder will receive probation or at most insignificant jail time, only to use his or her hacker experience to find fame and a lucrative job in network security.

Source: Salgado, Richard P. 2001. Working with victims of computer network hacks. U.S. Department of Justice. *United States Attorney's USA Bulletin.*www.usdoj.gov/criminal/cybercrime/usamarch2001_6.htm (accessed June 22, 2005).

The computer networks that have been attacked may also hold additional valuable evidence on which an investigator can follow up. First responders should not attempt to seize computers from a network or private or public sector environment unless they have been properly trained to do so. Improper handling of computers or other digital devices seized as evidence can result in loss, damage, or alteration of the evidence and could disrupt business, causing financial loss for which authorities could be held liable. If it's necessary to seize a computer from one of these environments, stop and notify a qualified computer crime investigator. If the exploits originate from an IP address outside the state where the victim is located, federal authorities should be notified for assistance and direction. State authorities or a local qualified high-tech crimes investigator/computer forensic examiner should be notified in cases where the IP address is traced to a location within the victim's state or community. See Chapter 9 for additional information regarding the seizure of a computer.

First responders' investigations must also focus on the human aspects of the situation. At some point in the investigation, it will be necessary to use traditional investigative techniques, such as speaking with potential witnesses and suspects. In addition to the high-tech evidence, victims can provide valuable investigative leads. For example, the network intruder could have been a former disgruntled employee who has since been hired by a competitor and who is stealing proprietary data. The hacker could also be a former contract employee who nefariously opened a "back door" to the system that allowed him or her remote access. He or she could also be a current employee, recently hired, who is actually working as an insider for another corporation to steal data. The weakest link, mentioned earlier, is often a human.

Learner Activity

Contact a local business in your community, preferably one that relies extensively on technology, and interview someone there about the company's response to a potential hacking incident. For example, you may ask, "If your customer files were taken by a hacker, what would you do?" Also, gauge the perceptions on the law enforcement response to hacking and what the local law enforcement may or may not be able to do for the company. Report your findings.

When interviewing a hacker, it's helpful to be aware of some of the underlying motivations for hackers' actions, which include the following:

- Intellectual challenge, curiosity, or "thirst" for knowledge
- Anarchy, dissent, or radical views
- Money, personal gain, or for hire

Prior to the interview, it's critical to determine the hacker's motivation. During the interview, first responders or investigators should focus on the motivation and downplay the unlawful aspects, encouraging the suspect to talk about what he or she has done. Remember, many hackers like to brag about their exploits and often view themselves as intellectually superior to the interviewer. Let suspects talk, and not only will this increase the chances of a confession, but at the same time will educate the interviewer.

In most states, it is unlawful to knowingly and without authorization modify, destroy, access, take possession of, or copy data from a computer or computer network. These statutes permit prosecution of hackers who exploit or gain access to computers within the first responder's jurisdiction or state. In addition, the federal Computer Fraud and Abuse Act of 1986 (18 U.S.C. 1030) makes hacking a "federal interest computer" illegal. This act has since been amended and broadened to protect essentially any computer with Internet access.

As technology continues to evolve and industry develops stronger measures to protect itself against hacking, hackers continue to evolve and figure out ways to continue to exploit or defeat computer systems. Law enforcement must take a proactive role in combating computer intruders.

5.4 TERRORISM, CYBERTERRORISM, AND ORGANIZED CRIME

This topic is discussed last because terrorist organizations and organized crime groups utilize many of the high-tech means discussed earlier to further their illicit activities. Some examples have already been provided, such as when organized crime members become involved in the lucrative mortgage fraud business. This section explores common types of terrorism, discusses cyberterrorism, and highlights examples of how terrorists and organized crime groups have used and are using technology to further their political and illegal activities.

Terrorism

There is not one accepted definition of terrorism. For the purposes of this section, **terrorism** is defined as a premeditated, politically motivated violence perpetrated against noncombatant targets by subnational groups or clandestine agents, usually intended to influence an audience (U.S.C. Title 22, Section 2656f(d)). Terrorism can also be broadly described as either domestic terrorism or international terrorism. According to the FBI, **domestic terrorism** is the unlawful use, or threatened use, of violence by a group or individual that is based and operating entirely within the United States or its territories without foreign direction and which is committed against persons or property with the intent of intimidating or coercing a government or its population in furtherance of political or social objectives. In contrast, **international terrorism** transcends national boundaries and is an act supported by and/or with foreign direction against the population or government of any other country outside the United State or its territories. International terrorism can further be divided into three distinct categories: loosely affiliated extremists, formal terrorist organizations, and state sponsors of terrorism (Freeh 2000), as described here:

Loosely Affiliated Extremists—Loosely affiliated extremists, motivated by political or religious beliefs, may pose the most urgent threat to the United States. Within this category, Sunni Islamic extremists, such as Osama bin Laden and individuals affiliated with his Al-Qaeda organization, have demonstrated a willingness and capability to carry out attacks against the United States resulting in large-scale casualties and destruction.

Formal Terrorist Organizations—Typically, these autonomous, generally transnational organizations have their own infrastructures, personnel, financial arrangements, and training facilities. These organizations are capable of planning and mounting terrorist campaigns on an international basis. A number of these organizations maintain operations and support networks in the United States. For example, extremist groups such as the Palestinian Hamas, the Irish

Republican Army, the Egyptian Al-Gama Al-Islamiyya, and the Lebanese Hizballah have a presence in the United States, and members are primarily engaged in fund-raising, recruiting, and low-level intelligence gathering.
State Sponsors Of Terrorism—These terrorists view terrorism as a tool of foreign policy. Presently, the Department of State lists six countries as state sponsors of terrorism: Cuba, Iran, Libya, North Korea, Sudan, and Syria. Sanctions against Iraq have been suspended. These countries will be removed from this list once a government is in place that pledges not to support acts of terrorism (U.S. Department of State 2006).

Domestic terrorism can also be divided into three distinct groups: right-wing extremist groups, left-wing and Puerto Rican extremist groups, and special interest extremists (Freeh 2000), as described here:
Right-Wing Extremists—Often, these groups adhere to the principles of racial supremacy and embrace anti-government, anti-regulatory beliefs. Generally, extremist right-wing groups engage in activity that is protected by constitutional guarantees of free speech and assembly. Law enforcement becomes involved when the volatile talk of these groups transgresses into unlawful action. Some examples include the World Church of the Creator and the Aryan Nations.
Left-Wing and Puerto Rican Extremists—These groups generally profess a revolutionary socialist doctrine and view themselves as protectors of the people against the "dehumanizing effects" of capitalism and imperialism. They aim to bring about change in the United States through revolution rather than through the established political process. From the 1960s to the 1980s, leftist-oriented extremist groups posed the most serious domestic terrorist threat to the United States. In the 1980s, however, the fortunes of the leftist movement changed dramatically as law enforcement dismantled the infrastructure of many of these groups and the fall of communism in Eastern Europe deprived the movement of its ideological foundation and patronage. Terrorist groups seeking to secure full Puerto Rican independence from the United States through violent means represent one of the remaining active vestiges of left-wing terrorism. Some other examples include anarchists and extremist socialist groups such as the Worker's World Party, Reclaim the Streets, and Carnival Against Capitalism, which has an international presence.
Special Interest Extremists—These groups differ from traditional right-wing and left-wing terrorism groups in that extremist special interest groups seek to resolve specific issues, rather than effect more widespread political change. Special interest extremists continue to conduct acts of politically motivated violence to force segments of society, including the general public, to change attitudes about issues considered important to the extremist group's causes. These groups occupy the extreme fringes of animal rights, pro-life, environmental, anti-nuclear, and other political and social movements. Some special interest extremists—most notably within the animal rights and environmental movements—have turned increasingly toward vandalism and

terrorist activity in attempts to further their causes. Some examples include the Animal Liberation Front (ALF) and the Earth Liberation Front (ELF).

Learner Activity

Using your text, the Internet, and other academic resources, select one example of international terrorists and one example of domestic terrorists and describe them. Locate a practical example of their activities and how they use technology to further their ideologies. In your own words, report your findings.

Historically, terrorists prefer explosives because it satisfies their primary goal—terror. Terrorist organizations are utilizing the Internet not necessarily to terrorize, but rather to support or promote their organizations and political goals. The Internet serves as a perfect vehicle for terrorist organizations. For example, computers seized from Al-Qaeda have revealed terrorists that are becoming more familiar with hacker tools that are freely available on the Internet (Clarke 2003). It is easily accessible with little consistent worldwide regulation and has the potential to reach and spread propaganda to large segments of the population throughout the world. There are eight different ways terrorists use the Internet (Weimann 2004):

- *Psychological Warfare*–PSYWAR, or psychological warfare, has been used by armies and terrorists around the globe to influence the enemy. PSYWAR is also synonymous with psychological operations (PSYOP) that are intended to convey selected information and indicators to foreign audiences to influence their emotions, motives, objective reasoning, and ultimately the behavior of foreign governments, organizations, groups, or individuals (Joint Chiefs of Staff 2003). Terrorist groups can use the Internet and Web sites to instill fear and panic by displaying images of their destruction, airing video footage of brutal murders, or claiming responsibility for their atrocities.

- *Publicity and Propaganda*–With the advent of the Internet, terrorists no longer have to rely on traditional television, radio, or print to spread their propaganda to a regional audience. Terrorists can now operate their own Web sites that are available worldwide to promote their agenda, appeal to sympathizers, and even recruit others to their cause.

- *Data Mining, Research, and Intelligence Gathering* –In the same way that law enforcement can use the Internet to gather information, terrorists use it to gather intelligence. A wide array of information of potential interest to terrorists is available, such as location of transportation facilities, water and electrical utilities, nuclear plants, airports, shipping ports, and even counterterrorism information. Law enforcement must be cautious of what it makes available for public consumption lest it fall into the wrong hands.

- *Fund-Raising*–Similar to how nonprofit organizations raise funds online, terrorists can use the Internet to appeal to potential donors. They can use it to set up "charitable" Web sites that serve as fronts to funnel money to terrorist organizations.

- *Recruitment and Mobilization*-Terrorists can use Web sites and multimedia technologies to glorify their message and attract others to the cause. They can also collect information, such as the IP addresses of visitors, and attempt contact with those who seem most interested. Terrorists can also surf chat rooms or message boards and recruit from potential interested sympathizers.
- *Networking*-The Internet serves as a great vehicle to bring together people with common interests. Terrorists can use it to contact one another or network and establish contacts throughout the world. Networking can take place via e-mail, in chat rooms, through instant messaging, or on message boards.
- *Sharing and Concealing* Information*-The Internet has made it much easier to share information about terrorism and even how to carry out terrorist acts. For example, bomb-making books titled *The Terrorist's Handbook* and *The Anarchist Cookbook* are widely available along with *The Mujhadeen Poisons Handbook* online. Terrorists can also use technology, such as steganography (discussed later), to hide data (e.g., terrorist plans) on the Internet.
- *Planning and Coordination*-Finally, terrorists can use the Internet to communicate, plan, and coordinate attacks. Communications can take place in secret or password-protected chat rooms, and terrorists also use encryption, which can make the communications difficult to intercept and/or decipher.

* Italicized text added by authors

Terrorists also use high technology to conceal their identities and carry out their missions. For example, Adam Adel Ali, Adam Khan Baloch, Richard Smith, Adam Ali, Paul Vijay, Alex Hume, Adel Sabah, and at least 30 other names were used by Ramzi Yousef, the mastermind behind the first World Trade Center attack. He created false photo identification cards for many of these names and in each photograph looked radically different (Reeve 1999). With matching false Social Security cards, Yousef would also have been able to obtain credit and establish false addresses, which would further conceal his activities. Terrorist organizations can also use the Internet to conceal funds by creating false online charitable organizations or fraudulent online auction sites where apparently legitimate transactions actually funnel illicit funds.

Steganography

It is well known to government officials that terrorist organizations, such as Al-Qaeda, are increasingly using computers and technology to further their goals. Prior to the September 11, 2001 attack, it was reported that Bin Laden and others were using **steganography,** the art of hiding messages within messages, to conceal and transmit terrorist plans, maps, and photographs (McCullagh 2001). When using steganography, the user hides a message, such as a secret terrorist plan, behind a photograph and then transmits or posts the photograph somewhere on the Internet. Unless investigators know where to look in cyberspace, the chances of randomly locating the hidden message are extremely low. Steganography is used also by other criminals who need to hide and share information, including drug traffickers, money launderers/embezzlers, gamblers, prostitutes, and child pornographers. Keyword searches for the term *steganography* will return several pages of information on the topic along with links to free software programs for practicing it, such as Dound's Steganography and Xiao Steganography, both of which can be downloaded from the Internet for free.

Detecting steganography can be very difficult. When dealing with a high-tech offender who might have a need to conceal data, first responders should look for any boxes or manuals about steganography in the area of the suspect's computer. If examining a computer in the field, during a consent search, for example, first responders should also note any icons that might be indicative of steganography use. These might be some of the best clues that a first responder could uncover. Knowing the type of steganography software program the offender is using increases the chances of the forensic examiner uncovering hidden data.

Cyberterrorism

Although terrorists use the Internet, they typically do not use it to commit **cyberterrorism** but may use it as a technique to enhance a traditional attack (e.g., jamming a 911 operations center during a terror attack to disrupt emergency response and communications). The word *cyberterrorism* comes from the combination of *cyberspace* (the computer-based world of information) and *terrorism*. Like terrorism, there is not one generally accepted definition of cyberterrorism. Cyberterrorism can be defined as unlawful attacks and threats against computers, networks, and the information stored therein when done to intimidate or coerce a government or its people in furtherance of political and social objectives (Federal Emergency Management Agency 2002). Cyberterrorist attacks typically focus on critical infrastructures, such as communications (see Figure 5–1), energy, water, and transportation, just to name a few. The impacts range from minor inconveniences to significant financial losses to private industry and business. As

Prosecutors in Wisconsin recently used the USA PATRIOT Act to investigate a case involving Rajib Mitra, a man who jammed the Madison, Wisconsin, police department's emergency radio system 21 times from January 2003 to August 2003 and for three hours on October 31, 2003, a day on which public safety concerns were heightened because of Halloween. Mitra was convicted in March 2004 for using computers to disrupt the administration of justice, national defense, and national security. Mitra was sentenced in May 2004 to a prison term of eight years.

Figure 5–1 Madison, Wisconsin, police emergency radio system jammed by cyberterrorist. *Source*: U.S. Department of Justice. 2004. Report from the field: The USA PATRIOT act at work. www.lifeandliberty.gov/doos/071304_report_from_the_field.pdf (accessed August 8, 2006).

critical infrastructure becomes more dependent on computer networks for operations, new vulnerabilities are created (Lewis 2002) and the more susceptible it becomes to a cyberterror attack.

There are three different types of computer (cyber) attacks: physical attack, electronic attack, and network attack (Wilson 2005), as summarized here:

Physical Attack—Involves conventional weapons (i.e., explosives) directed against a computer facility or its transmission lines.

Electronic Attack (EA)—Involves the use of electromagnetic energy as a weapon, more commonly as an electromagnetic pulse (EMP) to overload computer circuitry.

Computer Network Attack (CNA)—Involves malicious code (i.e., a virus) used as a weapon to infect enemy computers to exploit a weakness in software, in the system configuration, or in the computer security practices of an organization or computer user. Other forms of CNA are enabled when an attacker uses stolen information to enter restricted computer systems.

Cyberattacks alone are less effective, disruptive, and terrifying than traditional attacks. Furthermore, the built-in redundancy of modern critical infrastructures that include multiple avenues of communication (e.g., Internet, wireless, cell phones, LANs) along with strong network protection (e.g., firewalls, encryption, passwords) prevent long-term disruptions. Once a vulnerability is discovered, it is quickly corrected, forcing the cyberterrorist to discover another exploit, which can take considerable time. Observers also believe that mounting a coordinated attack against U.S. computer systems, using either large-scale, smaller scale, or even portable EMP weapons requires technical skills that are beyond the capabilities of most terrorist organizations (Wilson 2005). Terrorist organizations, however, do have the funding and networking available to hire individuals with the requisite skills to assist in carrying out some sort of cyberterror attack. Cyberattacks are also much too slow and require extensive planning and preoperational surveillance, in addition to testing of tools (i.e., weapons), which can take two to four years. A complex, coordinated attack could take 6 to 10 years of preparation (Wilson 2005); however, this ironically is similar to the preoperational strategy that goes into a traditional terrorist attack. The following box describes similarities between traditional terrorists and cyberterrorists.

Even though a cyberattack doesn't carry the same physical and emotional impact of a suicide bomber or car bomb and their technical skills may be lacking, terrorist organizations are attracted to using cyberterror in conjunction with traditional methods for several reasons (Federal Emergency Management Agency 2002):

Vulnerability—Society's sheer dependence on technology in all facets of life also creates sources of electronic vulnerability.

Fear Factor—To some, technology carries with it its own fear factor, stemming from its complexity, incomprehensibility, and seeming uncontrollability. The merger of traditional terror fear and cyberterror fear is a powerful one.

Anonymity—A cyberattack can be conducted remotely and anonymously, allowing the attacker to avoid detection and capture. Remote capability also

---

Similarities between Traditional Terrorists and Cyber terrorists

Terrorists	Cyberterrorists
Use a covert network structure to share information and move from one location to another, allowing them to disappear quickly and evade detection	Use a covert network structure to share information that moves from one virtual location (e.g., chat room) to another, allowing them to disappear quickly and evade detection
Use preattack surveillance over extended periods of time to gather information on a target's current patterns	Use social engineering and Dumpster diving to obtain passwords; install spyware to conduct virtual surveillance
Attack "soft targets," those that are unsecured or vulnerable	Attack unprotected computers—those without appropriate firewalls, virus protection, or network security in place
Utilize primary and secondary attacks on targets to prevent emergency services from assisting and causing maximum damage	Launch exploits from thousands of infected computers to produce waves of disruption

Source: Wilson, Clay. 2005. Computer attack and cyberterrorism: Vulnerabilities and policy issues for Congress. Federation of American Scientists. www.fas.org/sgp/ers/terror/RL32114.pdf (accessed June 22, 2005).

---

complicates the investigation, pursuit, and judicial processes because of differences in international laws.

Attention—Cyberterrorism provides a way to assert identity and command attention. If terrorists choose to forgo anonymity, an act of cyberterrorism would likely gain extensive media coverage as well as government and media attention.

Availability and Low Cost—Availability of cyberterror weapons and potential disruptive effects are rising, while the financial and other costs are decreasing.

Safety—Cyberterrorism doesn't require the handling of explosives or biochemical agents or a suicide mission.

Expertise—Many simple-to-use automated tools are available that the average user can execute. Hackers and insiders might be recruited by terrorists or become self-recruiting cyberterrorists.

First responders are on the front lines in the war against terrorism. A state trooper was responsible for apprehending Timothy McVeigh after the 1995 Oklahoma City bombing, and New Jersey first responders just missed apprehending Ramsey Yousef when they responded to a fire at his apartment that he accidentally started while boiling urea nitrate; Yousef fled before police arrived. First responders are also the first to encounter high-tech crimes in the field, and knowing the proper way to handle them is critical to the successful resolution of the case.

Organized Crime

Although terrorists may use cyberattacks more often in the future, there is growing evidence that organized crime groups or mafias are exploiting the new opportunities offered by the Internet (Dunlevy, Shimeall, and Williams 2002). Like cyberterrorism and traditional terrorism, there is not one commonly accepted definition of organized crime. According to Finckenauer and Voronin (2001), "Organized crime is crime committed by criminal organizations whose existence has continuity over time and across crimes and that use systematic violence and corruption to facilitate their criminal activities." Organized crime groups also tend to have the following common characteristics (Lyman and Potter 2004):

- Are nonideological (have no political goals)
- Have a hierarchical structure
- Have a limited or exclusive membership
- Are self-perpetuating (continue over time)
- Use violence (or threat of it) and bribery
- Demonstrate a specific division of labor
- Are monopolistic
- Are governed by explicit rules and regulations (including a code of secrecy)

Organized crime groups are well known for their use of sophisticated technology to commit crimes such as identity theft, credit card fraud (i.e., manufacturing cards and skimming data), adult pornography, and child pornography. Recently, it is believed that organized crime is behind many of the e-mail-based phishing attacks (Hansell 2004). These groups also use encryption, fraudulent e-mail accounts, and anonymous e-mail servers to communicate covertly. Orgnanized crime groups are also involved in telephone fraud, including telemarketing, calling card fraud, and cloning. In a 1999 case, a jailed member of the "phonemasters" sold thousands of stolen Sprint calling card numbers that ultimately ended up in the hands of organized crime groups in Italy (Etter, 2002). These are just a few of the illicit activities committed by organized crime groups, and each of the crimes discussed throughout this chapter have, at one time or another, been committed by organized crime groups. If organized crime groups do not have the requisite skills to pull off a particularly lucrative high-tech crime, they have the power and finances to pay for someone to do it. There will always be a black hat hacker out there willing to subcontract his or her skills to any organization for the right price.

5.5 PROTOCOLS FOR INVESTIGATING HIGH-TECH CRIMES

Many of the criminal offenses discussed in this chapter are facilitated in the online world. Some of them are also committed with other types of high-tech devices. Chapter 10 discusses in detail how to handle high-tech evidence properly. The investigative protocols that follow are intended to point the first responder toward the proper course of action when investigating an online-based high-tech crime. These are merely guidelines that are further expanded upon in later chapters.

- Receive and identify the nature of the complaint.
- Make evidentiary copy of the digital evidence.
- Expand the e-mail header/other Web address information on a nonevidentiary working copy.
- Read the address information to determine the originating source IP address.
- Use an IP lookup Web site to determine the originating source Internet service provider (ISP).
- Using the ISP administrative contact information; draft a subpoena/search warrant for ISP records pertaining to the e-mail message and its sender.
- Properly secure and document digital evidence while maintaining chain of custody in the electronic world.

In all criminal investigations, it's important to recognize, identify, interpret, document, and preserve evidence properly, regardless if it's in the real or digital world. The evidence must be correctly preserved so it can be tested, analyzed, or, in some cases, re-created.

The Internet and other technologies serve as yet another way for criminals to commit their crimes. First responders must also view technology as a vehicle that can lead them to a criminal or, at the very least, point them in the right direction. Drug traffickers, child pornographers, and terrorists all use technology in some shape, manner, or form to complete their illegal acts. Effectively combating such criminals requires first responders to understand the high-tech criminal mind-set and how these criminals operate.

■ SUMMARY

The Internet has, unfortunately, become the new vehicle that pedophiles use to collect and share their illicit images. Hidden behind the keyboard, the pedophile finds a sense of security in perceived anonymity. Combating the global child pornography problem begins with the first responder. A typical call for service, such as a loud-noise complaint, may lead to a plain-view observation of child pornography that must be properly seized. Law enforcement must be prepared to work with the computer repair technician who reports illicit images on a customer's computer. Properly preserving and seizing this digital evidence is essential for later forensic analysis and prosecution.

Like pedophiles, drug dealers and buyers use technology to their advantage. Purchase of illegal drugs online is common; and pagers, cell phones, and computers are part of the drug dealer's arsenal. The use of various technologies continues to expand: computers are used to track drug sales, chat rooms to attract customers, and digital cameras for countersurveillance. In addition to ensuring that drug dealers are not armed, law enforcement should look for digital devices that may be used in connection with drug sales, distribution, and possession.

Hacker, a familiar but frequently misunderstood term, is synonymous with computer crime. White hat hackers are needed in law enforcement to help combat the harmful effects of the black hat hackers. Hackers who illegally crack into systems simply because they can, or to exploit or steal sensitive information, are sought after by organized crime groups and even terrorist organizations. Cooperative efforts between businesses, network security personnel, and law enforcement are often needed to effectively investigate and track down the criminal hacker. Familiarity with the typical hacker profile, particularly their boastful nature, can increase the likelihood of obtaining a confession from a suspect.

Of greatest concern to law enforcement today is the ability of terrorists to use technology to carry out their acts. From the use of steganography to hide data or transmit plans, to online chat rooms where the plans are discussed and Web sites that promote their cause, terrorist groups take full advantage of these largely unregulated and inexpensive technologies. The digital world must be properly secured and policed in order to detect terrorists and prevent acts of cyberterrorism such as shutting down a 911 center to disrupt emergency response in connection with a traditional terrorist attack. Unfortunately it's not a question of *if* it could happten, but rather of *when.* We must be sufficiently prepared.

Regardless of the type of high-tech crime under investigation, established protocol must be followed in order to properly identify, collect, examine, investigate, and preserve digital evidence. Failing to follow protocol can result in altering the evidence or even destroying it, making a successful prosecution unlikely.

■ REVIEW QUESTIONS

1. What country is considered to be the capital of the child pornography trade and why?
2. What are the "typical" elements of child pornography statutes throughout the country that must be proved in child pornography cases?
3. What are Lolita images and what resources are available to law enforcement to help prove or disprove the legality of a questionable Lolita image?
4. What is the value of the MD5 message digest and how can it be used in child pornography investigations?
5. What are at least three ways drug dealers use technology and/or the Internet to further their elicit trade?

6. What is the difference between *white hat*, *black hat*, and *gray hat* hackers?
7. List and discuss at least five common forms of computer sabotage that are used by hackers.
8. Explain the difference between *terrorism*, *domestic terrorism*, and *international terrorism*.
9. List and discuss the eight different ways terrorists use the Internet.
10. Explain steganography and how terrorists are believed to use it.
11. Explain how organized crime groups use technology to further their criminal enterprises.
12. What are the seven investigative protocols for investigating high-tech crimes discussed in this chapter?

■ TERMS

black hat hackers	gray hat hackers	terrorism
crackers	hacker	Trojan horses
cyberterrorism	international terrorism	viruses
denial of service (DoS)	logic bomb	Web/IP spoofs
dictionary attacks	(aka "slag code")	white hat hackers
domestic terrorism	MD5	worms
e-mail bombs	sniffers	
	steganography	

■ REFERENCES

American Center for Law and Justice. 2001. The Child Pronography Prevention Act (CPPA) *Ashcroft v. The Free Speech Coalition*. www.aclj.org/news/read.aspx?ID=555 (accessed September 27, 2006).

Carr, J. 2001. Theme paper on child pornography for the 2nd World Congress on Commercial Exploitation of Children. National Children's Homes. www.ecpat.net/eng/Ecpat_inter/projects/monitoring/wc2/yokohama_theme_child_pornography.pdf (accessed June 22, 2005).

CBC News. 2003. Landslide: Child porn on the Internet. CBC News. www.cbc.ca/fifth/landslide/porn.html (accessed June 22, 2005).

Clarke, Richard. 2003. Vulnerability: What are Al Qaeda's capabilities? PBS Frontline: Cyberwar, April. www.pbs.org/wgbh/pages/frontline/shows/cyberwar/vulnerable/alqaeda.html (accessed June 22, 2005).

Dunlevy, C., Shimeall, T., and Williams, P. 2002. Countering cyber war. NATO Review, Winter. www.cert.org/archive/pdf/counter_cyberwar.pdf (accessed June 28, 2005).

Etter, B. 2002. Hi-tech crime: Global challenges for law enforcement. www.acpr.gov.au/pdf/Presentations/ASIC802.pdf (accessed October 14, 2006).

Federal Emergency Management Agency. 2002. Interim tool-kit: Appendix D. www.fema.gov/txt/onp/toolkit_app_d.txt (accessed July 4, 2005).

Finckenauer, J., and Voronin, Y. 2001. The threat of Russian organized crime. U.S. Department of Justice: Office of Justice Programs. www.ncjrs.org/pdffiles1/nij/187085.pdf (accessed June 30, 2005).

Finkelhor, D., and Ormrod, R. 2004. Child pornography: Patterns from NIBRS. *Juvenile Justice Bulletin*, December. www.ncjrs.org/pdffiles1/ojjdp/204911.pdf (accessed June 21, 2005).

Freeh, L. J. 2000. Cybercrime. www.fbi.gov/congress/congress00/cyber021600.htm (accessed June 22, 2005).

Goodman, M. 2001. Making computer crime count. *FBI Law Enforcement Bulletin*, 70. (August). www.fbi.gov/publications/leb/2001/aug01leb.pdf (accessed June 22, 2005).

Hansell, S. 2004. Organized crime may be behind phishing, fraudulent e-mail scams show more sophistication. *San Francisco Chronicle*. www.sfgate.com/cgi-bin/article.cgi?f=/chronicle/archive/2004/03/29/BUG8F5S1011.DTL (accessed July 5, 2005).

Hughes, D. R. 2001. Recent statistics on Internet dangers. ProtectKids.com. www.protectkids.com/dangers/stats.htm (accessed June 28, 2005).

Joint Chiefs of Staff. 2003. Doctrine for joint psychological operations. *Joint Publication 3-53*, (September 5). www.dtic.mil/doctrine/jel/new_pubs/jp3_53.pdf (accessed August 9, 2006).

Kovacich, G., and Boni, W. 1999. *High technology crime investigators handbook*. Burlington, MA: Butterworth-Heinemann.

Lewis, J. A. 2002. Assessing the risks of cyber terrorism, cyber war and other cyber threats. www.csis.org/tech/0211_lewis.pdf (accessed June 28, 2005).

Lourdeau, K. 2004. Online child pornography: Closing the doors on pervasive smut (witness testimony). http://energycommerce.house.gov/108/Hearings/05062004hearing1264/Lourdeau1970.htm (accessed October 14, 2006).

Lyman, Michael D., and Potter, Gary W. 2004. *Organized crime 3rd ed.* Upper Saddle Rivers, NJ: Pearson Education.

McCullagh, D. 2001. Bin Laden: Steganography master. *Wired News*. www.wired.com/news/print/0,1294,41658,00.html (accessed June 25, 2005).

McDonald, T. 2001. Anna virus author rewarded with job interview. *Newsfactor Technology News*. www.newsfactor.com/story.xhtml?story_id=7606 (accessed June 11, 2005).

Moore, C. 2005. Protecting your backdoor. *Law Enforcement Technology*, 32(6): 84–89.

Morris, D. A. 2005. Tracking a computer hacker. www.usdoj.gov/criminal/cybercrime/usamay2001_2.htm (accessed June 22, 2005).

National Drug Intelligence Center. 2005. National drug threat assessment 2005. www.usdoj.gov/ndic/pubs11/12620/ (accessed June 28, 2005).

Outpost9. n.d. New hackers dictionary. www.outpost9.com/reference/jargon/jargon_toc.html (accessed June 22, 2005).

Rantala, R. R. 2004. Cybercrime against businesses. *Bureau of Justice Statistics Technical Report*, (March). www.ojp.usdoj.gov/bjs/pub/pdf/cb.pdf (accessed June 22, 2005).

Reeve, S. 1999. *The new jackals: Ramzi Yousef, Osama bin Laden and the future of terrorism*. Boston: North Eastern University Press.

Rivest, R. 1992. RFC 1321—the MD5 message-digest algorithm. RFC 1321 (RFC1321). www.faqs.org/rfcs/rfc1321.html (accessed June 22, 2005).

Salgado, R. P. 2001. Working with victims of computer network hacks. www.usdoj.gov/criminal/cybercrime/usamarch2001_6.htm (accessed June 22, 2005).

Slatalla, M. 2005. A brief history of hacking. www.tlc.discovery.com/convergence/hackers/articles/history.html (accessed June 22, 2005).

Stambaugh, H., Beaupre, D., Icove, D., and Baker, R. 2000. State and local law enforcement needs to combat electronic crime. National Institute of Justice. www.ncjrs.org/txtfiles1/nij/183451.txt (accessed June 22, 2005).

Tjurjukanova, E., Rusakova, M., and Sakina V. 2003. Analysis of the situation and institutions in the field of sexual exploitation of children (CSEC) and counter-CSEC activities in Russia. www.ecpat.net/eng/Ecpat_inter/projects/monitoring/Russia/Situational_Analysis_Research__Russia_Feb2004.pdf (accessed July 3, 2005).

U.S. Department of Justice. 2004. Report from the field: The USA PATRIOT Act at work. (July). www.lifeandliberty.gov/docs/071304_report_from_the_field.pdf (accessed August 8, 2006).

U.S. Department of State. 2006. Country reports on terrorism, Chapter 6—State sponsors of terror overview. www.state.gov/s/ct/rls/crt/2005/64337.htm (accessed October 14, 2006).

Weimann, G. 2004. How modern terrorism uses the Internet. www.usip.org/pubs/specialreports/sr116.pdf (accessed June 28, 2005).

Wilson, Clay. 2005. Computer attack and cyberterrorism: Vulnerabilities and policy issues for Congress. Federation of American Scientists. www.fas.org/sgp/crs/terror/RL32114.pdf (accessed June 22, 2005).

chapter six

Tracking and Tracing
Internet Crimes

■ LEARNING OBJECTIVES

1. Examine IP addressing structure and how it is used to trace Internet activity.
2. Discuss laws pertaining to Internet communications and potential pitfalls for investigators.
3. Identify e-mail tracing procedures.
4. Discuss instant messaging, chat rooms, and ICQ, and the unique challenges they pose to law enforcement.
5. Examine the process of writing subpoenas and search warrants for Internet service providers and sample language commonly found within them.
6. Discuss the role of traditional investigative techniques for use in conjunction with technical investigative methods.
7. Discuss the investigatory challenges associated with wireless networks.

Although the Internet is an outstanding collection of knowledge and research, it can be used for good or ill. Like following footsteps in the snow from a burglary scene, it is sometimes possible to track crimes that are committed online. As discussed in earlier chapters, any data that travels across a network, such as the Internet or a small business network, has a source and a destination. Along the way, the data has to be routed in the proper direction to get from point A to point B. The addressing scheme on the Internet and on local computer networks is based on Internet Protocol (IP) addresses. The starting and ending points are the IP addresses of the source and destination computers as they are connected to the network or the Internet. This works just like the U.S. Postal Service in that there is a return address for the sender and a destination address for the recipient (see Figure 6–1). Continuing the analogy, mail has to stop at post offices in hub cities to be rerouted, just as data passes through computer routers to be routed most efficiently to the destination. For example, a letter sent from Wisconsin to New York likely passes through the hub city of Chicago.

Internet addresses are similar to mailing addresses in that there can be only one address for 1234 Main Street, Anytown, USA. Any computer that sends data to or receives data from a network or from the Internet must have its own unique IP address at the time that it sends or receives any data (see Figure 6–2). An IP address on the Internet can be allotted only to one computer at any given time. In other words, there cannot be two users simultaneously using the same IP address.

Although they area all routed by IP addresses, there are various different types of Internet communications and therefore numerous possible ways to trace or track them. Some communications are kept in server logs by the **Internet service providers (ISPs)** used to send or receive them (see Figure 6–3). Others are stored

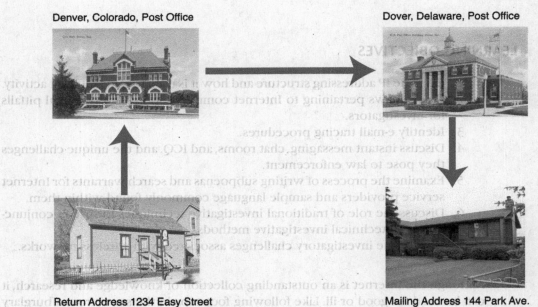

Denver, Colorado, Post Office

Dover, Delaware, Post Office

Return Address 1234 Easy Street

Mailing Address 144 Park Ave.

Figure 6–1 Diagram of how a letter might be routed through the U.S. Postal Service.

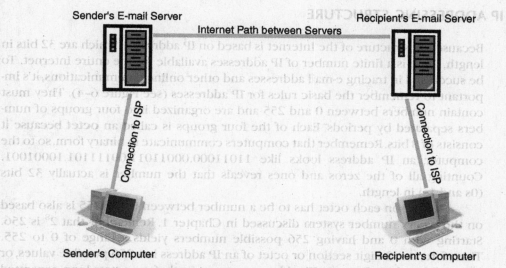

Figure 6–2 Simplified view of e-mail pathway between two users using different e-mail providers.

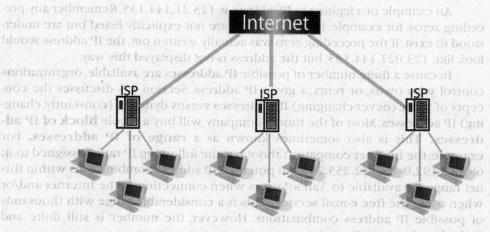

Figure 6–3 Example of customers connecting to Internet from three separate ISPs.

by recipients, either saved on their computer or in an e-mail folder. Others are stored automatically if a computer is set up to save transcripts. And last, some are stored locally on the computer that originally sent the message. In this chapter, we discuss the various types of Internet-related traffic, whether it can be traced, and what hurdles may have to be overcome in the process. In doing so, we examine the common types of crimes affiliated with a particular communication type.

6.1 IP ADDRESSING STRUCTURE

Because the structure of the Internet is based on IP addresses, which are 32 bits in length, there is a finite number of IP addresses available for the entire Internet. To be successful in tracing e-mail addresses and other online communications, it's important to remember the basic rules for IP addresses (see Figure 6–4). They must contain numbers between 0 and 255 and are organized into four groups of numbers separated by periods. Each of the four groups is called an **octet** because it consists of 8 bits. Remember that computers communicate in binary form, so to the computer, an IP address looks like 11011000.00011011.00111101.10001001. Counting all of the zeros and ones reveals that the number is actually 32 bits (0s and 1s) in length.

The reason each octet has to be a number between 0 and 255 is also based on the binary number system discussed in Chapter 1. Remember that 2^8 is 256. Starting with 0 and having 256 possible numbers yields a range of 0 to 255. Therefore, one 3-digit section or octet of an IP address has 256 possible values, or 2^8 possible values. Because IP addresses are currently four octets long, separated by periods, the potential number of possible IP addresses is $256 \times 256 \times 256 \times 256$, or stated another way, $2^8 \times 2^8 \times 2^8 \times 2^8$. There are, therefore, 4,294,967,296 possible IP address combinations under the current system.

An example of a legitimate IP address is 123.21.144.135. Remember any preceding zeros, for example, in the .21 octet, are not explicitly listed but are understood to exist. If the preceding zero was actually written out, the IP address would look like 123.021.144.135, but the address is not displayed this way.

Because a finite number of possible IP addresses are available, organizations control who owns, or rents, a given IP address. Section 1.3 discusses the concepts of static (never-changing) IP addresses versus dynamic (constantly changing) IP addresses. Most of the time, a company will buy a whole **block of IP addresses.** This is also sometimes known as a **range of IP addresses.** For example, the Internet company Yahoo! has the following IP range assigned to it: 68.142.192.0–68.142.255.255. All potential IP address combinations within this net range are available to Yahoo! users when connecting to the Internet and/or when using the free e-mail service. This is a considerable range with thousands of possible IP address combinations. However, the number is still finite and limited to that specific range.

- Each IP address must be 32 bits in length.
- It is divided into four octets (groups of 8 binary characters).
- Each octet must be a number between 0 and 255.
- Preceding zeros are not displayed for two-digit octets (below 100).

Figure 6–4 IP addressing rules summarized.

Because each address is assigned to an owner, IP addresses can be traced back to whatever company controls a given IP address number. Naturally, this can be used by a qualified investigator to find the source of the transmission. Because many Internet users have dynamic IP addresses that can change from day to day, or even hour to hour, the date and time of the violation become extremely important.

Timestamps within a communication greatly aid the investigator in narrowing the search. Remember the bowling shoe analogy from Chapter 1: if there are 10,000 bowlers in the world and only 5,000 pairs of bowling shoes, bowlers will have to rent shoes while bowling and return them when finished so other bowlers can use them. For the sake of example, say that one of the bowlers commits a murder while wearing a pair of rented bowling shoes. The murder happened at 1 P.M. on Sunday, March 5, 2006. The murderer leaves tracks in the mud, which have a distinctive pattern. Through pattern analysis, the police trace that pair of shoes back to the bowling alley that rented them out. Now all the police need to do is check the bowling alley records to see who rented the shoes at 1 P.M. on Sunday, March 5, 2006. In this analogy, the bowler is an Internet computer and the bowling alley is the Internet service provider.

Before law enforcement can begin to trace IP addresses, they must have a firm understanding of the laws pertaining to Internet communications and how they affect first responders investigating high-tech crimes involving IP addresses.

6.2 LAWS PERTAINING TO INTERNET COMMUNICATIONS

A variety of federal laws and state statutes governs the use of electronic communications in the United States. Two of the most well known federal statutes are the **Electronic Communications Privacy Act (ECPA)** and the **Privacy Protection Act (PPA)**.

The ECPA was passed in 1986 and has been amended several times since, including by the PATRIOT Act. Although commonly referred to as the ECPA, it is actually part of federal law. It is located in Title 18, Part I, Chapter 119 and is defined in Sections 2510–2522. The ECPA was essentially the modernization of the then-obsolete wiretapping statute. The original code was written to protect the privacy of telephone conversations and simply did not cover the emerging technologies involved with Internet communications. Thus, the ECPA was born to codify when government could and could not intercept Internet and/or stored electronic communications (i.e., those residing on a server). These Internet communications include e-mail that has been sent, is in transmission, has been received at the recipient's server, and/or has been received by the recipient. The ECPA mandates a court order demonstrating probable cause for law enforcement interception of electronic communications, and this is further discussed later in this chapter.

Another federal law, PPA, also had many purposes, but the most applicable was the protection of certain materials from government seizure. The PPA is located in Title 42, Chapter 21A, Subchapter 1 of the U.S. Code. The PPA arose because of perceptions that in seizing evidence, government entities were seizing materials that were not evidence and were not directly related to particular criminal investigations. In the computer age, this became even more problematic because a law enforcement officer might seize a computer that has multiple uses. A computer's hard disk drive could, for example, very easily store all of the files needed to run a legitimate business as well as spreadsheets detailing drug-trafficking transactions. Obviously, the drug transactions are of interest to the investigator, but the accounting files of a real, legal business might not be. Further, holding onto the legitimate business materials could damage or close down that business, which is not within the scope of an investigator's role.

The PPA, then, in part, makes it illegal to seize and hold materials not directly related to the crime being investigated. In common practice, investigators still seize the computer and its data in the entirety. Under the PPA, however, the investigators must make every possible effort to return to the owner everything that is not evidence or contraband, particularly if anything is a work product related to a legal or legitimate business. In practical cases, this generally means that investigators seize the entire hard disk drive and make several cloned images of it. These clones are exact copies in every way of the original. The original hard disk drive is then sealed into evidence. The investigators can then analyze one of the copies. To return the materials that are legal, and therefore irrelevant to the investigation, the investigator gives the suspect a hard disk drive clone that contains all nonevidentiary materials. In so doing, the investigators protect themselves and their government agency from being sued under the PPA.

One of the most famous examples of government being sued under the PPA and the ECPA is the **Steve Jackson Games** Case. Steve Jackson Games is a company that produces role-playing games in the form of booklets. In essence, then, it is a publishing company. The company had set up a bulletin board system where employees and game testers could log on and share information, drafts, and other messages. In 1990, the U.S. Secret Service raided the Steve Jackson Games facility in Austin, Texas, in connection with an investigation of data piracy. Agents seized many items, including the computers that hosted the bulletin board system. One item on the computers was a manuscript for a new role-playing game called "Cyberpunk." This manuscript was not related to the investigation, but was held, along with the other materials by the Secret Service. The Cyberpunk game manuals was a work product of a legitimate business entity and was not contraband or evidence of a crime. The gaming company argued that withholding that material could actually cause harm to its business by delaying production of the new game.

Steve Jackson Games sued the U.S. Secret Service under provisions of the ECPA and the PPA. It argued that the agents intercepted electronic communications in violation of the ECPA and that in keeping work materials unrelated to any criminal investigation, they also violated the PPA. Company representatives were largely unsuccessful in their argument that the agents intercepted electronic communications, although it was not disputed that the agents seized the computers on which all of the electronic messages were stored. The court ruled that although the messages were seized, they were seized after they had been transmitted and received and were therefore not truly intercepted. The courts found, however, that the Secret Service was liable under the PPA. This was based mostly on the holding of the manuscript for Cyberpunk. This booklet, or publication, fell under the PPA's **work product materials** definition (see Figure 6–5).

In the Steve Jackson Games case scenario, the basis of the lawsuit could have been avoided simply by giving copies of all legal work product materials back to the defendants. This should be considered a best practice or standard operating procedure for all high-tech crime units to avoid lawsuits under these laws.

Another case of interest is *Peter Hall and Big Bad Productions, Inc. v. Earthlink Network, Inc. (Hall v. Earthlink)*. Edited sections of the decision are included in Figure 6–6. When Hall initially brought the suit, he lost at the district

---

Part B—Remedies, Exceptions, and Definitions

Sec. 2000aa-7. Definitions
(a) "Documentary materials," as used in this chapter, means materials upon which information is recorded, and includes, but is not limited to, written or printed materials, photographs, motion picture films, negatives, video tapes, audio tapes, and other mechanically, magnetically or electronically recorded cards, tapes, or discs, but does not include contraband or the fruits of a crime or things otherwise criminally possessed, or property designed or intended for use, or which is or has been used as, the means of committing a criminal offense.
(b) "Work product materials," as used in this chapter, means materials, other than contraband or the fruits of a crime or things otherwise criminally possessed, or property designed or intended for use, or which is or has been used, as the means of committing a criminal offense, and—
(1) in anticipation of communicating such materials to the public, are prepared, produced, authored, or created, whether by the person in possession of the materials or by any other person;
(2) are possessed for the purposes of communicating such materials to the public; and
(3) include mental impressions, conclusions, opinions, or theories of the person who prepared, produced, authored, or created such material.

Figure 6–5 Title 42—The public health and welfare.
Chapter 21A—Privacy protection.
Subchapter I—First amendment privacy protection.

UNITED STATES COURT OF APPEALS FOR THE SECOND CIRCUIT

August Term, 2004
(Argued: September 30, 2004 Decided: January 25, 2005)
Docket No. 04-0384-cv

PETER HALL AND BIG BAD PRODUCTIONS, INC.,
Plaintiffs-Appellants,

- v. -

EARTHLINK NETWORK, INC.,
Defendant-Appellee.

POOLER, Circuit Judge:

Plaintiffs-appellants Peter Hall and Big Bad Productions, Inc. (collectively "Hall") appeal 2 from a final judgment and order of the United States District Court for the Southern District of New York (Richard Owen, Judge), entered December 30, 2003 dismissing all of Hall's claims by summary judgment. For the reasons specified below, we affirm the district court's dismissal of Hall's Electronic Communications Privacy Act, breach of contract, breach of the implied covenant of good faith and fair dealing, and tort claims.

BACKGROUND

Peter Hall, a self-employed independent film producer, wrote and filmed his first movie, entitled Delinquent, from 1992 to 1999. Hall marketed Delinquent through his corporation, Big Bad Productions Incorporated. In July 1996, Hall opened an account with EarthLink Network Incorporated ("EarthLink"), an Internet Service Provider ("ISP"), for Internet services and personal use of e-mail. Hall claims that he was known in the independent film community by his EarthLink e-mail username, lot99@earthlink.net ("lot99"). When Hall signed up for the EarthLink account, he agreed to EarthLink's subscriber agreement ("contract") which stipulated that California law governed the contract.

According to the complaint, Hall planned to use his EarthLink lot99 e-mail account to promote the two September 12, 1997, premieres at the upcoming Chicago Underground Film Festival on August 13, 1997. On August 5, 1997, UUNet, which provided "backbone" Internet services to EarthLink informed EarthLink that lot99 was sending mass junk e-mail, or "spam."

EarthLink immediately terminated Hall's access to the lot99 e-mail account. Six days later, on August 11, 1997, after a series of exchanges between EarthLink, Hall, and Wired News (an Internet industry magazine), EarthLink determined that lot99 was not a source of spam. EarthLink posted a retraction on the Net Abuse Report website and sent sixteen lot99 e-mails to Hall's new non-EarthLink e-mail account. Hall claims that he requested that EarthLink turn his service back on but that EarthLink failed to do so. EarthLink claims

(continued)

Figure 6–6 Sections of the *Peter Hall and Big Bad Productions, Inc. v. Earthlink Network, Inc.,* decision.

that Hall, "with shouted obscenities," refused its offers to reconnect the account. Hall's EarthLink account was not reopened, and between mid-August 1997 and July 1998, EarthLink received and stored 591 e-mails sent to the lot99 address. In July 1998, EarthLink sent the 591 stored e-mails to Hall. Hall then filed suit.

Hall's ECPA claim was that EarthLink "illegally intercepted" his e-mail in violation of 18 U.S.C. § 2511(1)(a) by intentionally continuing to receive messages sent to lot99 after the termination of his account. The district court dismissed this claim, reasoning that EarthLink's acts did not constitute an "intentional interception" under ECPA.

DISCUSSION

I. Electronic Communications Privacy Act
We review the district court's summary judgment dismissal of Hall's ECPA claim de novo. Perry v. Dowling, 95 F.3d 231, 235 (2d Cir. 1996). We agree with the district court's conclusion that EarthLink did not violate 18 U.S.C. § 2511(1)(a) but write to further clarify the proper interpretation of this section.

Through the enactment of ECPA, Congress amended the Federal wiretap law in order to "update and clarify Federal privacy protections and standards in light of dramatic changes in new computer and telecommunications technologies." Sen. Rep. No. 99-541, at 1 (1986), reprinted in 1986 U.S.C.C.A.N. 3555, 3555.

ECPA is divided into Title I, which governs unauthorized interception of electronic communications, 18 U.S.C. §§ 2510-2522, and Title II, which governs unauthorized access to stored communications, 18 U.S.C. §§ 2701-2711. Organizacion JD Ltda. v. United States Dep't of Justice, 124 F.3d 354, 356 (2d Cir. 1997). This appeal concerns Title I exclusively.

Section 2511(1)(a) states that, except as otherwise provided, anyone who "intentionally intercepts, endeavors to intercept, or procures any other person to intercept or endeavor to intercept, any . . . electronic communication" violates ECPA. 18 U.S.C. § 2511(1)(a). The district court held that EarthLink did not "intentionally intercept anything" in violation of Section 2511(1)(a) because EarthLink "merely received and stored e-mails precisely where they were sent—to an address on the EarthLink system."

We hold that EarthLink's continued reception of e-mails sent to lot99 did not constitute an "interception" under ECPA because it was conducted as part of the "ordinary course of [EarthLink's] business." See 18 U.S.C. § 2510(5)(a). Because we hold that EarthLink did not intercept electronic communications in violation of ECPA, we do not need to decide whether EarthLink's acts were intentional.

Moreover, an interpretation that excludes ISPs from the ordinary course of business exception should be avoided because it would lead to an absurd result. If ISPs were not covered by the ordinary course of business exception, ISPs would constantly be intercepting communications under ECPA because their basic services involve the "acquisition of the contents" of electronic communication. See 18 U.S.C. § 2510(4). Congress could not have intended this absurd result. Thus, we hold that ISPs do not "intercept" if they are acting within the ordinary course of their businesses.

We must next determine, therefore, if there is a material issue of fact as to whether or not EarthLink was acting within the ordinary course of business when it continued to receive messages sent to Iot99. EarthLink argues that it used its routers, servers and other computer equipment as part of its e-mail service to all customers, including Hall, in the ordinary course of its business.

CONCLUSION

For the reasons we have discussed, we affirm the judgment of the district court. Through the enactment of ECPA, Congress amended the Federal wiretap law in order to "update and clarify Federal privacy protections and standards in light of dramatic changes in new computer and telecommunications technologies."

Section 2511(1)(a) states that, except as otherwise provided, anyone who "intentionally intercepts, endeavors to intercept, or procures any other person to intercept or endeavor to intercept, any . . . electronic communication" violates ECPA. 18 U.S.C. § 2511(1)(a). The district court held that EarthLink did not "intentionally intercept anything" in violation of Section 2511(1)(a) because EarthLink "merely received and stored e-mails precisely where they were sent—to an address on the EarthLink system." Hall, 2003 WL 22990064, at *2. The district court did not specify whether it based this holding on a determination that EarthLink's actions were not an interception, not intentional, or both. We hold that EarthLink's continued reception of e-mails sent to Iot99 did not constitute an "interception" under ECPA because it was conducted as part of the "ordinary course of [EarthLink's] business." See 18 U.S.C. § 2510(5)(a). Because we hold that EarthLink did not intercept electronic communications in violation of ECPA, we do not need to decide whether EarthLink's acts were intentional. EarthLink's act did not constitute an interception.

Figure 6–6 *(continued)*

court level. He then appealed, and the case was heard by the U.S. District Court of Appeals for the Second Circuit. As the plaintiffs, Hall and the movie company alleged that Earthlink violated the ECPA by "intercepting" his e-mail. He had sent out very large numbers of e-mail messages in an attempt to advertise for a new movie that was set to premier. His sending of mass e-mail messages was initially interpreted to be spam by an Internet monitoring organization, and his e-mail account was frozen by Earthlink.

Then, there was a dispute over whether or not Hall requested Earthlink to turn e-mail services back on for his account, with Hall claiming Earthlink never turned services back on, and with Earthlink claiming that Hall refused reconnection offers "with shouted obscenities." Hall's service was not reconnected; however, the account still existed on Earthlink servers and received more than 500 e-mail messages over the course of about a year. Toward the end of that year, Earthlink sent all of those e-mail messages to Hall. Hall then sued under the ECPA, claiming that Earthlink had illegally intercepted the e-mail contrary to his ECPA rights. Earthlink ultimately won, and Hall's appeal was denied because the storage of the e-mail was found to be within the scope of Earthlink's normal business procedures, and therefore not considered an interception. The court went on to say that because there was no interception, it did not need to examine if there was an **intentional intercept.**

In addition to all of the attention paid to electronic communications by the federal government, individual states have also drafted new statutes or amended existing ones to address the challenges of the information age. Because of e-mail and other forms of online harassment, most states have statutes prohibiting harassing or intimidating communications. Some have even written statutes that specifically address such communications of an electronic nature. In addition to Wisconsin's e-mail Harassment State Statute 947.0125 (discussed earlier), Maryland State Statute/Article 27 (Crimes and Punishment), 555C (see Figure 6–7) also outlaws sending threatening, harassing, profane language and so forth via electronic communications. Because it is vaguely worded, like a disorderly conduct type statute, it

---

Article 27 - Crimes and Punishments

(a) In this section, "electronic mail" means the transmission of information or a communication by the use of a computer or other electronic means sent to a person identified by a unique address and received by that person.

(b) This section does not apply to any peaceable activity intended to express political views or provide information to others.

(c) A person may not use electronic mail for a communication made with intent to harass:

    (1) One or more persons; or

    (2) By sending lewd, lascivious, or obscene material

Figure 6–7   Statute example § 555C Maryland criminal code.

can easily be applied to most online communications of an inappropriate, harassing, or disorderly nature.

The challenge with many of these crimes, then, is not finding an applicable statute to define and explicitly outlaw the violation; the challenge lies in tracing the violation back to the offender to prove guilt. In many cases, the offender is somewhat local to the victim's area because he or she generally knows the victim. In some rarer cases, it may be a long-distance or even international crime. Even if we have an e-mail address or other contact information for the user account that sent the information, we still have the problem of identifying who was between the chair and the keyboard when the communication was sent. In other words, finding who was sitting at the computer from which the message came can be the most challenging element of these offenses to prove. In many cases, this is determined by the content of the message because it may be specific to one party. Information known only to the suspect might be contained in the message, thus eliminating the possibility that someone else sent the message. In other cases, traditional investigative techniques such as interview and interrogation may be relied upon.

6.3 E-MAIL TRACING PROCEDURES

E-mail is one of the most common and most recognizable forms of online communication, and therefore it is commonly used for illegal acts. In general, e-mail is also one of the easiest forms to track and trace because e-mail service providers plan for and provide online mailbox storage for messages, usually for the sender and the recipient. Second, e-mail messages have the source and destination information encoded right into the e-mail message to ensure proper routing. This encoded addressing scheme is usually not seen by the average e-mail user. Most users generally see only lines such as To:, From:, Re:, and the date. This information is commonly referred to as **brief headers.** Behind the scenes in the full e-mail header (i.e., **full headers**), the actual message routing code is present. When someone views the full header, he or she can examine the source and destination information in its entirety. Additionally, as the message travels across the Internet, it will likely pass through other computers (routers) on its way to the recipient. Each routing server or other computer it touches generally adds a piece of code to the header containing the IP address of that machine along with a timestamp indicating the date and time the message passed through that system. This is similar to a postmark stamp placed on a piece of mail as it passes through a post office in a given city, and it helps to confirm how the e-mail was routed.

It stands to reason that the first step in tracing any e-mail message would be to examine the full header. There is one other step that should be taken, however, and this is the case for all digital evidence. To ensure that investigators do not modify, alter, or destroy digital evidence it should be a standard operating procedure to first make an exact digital copy or clone of the evidence, or in this case, the e-mail message. In some major cases, this means cloning an entire hard disk drive.

In the case of a lower-level e-mail, it could mean simply saving the e-mail to a disk or other storage device, such as a universal serial bus (USB) key. Remember that some jurisdictions may have simply adopted their state's e-mail harassment statute as a municipal ordinance violation. Cloning an entire hard disk drive definitely seems like overkill when prosecuting an e-mail harassment case in municipal court with a civil forfeiture penalty. Circuit court criminal matters, on the other hand, have a much higher standard of evidence, and evidence in these cases should be treated accordingly.

Once investigators have ensured the safety of at least one exact copy, they can begin to analyze an evidentiary copy. In the evidence copy, then, the first step is to analyze the full headers of that e-mail message. Most e-mail programs by default display only the brief headers, but all types of e-mail, including **Web-based e-mail** such as Hotmail and Yahoo! mail, can be set up to display the full e-mail headers. A keyword search on the Internet for "reading full e-mail header" or similar phrases will reveal several Web pages discussing how to expand e-mail headers. An example of how to expand three common e-mail programs are listed in Table 6-1.

The full e-mail routing header displays many lines of data, including names of servers, e-mail addresses, IP addresses, and **timestamps** (see Figure 6-8). The investigator will need to go through this material in chronological order to see how the message traveled. Generally speaking, investigators should work from the most recent timestamp (at the recipient) backward to the oldest timestamp (at the sender). The first timestamp occurred when the sender clicked the Send button in the e-mail application and the message first reached the e-mail server of the sender's Internet service provider. It lists the IP address the sender's personal computer was assigned at the time the computer connected and sent that message. The next IP address and timestamp in line generally will be the IP address of the sender's Internet service provider's e-mail server. The third will usually be the e-mail server of the recipient's ISP. Last, the final IP address will be the IP address that was assigned to the recipient's computer at the time the e-mail message was received from the ISP server.

Table 6-1 Expanding Full Headers for Common E-Mail Programs

Microsoft Outlook	Yahoo!	Hotmail
1. Select the e-mail message to be traced.	1. Select the e-mail message to be traced	1. Select the e-mail message to be traced.
2. Right-click the e-mail message and select Options.	2. Scroll down to the bottom of the inbox and click Full Headers.	2. Navigate to and click Options.
3. A Message Options dialog box will open and display the full header under the title Internet Headers.	3. The e-mail message screen will refresh and display the full header.	3. Navigate to and click Preferences.
		4. Select Advanced Headers and full headers will be displayed.

```
Return-path: <**********@aol.com>
Envelope-to: gbp****pop.bi***.com
Delivery-date: Fri, 28 Jul 2006 06:25:55 -0400          (Most Recent Timestamp)
Received: from mail05.yourhostingaccount.com ([10.1.1.85] ident=exim)
      by mailscan30.yourhostingaccount.com with spamscanpop (Exim)
      id 1G6PXW-0000ye-QK
      for gbp****pop.bi***.com; Fri, 28 Jul 2006 06:25:54 -0400
Received: from mail05.yourhostingaccount.com ([10.1.1.85]
helo=mail05.yourhostingaccount.com)
      by mailscan30.yourhostingaccount.com with esmtp (Exim)
      id 1G6PXJ-0000yb-Ma
      for we******@gbp*****.org; Fri, 28 Jul 2006 06:25:41 -0400     (Earliest IP)
Received: from imo-m23.mx.aol.com ([64.12.137.4] helo=imo-m23.mail.aol.com)
      by mail05.yourhostingaccount.com with esmtp (Exim)
      id 1G6PXJ-0000NM-1i
      for we******@gbp*****.org; Fri, 28 Jul 2006 06:25:41 -0400
Received: from *********@aol.com
      by imo-m23.mx.aol.com (mail_out_v38_r7.5.) id 9.470.4fbd2100 (62952)
      for < we******@gbp*****.org >; Fri, 28 Jul 2006 06:25:35 -0400 (EDT)
From: *********@aol.com                                    (Earliest Timestamp)
Message-ID: <470.4fbd2100.31fb401f@aol.com>
Date: Fri, 28 Jul 2006 06:25:35 EDT
Subject: bounty hunters license
To: we******@gbp*****.org
MIME-Version: 1.0
Content-Type: multipart/alternative;
boundary="part1_470.4fbd2100.31fb401f_boundary"
X-Mailer: 6.0 sub 10552
X-EN-OrigSender: *******@aol.com
X-EN-OrigIP: 64.12.137.4
X-EN-OrigHost: imo-m23.mx.aol.com
X-EN-OrigRcptDomain: gbpolice.org
```

Figure 6–8   Full e-mail header.

Once an investigator has isolated the IP addresses and timestamps in the full header of a message, the next step is to verify who is responsible for that IP address. On the Internet, domain name information and IP address information can be tracked using a **WHOIS query** (see Figure 6-9). Many agencies are responsible for the sale and registration of IP addresses and domain names. The most wide reaching agency is the American Registry for Internet Numbers (ARIN), which can be accessed at www.arin.net. Investigators can type any domain name or IP address into the WHOIS search function and the databases of registry will supply registration information, including what company owns or maintains a given IP address or range of addreses. If, for example, an e-mail message appears to be from emailaddress@yahoo.com, the IP address and timestamp associated with the sender could be isolated. Running that IP address through a WHOIS search should yield an IP address that is registered to Yahoo and therefore falls within the realm of Yahoo's control. (Remember, however, users' an computers must be connected to the Internet service provider, so another IP address will be associated with their basic connection to the Internet.) If, for example, a user has an Internet service account through the local cable company, the timestamp and IP address

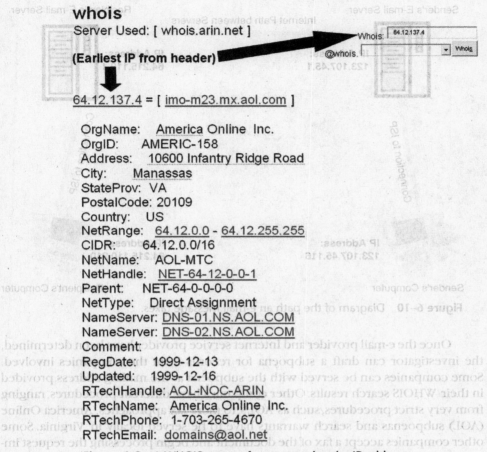

whois

Server Used: [whois.arin.net]

(Earliest IP from header)

Whois: 64.12.137.4
@whois.   Whois

64.12.137.4 = [imo-m23.mx.aol.com]

OrgName: America Online Inc.
OrgID: AMERIC-158
Address: 10600 Infantry Ridge Road
City: Manassas
StateProv: VA
PostalCode: 20109
Country: US
NetRange: 64.12.0.0 - 64.12.255.255
CIDR: 64.12.0.0/16
NetName: AOL-MTC
NetHandle: NET-64-12-0-0-1
Parent: NET-64-0-0-0
NetType: Direct Assignment
NameServer: DNS-01.NS.AOL.COM
NameServer: DNS-02.NS.AOL.COM
Comment:
RegDate: 1999-12-13
Updated: 1999-12-16
RTechHandle: AOL-NOC-ARIN
RTechName: America Online Inc.
RTechPhone: 1-703-265-4670
RTechEmail: domains@aol.net

Figure 6–9   A WHOIS query of a message header IP address.

of the sender should fall within the range of IP addresses owned and maintained by the cable company. (see Figure 6–10.)

The easiest scenario to envision is the case where a user has Internet service and e-mail accounts with the same company. Many higher end users, however, have many different e-mail accounts used for different purposes. It is not uncommon for one person to have the cable company provide the Internet connection, maintain an e-mail address through the cable company, and keep several separate e-mail address accounts with online mail providers such as Yahoo!, Hotmail, or other Web-based or work-related providers.

The example shown in Figure 6–11 lists the results from a WHOIS search of the domain name www.yahoo.com. Domain names can be searched by WHOIS just like a specific IP address can be searched. Notice that the mailing address for the entity is provided in the report. Also note the "NetRange" showing 66.218.64.0–66.218.95.255. This is the range of IP addreses controlled by Yahoo!

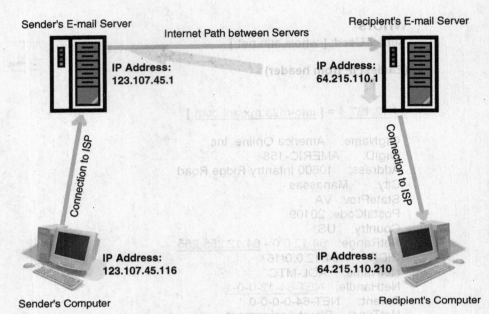

Sender's E-mail Server

Internet Path between Servers

Recipient's E-mail Server

IP Address:
123.107.45.1

IP Address:
64.215.110.1

Connection to ISP

Connection to ISP

IP Address:
123.107.45.116

IP Address:
64.215.110.210

Sender's Computer

Recipient's Computer

Figure 6–10 Diagram of the path an e-mail message takes.

Once the e-mail provider and Internet service provider have been determined, the investigator can draft a subpoena for records from the companies involved. Some companies can be served with the subpoena at the mailing address provided in their WHOIS search results. Other companies have different procedures, ranging from very strict procedures, such as AOL's, to more lax approaches. America Online (AOL) subpoenas and search warrants have to be served locally in Virginia. Some other companies accept a fax of the document and begin processing the request immediately. Ultimately, each company is somewhat different, but most have a designated point of contact for questions regarding subpoenas and search warrants.

If approved by a judge, the subpoena will compel the company to turn over any and all records it has regarding the questioned user's account. Naturally, this will include a billing name and billing address for the user. Depending on the severity or nature of the offense, the billing information and address could then be used for drafting a search warrant for the suspect's home, which could ultimately result in the search/seizure of a suspect's computer.

There are other ways to trace and track e-mail, particularly if the sender continually sends e-mails or is expecting some sort of a reply from the victim. Certain Web sites can be used to send traceable e-mail messages. This works kind of like sending a registered letter via the postal service in that the sender receives confirmation that the message was received. One example of such a service is Confirm.To. For a modest fee, this Web site attaches a line of code to a sender's e-mail message and then sends it to the intended recipient. As soon as the recipient opens the e-mail message, a message is automatically sent to the sender by

```
OrgName:   Yahoo!
OrgID:   YAOO
Address:   701 First Ave
City:   Sunnyvale
StateProv:   CA
PostalCode:   94089
Country:   US

NetRange:   66.218.64.0 - 66.218.95.255
CIDR:   66.218.64.0/19
NetName:   A-YAHOO-U23
NetHandle:   NET-66-218-64-0-1
Parent:   NET-66-0-0-0-0
NetType:   Direct Allocation
NameServer:   NS1.YAHOO.COM
NameServer:   NS2.YAHOO.COM
NameServer:   NS3.YAHOO.COM
NameServer:   NS4.YAHOO.COM
NameServer:   NS5.YAHOO.COM
Comment:   ADDRESSES WITHIN THIS BLOCK ARE NON-PORTABLE
RegDate:   2002-01-15
Updated:   2002-06-27

RTechHandle:   NA258-ARIN
RTechName:   Netblock Admin
RTechPhone:   +1-408-349-3300
RTechEmail:   netblockadmin@yahoo-inc.com

OrgAbuseHandle: NETWO857-ARIN
OrgAbuseName:   Network Abuse
OrgAbusePhone:   +1-408-349-3300
OrgAbuseEmail:   network-abuse@cc.yahoo-inc.com
OrgTechHandle:   NA258-ARIN
OrgTechName:   Netblock Admin
OrgTechPhone:   +1-408-349-3300
OrgTechEmail:   netblockadmin@yahoo-inc.com
```

Figure 6–11   Sample WHOIS record for www.yahoo.com.

Confirm. To that includes the IP address, date, and time the e-mail message was opened. This is generally unrecognizable to recipients because they see nothing unusual about the original the e-mail. Unless the recipient is suspicious enough to look closely at the full e-mail header, he or she will not realize what has occurred. By utilizing this tool, investigators can easily find out the IP address used by the offender at that date and time; if the offender checks e-mail from his or her usual computer, this greatly aids the investigator in getting a subpoena for documents for ISP records, or possibly a search warrant for the suspect's address. A variety of these kinds of confirmed mail services is available at varying rates. Some even offer a brief free trial period.

Figure 6–12 lists the basic steps taken to trace a suspect's e-mail. E-mail tracing is not foolproof. Experienced hackers can use certain tricks to strip IP addresses from e-mail headers, and there are anonymous e-mail services. Finally, a user could also utilize a public computer at a library or college, which enables investigators to trace the message, but only back to the public institution. This is similar to using a pay phone to make harassing phone calls; these cases rely more heavily on the traditional investigative skills of the responding investigator.

Learner Activity

Obtain an e-mail message from your own e-mail account or elsewhere. Find the correct method for displaying the full e-mail headers. Note the time zones or GMT differential for each timestamp within the e-mail header. Trace each IP address within the e-mail header utilizing a WHOIS query tool such as www.arin.net, www.samspade.org, or www.geektools.com to verify with which Internet service provider the IP address is associated. Working from the most recent IP address backward in time to the oldest IP address, document the exact path the e-mail took from recipient to the original sender. Make sure to document the name of the ISP of the original sender as well as the mailing address where a subpoena could be served on that ISP.

1. Make an evidentiary copy or copies of the e-mail message.

2. While working with an evidentiary copy, expand the e-mail message to view the full e-mail header, which contains routing, IP address, and timestamp information.

3. Work backward chronologically from the most recent timestamp to the oldest timestamp and examine the associated IP addresses.

4. Perform a WHOIS search on the IP addresses to ascertain who is responsible for those IP addresses.

5. Subpoena records from the appropriate company or entity to get user account information, billing address, and so forth.

Figure 6–12 Overview of e-mail tracing steps.

6.4 INSTANT MESSAGING/CHAT, ICQ, AND OTHERS

Another one of the wonderful and very popular communications tools on the Internet is **instant messaging**, also known as **IM**. Instead of waiting for a recipient to receive, open, and read an e-mail message, whenever that is, before a response is made, two users can meet online and type messages back and forth to each other in real time. This method of communication is extremely fast and is limited only by the distance the electrical impulses have to travel between users. Even users on different continents might only experience a delay of a few seconds, hence the name "instant messaging." There are various types of instant messaging, including personal messaging and use of chat rooms. One of the most popular versions of IM is **ICQ**, which is slang for "I seek you." With ICQ, users can type messages back and forth, but they also have other ways to connect. Users with speakers and a microphone attached to their computer can talk to each other over the Internet. This is sometimes referred to as **Voice over IP**, or **VoIP.** The audio is converted to digital signals, sent via the IP address connection, and converted back to audio again. Likewise, users with a camera connected to their computer can communicate with video and audio. The various online service providers have their own versions of these products, but the most common are MSN Messenger, Windows Messenger, and AOL Instant Messenger. As these programs have evolved, they have developed new features such as PC-to-PC direct file transfer. The newest versions even allow users to synchronize folders on their individual computers. If user 1 places a file in an online sync folder, the program automatically copies that file to the folder on the other user's computer. Direct file transfer is limited only by the users' Internet connection speed or bandwidth, and virtually any type of file can be transferred very quickly.

It is easy to see the multitude of uses for this technology in business or government because it allows instant online collaboration. Investigators must also think like criminals and figure out ways this technology could be used to commit crimes. As you will read in Chapter 7, this technology could be used by a pedophile to try to entice a child into committing a sexual act. A sex offender could literally videoconference with a teenager or child and expose sex organs to a minor right on the Webcam without having to buy any fancy equipment or software. Any Internet-capable computer with a $25 Webcam can use these features. A sex offender could also easily transfer pornographic or other harmful materials to a victim. (See Chapter 7 for more on victim grooming techniques.)

Instant messaging, VoIP, and videoconferencing investigations all have one major hurdle and several smaller problems to overcome. First, records of these conversations are kept only for a very short time by Internet service providers. Service providers can literally have millions or billions of instant messages per day pass through their servers. They simply do not have enough storage capacity to store them all for any great length of time.

Second, it takes very little information to sign up for an e-mail account or instant messaging service. A user can literally sign up for a screen name using completely bogus information, and signing up may take only a few minutes. A user could easily create dozens of online profiles in an afternoon. The only information a user might have about someone else who communicates via IM is the sender's screen name or e-mail address. It becomes much harder, therefore, for investigators to trace back an instant communication to the person who sent it. And time is not on the investigator's side.

However, once the screen name or e-mail address of the sender is determined, a subpoena for records can be drafted to get all records the ISP has on the person that uses that name or address. The investigator should, again, pay close attention to the time and date of the offending communication. If the investigator can narrow down that time period, the ISP might have a record of which IP address the offending user was assigned at the time the message was sent. The investigator can WHOIS that IP address to determine what Internet service provider the offender was using and subpoena name, address, and billing information from that Internet service provider. A confirmed e-mail message could also be sent to verify the user's IP address if the suspect's screen name or associated e-mail address is known. In reality, though, instant messaging records may be kept only for a day or two, if at all. Unless a violation is immediately reported and immediately investigated, there may be little information an investigator can use. One piece of good news, however, is that many instant messaging programs save logs or transcripts of all **chat** sessions right on the computer used for the communication. Some have this feature enabled by default, others require the user to specifically turn on the logging feature. In a child enticement investigation, for example, this feature can be very valuable because it will clearly document conversations between the victim and offender and may even contain specific statements of the offender's criminal intent. Like other forms of digital evidence, the logs might be on the victim's computer, the suspect's computer, or both.

Once the digital trail has been traced back to a specific company or Internet service provider, it is time to use that information to justify further evidence collection. By compelling a disclosure of customer records, the investigator narrows down the search from the service provider to the specific customer.

6.5 SUBPOENAS AND SEARCH WARRANTS FOR ISP RECORDS

Sometimes in the course of investigations, investigators are able to determine what Internet service provider is responsible for the IP address they are interested in tracing. The next hurdle then becomes requesting or compelling the Internet service provider to share those records with the investigating agency. The U.S. Attorney's bulletin *Tracking a Computer Hacker,* written by the assistant U.S. Attorney, describes five possible ways to obtain these records:

> Section 2703 of ECPA provides investigators with five mechanisms for compelling an Internet Service Provider to disclose information that might be useful in an investigation of a hacker.
> The mechanisms, in ascending order of the threshold showing required, are described below:

1. Subpoenas can be used by an investigator to obtain basic subscriber information from an Internet Service Provider, including "the name, address, local and long distance telephone toll billing records, telephone number or other subscriber number or identity, and length of service of a subscriber to or customer of such service and the types of service the subscriber or customer utilized." 18 U.S.C. & 2703(c)(1)(C).

2. Subpoenas also can be used to obtain opened e-mails, but only under certain conditions relating to notice to the subscriber. See 18 U.S.C. § 2703(b)(1)(B). Notice may be delayed under Section 2705 for successive 90-day periods. Subpoenas may be issued for e-mails that have been opened, but a search warrant is generally needed for unopened e-mails.

3. Court orders under 18 U.S.C. § 2703(d) can be obtained by investigators for account logs and transactional records. Such orders are available if the agent can provide "articulable facts showing that there are reasonable grounds to believe that the contents of a wire or electronic communication, or the records or other information sought, are relevant and material to an ongoing criminal investigation."

   The government must offer facts, rather than conclusory statements, in an application for a 2703(d) order. A one- to three-page factual summary usually is sufficient for this purpose. The standard for issuing such an order is not as high as for a search warrant.

4. Investigators who obtain a court order under 18 U.S.C. § 2703(d) can obtain the full contents of a subscriber's account (except for unopened e-mail stored with an ISP for 180 days or less and voice-mail), if the order complies with a notice provision in the statute. 18 U.S.C. § 2703(b)(1)(B)(ii) and (b)(2). Notice to the subscriber can be delayed for up to ninety days when notice would seriously jeopardize the investigation. 18 U.S.C. § 2705(a).

5. Search warrants obtained under Rule 41 of the Federal Rules of Criminal Procedure or an equivalent state warrant can be used to obtain the full contents of an account, except for voice-mail in electronic storage (which requires a Title III order). The ECPA does not require notification to the subscriber when the government obtains information from a provider using a search warrant.

   Warrants for information regarding evidence of a computer intrusion are usually obtained like all other search warrants but are served like subpoenas. That is, the agents serving the warrants on an ISP ordinarily do not search through the provider's computers. Instead, they serve the warrants on the provider and the provider produces the material described in it. (Morris 2001)

   Note that there are several instances listed in the preceding five procedures where a **search warrant** is preferable to a simple **subpoena.** Subpoenas aren't good enough for obtaining unopened e-mail messages as listed in paragraph 2. Further, under paragraph 5, the "ECPA does not require notification to the subscriber" when using a search warrant. Although both procedures can request nondisclosure, or at least a delay of disclosure to the defendant, a search warrant has more power.

   A well-written subpoena or search warrant enables the person investigating a high-tech crime to obtain evidence in an efficient manner. Improperly writing a search warrant, or failing to demonstrate probable cause that will justify a search warrant, can cause frustrating delays in an investigation. In the worst-case scenario, a delay of even a few days could result in the permanent loss of damning evidence. A detailed and well-written search warrant example is shown in Figure 6–13.

Although the search warrant in Figure 6–13 might be used for searching property, it could also be used in cases where the search of an offender's home, vehicle, or other property is necessary. Search warrants for computer-based evidence are discussed further in Chapter 9. In the case of many Internet crimes, however, investigators need to obtain records from a business, such as an Internet service provider (ISP). In this case, they either serve a search warrant on the ISP or draft a subpoena for records, if disclosure of that action to the suspect will not harm the investigation. A subpoena for records is still based on demonstrable probable cause. The subpoena, however, merely commands the business to turn records over to law enforcement instead of allowing for investigators to go and conduct an in-person search and/or seizure. Most reputable businesses have a point of contact for subpoena service and a procedure for complying with the orders.

One major factor to consider when utilizing subpoenas and search warrants is the element of secrecy. If an officer drafts a subpoena for records to an ISP, the ISP may have a policy in place that states it will notify the customer that the customer's records have been turned over to law enforcement. This can cause problems in an ongoing case by alerting the suspect that law enforcement is hot on the trail. In the worst-case scenario, this information could give suspects all the advanced notice they need to destroy evidence before law enforcement is able to secure it. This is why many subpoenas for records include language that commands the recipient as follows: "You are not to disclose the nature of this request to anyone." A search warrant with the same language carries more weight relative to nondisclosure orders. As part of the court order, therefore, whoever receives the search warrant cannot lawfully advise the suspect of the search or subsequent action taken by the company in reference to the suspect's account records.

A second factor to consider when gathering documentary evidence is the timeliness of the subpoena for documents. Although many corporations maintain records for years, Internet activity logs maintained by ISPs may be preserved only for a month or two. In the context of an investigation, 30 days is not a long time. An investigator can, therefore, write a **records retention letter,** or data preservation request and send it to the ISP or other record holder, requesting that it maintain records for that account for an extended period of time to assist with the investigation. Investigators should recognize that unless this is explicitly stated in and/or in support of a subpoena and/or search warrant, this letter is essentially a request. Most reputable businesses will likely comply with this request, but such a request is not enforceable. Even if a business receives an enforceable court order, there is no guarantee it won't purge all its data and deny having any stored records, especially if it is a fly-by-night-type organization. Sample language for a records preservation letter is noted in Figure 6–14.

CIRCUIT COURT BRANCH   ANY COUNTY   STATE OF ANY

State Of Any   )
)   SS   **SEARCH WARRANT**
COUNTY OF ANY   )

    THE STATE OF Any, To Detective Joe Blank, a law enforcement officer of the Anytown Police Department:

    Whereas, Detective Joe Blank has this day complained in writing to the said court that certain property located in evidence at the Anytown Police Department, in the City of Anytown, in said county, owned by Joseph K. Suspect, DOB 01-11-61, and more particularly described as follows:

> Compaq Presario 1255 laptop computer, serial # 1345ZXCV0EK, in a black nylon laptop computer case, and identified as exhibit number 2-238-SK for Anytown Police Department case number 05-123456

there are now or will be located and concealed certain things, to wit:

    Internal and peripheral storage devices, to include but not limited to, ROM memory, hard drives, floppy disks, CR-R/RW disks, DVD +/– R/RW disks, compact flash memory cards, memory sticks, and other magnetic media and non-volatile memory storage devices, that can be used to transmit or receive information to or from a computer.

    Records or other items which evidence ownership or use of the above listed computer equipment, including but not limited to, sales receipts or repair receipts.

which is contraband and/or was used in the commission of, or may constitute evidence of illegal activity, to wit:

Any ss948.07	**Child enticement.**
Any ss948.075	**Use of a computer to facilitate a child sex crime.**
Any ss948.09	**Sexual intercourse with a child age 16 or older.**
Any ss948.12	**Possession of child pornography**

and prayed that a search warrant be issued to search said property. For any digital storage media located the search would consist of making a forensic copy of the digital storage media and then conducting a forensic examination and analysis of the evidence files created during the copying process.

    Now, therefore, in the name of the state of Anystate you and any necessary assisting law enforcement personnel are commanded forthwith to search the said property for said things and if the same or any portion

(continued)

Figure 6–13   Example of search warrant.

thereof are found, to bring the same and return this warrant within 48 hours before the said court to be dealt with according to law.

Dated August 14, 2006.

Honorable _____   Honorable _____
Judge of the Circuit Court,
Branch _____   Court Commissioner _____
Any County, Anystate   Any County, Anystate

ENDORSEMENT OF LAW ENFORCEMENT OFFICER
Received by Detective Joe Blank on August 14, 2006, at 6:13 PM.
_____
Detective Joe Blank

CIRCUIT COURT BRANCH   ANY COUNTY   STATE OF ANY

STATE OF ANYSTATE   )
)   SS   **AFFIDAVIT IN SUPPORT OF**
)   **SEARCH WARRANT**
COUNTY OF ANY   )

In the Circuit Court of Any County.

Detective Joe Blank, a law enforcement officer of the City of Anytown Police Department, being duly sworn, says that on August 14, 2006, in and upon certain property located in evidence at the Anytown Police Department, in the City of Anytown, in said county, owned by Joseph K. Suspect, DOB 01-11-61, and more particularly described as follows:

Compaq Presario 1255 laptop computer, serial # 1345ZXCV0EK, in a black nylon laptop computer case, and identified as exhibit number 2-238-SK for Anytown Police Department case number 05-123456

there are now or will be located and concealed certain things, to wit:

Internal and peripheral storage devices, to include but not limited to, ROM memory, hard drives, floppy disks, CR-R/RW disks, DVD +/− R/RW disks, compact flash memory cards, memory sticks, and other magnetic media and non-volatile memory storage devices, that can be used to transmit or receive information to or from a computer.

Records or other items which evidence ownership or use of the above listed computer equipment, including but not limited to, sales receipts or repair receipts.

Figure 6–13   *(Continued)*

which is/are contraband and/or was used in the commission of, or may constitute evidence of illegal activity, to wit:

Any ss948.07	**Child enticement.**
Any ss948.075	**Use of a computer to facilitate a child sex crime.**
Any ss948.09	**Sexual intercourse with a child age 16 or older.**
Any ss948.12	**Possession of child pornography**

The facts tending to establish the grounds for issuing a search warrant are as follows:

On May 31, 2005, I called and spoke with Police Chief Gerald Smith of the Little Town Police Department, LittleTown, ANYSTATE, in reference to a case his agency investigated that involved a missing/endangered 16-yr-old female from Tinyberg, ANYSTATE. That 16-yr-old female, further identified in this affidavit as A.R.E., had been reported missing on May 23, 2005. Based upon information received from the Littletown Police Department on May 25, 2005, Anytown Police Department Officers James and Johnson were dispatched to 319 N. Oakland Ave., lower apt, Anytown, ANYSTATE, to check for A.R.E. A.R.E. was located inside the residence and taken into custody. Also in the apartment at the time was the renter, Joseph K. Suspect, DOB 01-11-61.

Officer James completed an Anytown Police Department incident report and wrote details about this incident. Officer James's details state that he interviewed A.R.E. and she said that she had previously conversed with Mr. Suspect in an Internet chat room. A.R.E. also stated that she sent Mr. Suspect an e-mail message from a residence in Sheboygan on May 21, 2005, asking him to come there and pick her up. A.R.E. said that Mr. Suspect did come to Sheboygan and pick her up and brought her to his apartment at 319 N. Oakland Ave. A.R.E. said that she had never seen Mr. Suspect prior to this encounter. A.R.E. said that she did not have any sexual relations with Mr. Suspect while she stayed at his apartment and said that she slept on the couch and Mr. Suspect slept in his bedroom.

Officer James's details also state that he spoke with Mr. Suspect. When Officer James first spoke with Mr. Suspect he admitted knowing A.R.E. but said she was not at his apartment. Mr. Suspect at first refused to let Officer James and Johnson into the apartment to check for A.R.E. Mr. Suspect then changed his mind and gave Officer James and Johnson permission to search his apartment for A.R.E. Officer James said A.R.E. was located in Mr. Suspect's bedroom. Mr. Suspect told Officer James that he had spoken to A.R.E. in the past

(continued)

using the Internet and also talked about the e-mail he received from A.R.E. asking him to come to Sheboygan to pick her up. Mr. Suspect said he went to Sheboygan and picked up A.R.E. Mr. Suspect said he knew A.R.E. was 16 yr old and denied have any sexual contact with her. Officer James located some pornographic videos in the apartment by the television. Mr. Suspect said he is an exotic dancer and likes pornography. Mr. Suspect said he did not watch any of the pornographic movies with A.R.E.

Chief Smith told me that on May 25, 2005, he contacted A.R.E.'s mother and was able to receive their home computer, as he believed it might contain information on A.R.E.'s whereabouts. Chief Smith told me the computer was turned over to the Anystate Dept. of Justice, DCI (Dept. of Criminal Investigation) to be analyzed.

Chief Smith said that on May 27, 2005, he received a CD containing files that had been copied off of A.R.E.'s home computer by the DCI agents. Chief Smith said the files were text and chat room logs. Chief Smith said that the CD did contain chat logs between A.R.E. and Mr. Suspect. Chief Smith said the chat logs contained discussion about Mr. Suspect wanting to have sex with A.R.E., knowing she was only 15 years old at the time of the chat.

Chief Smith asked for our assistance in obtaining a search warrant for Mr. Suspect's apartment to gather additional computer evidence from Mr. Suspect's computer as well as any evidence that may indicate that sexual contact had occurred between Mr. Suspect and A.R.E. Chief Smith told me that he was meeting with the District Attorney's Office in his jurisdiction regarding possible charges against Mr. Suspect based upon the information contained in these chat logs.

Chief Smith faxed me a copy of his report that contained copies of the chat logs between Mr. Suspect and A.R.E. I read through the chat logs and observed conversation between screen names ash_r_end and stripperinanytown dated March 1, 2005, chat logs between screen names cuttie_stoner_chick and stripperinanytown dated March 2, 2005, chat logs between shaneishott@anytownmail.com and strippin4u@genericmail.com dated March 2, 4, and 7, 2005, and April 20 and 25, 2005. Chief Smith's details explain that he knows A.R.E. uses the screen name ash_r_end and cuttie_stoner_chick. Chief Smith also reports that he believes content of one chat log is from A.R.E. as she describes where she lives and her age. Chief Smith's report also states that he believes the screen name stripperinanytown belongs to Mr. Suspect because the Yahoo screen name stripperingreenbay@yahoo.com is posted on the Web site www.genericexoticdancing.com and that Web page is listed to a Joseph Suspect. Chief Smith states that this Web page also states that Joseph is a student at UWGB and NWTC. Chief Smith states that he was able to confirm that Mr. Suspect is a student at UWGB and NWTC and registration records list

Figure 6–13 (*Continued*)

an e-mail address for Mr. Suspect as stripperingreenbay@yahoo.com and an address of 319 N. Oakland Ave., Anytown. I read through the chat logs and there is talk of sexual contact occurring between the two screen names and specifically getting together Memorial Day weekend to have sex together.

On June 01, 2005, I called and spoke with Chief Smith. Chief Smith told me that the Any County District Attorney's Office had issued an arrest warrant for Joseph K. Suspect, DOB 01-11-61, for Child Enticement and Use of a computer to facilitate a child sex crime. Chief Smith asked that we take Mr. Suspect into custody. Chief Smith faxed me a copy of the warrant and criminal complaint.

On June 01, 2005, I spoke with Officer James. Officer James told me that he entered Mr. Suspect's residence using the front door. Officer James told me that he observed one computer in the residence. He said the computer was located in Mr. Suspect's bedroom.

On June 2, 2005, I spoke with Officer Johnson. Officer Johnson told me that he also saw the computer in Mr. Suspect's bedroom. Officer Johnson said the computer monitor screen was blank, but the URL address for the Web page contained the word *sex*. He did not remember the exact Web page address.

On June 2, 2005, at approximately 1:30 pm I along with other officers of the Anytown Police Department executed a search warrant at Mr. Suspect's residence located at 319 N. Oakland Ave., lower apartment. Mr. Suspect was not home at the time. A number of items were taken as evidence during the search of Mr. Suspect's residence, including a desktop computer.

On June 5, 2005, at approximately 7:59 am Anytown Police Department officers James and Weiss stopped Mr. Suspect as he drove away from his residence in his 1997 Ford Focus, Anystate license #WXK905. Officer James took Mr. Suspect into custody for the arrest warrants issued by Any County. Officer James conducted a search of Mr. Suspect's vehicle and located a laptop computer. Officer James was aware of the search warrant I executed at Mr. Suspect's apartment on June 2, 2005, and familiar with the investigation. Officer James confiscated the laptop computer from Mr. Suspect's vehicle because he believed it may contain evidence related to the investigation. Officer James placed the laptop into evidence at the Anytown Police Department and identified it with exhibit #2-238-SK.

I have received reports and information from officers of other police departments in the past and have found the information to be truthful and accurate. I also have received reports and information from Officers James and Johnson in the past and found the information to be truthful and accurate.

(continued)

Based upon my training and experience as a detective with the Anytown Police Department assigned to the Computer Forensic Unit and doing computer forensic investigations I know that chat logs can be stored on a computer, and even if the logs have been deleted, they may still be recovered. Based upon this, I believe Mr. Suspect's computer may still contain chat log evidence related to this investigation. The files maintained on a computer may also be transferred or copied to other types of digital storage media, such as CDs, DVDs, USB devices, etc. It may also be necessary to view certain file types with the software that produced it or to use certain peripheral devices to reproduce evidence. Mr. Suspect stated to Officer James that he likes pornography. Based upon my training and experience individuals involved in sexual crimes against children may possess child pornography images or photographs of the child victim. These individuals will then save and preserve this material.

Figure 6–13　(*Continued*)

The previous section on documentary evidence assumes that records are actually available for gathering and compilation. A search warrant to a reputable business will ensure access to those materials and can also prevent the suspect from knowing that investigators have gathered them. In many cases, this evidence will not paint the entire picture, and in others there may not be any useful evidence to gather. The investigator then must fall back on traditional skills for assembling as many other pieces of the puzzle as possible.

Learner Activity

Search warrants and subpoenas can be lengthy and complicated to write, particularly when discussing technical devices and operations. It is usually easiest, particularly for a novice warrant writer, to use a template or other predesigned search warrant language. It is very likely that warrant language already exists for the materials an investigator may wish to seize. Instead of writing definitions of technical components and terms from scratch, it would be easier and less mistake-prone to use government definitions for terms. For this activity, go to Google or another search engine and conduct an Internet search for sample search warrant language. Another excellent place to start is "Searching and Seizing Computers and Obtaining Electronic Evidence in Criminal Investigations," at www.usdoj.gov/criminal/cybercrime/s&smanual2002.pdf. This federal government manual has numerous terms already defined, including Internet, Internet Relay Chat, and IP address. For this activity, compile sample search warrant language from at least three different sources. List three different sections of example search warrant language and cite its source within your document. This

Dear   :

I am writing to [confirm our telephone conversation earlier today and to] make a formal request for the preservation of records and other evidence pursuant to 18 U.S.C. § 2703(f) pending further legal process.

You are hereby requested to preserve, for a period of 90 days, the records described below currently in your possession, including records stored on backup media, in a form that includes the complete record. You also are requested not to disclose the existence of this request to the subscriber or any other person, other than as necessary to comply with this request. **If compliance with this request may result in a permanent or temporary termination of service to the accounts described below, or otherwise alert the subscriber or user of these accounts as to your actions to preserve the referenced files and records, please contact me before taking such actions.**

This request applies only retrospectively. It does not in any way obligate you to capture and preserve new information that arises after the date of this request.

This preservation request applies to the following records and evidence:

A. All stored communications and other files reflecting communications to or from [e-mail account / user name / IP address or domain name (between DATE1 at TIME1 and DATE2 at TIME2)];

B. All files that have been accessed by [e-mail account / user name / IP address or domain name (between DATE1 at TIME1 and DATE2 at TIME2)] or are controlled by user accounts associated with [e-mail account / user name / IP address or domain name (between DATE1 at TIME1 and DATE2 at TIME2)];

C. All connection logs and records of user activity for [e-mail account /user name / IP address or domain name (between DATE1 at TIME1 and DATE2 at TIME2)], including:

  1. Connection date and time;

  2. Disconnect date and time;

  3. Method of connection (e.g., Telnet, FTP, HTTP);

  4. Type of connection (e.g., modem, cable / DSL, T1/LAN);

  5. Data transfer volume;

  6. User name associated with the connection and other connection information, including the Internet Protocol address of the source of the connection;

(continued)

Figure 6–14 Sample language for preservation request letters.

7. Telephone caller identification records;

8. Records of files or system attributes accessed, modified, or added by the user;

9. Connection information for other computers to which the user of the [e-mail account / user name / IP address or domain name (between DATE1 at TIME1 and DATE2 at TIME2)] connected, by any means, during the connection period, including the destination IP address, connection time and date, disconnect time and date, method of connection to the destination computer, the identities (account and screen names) and subscriber information, if known, for any person or entity to which such connection information relates, and all other information related to the connection from ISP or its subsidiaries.

All records and other evidence relating to the subscriber(s), customer(s), account holder(s), or other entity(ies) associated with [e-mail account / user name / IP address or domain name (between DATE1 at TIME1 and DATE2 at TIME2)], including, without limitation, subscriber names, user names, screen names or other identities, mailing addresses, residential addresses, business addresses, e-mail addresses and other contact information, telephone numbers or other subscriber number or identifier number, billing records, information about the length of service and the types of services the subscriber or customer utilized, and any other identifying information, whether such records or other evidence are in electronic or other form.

Any other records and other evidence relating to [e-mail account / user name / IP address or domain name (between DATE1 at TIME1 and DATE2 at TIME2)]. Such records and other evidence include, without limitation, correspondence and other records of contact by any person or entity about the above-referenced account, the content and connection logs associated with or relating to postings, communications and any other activities to or through [e-mail account / user name / IP address or domain name (between DATE1 at TIME1 and DATE2 at TIME2)], whether such records or other evidence are in electronic or other form.

Very truly yours,

_____

Assistant United States Attorney

Figure 6–14 (*Continued*)

Source: U.S. Department of Justice. 2002. Searching and seizing computers and obtaining electronic evidence in criminal investigations. www.usdoj.gov/criminal/cybercrime/s&smanual2002.pdf (accessed May 5, 2005).

activity will give you a head start on assembling your own search warrant templates by demonstrating that search warrant language can be located and saved for future use in a search warrant template. A good search warrant template can save investigators a great deal of time.

6.6 TRADITIONAL INVESTIGATIVE TECHNIQUES

One problem that plagues those who investigate high-tech crimes is how to place blame on the human being who was using the computer at the time the crime was committed. In other words, investigators can trace the criminal activity to a specific IP address or a specific computer, but how can they prove who was sitting at that computer at the time of the crime? One term often used to describe this phenomenon is **PEBCAK.** This acronym stands for *problem exists between the chair and the keyboard.* This term was initially used in help desk circles by computer professionals. If the help desk received numerous calls from one person, they would often joke that there was no problem with the computer, only with its user. In some cases, with particularly troublesome users, they might even make a notation in that user's call files using the PEBCAK acronym so that other help desk staffers would realize the true nature of the problem.

In many cases, investigators can solve this problem only by utilizing traditional investigative techniques such as interview, interrogation, the process of elimination, and alibi confirmation/destruction. One of the easiest ways to prove a specific person committed an act is to eliminate the possibility that anyone else could have been on that computer at that time. This is effective because it is highly unlikely that a savvy criminal will simply admit to committing the crime. One way of determining this is discovering whether the computer is available to the public. Is there more than one user name and account password on the system? Does the system have a power-on password or biometric security system? Is the computer located in a private residence with access only open to the resident(s)? If the suspect user routinely allows others access to his or her computer, what are their names, dates of birth, and have they been interviewed? Is the content of the e-mail or other online activity specific to that sender? Are other personality traits, speech patterns, or mannerisms included in the text that are indicative of the suspect user? These are all examples of starting-point questions to help isolate the suspect users and eliminate the possibility of other users.

Another potential hurdle to the investigation could be the use of a public computer, such as those found in public libraries and educational institutions. Similar to the old problem of tracing bomb threats or prank calls to pay phones, this scenario poses its own challenge to the high-tech crime investigator. One thing that assists investigators is that many such institutions require users to sign in and out of the computer lab using photo identification, and they maintain logs of the users. If an institution is strict in using this procedure, it can make the investigator's job very easy. Unfortunately, many institutions either have no such policy or are very lax in their enforcement of it. Further compounding the problem is the trend of educational centers providing campus-wide wireless Internet connections.

6.7 WIRELESS NETWORKS AND WARDRIVING

A rapidly growing problem facing investigators of Internet crime is the widespread availability of **open wireless networks,** commonly referred to as **Wi-Fi.** One can hardly drive around with a wireless-capable laptop computer without noting the presence of dozens, if not hundreds, of open wireless networks. In some cases, the networks are left open intentionally as a customer service to a particular business's patrons. For example, many popular coffee shops are also Internet cafés where users can use a wide open wireless network to connect to the Internet to browse Web sites, check e-mail, or perform just about any other Internet task. Any online communication sent from a wireless network will be traced to the Internet café because its router assigned temporary IP addresses to the suspect user's computer. Hotels, airports, and other transportation depots are also providing Wi-Fi service. These businesses generally do not keep track of who their network users are.

Another type of open network is the kind that is left open and vulnerable either by oversight or a lack of technical knowledge on the part of the operator. It is not uncommon for many home users simply to accept the default security settings of their new wireless router out of the box. One may easily find open networks with router names of "default" or in many cases the brand name of the router, such as "Linksys" simply by driving around with a wireless-enabled laptop. There are also numerous programs to aid in searching for and documenting open networks. One example of such a program is called NetStumbler. It locates and logs the open networks it discovers. There is also a smaller version of the program for use on a wireless-enabled personal digital assistant (PDA) or similar device. Most wireless-enabled laptops automatically seek out wireless networks and advise the user when a wireless network is detected. Some laptops even come preconfigured to auto connect to an available wireless source.

The problem with users not securing their personal wireless routers is that any illegal Internet activity performed by someone connected to that network may be traced back to the router owner, not to the true criminal who used the connection. There are cases of suspects downloading child pornography while parked outside of a private residence, siphoning off that household's wireless connection. Because they are using someone else's connection these suspects are much more elusive and difficult, if not impossible, to track. In some cases, only good old-fashioned police work, such as canvassing a neighborhood for descriptions and license plates of suspicious vehicles seen in the area, can give investigators leads as to a suspect's identity. It is in all users' best interest to secure their networks to avoid having a search warrant served at their residence based on Internet activity on their wireless router. Securing a wireless router or other wireless access point is the responsibility of the network's owner. Failing to secure a wireless network could cause a number of headaches for wireless network owners, especially if illegal activity, such as the downloading of child pornography, is traced back to their network. The trend seems to be toward more Wi-Fi networks, not fewer. Many municipalities have Wi-Fi service citywide, and the day is coming when most urban areas will have hotspots or connection points in most areas.

An example of how having an open wireless network is problematic is the case of Auburn University. During an online vote for Miss Homecoming in 2004, it was discovered that 37 students' votes had been cast fraudulently for them after someone obtained the students' Social Security numbers. The victims did not know this had happened until they tried to log on and cast their own vote, at which time they were advised on screen that they had already voted. The school's director of Information Technology traced the votes back to an IP address. The investigation stalled, however, when it was discovered that this IP address belonged to an open network in a residential area cul-de-sac. Numerous students who live within the estimated range of the open network were questioned, particularly those who had been known to use the network in the past. No one admitted wrongdoing, and without further evidence the public safety department has not been able to bring charges (Evans and McVay 2004). Although this example seems relatively harmless on the face of it, it is important to remember that this particular incident involves 37 counts of identity theft in the form of stolen Social Security numbers and also demonstrates the protection offered by the cloak of anonymity associated with wireless networks. Although the identity information was used only for a relatively minor fraud in fixing the homecoming election, the information could just as easily been used to obtain loans, goods, or other services in the stolen names.

Open networks are a relatively new phenomenon, but have also spawned related problems. In a process called **wardriving,** a user drives around an urban area, say a business district, looking for and noting all open networks in that area. If the wardriver wants to share this information, he or she might engage in **warchalking,** the process of making marks on the sidewalk or buildings to tell other wireless users where an open network is available. Wardriving and war chalking encourage and facilitate the exploitation of open networks, and open networks are problematic for law enforcement when they are used to commit crimes online. Further, a business is exposing its network to potential infiltration by making it readily accessible wirelessly from some distance away, removing one layer of security against potential theft of intellectual property. For this reason alone, many companies forbid the use of Wi-Fi networks in their computer security policies. A keyword search for "wardriving" or similar terms will reveal several Web sites devoted to the topic, including wardriving maps to find open networks at any location.

In an effort to combat this anonymity, and the potential safe haven it offers computer criminals, some cities have recently taken the extraordinary step of requiring businesses to secure their networks. One such law, proposed in Westchester County, New York, states that businesses offering "public Internet access" must have minimum security measures installed, including installing a firewall for their network and changing the default network name (Scannell 2006). Because Wi-Fi is a relatively new technology, there are sure to be cases and challenges associated with these networks. Case law and other regulations of these networks are forthcoming and evolving.

■ SUMMARY

This chapter focuses on the structure of the global information network called the Internet and the way that information travels across it. It also examines specific laws and cases dealing with Internet communications. The real heart of the matter for the first responder, however, is the methods employed to actually follow the path that the data traveled so its source can be found. Once the source ISP is found, the investigator can compel the production of records to further cement the case. Those materials can then be used to justify a search warrant for the search and seizure of a suspect's computer. Taking the suspect's computer away is a very good thing; however, this chapter also focuses on what to watch out for when this is required. By following the procedures outlined and always making sure not to deprive suspects of legitimate work products, investigators can gather needed evidence to prosecute the case while avoiding a lawsuit.

■ REVIEW QUESTIONS

1. IP addresses are broken down into _____ sections called octets, which are separated by _____.
2. IP addresses consist of numbers between _____ and _____.
3. Discuss the concept of dynamic allocation of IP addresses and how it can be compared to bowling.
4. What does *GMT* refer to and why are time and date stamps extremely important in tracking and tracing Internet crimes?
5. List the names of the two major federal statutes relating to tracing Internet crimes. Briefly discuss what each statute intends to accomplish.
6. What is the difference between a brief e-mail header and the full e-mail header?
7. What is a WHOIS query and what information does it provide an investigator?
8. What is a confirmed e-mail and how is it utilized by investigators?
9. Which method of compelling information disclosure is better, a subpoena for documents or a search warrant? Why is it better?
10. What is PEBCAK and how can an investigator deal with it?
11. What problems do wireless networks pose for investigators? How can these be overcome?

■ TERMS

block of IP addresses	chat	full headers
brief headers	Electronic Communications Privacy Act (ECPA)	*Hall v. Earthlink*

ICQ
Instant messaging (IM)
intentional intercept
Internet Service Provider (ISP)
octet
open wireless networks
PEBCAK
Privacy Protection Act (PPA)

range of IP addresses
records retention letter
search warrant
Steve Jackson Games
subpoena
timestamps
Voice over IP (VoIP)
warchalking

wardriving
Web-based e-mail
WHOIS query
Wi-Fi
work product
  materials

■ REFERENCES

Children's Internet Protection Act. 42 U.S.C. § 8323 (2000).

Electronic Communications Privacy Act. 18 U.S.C. §2510–2522 (1986 revised 2006).

Evans, Lindsay, and McVay, Richard. 2004. Seven questioned, none charged in online voting investigation. Auburn University, Auburn, AL: *Auburn Plainsman*, March 11.

Morris, Daniel A. 2001. Tracking a computer hacker. U.S. Department of Justice. www.usdoj.gov/criminal/cybercrime/usamay2001_2.htm (accessed September 27, 2006).

Peter Hall and Big Bad Productions, Inc. v. Earthlink Network, Inc. 04-0384-cv (2d Cir. 2004). www.ca2.uscourts.gov/ (accessed January 16, 2006).

Privacy Protection Act. 42 U.S.C. §2000aa (2004).

Scannell, Tim. 2006. Lawmakers crack down on Wi-Fi crime. InternetNews, April 26. www.Internetnews.com/wireless/article.php/3601886 (accessed June 16, 2006).

Wisconsin Statutes and Annotations. §947.0125 (2004).

chapter seven

Pedophiles, Online Child Enticement, and Child Pornography

■ LEARNING OBJECTIVES

1. To define the disease of pedophilia and profile a common pedophile.
2. To explore the three personality classifications of pedophiles.
3. To explore the modus operandi of a pedophile's child enticement acts in traditional and online settings.
4. To learn about law enforcement efforts and methods to combat online child enticement.
5. To define child pornography and explore criminal statutes against it.
6. To define child pornographers' modus operandi and potential challenges to prosecution.
7. To explore the law enforcement response to child pornography.

Sex offenders are one type among a host of Internet-based predators. **Pedophiles** have been around for all or most of recorded history—mention of grown men having sexual relations with boys appears in ancient Greek writings and Egyptian hieroglyphics. The older term, **paederast** (a man who has intercourse with a boy), comes from two Greek words, *pais/paid* the word for "child," and *erastes*, the word for "lover." Most people are probably more familiar with the term *paedophile*, which is an adult who is sexually attracted to children. In modern spelling, the *a* is dropped, yielding the word *pedophile*.

In modern times, numerous media accounts describe children being approached, abducted, sexually assaulted, and oftentimes murdered afterward. One can hardly turn on a news program or visit a news Web site without seeing a story on **pedophilia.** This problem appears to be getting worse instead of better, and the use of the Internet certainly exacerbates this problem. According to *Highlights of the Youth Internet Safety Survey* conducted by the U.S. Department of Justice, "one in five children (10 to 17 years old) receives unwanted sexual solicitations online." The study from June 2000 also finds that 1 in 33 received an "aggressive sexual solicitation" defined as the subject asking for a physical meeting, calling the youth on the telephone, or sending gifts, money, or mail. One in 33 may not sound like a large number, but that represents approximately 3% of all respondents. The U.S. Census Bureau estimates there are approximately 72 million children in the United States. Even if only half of them used the Internet, 3% of 36 million is 1,080,000 potential victims of online child enticement. These numbers paint a very dark picture of the online world. This chapter discusses how pedophiles work and how law enforcement can work to stop them. The Internet and its inherent anonymity have emboldened sexual predators; it is now up to law enforcement to establish a noticeable presence online and deter this behavior.

7.1 PROFILING A PREDATORY PEDOPHILE

The July 2000 report from the U.S. Department of Justice Bureau of Justice Statistics (2002) titled "Sexual Assault of Young Children as Reported to Law Enforcement: Victim, Incident, and Offender Characteristics," reveals sex offender profile information. This study found, "Nearly all of the offenders in sexual assaults reported to law enforcement were male (96%)." In regard to the age of the offender, the study found that "overall, 23% of sexual assault offenders were under age 18 and 77% were adults." Therefore, in most cases, the pedophile sex offender is an adult male.

It is important to note that the vast majority of pedophiles are men, but that does not mean that pedophilia is limited only to men. There have been several famous examples of female schoolteachers having sexual relations with 13- and 14-year-old male students. Figures from the Bureau of Justice Statistics appear to indicate, however, that women are more likely to sexually assault younger victims and are very unlikely to assault adults.

Pedophilia is a documented psychological disorder and is described and defined in the *Diagnostic and Statistic Manual of Mental Disorders—4th Edition,* commonly known in psychology circles as the *DSM-IV.* According to the *DSM-IV,* three criteria must be met for a diagnosis of pedophilia. The criteria are paraphrased here in simple language:

1. For at least a half year, the person has experienced sexual fixation, fantasizing, or sexual activities with a preadolescent child.
2. The fixations, fantasizing, or activities will have caused problems for the pedophile in the person's public life, job, or some other important area. Examples could include arrest, termination of employment, divorce, and so forth.
3. The pedophile must be 16 years old or older, and the victim (or fantasized victim) must be a minimum of 5 years younger than the pedophile. (American Psychiatric Association 2000)

Most psychologists agree that there is no known cure for pedophilia, but some believe that some of the symptoms can be controlled or limited. Some advocate the use of hormone therapy to try to limit the manifestation of sexual desire in the pedophile. Others believe that pedophilia can only be dealt with "one day at a time" and that the pedophile must learn how to limit his or her desire much the same way an alcoholic struggles each day not to take a drink. One thing is certain, however; many people are pedophiles, and many of them commit sexual crimes against children. Many of them are arrested for their crimes, serve time, and are later arrested for a similar crime again. The rate of recidivism for pedophiles is extraordinarily high. Sex offenders are four times more likely to be rearrested for another sex crime than released nonsex offenders are (Langan, Schmitt, and Durose 2003). In some cases, pedophiles also kill their victims after sexually assaulting them.

7.2 ACTIVITY CLASSIFICATIONS OF PEDOPHILES

Pedophiles can be further broken down into thee categories, each more dangerous than the last. The first category is the **secretive pedophile.** This person may appear to be totally normal, may be married, may have children of his or her own, and may never sexually assault a child. These pedophiles still embody the trait of becoming sexually aroused by children, but may never act on it. If they do act upon their urges, they may limit their action to acquiring child pornography for the purposes of sexual gratification.

The second type of pedophile is the **child pornography collector.** This person is an avid collector of child pornography for sexual gratification and for trading these illicit images or videoes to other pedophiles. This person may also never physically victimize a child, although possessing a photograph or video of child or sharing it with others victimizes that child one viewing at a time, albeit at a somewhat milder level. Some have argued that the secretive pedophile and child pornography collector are just as bad as the third category of pedophile, described later, because they are fueling the market demand for illicit child pornography. This ultimately results in children being victimized in an effort to create a large enough supply of these materials.

The third and most dangerous type of pedophile is the **active pedophile.** This is the person who performs some physical act against a child or several children. The active pedophile is one of the people who actually create or manufacture child pornography by photographing or taking video of sexual acts against or with a child. The active pedophile is also likely to keep souvenirs from victims such as the victim's underwear or other articles of clothing. This is the pedophile that fits the stereotype of the "dirty old man in a van who gives out candy" to little kids. In the past, this stereotype is what people envisioned the pedophile child enticer to be.

7.3 MODUS OPERANDI OF THE ACTIVE PREDATORY PEDOPHILE

In the days before the Internet, pedophiles had no choice but to try and approach potential victims in person. They could, for example, park their vehicle near a school, playground, or other area where children frequented and try to get a victim's attention by asking directions, pretending to need help, passing out candy, or doing something else likely to draw attention from a child victim without arousing general alarm.

Traditionally, pedophiles have also tended to look for vocations that allow them the advantages of working with children and acquiring a position of trust and responsibility. There have been many examples of this in recent years such as stories about predatory teachers, clergy, athletics coaches, and yes, even police officers. In addition to implied trust, these occupations also have another advantage for a would-be pedophile: a perception of power or control. In the case of clergy, the belief that the clergy member is doing God's work can be a very powerful force in motivating a naïve youngster to do as the offender says. Likewise with a teacher or police officer there is a certain aura of power or authority, and the victim may fear repercussions in the form of bad grades, expulsion from school, or even arrest. The offender may take further advantage of the victim's perception of inferiority by making threats or telling the victim that no one would believe the victim's story over that of a "respected" police officer or teacher. Add to all of this the fact the most children are constantly reminded to listen to and respect adults, and the child victim is in a very vulnerable position.

In addition to exercising their positional superiority, pedophiles make use of another technique to prepare their victims. This process of breaking down a victim's barriers or objections is called **grooming** the victim. This is not grooming in the traditional sense—combing hair, brushing teeth, and so forth. *Grooming,* in this sense, is the process of preparing a victim, overcoming the victim's sense of right and wrong, and lowering the victim's inhibitions about a sexual act. For example, if a sex offender wants to have sexual intercourse with a young child, he may show that child numerous images of child pornography to desensitize the child. Then, he will appeal to the child's naïve logic and say something like, "It can't be wrong if they are all doing it." In the case of an older victim, the pedophile may show images or videos of other teens engaged in sexual conduct. It is widely believed that pornography desensitizes the pedophile as well, and this can actually cause a cycle of pedophilia, similar to a narcotics addiction. Pedophiles will eventually believe there is nothing wrong with their pedophilia if they become desensitized enough. Some even believe they are simply more enlightened than the rest of society is in regards to sexual relations with children. Organizations have formed around this concept, such as NAMBLA, the North American Man/Boy Love Association. On the group's Web site, Nambla.org, the organization states as one of its goals "To end the extreme oppression of men and boys in mutually consensual relationships." Most state legislatures, however, recognize that children are incapable of giving knowledgeable consent for sexual relations until they reach the age of majority, usually 18 years of age.

7.4 ONLINE PREDATION AND CHILD ENTICEMENT

Pedophiles operate online in a wide variety of ways, and the online mechanism of anonymous communications can be a very powerful ally. **Online child enticement** statistics are truly frightening and demonstrate that this type of activity has increased tremendously. Studies have estimated that approximately 1 out of every 5 children 10 to 17 years old receives an unwanted sexual solicitation each year (Office of Juvenile Justice and Delinquency Prevention 2001).

In the past, a pedophile would have to go to a park or school and try in person to talk to a child one child at a time. Think of going fishing using one fishing pole. Then, compare that to talking to hundreds of different kids every day in an online chat room, where anonymity can be maintained. This is similar to casting a wide commercial fishing net into a large body of water. A sex offender may entice so many potential victims to respond that he or she may actually have to work to filter choices to a more manageable number before determining which victims to try to meet in the real world. The larger pool of potential victims and the feeling of anonymity likely emboldens pedophiles and exacerbates the problem of child enticement and sexual assault.

Emboldened pedophiles online also have one other advantage. They can gradually introduce themselves to younger children. In person, it is obvious right away that they are much older than their victim, or are "scary looking," or perhaps even physically unattractive. Online they can portray whatever persona they devise using names and photos they choose. A male pedophile who likes teenage boys might even pose online as an attractive female and propose a meeting with the unwitting victim. By the time the victim sees the true form of the pedophile, it will be too late. The wider net, the feeling of anonymity, the ability to transfer photos and videos almost instantly, and the emboldened pedophile are an explosive combination that law enforcement must address in a proactive manner.

One of the ways law enforcement can combat these trends is to establish a proactive presence online. Online communications, including chat rooms, have their own jargon or abbreviated language. There are too many abbreviations and variants to describe here; however, many common ones are used by sex offenders. Law enforcement should become familiar with such online jargon. One such example is the shorthand text **A/S/L**, or asl?. If someone sends a message that says A/S/L, they are asking for the recipient's age, sex, and location. This is a very common online question because people usually seek out someone to chat with in their age group, of their gender, and somewhere in their area, and it is very often on the first line of a communication someone sends or may come just after the initial greeting. In addition to its legitimate use, this phrase is a perfect tool for the sex predator because it filters potential victims from the thousands of potential victims online by quickly determining if the other party is close by and is a member of the offender's preferred victim age and gender. Other examples of online shorthand include LOL (laugh out loud) and 1..2..3..4..5, which is a shorthand warning to other people in the chat room that means, "keep the language clean, my parents are watching." Responsible parents and teachers should be aware of this particular shorthand message because its use may indicate unlawful or inappropriate activity in the chat session (see Figure 7–1).

Figure 7–1 is just an abbreviated list of common chat jargon or slang that can be found in various chat room environments. A keyword search for "common chat jargon," "chat slang," or "Internet slang" can reveal several pages with many more examples and definitions.

Once a person of the right age and gender is located, the pedophile may quickly turn to the topic of sex or pornography. Often sex predators will ask victims if they have a photograph of themselves and will ask to see it. They may provide victims an e-mail address to send the photograph to. This online exchange is a two-way street, naturally, and the offender may then send a picture to the victim, too. In some cases, predators may represent themselves as a boy or girl of the same age as the victim, assuming a false identity and sending a bogus photograph. Often they will also begin the process of grooming potential victims by e-mailing images of pornography or child pornography to them.

After some days, weeks, or even months of communications, the last step is to try to set up a real-world meeting between themselves and a victim. In some cases, the offender will invite the victim to some event such as a rock concert or sporting event. In other cases, the pedophile will be explicit, asking to meet for sex. In most cases, the offender will meet the victim and sexually assault him or her. In some cases, an offender might kidnap the victim and repeatedly sexually assault the child. In the worst cases, offenders kidnap, rape, and finally kill a victim. The best possible outcome is for the offender to show up intending to assault a victim only to discover that he is actually meeting a police officer who performed an undercover child enticement sting. Some defendants have attempted to argue that they should not be charged as a result of these stings because no actual victim exists. They argue that because they had actually been communicating with an adult (the undercover officer), there was no ability or intent to harm a child.

Letters and numbers are often interchangeable:

1—Won or one (1dr = wonder, 1drful = wonderful)

2—Too, to, or two

3—The letter E (I s33 U = I see you)

4—For, four, fore (b4 = before, b4warned = be forewarned)

8—Used for a pair of eyes, glasses, and to mean taking pictures

9—A good thing (i.e., she dressed to the 9s = she is all dressed up)

Some combinations of numbers have their own meanings:

12345	Warning, other people around (parents), keep it clean
10-4	Message acknowledged
224	Today, tomorrow, forever
46	Pleased to meet you
20	Your location
143	I love you
420/4life	Marijuana
53x	Sex

Some combinations of letters have their own meaning:

A/S/L	Age, sex, location	FOAD	**** off and die
NSL	Name, sex, location	FOTCL	Falling off the chair laughing
ASLP	Age, sex, location, picture	FYEO	For your eyes only
AWHFY	Are we having fun yet?	GAL	Get a life
BAK	Back at the keyboard	GFETE	Grinning from ear to ear
BRB	Be right back	GNOC	Get naked on cam
BBS	Be back soon	HAGN	Have a good night
CAD	Control, Alt, Delete	HF	Have fun
CWYL	Chat with you later	HSWM	Have sex with me
CYO	See you online	IAG	I am gay
DIKU	Do I know you?	IBM	I'm buck naked
DND	Do not disturb	IHU	I hate you
DYK	Do you know	JJWY	Just joking with you
EG	Evil grin	JK	Just kidding
EMSG	E-mail message	JP	Just playing
EYC	Excitable, yet calm	KB	Kiss back
F/F	Face to face	KMB	Kiss my butt

Figure 7–1 Common chat jargon. *(continued)*

KPC	Keeping parent clueless	RUMOF	Are you male or female?
LBR	Little boys room	RUTTM	Are you talking to me?
LMIRL	Lets meet in real life	SH	So hot, or same here
LTR	Long-term relationship	SHMILY	See how much I love you
MB	Maybe	SO	Significant other
MYOB	Mind your own business	TAW	Teachers are watching
MWBRL	More will be revealed later	THTH	Too hot to handle
NIFOC	Nude in front of computer	TMS	Too much showing
NC	Not cool	URAQT	You are a cutie
NOYB	None of your business	VBG	Very big grin
OLL	Online love	VBS	Very big smile
OBTW	Oh, by the way	WTGP	Want to go private
OOC	Out of character	WUF	Where are you from?
PAW	Parents are watching	WYRN	What you see is
PM	Private message		what you get
POS	Parents over shoulder	YWTHM	You want to hug me
QT	Cutie	YWTLM	You want to love me
RAT	Remote activated Trojan	YWTKM	You want to kiss me

Figure 7–1 *(Continued)*

These defense arguments have been routinely defeated because the court generally determines that, although no actual child victim exists, the defendant did not know that fact at the time, and therefore the defendant's intent remained the same. This is similar to many cases that are charged as an attempted crime. The mere fact that the defendant is either incompetent or unsuccessful is not a valid defense against charges. This was the nature of the defense presented in a Wisconsin Case, *Wisconsin v. Robins* (see Figure 7–2).

Overview of State Laws on Child Enticement Involving a Computer

All 50 states have statutes outlawing the use of a computer to commit a sex crime against a child. Although the statutes have slightly different titles and terminology, they are united in their purpose to outlaw using computers for locating, grooming, or luring underage victims. The chapter locations of many states are summarized briefly below.

Alabama—Ala. Code §§ 13A-6-110 to 111—Soliciting a child by computer for the purposes of committing a sexual act and transmitting obscene material to a child by computer.
Arkansas—Ark. Code § 5-27-603—Knowingly utilizes a computer online service, Internet service, or local bulletin board service to seduce, solicit, lure, or entice or attempt to seduce, solicit, lure, or entice a child or another individual believed by the person to be a child, to engage in sexually explicit conduct.

"¶1. DIANE S. SYKES, J. This is a prosecution for attempted child enticement arising out of an Internet "sting" operation by the Department of Justice (DOJ). The primary issue is whether the child enticement statute is violated when there is no actual child victim, but, rather, an adult government agent posing online as a child."

"¶3. We conclude that an attempted child enticement under Wis. Stat. § 948.07 (1999–2000) may be charged where the intervening extraneous factor that makes the offense an attempted rather than completed crime is the fact that unbeknownst to the defendant, the "victim" is not a child at all, but an adult posing as a child."

The chat room conversation transcript kept by the investigation shows the following:

Benjm13: ru my age
Benjm13: im 13
Wl4kink: no older

[Later in a conversation]

Wl4kink: cool so how would we ever meet?
Benjm13: i dont know u can come here if u want
Wl4kink: ya that is true
Wl4kink: you have a place we could go?
Benjm13: just my house but thats scary
Wl4kink: ya it would be, specially [sic] if someone comes home :)
Benjm13: wow not cool
Wl4kink: no
Benjm13: i dont know were [sic] to go
Wl4kink: could just get a room somewhere
Benjm13: oh that would be cool—like a motel
Wl4kink: yup
[Robins acknowledged that what he was proposing to do was illegal:]
Benjm13: im getting nervus [sic] already
Wl4kink: ok I understand well I am a little to [sic] this isn't legal you know
Benjm13: i geus [sic] so

Figure 7–2 Chat room investigation case study: *Wisconsin v. Robins* 00-2841-CR (2002).

California—Cal. Penal Code § 288.2—Making criminal the act of knowingly sending harmful matter (as defined in Section 313) to a minor through the Internet, "with the intent of arousing, appealing to, or gratifying the lust or passions or sexual desires of that person or of a minor, and with the intent, or for the purpose of seducing a minor . . .".

Connecticut—Conn. Gen. Stat. § 53a-90a—A person is guilty of enticing a minor when such person uses an interactive computer service to knowingly persuade, induce, entice or coerce any person under sixteen years of age to engage in prostitution or sexual activity for which the actor may be charged with a criminal offense. For purposes of this section, "interactive computer service" means any information service, system or access software provider that provides or enables computer access by multiple users to a computer server, including specifically a service or system that provides access to the Internet and such systems operated or services offered by libraries or educational institutions. Enticing a minor is a class A misdemeanor for a first offense, a class D felony for a second offense and a class C felony for any subsequent offense.

Delaware—Del. Code. tit. 11 § 1112A—Sexual solicitation of child.

Florida—Fla. Stat. § 847.0135—Any person who knowingly utilizes a computer on-line service, Internet service, or local bulletin board service to seduce, solicit, lure, or entice, or attempt to seduce, solicit, lure, or entice, a child or another person believed by the person to be a child, to commit any illegal act described in chapter 794, relating to sexual battery; chapter 800, relating to lewdness and indecent exposure; or chapter 827, relating to child abuse, commits a felony of the third degree.

Georgia—Ga. Code § 16-12-100.2—It shall be unlawful for any person intentionally or willfully to utilize a computer on-line service, Internet service, or local bulletin board service to seduce, solicit, lure, or entice, or attempt to seduce, solicit, lure, or entice a child or another person believed by such person to be a child, to commit any illegal act described in Code Section 16-6-2, relating to the offense of sodomy or aggravated sodomy; Code Section 16-6-4, relating to the offense of child molestation or aggravated child molestation; Code Section 16-6-5, relating to the offense of enticing a child for indecent purposes; or Code Section 16-6-8, relating to the offense of public indecency; or to engage in any conduct that by its nature is an unlawful sexual offense against a child.

Hawaii—Rev. Stat. § 707.756, 707.757—Electronic enticement of a child in the second degree.

(1) Any person who, using a computer or any other electronic device:

    (a) Intentionally or knowingly communicates:

        (i) With a minor known by the person to be under the age of eighteen years;

        (ii) With another person, in reckless disregard of the risk that the other person is under the age of eighteen years, and the other person is under the age of eighteen years; or

        (iii) With another person who represents that person to be under the age of eighteen years; and

(b) With the intent to promote or facilitate the commission of a felony, agrees to meet with the minor, or with another person who represents that person to be a minor under the age of eighteen years; and

(c) Intentionally or knowingly travels to the agreed upon meeting place at the agreed upon meeting time is guilty of electronic enticement of a child in the second degree.

(2) Electronic enticement of a child in the second degree is a class C felony.

Idaho 2003 H.B. 266, Chapter 145—ENTICING OF CHILDREN OVER THE INTERNET

(1) A person aged eighteen (18) years or older shall be guilty of a felony if he or she knowingly uses the Internet to solicit, seduce, lure, persuade or entice by words or actions, or both, a minor child under the age of sixteen (16) years or a person the defendant believes to be a minor child under the age of sixteen (16) years to engage in any sexual act with or against the child where such act is a violation of chapter 15, 61 or 66, title 18, Idaho Code.

Illinois 720 Ill. Comp. Stat. § 5/11-6—Indecent solicitation of a child. "Solicit" means to command, authorize, urge, incite, request, or advise another to perform an act by any means including, but not limited to, in person, over the phone, in writing, by computer, or by advertisement of any kind.

Indiana—Ind. Code § 35-42-4-6—A person eighteen (18) years of age or older who knowingly or intentionally solicits a child under fourteen (14) years of age to engage in: (1) sexual intercourse; (2) deviate sexual conduct; or (3) any fondling or touching intended to arouse or satisfy the sexual desires of either the child or the older person; commits child solicitation, a Class D felony.

Maine Title 17—A Maine Criminal Code—Chapter 11: Sex Assaults § 259. Solicitation of Child by Computer to Commit a Prohibited Act.

Maryland—Md. Stat. § 11-207—Solicitation of an individual under the age of 18 to engage in sexual conduct.

Michigan—Mich. Comp. Laws § 750.145c, 750.145d—Any person who accosts, entices, or solicits a child under the age of sixteen with intent to induce or force the child to commit an immoral act, or to submit to an act of sexual intercourse, or an act of gross indecency, or any other act of depravity or delinquency, or who suggests to the child any such acts, is guilty of a misdemeanor punishable by imprisonment in jail for not more than one year.

Minnesota—Minn. Stat. § 609.352—A person 18 years of age or older who solicits a child or someone the person reasonably believes is a child to engage in sexual conduct with intent to engage in sexual conduct is guilty of a felony and may be sentenced to imprisonment for not more than three years, or to payment of a fine of not more than $5,000, or both.

Mississippi—Miss. Code § 97-5-27—Dissemination of sexually oriented material to children.

Missouri—Mo. Rev. Stat. § 566.151—A person at least twenty-one years of age or older commits the crime of enticement of a child if that person persuades, solicits, coaxes, entices, or lures whether by words, actions or through communication via the Internet or any electronic communication, any person who is less than fifteen years of age for the purpose of engaging in sexual conduct with a child.

Nevada—Nev. Rev. Stat. § 201.560, 207.260—Luring a child using a computer, system or network.

New Hampshire—N.H. Rev. Stat. § 649-B:3, 649-B:4—Any person who knowingly utilizes a computer online service, Internet service, or local bulletin board service to seduce, solicit, lure, or entice, or attempt to seduce, solicit, lure, or entice, a child or another person believed by the person to be a child, to commit any of the following is guilty of a class B felony.

New Jersey—N.J. Stat. § 2C:13-6—A person commits a crime of the third degree if he attempts, via electronic or any other means, to lure or entice a child or one who he reasonably believes to be a child, via electronic or other means, into a motor vehicle, structure or isolated area, or to meet or appear at any other place, with a purpose to commit a criminal offense with or against the child.

New Mexico—N.M. Stat. § 30-37-3.2(B)—Criminalizes child luring by means of the computer.

New York—N.Y. Penal Law § 235.22—Criminalizes the use of sexually explicit communications which lures children into harmful conduct. On April 11, 2000, the New York Court of Appeals held that this law is not in violation of the First Amendment or the Commerce Clause. The court clarified that this law was not a bar to certain communication, but rather bars the act of luring children into sex.

North Carolina—N.C. Gen. Stat. § 14-202.3—Computer solicitation of a child for sexual purposes by a perpetrator at least 16 with a victim under age 16 and at least 3 years younger than the perpetrator.

North Dakota—N.D. Cen. Code § 12.1-20-05.1—An adult is guilty of luring minors by computer when . . .

> (1) The adult knows the character and content of a communication that, in whole or in part, implicitly or explicitly discusses or depicts actual or simulated nudity, sexual acts, sexual contact, sadomasochistic abuse, or other sexual performances and uses any computer communication system that allows the input, output, examination, or transfer of computer data or computer programs from one computer to another to initiate or engage in such communication with a person the adult believes to be a minor; and
>
> (2) By means of that communication the adult importunes, invites, or induces a person the adult believes to be a minor to engage in sexual acts or to have sexual contact with the adult, or to engage in a sexual performance, obscene sexual performance, or sexual conduct for the adult's benefit, satisfaction, lust, passions, or sexual desires.
>
> (3) A violation of this section is a class A misdemeanor, but if the adult is twenty-two years of age or older or the adult reasonably believes the minor is under the age of fifteen, violation of this section is a class C felony.

Oklahoma—Okla. Stat. tit. 21, § 1040.13a—A person is guilty of violating the provisions of this section if, for the purposes of facilitating, encouraging, offering or soliciting sexual conduct with any minor, the person knowingly transmits by means of computer, or prints, publishes or reproduces by other computerized means, or buys, sells, receives, exchanges, or disseminates, any notice, statement, or advertisement of any minor's name, telephone number, place of residence, physical characteristics or other descriptive or identifying information.

South Dakota—S.D. Codified Laws §§ 22-22-24.4, 22-22-24.5—Knowingly compiles or transmits by means of a computer; or prints, publishes or reproduces by other computerized means; or buys, sells, receives, exchanges or disseminates, any notice, statement or advertisement of any minor's name, telephone number, place of residence, physical characteristics or other descriptive or identifying information for the purpose of soliciting a minor or someone the person reasonably believes is a minor to engage in a prohibited sexual act.

Tennessee—Tenn. Code § 39-13-528—Solicitation of minors for sexual acts.

Utah Code § 76-4-401, 2003 H.B. 334—A person commits enticement of a minor over the Internet when the person knowingly uses a computer to solicit, seduce, lure, or entice, or attempts to use a computer to solicit, seduce, lure, or entice a minor or a person the defendant believes to be a minor to engage in any sexual activity which is a violation of state criminal law.

Vermont—Vt. Stat. tit. 13 § 2828—No person shall knowingly utilize an electronic communication to solicit, lure, or entice, or to attempt to solicit, lure, or entice, a child under the age of 16 or another person believed by the person to be a child under the age of 16, to engage in a sexual act as defined in section 3251 of this title or engage in lewd and lascivious conduct as defined in section 2602 of this title.

Virginia—Va. Code § 18.2-374.3—Prohibits the use of any communications system, including computers, computer networks, bulletin boards and other electronic means of communicating, for the purpose of procuring or promoting the use of a minor for any activity in violation of Virginia Code Sec. 18.2-370 (taking indecent liberties with a minor) or Sec. 18.2-374.1 (using a person less that 18 years of age in sexually explicit visual material).

Wisconsin—Wis. Stat. § 948.075—Use of a computer to facilitate a child sex crime. (1) Whoever uses a computerized communication system to communicate with an individual who the actor believes or has reason to believe has not attained the age of 16 years with intent [to] have sexual contact or sexual intercourse with the individual in violation of s. 948.02 (1) or (2) is guilty of a Class D felony.

Bear in mind that most of the preceding statutes relate only to the attempt to entice the child into a meeting for the purposes of sexual relations. If a pedophile sends images of pornography or child pornography to the victim during the "grooming phase," the offender is committing a separate offense by exposing the minor to harmful or illicit materials and/or possession/distribution of child pornography.

7.5 THE LAW ENFORCEMENT RESPONSE TO ONLINE CHILD ENTICEMENT

Law enforcement professionals can respond to the online child enticement epidemic in several different ways. The first and least effective response method is a passive, reactionary response paradigm. Under this model, police wait until a juvenile victim is reported missing or reports being sexually assaulted. After the fact, the police during their investigation determine that the child victim met the predator online and communicated via e-mail, a chat room, or an instant messaging service. The police then try to trace and reconstruct the conversations and messages that were exchanged. Very often, the habits of the victim or other people using the victim's computer may result in evidence being lost. If, for example, the victim routinely deletes e-mail messages from the offender, officers may not have much to work with.

If there are a sufficient number of messages remaining on the victim's computer, officers can attempt to use the messages to trace a link back to the suspect to identify the suspect. Officers can trace e-mail message headers back to a source Internet Protocol (IP) address. Once the owner or administrator of that IP address is found, officers can subpoena records from the IP address owner to get personal information about who was using that IP address at the time of the offense.

If there are no e-mail messages involved, the victim's computer and software may have been configured to automatically log chat transcripts or to otherwise log messages that have been sent and received. If this is the case, officers may still have enough information to be able to trace the Internet activity back to a user account name for the suspect. If they get a user name, they can subpoena records from the offender's Internet service provider. Suppose an offender has a user name of pervert1@localnet.net. This user name will probably appear in the chat message log or in the e-mail messages exchanged. Law enforcement needs to find out all of the information it can regarding pervert1. If law enforcement officers have established probable cause to believe the owner of this account has committed a crime, they can subpoena account records from localnet.net. The subpoena will generally require localnet.net to give law enforcement all user account records, including name, billing address, and so forth for the pervert1@localnet.net user account.

This reactive approach has several inherent weaknesses. The first, and most glaring, is the fact that it does nothing to prevent the victimization of a child in the first place. Second, high-tech evidence is extremely fragile. Important messages, logs, e-mail addresses, and other electronic evidence can very easily be deleted by the victim or by the system if configured to do so automatically. Therefore, a proactive approach is preferred.

The proactive method for dealing with predatory pedophiles online is to perform an online enticement sting. Every state or region in the United States now has an Internet Crimes Against Children (ICAC) task force. Often, these task forces are run by the state government in conjunction with national standards and training. Nationally recognized ICAC courses are available nationwide. One of the best resources is the ICAC Technical and Training Assistance Program. This program's Web site is www.icactraining.org/default.htm. Among other things, this program offers a weeklong class in the intricacies of conducting an undercover chat room sting.

The proactive sting is accomplished by a law enforcement officer going online into chat rooms or other areas frequented by young people (and hence targeted by the predators). In these chat rooms, the undercover officer poses as a young person. Many times, chat room user names or e-mail addresses feature either the child's age or year of birth. Therefore, "Jenny14" implies a 14-year-old girl user, and "Christy92" implies a girl user that was born in 1992. Officers, like pedophiles, can easily set up and use whatever user name or nickname they want. There are, at present, no rules in place governing the creation of screen names or for verifying the user's true identity.

After creating the user name, the officer generally waits to be contacted by other users in that particular chat room or online community. It is important to avoid the pitfall of **entrapment** in any kind of sting operation (see Figure 7–3), and this is especially true in a child enticement sting. Officers must be careful to be passive actors in all that they do. They can respond to messages or requests, but should not initiate contacts. In many chat rooms, it will not take long for other users in the room to contact the officer. The most common first line of contact is A/S/L, asking for the chatter's age, sex, and location. Legitimate chatters use this to ensure that they are talking to someone they can relate to. As discussed earlier, this is the first-line filter of the predator as well.

Many times, the chatter contacting the officer will not appear to care that the officer's user name or implied persona is an underage minor. The predator may ask questions like, "Do you have a boyfriend?" or "do you like older men?" In some cases,

Entrapment is a lawful defense to criminal activity. Entrapment occurs when a government agent (i.e., police) induces a person to commit a crime that he/she wouldn't have ordinarily committed. To be proven entrapment requires the defense to show that the police induced the unwilling person to commit a crime. Merely being present in a chat room and posing undercover as a young child is not entrapment. Responding to messages from potential sexual predators is not entrapment. Merely providing other chatters with an opportunity to share photographs, such as child pornography, would not be considered entrapment. However, if there is any evidence of persuasive communications (i.e., multiple requests made by the undercover officer for the photographs, which are eventually sent) or promises for rewards (i.e., an offer and promise to pay for the illegal photographs), entrapment might be raised as a legal defense. Again, merely mentioning "sex" or "pics" and providing the context in which an exchange might take place is not normally considered entrapment. It is recommended that the undercover officer "go with the flow" of the conversation, and once the bait is taken, to just "roll with it." First responders will quickly realize that it doesn't take much for these online predators to turn the conversation from apparent "curiosity" to outright deviance and disgust. Last, to avoid claims of entrapment, officers should be sure to properly record and preserve all chat logs.

Figure 7–3   Avoiding entrapment in online undercover operations.

predators may be even more blatant and say things like, "I'm 25, is that okay?" The officer or "victim" can answer all of these questions and can engage in normal conversations. The officer has to use caution, however, not to initiate any act that would satisfy an element of the criminal offense of enticement. For example, the officer can respond when asked about exchanging photographs, but should never suggest it. The offender may ask for a picture of the "victim." It has been long established by the Supreme Court that police can lie during sting operations. If a drug dealer asks an undercover agent if he or she is a cop, the officer can deny it all day long without jeopardizing the case. The same is true of an officer posing as a minor online. Further, the officer can send a fake photograph or give other bogus information so as not to give away his or her true identity. The officer could, therefore, respond to the offender's request for a photo by sending a photograph scanned from a magazine or school yearbook. If the offender wants to send e-mail messages or other messages containing photographs, the officer can give out an e-mail address or otherwise make arrangements to receive those photos. If the offender sends images of a pornographic nature to the officer, this likely violates state statutes in most states. Most states have obscenity laws against showing harmful or pornographic materials to a minor. If the offender sends child pornography to the "victim," this violates the possession of child pornography laws that exist in every state.

In courses the authors have taught, students log into chat rooms with a user name indicative of a child or teenager. It normally doesn't take long, sometimes less than 60 seconds, for the students to be contacted with an A/S/L request. Although the A/S/L request does not alone constitute a potential victimization, it is often the first step employed by pedophiles (and legal chatters as well). During our courses, we have seen countless examples of adults who are willing to chat with minors when we or students pose as 13- or 14-year-olds and answer the A/S/L question accordingly. Some chatters comment on the chatter's age before continuing to chat with sexually explicit text. In numerous cases, the males were from overseas, predominantly from the Middle East. It also became common for the males to send photographs of themselves to our students via direct file transfer. These photos were usually sexual in nature (e.g., naked pictures of the male). This is an example of exposing a minor to harmful materials. Often, the person who sends the photo follows up with questions about the receiving child (or undercover investigator posing as a child). They may ask if the child likes the photo or wants to "get together to meet." This phase of the conversation begins the act of child enticement.

Some states also have separate statutes that prohibit the transmission of child pornography, which could be a separate charge from the possession charge. For example, the state of Michigan statute states:

752.365 Obscenity; elements; misdemeanor; penalty; second or subsequent offense as a felony.
Sec. 5.

(1) A person is guilty of obscenity when, knowing the content and character of the material, the person disseminates, or possesses with intent to disseminate, any obscene material.

(2) Obscenity is a misdemeanor, punishable by imprisonment for not more than 1 year, or by a fine of not more than $100,000.00, or both.

(3) A person convicted of a second or subsequent offense under this section is guilty of a felony and may be imprisoned for not more than 2 years, and shall be fined not less than $50,000.00 or more than $5,000,000.00. For purposes of this section, an offense is considered a second or subsequent offense if the defendant has previously been convicted under this section or under any similar statute of the United States or of any state. (Michigan Statutes, Act 343 of 1984)

The state of Texas has the following statute:

§ 43.24. SALE, DISTRIBUTION, OR DISPLAY OF HARMFUL MATERIAL TO MINOR.

(a) For purposes of this section:

(1) "Minor" means an individual younger than 18 years.

(2) "Harmful material" means material whose dominant theme taken as a whole:

(a) appeals to the prurient interest of a minor, in sex, nudity, or excretion;

(b) is patently offensive to prevailing standards in the adult community as a whole with respect to what is suitable for minors; and

(c) is utterly without redeeming social value for minors.

(b) A person commits an offense if, knowing that the material is harmful:

(1) and knowing the person is a minor, he sells, distributes, exhibits, or possesses for sale, distribution, or exhibition to a minor harmful material;

(2) he displays harmful material and is reckless about whether a minor is present who will be offended or alarmed by the display; or

(3) he hires, employs, or uses a minor to do or accomplish or assist in doing or accomplishing any of the acts prohibited in Subsection (b)(1) or (b)(2).

(Texas Penal Code 2005)

Although the officer could request charges for the distribution of harmful material to a minor or for the possession or distribution of child pornography—both serious charges—the officer may wish to continue the enticement investigation. Often, these materials are sent to further groom the victim because it is the offender's ultimate goal to arrange a real-life meeting so as to sexually assault the victim. If the offender asks for a meeting, the undercover officer should agree to a date and time and set up the meeting. Officers will then set up an undercover sting to meet the subject at the agreed-upon spot on that date and time. Some law enforcement agencies have utilized young-looking police officers, explorers, or cadets to pose as the victim; others rely upon the explicit nature of messages before the meeting to meet the statutory elements of attempted child enticement.

Currently, pedophiles and online child predators are attempting to protect themselves from online stings in a variety of ways. Online investigators of these types of crimes, particularly those posing as victims, should take certain steps to ensure success. The predators are starting to check up on potential victims in an attempt to make sure the "victim" is a real child and not a law enforcement officer. They may attempt contact from different screen names or e-mail addresses and ask questions in hopes of verifying the information. It is important, therefore, for those posing as victims to stay consistent in their persona. Investigators may write down relevant persona details such as height, weight, hair color, and description so they can answer quickly and consistently when asked for these details

From a more technical perspective, the investigative PC should not be located on a police department or government network because the predators often check on IP addresses. Tracking the IP address of the "victim" back to a government entity would quickly kill the suspect's interest. If possible, the standalone PC, connected to a "normal" Internet service provider such as a local cable or telephone company, should have a dedicated IP address so that it will not change. This will aid in documenting traffic as routed on the Internet. The standalone PC should be physically secured or locked into a room for this specific purpose, used only by Internet investigative staff, and not utilized for any purpose other than communicating with suspects. All reporting and documentation work should be performed at a separate workstation.

Summary of Chat Investigation Protocols

The following points summarize the protocols that investigators should utilize when conducting online investigations of pedophiles using chat rooms, e-mail, instant messenger, or other online communications systems. These protocols emphasize a thorough online persona, thorough documentation of all communications and violations, and reacting passively to avoid entrapment issues.

1. Create an undercover online identity including user names, e-mail addresses, photos, and so forth that make the investigator appear to be an underage child.
2. Set up chat room applications to automatically log all chats and other activities to keep ongoing records of all online activity performed while investigating.
3. Visit online chat rooms that might be commonly used by teenagers or underage children.
4. *Reactively* engage in conversations with other chatters and people that contact you.
5. Document any attempts to transmit pornography, child pornography, or other harmful materials to a minor (even if the minor is really the adult investigator).
6. Document any attempts to entice a child into meeting for the purpose of sexual activity.

7. If a meeting is proposed, *reactively* agree to the meeting and set up a sting operation to apprehend the adult suspect upon arrival at the agreed time and place.
8. Make the arrest.

Learner Activity

Create an online persona as if you would be conducting an undercover sting investigation. A full persona generally includes an e-mail address, screen name, and instant messaging ID. Next, locate a picture to be used as the virtual person whose identity you are creating. Use a Google search to locate an appropriate image. Finally, once you have created an ID, locate an online IRC or chat service, such as MIRC. Log in using your profile and engage in a chat with someone. Make sure that the chat logging function is enabled. Engage in a brief chat and save the log from that chat session for presentation in class.

Numerous organizations online bill themselves as vigilante justice groups or civilian investigators who pose as children online in an attempt to lure these predators out into the open. One example is a Web site called www.perverted-justice.com. This Web site recruits people to follow the preceding investigative protocols, posing as children between 10 and 15 years of age. Once they have received inappropriate materials or have been propositioned for sex, they turn all documentary materials over to the appropriate law enforcement agency. This site is also an excellent resource because it lists numerous sample chat logs from these sessions. Examining these chat logs is a great way to see real-life examples of the material discussed in this chapter.

7.6 CHILD PORNOGRAPHY OVERVIEW

The creation, possession, and/or transmittal of child pornography is a crime of epidemic proportions. Although no one can say with certainty exactly how widespread the problem is, the trends and indicators that are measurable are truly frightening. A problem-oriented manual for police published by the U.S. Department of Justice illustrates this problem:

> It is difficult to be precise about the extent of Internet child pornography, but all of the available evidence points to it being a major and growing problem. At any one time there are estimated to be more than one million pornographic images of children on the Internet, with 200 new images posted daily. One offender arrested in the U.K. possessed 450,000 child pornography images. It has been reported that a single child pornography site received a million hits in a month. As noted above, one problem in estimating the number of sites is that many exist only for a brief period before they are shut down, and much of the trade in child pornography takes place at hidden levels of the Internet. It has been estimated that there are between 50,000 and 100,000 pedophiles involved in organized

pornography rings around the world, and that one third of these operate from the United States. (Wortley and Smallbone 2006)

Although states may differ on the precise definition of child pornography, it is generally defined as the visual representation of a child engaged in sexually explicit conduct or a sexual act. The possession of child pornography is criminalized by Title 18 of U.S. federal code. Federal law defines a child as anyone under the age of 18 years.

Title 18, Chapter 110: Sexual Exploitation and Other Abuse of Children. 18 U.S.C. § 2256 defines "Child pornography" as:
any visual depiction, including any photograph, film, video, picture, or computer or computer-generated image or picture, whether made or produced by electronic, mechanical, or other means, of sexually explicit conduct, where—

(a) the production of such visual depiction involves the use of a minor engaging in sexually explicit conduct;

(b) such visual depiction is, or *appears to be*, of a minor engaging in sexually explicit conduct;

(c) such visual depiction has been created, adapted, or modified to appear that an identifiable minor is engaging in sexually explicit conduct; or

(d) such visual depiction is advertised, promoted, presented, described, or distributed in such a manner that *conveys the impression* that the material is or contains a visual depiction of a minor engaging in sexually explicit conduct. . . .

In 1996, Congress adopted the Child Porn Prevention Act of 1996 (CPPA). This law, now included within the preceding section 2256, attempts to outlaw "virtual child pornography," which is defined as an image depicting a child engaged in sexual activity that may have been created or modified by a computer. Virtual child pornography may make it impossible to determine if there is an actual child victim that was photographed. The original law, as written in 1996, criminalizes the possession of "visual depictions of what 'appears to be' minors engaging in sexual conduct," even in those cases where prosecutors could not prove that an actual child existed.

One of the common defenses in this type of case is a First Amendment challenge, citing free speech. Child pornography is not protected by the First Amendment, although there have been several challenges to child pornography laws, often under the auspices of a free speech restriction. Oftentimes, the material is presented as artwork, and thus an expression of free speech.

The virtual child pornography clause spawned a Supreme Court challenge in *Ashcroft v. Free Speech Coalition (2002).* In *Ashcroft*, at issue was whether two provisions of a federal law that criminalizes computer-generated images of minors engaged in sexually explicit conduct but that may not involve actual minors violate the First Amendment. Perhaps surprisingly, the court struck down the "appears to be" and "conveys the impression" provisions of the **Child Pornography Prevention Act** (see the italicized text in the statute cited previously). The rationale behind the Court's decision is that these portions of the Child Pornography Prevention Act prohibit speech that records no crime and creates no victims by its production. In other words, there is no crime because the image is not a real person.

Many states have very specific child pornography statutes. The Wisconsin Statute from Chapter 948: Crimes Against Children is included here as an illustration of a common child pornography statute.

> Wisconsin Statute 948.12 states:
> Whoever possesses any undeveloped film, photographic negative, photograph, motion picture, videotape, or other recording of a child engaged in sexually explicit conduct under all of the following circumstances is guilty of a Class I felony.

Another potential hurdle encountered during child pornography investigations is determining if the subject in the photograph is actually a minor, or has attained 18 years of age. There are many **Lolita** or **barely legal** Web sites that feature models who may be of legal age, but who look younger. This perception of youth is enhanced with youthful outfits, hairdos, or other props to add to the perception that the model is underage to appeal to the pedophile's compulsions. One common stereotype is the image of a girl with pigtails, a school uniform dress, and maybe a lollipop for added emphasis of youth. The term *Lolita* originates from a Russian novel titled *Lolita* by Vladimir Nabokov. Nabokov's work, published more than 50 years ago, was extremely controversial for its time and features a main character who becomes enthralled with a pubescent female character. In the novel, the females were generally between the ages of 9 and 14. When the term is used in the Internet sense, the girls are 18- or 19-year-olds who appear to be underage. In addition to Lolita sites there are many sites that cater to teens, and many others that feature images of teens. Sexual exploitation of teens is very common overseas as a commercial venture. Countries such as Russia and the Netherlands have demonstrated a capacity for producing a large percentage of the world's teen sex or naked teen images. In Russia, this can be partially attributed to the country's struggling economy and organized crime problem. In the Netherlands, where prostitution is legal in certain areas and drugs can be purchased in deli-like storefronts, it can perhaps be attributed to a much more decadent lifestyle in general.

Defendants in child pornography cases have attempted to argue that the people represented in the explicit images are not children, but rather Lolitas, or legal adults posing as children. To successfully prosecute a child pornography matter, the state has the burden of proving the people in the images are, in fact, underage. An Illinois Appeals Court decision spells this out: "The determination of the age of the subjects in each photograph is for the trier of fact, relying on 'everyday observations and common experiences.'" (*People v. Thomann*, 554 N.E.2d 748, 755 [Ill. App. Ct. 1990]). In most cases, the "trier of fact" is the jury.

In other cases, individuals have been charged with the possession and distribution of child pornography after posting sexually explicit pictures of themselves. In one case from Providence, Rhode Island, a 16-year-old girl took photographs of a 16-year-old girl and a 19-year-old girl. These photos were posted on www.myspace.com. Because of the sexually explicit nature of the photographs, all three girls were charged with the transmission of child pornography. Myspace is a tremendously popular social networking Web site with membership measured in the millions. As such, there are numerous news items associated with Myspace that can be found via a Google search.

7.7 THE LAW ENFORCEMENT RESPONSE TO CHILD PORNOGRAPHY

The victimization of a child has a galvanizing effect upon the human community. Once any form of sexual victimization is factored in, society demands swift, sure action to prevent other such tragedies. Nowhere is this more evident than in the arena of child pornography. There are numerous citizen groups whose missions is to stamp out child pornography. A few examples of such groups are as follows:

www.antichildporn.org/—The AntiChildPorn.Org Web site (APCO) is a Web site and organization made up of volunteers who endeavor to combat online child exploitation. They have news and resources for parents and law enforcement, including a freely downloadable software utility called Reveal that allows parents to search their computer for illegal activity, pornographic images, or alarming text.

www.asacp.org/index.php—The Association of Sites Advocating Child Protection Web site attempts to combat child pornography online by utilizing a child porn reporting hotline and organizing the adult pornography industry. Adult pornography sites can join this organization and also receive guidance in "best practices" for their "industry."

www.pedowatch.com—Pedowatch is named for its efforts to monitor sexual predators on the Internet while, at the same time, stressing the protection of children by promoting education, awareness, and crime prevention. The site offers links to state sex offender registries and state criminal records Web sites, articles on the topic of Internet crimes, and child and teen safety tips.

www.missingkids.com—The National Center for Missing and Exploited Children is a nationwide clearinghouse for missing children reports. It offers a number of features, including a state-by-state search that allows people to print their own missing persons posters. The site also has a cyber tipline for submitting information, as well as Amber Alert information and Wireless Phone Amber Alert information to enable people to sign up to receive Amber alerts for missing children.

What these groups all have in common is an intense desire to assist law enforcement in the detection of child pornography Web sites. Most of these groups have a mechanism in place that allows anyone with Internet access to report a known instance of child pornography. Law enforcement can then follow up on this information, locating owner information for the Web site, or in the case of an e-mail advertisement, tracing the e-mail message to its source. Many times, investigations may utilize an undercover law enforcement officer who attempts to join a subscription-based Web site or an online group of people trading in illicit images or videos. The protocol is actually quite similar to making undercover narcotics buys and finding out whom the main distributors are.

The Federal Bureau of Investigation (FBI) has also launched the **Innocent Images National Initiative (IINI)**. The FBI states:

> The mission of the IINI is to:
> - Identify, investigate, and prosecute sexual predators who use the Internet and other online services to sexually exploit children.
> - Identify and rescue witting and unwitting child victims.
> - Establish a law enforcement presence on the Internet as a deterrent to subjects that exploit children.

As part of its mission to help identify the child victims shown in child pornography images, the FBI has created a database of known child pornography images. In addition, for those known images where the victim has been identified, the victim's information is also kept on file. This database of known images can be utilized by a computer forensic examiner in a forensic search of a suspect's computer. Using known hash values, the examiner can quickly locate on a suspect's computer any of the files included in the FBI database. The FBI makes this database available to law enforcement, which enables law enforcement to quickly find any matching files contained on the suspect's computer. Further, law enforcement can also submit new images to the FBI for possible identification of the victims or to catalog the images in the national database of known illegal child porn. (See Chapter 10 for further information).

The FBI also lists the following sections of U.S. Code as some of those most likely to be investigated in association with the Innocent Images National Initiative:

- 18 U.S.C. § 1462. Importation or Transportation of Obscene Matters
- 18 U.S.C. § 1465. Transportation of Obscene Matters for Sale or Distribution
- 18 U.S.C. § 1466. Engaging in the Business of Selling or Transferring Obscene Matter
- 18 U.S.C. § 1470. Transfer of Obscene Material to Minors
- 18 U.S.C. § 2251(a)(b)(c). Sexual Exploitation of Children
- 18 U.S.C. § 2252. Certain Activities Relating to Material Involving the Sexual Exploitation of Minors
- 18 U.S.C. § 2252A. Certain Activities Relating to Material Constituting or Containing Child Pornography
- 18 U.S.C. § 2422. Coercion and Enticement
- 18 U.S.C. § 2423(a). Transportation of Minors with Intent to Engage in Criminal Sexual Activity
- 18 U.S.C. § 2423(b). Interstate or Foreign Travel with Intent to Engage in a Sexual Act with a Juvenile

The other way in which government has responded to sex crimes against children is by passing several different laws to help protect children. One such law is titled Megan's Law. In 1994, a 7-year-old girl was raped and murdered by a recently released sex offender. This event sparked public outrage and resulted in a law that required a widespread community notification any time a sex offender was being released into that community. It is also this law that prompted most states to institute Web sites listing all known sex offenders. Numerous Web sites are devoted to protecting children, offering sex offender notification, and supporting other Megan's Law issues. Some of the best are these:

- www.klaaskids.org/index.htm
- www.ncmec.org/ (can also be accessed at www.missingkids.com/)
- www.teamhope.org/
- www.beyondmissing.com/main.shtml

7.8 SUMMARIES OF WELL-KNOWN LAW ENFORCEMENT STING OPERATIONS

In an attempt to stem the tide of child pornography into the United States, Federal law enforcement agencies have conducted several national sting operations. Some of these stings were Operation Artus, Operation Avalanche, Operation Blue Orchid, Operation Candy Box, Operation Candyman, Operation Cyber Sweep, Operation E-con, Operation Falcon, Operation Hamlet, Operation Ore, Operation Pipe Dreams, Operation Predator, Operation Snowball, Operation Twins, Operation Web Sweep, and Project Exile. A few of these are summarized here.

Operation Hamlet was announced by the U.S. Customs Service in August 2002. This operation focused on approximately 20 different families who were molesting their own children and recording the molestations by taking still photos and videos. The members of the group would then trade the images and videos with other like-minded individuals. The first detected member of this group was located in the European nation of Denmark. A citizens' action group called Save the Children was alerted to an image of a young girl being molested. Unfortunately for the suspect, a company logo was visible in the picture, which eventually led to his being identified. Subsequently, after searching and analyzing his computer, 10 other Europeans and 12 Americans were identified as participating in molestation and image trading. One member of the group was found to be in possession of more than 1 million images of child pornography. He had approximately 450 CDs worth of illicit material. Additionally, 37 American children and 8 European children were taken into protective custody. (U.S. Customs and Border Protection 2002).

A popular way for child pornographers to gather involves forming an online affiliation, or e-group. **Operation Candyman** focused on such a group. This investigation was announced by the FBI in 2002. The e-group in question invited members to trade images of child pornography. The results of the investigation indicated that there were approximately 7,000 subscribers, or members, of this group, with around 2,400 of them living overseas. Operation Candyman really got started when an undercover agent joined the group. Upon joining the group, he had instant access to several dozen images and some video clips of children engaged in sexual acts. Within one month of joining, the agent had received several hundred e-mail messages from other members, some of which had file attachments that included child pornography. In total, more than 100 people, most of them American, were arrested (Federal Bureau of Investigation 2005).

Operation Avalanche started in Forth Worth, Texas, in 2001. The operation's name was a play on words because the company being investigated was called Landslide Productions, Inc., an Internet-based company that offered pay subscriptions to more than 250 Web sites, many of which contained child pornography. The corporation amassed more than 300,000 subscribers and at various times had monthly earnings in excess of $1 million. It is widely believed to be the largest commercial child pornography site known to law enforcement. Thomas Reedy, the owner, was sentenced to 1,335 years in prison. His wife, Janice, received a lighter sentence of 14 years as a result of her lesser involvement.

The operations mentioned here have also spawned other international investigations. **Operation Snowball** is a spin-off of Operation Avalanche and took place in Canada. This investigation centers around approximately 2,300 Canadian citizens who bought subscriptions to the Landslide Productions Web site (U.S. postal service, n.d.).

Learner Activity

Research a law enforcement sting (other than the ones summarized here) in the area of child enticement or child pornography. Write a research paper summarizing the investigation along with the methods employed by those committing the crime. In addition, discuss the scope of the crime such as the number of victims and suspects. Also, examine the tools and methods used by law enforcement to solve the crime.

■ SUMMARY

This chapter explores the troubling world of high-tech crimes against children. Crimes against children are generally the most disturbing because they victimize the most innocent in society, those most unable to defend themselves. Because these crimes are sexual in nature, they can arouse a great deal of outrage among those who investigate them. The chapter begins by exploring the psychological disorders and abnormalities of the pedophile. It continues by classifying pedophiles into three types and examines the methods they use in committing these crimes. Next discussed are the methods, both reactive and proactive, law enforcement can use for dealing with pedophilia. This chapter also briefly described several of the most widely known law enforcement operations in this arena.

■ REVIEW QUESTIONS

1. Is there any known cure for pedophilia? If so, what is it? If not, what does it mean in terms of a sex offender's likelihood of reoffending?
2. Pedophiles are broken down into three categories or severity levels. List the three levels and define them in your own words, focusing on how they are different from each other.
3. In what ways has the Internet emboldened pedophiles? How are their techniques different in an online world than they were years ago?
4. Define *grooming*. How do pedophiles use the Internet to groom potential victims? How did pedophiles attempt to groom victims before the days of the Internet?
5. The law enforcement response to these crimes can be reactive or proactive. Discuss why the proactive response is preferred, and give an example of a proactive technique that can be employed by an investigator.
6. Consult your state's statutes. Locate the state laws against possession of child pornography, transmission of porn or other harmful materials to a minor, and child enticement. Does your state have a specific law against using a computer or the Internet in conjunction with child enticement?
7. Does your state have a sex offender registry available online? If so, list the Web site address where it can be accessed.
8. Define *entrapment*. What can investigators do to ensure that they will not lose their case to an entrapment defense?

■ TERMS

active pedophile	entrapment	Operation Snowball
Ashcroft v. Free	grooming	paederast
Speech Coalition(2002)	Innocent Images National	pedophile
A/S/L	Initiative (IINI)	pedophilia
barely legal	Lolita	secretive pedophile
child pornography	online child enticement	*Wisconsin v. Robins*
collector	Operation Avalanche	
Child Pornography	Operation Candyman	
Prevention Act	Operation Hamlet	

REFERENCES

American Psychiatric Association. 2000. *Diagnostic and Statistical Manual.* 4th ed. Washington, D.C.: American Psychiatric Association.

Appeals Court of Illinois. 1990. *People v. Thomann*, 554 N.E.2d 748, 755.

Bonner, R. 2002. Remarks of U.S. Customs Commissioner Robert C. Bonner: Press Conference on Operation Hamlet. U.S. Customs Service. www.customs. gov/xp/cgov/newsroom/commissioner/speeches_statements/archives/ 2002/aug092002.xml (accessed June 12, 2005).

Federal Bureau of Investigation. 2005. Innocent Images Operation Candyman PhaseI.www.fbi.gov/pressrel/pressreloz/cm031802.htm (accessed October 14, 2006).

Langan, P., Schmitt, E., and Durose, M. 2003. *Recidivism of sex offenders released from prison in 1994*. Washington, DC: U.S. Department of Justice. Bureau of Justice Statistics. www.ojp.usdoj. gov/bjs/pub/pdf/rsorp94.pdf. (accessed July 20, 2006).

Office of Juvenile Justice and Delinquency Prevention. 2001. *Highlights of the Youth Internet Safety Survey.* Washington, DC: U.S. Department of Justice.

Supreme Court of Wisconsin. 2002. *Wisconsin v. Robins* 00-2841-CR.

U.S. Customs and Border Protection. 2002. Remarks of U.S. Customs Commissioner Robert C. Bonner: press conference on Operation Hamlet. www.customs. gov/xp/cgov/newsroom/commissioner/speeches_statements/archives/ 2002aug092002.xml (accessed September 29, 2006).

U.S. Department of Justice, Bureau of Justice Statistics. 2002. *Sexual assault of young children as reported to law enforcement: Victim, incident, and offender characteristics*. Washington, DC: U.S. Department of Justice, Bureau of Justice Statistics.

U.S. Postal Service. (n.d). The U.S. Postal Inspection Service teams with Internet Crimes Against Children Task Forces in Operation Avalanche. www.usps. com/postalinspectors/avalanch.htm (accessed June 12, 2005).

Wortley, R., and Smallbone, S. 2006. *Child pornography on the Internet.* Problem Oriented Guides for Police 41. www.cops.usdoj.gov/mime/open.pdf? Item=1729 (accessed August 1, 2006).

chapter eight

High-Tech Intelligence Gathering and Online Resources

■ LEARNING OBJECTIVES

1. Explain the difference between open and closed sources of data.
2. Explain the difference between *information* and *criminal intelligence*.
3. Explain how the Internet can be used to gather intelligence information.
4. Explain and demonstrate common Boolean search techniques.
5. Explain what a search engine is.
6. Explain how to properly identify, analyze, and disseminate intelligence information.
7. Identify online sources that can be used for intelligence gathering.

The Internet is a valuable source of information that is just waiting to be tapped. The good, bad, and the ugly—it can all be found online. However, law enforcement can also utilize it for intelligence gathering at a local, state, or even national level. Like law enforcement, criminals use the Internet on a daily basis. But they use it to facilitate and commit criminal acts or communicate with accomplices. Some criminals brag about their latest crime or exploit and display their "trophies" for others to see. Law

211

enforcement just needs to know how to search and where to find valuable online information that may lead to the discovery or evidence of a crime.

8.1 TYPES OF INFORMATION AVAILABLE ONLINE

Before getting into the types of information available online, it's important to first understand the difference between *information* and *criminal intelligence.* *Information,* in the context of an intelligence process, can be defined as "pieces of raw, unanalyzed data that identifies persons, evidence, events, or illustrates processes that indicate the incidence of a criminal event or witnesses or evidence of a criminal event" (Carter 2004). *Criminal intelligence* is defined as "information compiled, analyzed, and/or disseminated in an effort to anticipate, prevent, or monitor criminal activity" (U.S. Department of Justice 2003). Examples of information include criminal history and driving records, police reports, witness/suspect statements, and license plate information, whereas criminal intelligence includes "a report by an analyst that draws conclusions about a person's criminal liability based on an integrated analysis of diverse information collected by investigators and/or researchers" (Carter 2004). The Internet contains a wealth of criminal intelligence and information just waiting to be found.

The Internet also contains both "open" and "closed" sources of information. **Open source** information consists of databases, message boards, media sources/outlets, photographs, tape/video recordings, satellite images, and government and private sector Web sites that are searchable by anybody with an Internet connection for free or for a fee. **Closed source** data include the same general types of information that can be found in open sources, but require authorization to access that is generally controlled by using an encrypted user name and password. Closed-source data is highly secured and controlled. Unauthorized access is not only a violation of the entities' policies and procedures, but likely a violation of applicable state and federal laws. Some examples of closed-source information include the National Crime Information Center (NCIC) database maintained by the Federal Bureau of Investigation (FBI) and the Wisconsin Transaction Information for Management of Enforcement (TIME) system, which contains restricted access to criminal justice information. The primary focus of this chapter is on open sources available on the Internet. It's also important to note that digital intelligence does not replace the value of human intelligence (e.g., informants, citizen witnesses).In fact, the Internet can be used to locate experts in any field who can serve as valuable sources of information.

It is also important to note that the nature of the information or intelligence obtained from open sources needs to be scrutinized for bias and reliability. Great caution needs to be taken when determining the reliability of the information obtained. The Internet is not highly regulated, which means anybody can post and display information. From legitimate research documents and media outlets to terrorist propaganda, it can all be found on the Internet, and it's important to always "consider the source" when evaluating the information obtained. For example, information from a blog page where people can post opinions and comments on any topic is considered much less reliable than information from a pay site, such as Lexis-Nexis, which is subject to industry scrutiny and regulations. Like investigations in real life, ask *who* published it, *what* was published, *when* was it published, *where* is it published, and on what server.

Online intelligence information can not only assist law enforcement with their investigations, it can also help them learn more about and/or identify people of interest living in their communities. The post-9/11-world highlights the importance of being vigilant and aware of suspicious behavior or people. Online databases can help identify the listed owners of property or even their criminal records. Online intelligence information can benefit law enforcement and assist in criminal investigations through the following means: filling in investigative gaps; confirming information obtained; gathering full names, dates of birth, addresses, and phone numbers of suspects; maps or images of target locations; interagency communications; and more.

When preparing to utilize the Internet as an intelligence-gathering tool, certain hardware and software considerations should be addressed. Availability of foreign language translation software, multiple browsers, color printer, dedicated Internet access, image processing, link-analysis programs, word processing programs, spread sheets, and the like needs to be determined. Many of the default programs that come with common operating systems today will suffice, and sometimes other high-end software programs might be necessary. This is all dependent upon the type of intelligence gathering to be conducted.

8.2 LOCATING ONLINE INTELLIGENCE INFORMATION

The Internet is so vast that one can easily conduct a keyword search and obtain thousands of results, which would take countless hours to view. Current estimates indicate that there are more than 250,000 databases available on the Internet, many of which have potential intelligence value (North Atlantic Treaty Organisation 2001). To use the Internet as an intelligence-gathering source requires law enforcement to efficiently and effectively conduct searches that provide them with the most specific and useful information. Effectively searching the Internet for intelligence information has three basic requirements:

1. Knowing where to search
2. Knowing how to search effectively
3. Knowing what to do with the information

Using Search Engines

To search the Internet effectively first requires knowing where to search. The most common way to search the Internet is by using **search engines,** which are

Web sites dedicated to retrieving data from the Internet. Some of the more common search engines include www.google.com and www.altavista.com. A comprehensive search engine that searches several other search engines at once is called www.dogpile.com. A keyword search for "search engine" will reveal many others. These search engines or Web sites enable Internet users to submit keywords related to information they are seeking. The more general the search, the more responses will be returned. For example, entering the keywords "police officer" at www.google.com nets a return of 50,300,000 Web sites related to police officers. It would take a significant amount of time to go through all of these Web sites to find the information you are searching for. To limit the amount of returns, **Boolean search techniques** can be used.

Boolean logic, developed by a nineteenth-century English mathematician named George Boole, allows an Internet searcher to use three primary commands to help reduce and/or expand return results. The three standard Boolean search terms are the plus sign (e.g., police +officer) or the *AND* term (e.g., police AND officer); the minus sign (e.g., police − officer) or the *NOT* term (e.g., police NOT officer); and the *OR* term (e.g., police OR officer). We use the search engine www.google.com to demonstrate each search technique, as summarized in the following subsections.

Plus (+) Sign or AND

The plus sign (+) or the term *AND* generates a return of Web pages that include both of the terms that appear before and after the AND or + command. In other words, when conducting a keyword search for "police AND officer," the Web page results will include only those pages that include both the search terms. The plus sign can be inserted in place of the AND, but the + must appear alongside the second term or in front of it (e.g., police +officer). To demonstrate how this type of search command reduces the number of returns and helps to filter the response, the results of the searches for "police," "officer," and "police AND officer" are as follows:

Boolean + or AND

Search Terms	Results
Police	242,000,000 Web pages
Officer	305,000,000 Web pages
Police AND officer	44,000,000 Web pages

In the preceding example, using the AND Boolean search technique created a significant reduction in the number of returns. Granted, 44,000,000 Web pages is still an unreasonable number to read, and making the search more specific to reduce that number even more would be helpful. The more specific and unique the search terms, the better and more manageable the results.

Minus (–) Sign or NOT

The NOT term or minus sign (–) retrieves information related only to the first term and excludes the second. For example, when searching for information related to "capital offenses," which will commonly include returns for murder, the most common capital offense, you can narrow and/or filter that search by eliminating "murder." The search string would look like this, "capital offense –murder":

Boolean – or NOT

Search Terms	Results
Capital offense	3,630,000 Web pages
Capital offense –murder	2,160,000 Web pages

Using the NOT or – Boolean search terms, significantly reduces the number of pages returned. Again, 2,160,000 pages are impossible to read through in a timely fashion, but a reputable search engine, such as Google or Alta Vista, can provide the most relevant results first and greatly increases accessibility of relevant information the user is seeking.

OR Search Term

In contrast to AND and NOT Boolean search terms, the OR command broadens the number of return results. The Boolean OR provides results that include either of the keywords that were entered. For example, searching for "police OR Tasers" produces a list of Web pages that include "police," "Tasers," or "police and Tasers."

Using Quotation Marks

Another way to limit the number of returns and search for more specific information is to use quotation marks. For instance, when seeking information on popular topics, such as deaths related to Taser use, using quotation marks around the search phrase, such as "TASER related deaths" produces results that contain the keywords used in the exact order they were entered. Using quotation marks could make a search too restrictive, resulting in few or no results, so caution must be exercised.

Using Quotes

Search Terms	Results
Taser related deaths	176,000 Web pages
"Taser related deaths"	591 Web pages

As you can see, placing quotes around the search term greatly reduces the number of returns. In this case, 591 Web sites seems manageable compared to 176,000. Furthermore, the returns for "Taser related deaths" will be very specific to that topic.

Other Techniques for Gathering Online Intelligence

Using proper search techniques can help locate valuable intelligence information. However, intelligence information can also be obtained from suspects themselves. Asking suspects their e-mail address, user name, passwords, and even which Web sites they frequent can provide valuable leads. Figure 8–1 highlights the value of gathering this type of information.

In addition to searching Web sites, another place to look for useful intelligence information are Web sites that cater to groups or other online communities. Three of the more popular groups sites are www.groups.google.com, Internet Relay Chat (IRC) and, most recently, www.myspace.com. Myspace.com is currently the leader in online communities, especially among teens and young adults. Each of these is discussed in this section.

The groups sites hosted at www.groups.google.com contain groups or communities of people that can join any group based upon subject matter. Any conceivable topic can be found within these groups. For example, anybody can join the alt.pot.drugs group for discussions regarding the use of marijuana or where to

During the summer of 2004, law enforcement officers in northeast Wisconsin were receiving several complaints of homosexual men engaging in sexual activity in a park frequented by families. The park had several nature trails in a densely wooded area that lead to the Bay of Green Bay. The sexual activity was occurring alongside the trails. Parents complained of their children potentially witnessing this activity. In addition, several used condoms were found on the ground, which created a potential biohazard, especially if they are contaminated with sexually transmitted diseases. Undercover officers were placed in the area and within a matter of days an arrest was made for lewd and lascivious behavior. An interview with the offender revealed that all of the "meetings" for the sole purpose of sexual gratification were made at a particular Web site. Investigators went to the Web site and discovered a bulletin board that was being utilized by surfers to arrange meetings. Users would post their sexual preferences and those interested would respond and ultimately set up a meeting. For several weeks investigators monitored the postings and each time a date and time at the park was arranged, undercover officers were placed in the area and three consecutive arrests were made. Shortly thereafter, a message was posted on the bulletin board that read something like, "Use caution, the police are monitoring this board." It was just a matter of time until the word got out as a result of the number of arrests that were made. The intelligence information obtained from the Web site ended the lewd and lascivious behaviors that were occurring at the park.

Figure 8–1 Obtaining intelligence information directly from suspects.

purchase it. Or users can join the alt.tv.csi for discussions about the TV show *Crime Scene Investigation* and the like. All of the messages archived at www.groups.google.com are keyword searchable. Millions of messages have been posted, and they can all be searched. Boolean search techniques can be used to locate specific information, and an advanced search feature is also available. Law-abiding citizens and criminals alike spend time in these groups. Some have discussions about the latest business trends, while others coordinate or even advertise their criminal activities and intentions. Occasionally, surfing these sites can reveal useful leads for a crime that has already been committed or for crimes that have yet to be committed. Figure 8–2 highlights how intelligence information can be gathered by searching groups.

Google Groups is just one of the many groups sites that are available on the Internet, and it's one of the most comprehensive.

When conducting keyword searches on the Internet, it is recommended that street slang and words associated with crime and/or the criminal element be used. For example, a keyword search for "narc" could reveal responses associated with drug agents, informants, or those involved in anarchy. It also helps to use keywords that are consistent with the region.

Internet Relay Chat (IRC) is similar to Google Groups in that it can be searched, but it functions more like an instant messaging (IM) system. IM is very popular today, especially among young adults, and allows for instantaneous communications in a chat room environment. The IRC system contains servers from around the world that host chat rooms or chat channels. Like groups, the topics of these chat rooms range from business and sports to pornography and credit card fraud. Pedophiles use IRC to surf channels that cater to children and teens, hoping

While conducting some random keyword searches at www.groups.google.com, investigators discovered a death threat against a fellow officer's 16-year-old son. The threats were very specific and appeared to be more than just harassment or "flaming" via the Internet. The threats discussed the manner of death, where the victim attended school, and the fact that he was the son of a police officer. Investigators alerted the officer and his son, neither of whom where aware of these death threats. The primary suspect, who lived in the same community, was careless and left an actual e-mail address and signed the post by name. A subsequent interview of the targeted victim revealed the actual name of the suspect, which matched the name that he used to sign the post. An interview with the suspect revealed that both the targeted victim and suspect had been involved in drug activity and their relationship had recently gone bad. Although no official law enforcement action was taken, the discovery of this information likely prevented a tragedy.

Figure 8–2   Searching online groups for intelligence information.

to find their next victim. Identity thieves use IRC to trade stolen identities and credit card numbers. Law enforcement can also use IRC to surf undercover in an effort to lure and arrest these offenders (see Chapter 7 for a full discussion on this topic).

The most effective way to search the IRC system is by going to www. searchirc.com. This Web site serves as a search engine of the IRC system. For example, conducting a keyword search for "credit card" can reveal several responses, including messages that have been posted either seeking or offering stolen credit card numbers to those warning that offenders will be prosecuted to the fullest extent of the law. It is of concern that such information can be so easily obtained. As with searching groups, using street slang common to the criminal element can reveal investigative leads.

Myspace.com is one of the most popular social networking Web sites for the typical teen blogger and music and movie stars, who use it stay in touch with their fan base. Membership is free to anybody age 14 or older, and signing up is simple. Outside of a date-of-birth entry, there is no other age verification mechanism, and users can lie about their birth date to become a member. Once a member, users can create a personal Web page or profile that contains personal photos, first name and/or unique screen name, likes/dislikes, blogs (Web logs frequently updated and for public consumption), geographical location (city and state), e-mail addresses, and much more. Although Myspace.com does its best to police the service and even prohibits sexually explicit, harassing, obscene, lewd, excessively violent, or otherwise objectionable subject matter, it's nearly impossible to prevent it all. The Web site does reserve the right to remove any subject matter that it deems inappropriate, but some objectionable content and even information about illegal acts can still be found on Myspace.com and can be of value to law enforcement. Myspace.com can be searched from the homepage by name, display name, e-mail address, school name, or various affiliations (e.g., dance, fashion, film). Getting in the habit of asking offenders, especially teens and young adults, if they have a Myspace.com page is advisable.

The investigative value of Myspace.com is highlighted in a recent 2006 case out of Washougal, Washington, where police, following an anonymous tip, visited the Myspace profile of two brothers who were responsible for large amounts of graffiti in the community. The tip came in response to $150.00 reward posters that had been placed throughout the community. The suspects, two brothers, were so proud of their work that they posted pictures and took credit for their crimes on their Myspace page. This alone gave officers enough evidence to obtain a search warrant, make an arrest, and recover the paint, pens, and markers that the suspects used along with a CD containing more photos of their graffiti. Further investigation also revealed chat transcripts related to what the graffiti meant, what they used to create it, and even where they obtained the paint (Sgt. Kim Yamashita, personal communication, July 26, 2006).

In another 2006 case, officials in Montgomery County (Maryland) utilized Myspace, in part, during their investigation of two serial arsonists. Traditional investigative techniques had failed, and during an information-sharing session with other law enforcement officials, Lt. Brian Anderson was shown some pictures of a playground fire that had been sent to another agency by a concerned citizen. The citizen witness had obtained them on Myspace, and the owner of that particular Web page also took credit for setting the fire. The playground fire scene matched one that Lt. Anderson had been investigating. With guidance from the local computer crimes unit, Lt. Anderson subpoenaed Myspace and obtained the individual's account name, chat logs, and IP addresses, which were subsequently traced to America Online (AOL). Legal documents were also served upon AOL, which provided the individual's subscriber information. The chat logs also revealed the identity of a coconspirator, and search warrants were executed. All electronic items that could potentially contain stored data, including their computers, were seized, and both 17-year-old suspects were charged with 17 counts of arson-related crimes and 3 counts of reckless endangerment (Lt. Brian Anderson, personal communication, July 26, 2006).

One of the best software programs for searching the Internet is offered by www.copernic.com. Copernic offers free basic search engine software with a powerful search engine technology that searches multiple search engines at once. Other features include the ability to verify valid links and avoid viewing broken ones; to sort results by title, search engine, or address; and to recall searches that have already been conducted. This program is a must-have for the first responder who wishes to gather intelligence information on the Internet.

When surfing the Internet for intelligence information, it's important to keep in mind that the Internet Protocol (IP) address associated with the government/law enforcement computer can be "seen" by the servers hosting those sites. All Internet traffic is subject to monitoring by the host server. If it's necessary to surf anonymously, law enforcement should use a dedicated connection that is not associated with the agency, turn off cookies, clean out history folders, and routinely remove cached files. Or consider using an anonymizer that masks the IP address used to connect to the servers and/or Web sites. Some of the more popular anonymizer's include Ghostsurf, Anonymizer, and Webtunnel. This is especially important when doing undercover online investigations, as discussed in Chapter 5. Also, be sure to not leave the Internet connection open and be sure to surf behind a firewall.

Learner Activity

Using the Boolean search techniques described earlier, visit some of the following Web sites: www.searchirc.com, www.groups.google.com, and www.google.com. Practice each of the Boolean search techniques. Describe, typically, the return results when using the + or AND, – or NOT, the OR limiter, and quotation marks in contrast to when not using them.

Using the Gathered Intelligence

What to do with the information is the final step. All of the information obtained has to be scrutinized for its overall evidentiary or intelligence value. The *NATO Open*

Source Intelligence Handbook (North Atlantic Treaty Organization, 2001) provides an Open Source Intelligence (OSINT) process that provides guidelines on how to handle intelligence information. The OSINT process includes the following steps:

1. **Discovery** Know who knows the information
2. **Discrimination** Know what's what
3. **Distillation** Know what's hot
4. **Dissemination** Know who's who

The discovery step not only includes knowing who in the organization knows the information, but who on the outside knows as well. Does the criminal element know of the information? Do the criminals know that law enforcement knows the information?

The discrimination process requires the analyst or investigator to correctly recognize and identify useful information. What is the worth or value of the information? How does it apply to the investigation or intelligence that is being sought?

Distillation is the process of prioritizing the information from most valuable to least valuable and preparing it for dissemination, the final step. When disseminating the information, it's critical to know who needs it and why. How is the information going to benefit the investigation?

The OSINT process works well in organizations that require intelligence information to pass through many hands. The concept also works well when an investigator is searching and/or discovering the intelligence information.

Learner Activity

Conduct keyword searches on the Internet for potential open-source intelligence information that might be useful to law enforcement. Avoid using typical news sources, and conduct keyword searches in some areas of the Internet that have been discussed earlier. Presume that any information found is not known to law enforcement. Apply the four-step Open Source Intelligence (OSINT) process to the open-source information and/or intelligence you found. Explain each step of the process, and apply it to the information you located. In your own words, report your findings.

8.3 HIGH-TECH CRIME WEB SITES

The Internet contains valuable information that law enforcement can use to inform, network, communicate, and assist with investigations. The key is knowing where to look. This section contains listings of useful Web sites, categorized by topic, that law enforcement and criminal justice students alike can find beneficial. Brief summaries of the types of information that can be found at each site are also included. It would be fair to identify some of these sites as "criminal sites" that cater to the criminal element. However, effectively combating high-tech criminals requires law enforcement and criminal justice students to "know thy enemy." This is not a conclusive list, but includes sites we and others have used with success. We do not endorse any of these Web sites, and the web addresses were current at the time of writing, although they are subject to change.

E-Mail Harassment, Threats, and Cyberstalking

E-mail harassment, threats, and cyberstalking can be just as terrifying as similar real-world events. The following Web sites contain information on organizations dedicated to fighting online harassment/threats along with providing helpful resources for victims.

www.cyberangels.org/—Cyber Angels
Considered the oldest and world's largest Internet safety organization, Cyber Angels, a program of the Guardian Angels, is a source for first responders to obtain information on Internet safety and refer victims to report child pornography, cyberstalking, identity theft, fraud, and hacking. Cyber Angels offers helpful tips for crime victims and also assists first responders investigating these online crimes.

www.haltabuse.org/—Working to Halt Online Abuse (WHO@) A volunteer organization founded in 1997 to fight online harassment through education of the general public, education of law enforcement, and the empowerment of victims. WHO@ offers training for both online and offline stalking and harassment along with tips for victims and intvestigative assistance.

www.cotse.net—Your Shield from the Internet
A comprehensive source to which first responders can refer victims of cyberstalking to help them protect their privacy rights and learn more about offline and online legal issues. Of particular interest are the many free privacy tools offered that help victims protect their computers and files from intruders.

www.ncvc.org—The National Center for Victims of Crime
A comprehensive Web site for crime victims, it also contains an excellent Stalking Resource Center that includes a listing of state stalking laws and an information clearinghouse along with links for victim assistance, actual stalking cases, statistics, resources, publications, and more.

www.atapusa.org/—Association of Threat Assessment Professionals
Founded in 1992 by the Los Angeles Police Department Threat Management Unit, this site is composed of law enforcement, prosecutors, mental health professionals, and corporate security experts who are dedicated to the prevention of stalking, workplace violence, and attacks or threats of attacks against public figures. First responders can obtain useful information related to these topics and also find information on how to become a member of this unique organization.

www.emailman.com/finger/—eMailman Finger
This Web page is hosted by Emailman, LLC, and the Web site is "meant to provide information and resources for electronic mail, as well as point to other

information and sources." The Finger page provides information on how obtain the name of a person associated with some e-mail accounts and also provides excellent links on how to find someone's e-mail address. This Web site can be used by the first responder when investigating e-mail harassment or cyberstalking cases. It is also a great resource for criminal justice students to learn more about the techniques needed to investigate such cases.

www.cybercrimes.net/persons/stalking/stalking.html—University of Dayton Law School Cybercrimes Stalking page
This page, created by University of Dayton Law School Professor Susan Brenner, is dedicated to cyberstalking and provides excellent links on the topic, including links to case studies and legal issues dealing with this contemporary criminal activity.

www.getnetwise.org/—Get Net Wise
Get Net Wise is a site created through a partnership of Internet industry corporations and public interest organizations, and it advertises itself as a one-stop source of information to assist families in making informed decisions about Internet use. It also offers a kids safety page that provides an online safety guide, online filtering tools, and a link to report illegal activity to state police in all 50 states.

www.cybersnitch.net—Cyber Snitch
A premier Web site for reporting high-tech crimes ranging from child pornography, e-mail harassment, and auction fraud to illicit drug sales and prostitution. The online dispatch center allows complainants or victims to submit reports of illegal activity and they can also do it anonymously. The reports are then "dispatched" to all Cyber Snitch members who comprise the law enforcement community. Law enforcement officers can then dispatch themselves to the call and conduct appropriate follow-up investigation or, at the very least, get the complainant in touch with somebody who can assist.

Auction/Online Fraud

As alluded to earlier in this text, according to the Federal Trade Commission (FTC) *National and State Trends in Fraud* and *Identity Theft* (2005), Internet auction fraud is the second most common form of fraud, accounting for 16 percent of all complaints. The following Web sites contain information on reporting auction fraud, filing reports of auction fraud victimization, and how to search for eBay members in conjunction with an auction fraud investigation. The slang term we coined for this illegal activity is "frauction."

www.reportauctionfraud.com/main.php4—Report Auction Fraud
A Web site based in the United Kingdom that is dedicated to the fight against the growth of online auction fraud. It also contains a useful list of advice for online buyers to help them avoid becoming a victim of online auction fraud.

www.ifccfbi.gov/index.asp—Internet Fraud Complaint Center (IFCC)
IFCC is a partnership between the Federal Bureau of Investigation (FBI) and the National White Collar Crime Center (NW3C). For victims of Internet fraud, IFCC provides a convenient and easy-to-use reporting mechanism that alerts authorities of a suspected criminal or civil violation. For law enforcement and regulatory agencies at all levels, IFCC offers a central repository for complaints related to Internet fraud, works to quantify fraud patterns, and provides timely statistical data of current fraud trends. The site also contains a 2001 Internet auction fraud study that highlights the continued worldwide nature of the problem.

www.fraud.org—National Internet Fraud Watch Information Center
This site contains information about telemarketing fraud, Internet fraud, scams against businesses, elder fraud, and more. There is also an online complaint form that consumers can fill out to obtain assistance and forward their complaints to the appropriate law enforcement agencies.

search.ebay.com/—Search for eBay Members
eBay is the most popular auction site on the Internet, and all of the auction fraud cases we have investigated have involved sellers and/or buyers using eBay. eBay is very proactive in its efforts to thwart this illegal behavior, and it cooperates fully with law enforcement when necessary. When investigating an auction fraud involving eBay, you can also search for members at the Web site. You can search by e-mail address or member ID number.

Identity Theft

According to the Federal Trade Commission (FTC) *National and State Trends in Fraud and Identity Theft* (2005), identity theft is still ranked number 1, accounting for 39% of all complaints received. These resources are links for the FTC identity theft Web site, the Identity Theft Resource Center, the Privacy Rights Clearinghouse, and other Web sites of interest to consumers and/or victims of identity theft. Providing victims with these resources can help them begin the repair process.

www.consumer.gov/idtheft/—Federal Trade Commission National Resource for Identity Theft
The premier U.S. government Web site for increasing awareness, reporting, investigation, and prevention of identity theft. The site contains a members-only area for restricted law enforcement access to the Identity Theft Clearinghouse, which searches for other identity theft complaints nationwide that may be related to one currently being investigated. The site also contains useful links and free educational resources for law enforcement, victims, and businesses.

www.idtheftcenter.org—Identity Theft Resource Center
The Identify Theft Resource Center is a nonprofit Web site dedicated to consumer protection from and prevention of identify theft. It also supports and

advises government agencies, legislators, and companies on identify theft. It provides links for victim resources, consumer resources and scam alerts, law enforcement, media sources, and a reference library. This Web site should be provided as a source for any victim of identify theft.

www.privacyrights.org—Privacy Rights Clearinghouse
The Privacy Rights Clearinghouse is a nonprofit consumer information and advocacy organization. It provides a wealth of information on identity theft, background checks, and other privacy issues related to financial, Internet, telecommunications, public records, and direct marketing of information. A most useful part of the Web site associated with identity theft is the Sample Letters page, which provides victims with samples of appropriate letters to write to dispute inaccuracies on credit reports effectively, to stop contacts by collection agencies, and for other uses that are specific to California. This is another Web site that should be provided to victims of identify theft.

www.usdoj.gov/criminal/fraud/idtheft.html—U.S. Department of Justice Identity Theft and Fraud
This Web site is administered by the U.S. Department of Justice and provides consumers and victims with information related to common ways identity theft is committed, how to respond to it and, most important, how to avoid becoming a victim. It also contains information related to what the DOJ is doing about identify theft along with recent examples of successful investigation and prosecution.

www.ftc.gov/sentinel—Federal Trade Commission Consumer Sentinel
The Consumer Sentinel is a unique investigative cybertool that allows law enforcement members secure, online access to hundreds of thousands of consumer complaints dealing with Internet, telemarketing, and other types of distant-selling fraud. Membership is restricted to law enforcement only and certain Better Business Bureaus. This site also contains an identity theft database where law enforcement can submit complaints and/or view other complaints that have been filed. It allows law enforcement to track identity theft trends and suspects across the nation.

Credit Card Fraud and Other White-Collar Crimes

Credit card fraud is not a new phenomenon and has been around since plastic cards were introduced to the masses. Unfortunately, technology, such as skimmers and the Internet, have made credit card fraud and other white-collar crimes easier. The following Web sites contain intelligence, educational, and investigative resources to use to combat white-collar crime.

www.ckfraud.org—National Check Fraud Center
The National Check Fraud Center is a private organization that provides nationwide, updated multisource information and intelligence to support local law

enforcement, federal agencies, financial and retail communities in the detection, investigation, and prosecution of known check fraud and white-collar crimes. The site also includes a link victims can use to report a white-collar crime.

www.fincen.gov/—Financial Crimes Enforcement Network (FINCEN)
FINCEN is a network managed by the U.S. Department of Treasury. The primary mission is to fight the complex problem of money laundering, including terrorist financing and other illicit activity. One primary goal of FINCEN is to support federal, state, and local law enforcement through information sharing and investigative assistance.

www.einformation.usss.gov—United States Secret Service (USSS) eInformation Network
This USSS network contains a unique collection of resources and databases that help financial institutions and law enforcement with the investigation of financial crimes, primarily the suppression of counterfeiting currency. All secure databases are law enforcement restricted. Law enforcement personel must register to be granted access. The Counterfeit Note search site allows qualified users to search on and identify U.S. counterfeit currency. The site also contains links to electronic crimes task forces throughout the country.

www.imolin.org—International Money Laundering Information Network
This site is administered by the United Nations and serves as an Internet-based network assisting governments, organizations, and individuals in the fight against money laundering. It is a great resource for practitioners and researchers to find the latest information on efforts to combat counterfeiting and money laundering along with the latest trends on these topics.

4-1-9 Scams—Advanced Fee Fraud and Other Scams

Advanced fee fraud is also a tried and true fraud that found early success with the fax machine. Today, e-mail has made it simpler and more efficient, allowing the fraudster to reach hundreds of potential victims with the click of a mouse. The following Web sites contain information on protecting citizens from scams, resources for law enforcement, and mechanisms alerting the public to the most recent scams.

www.scamshield.com/default.asp—Scam Shield
Scam Shield is a Florida-based nonprofit organization that is dedicated to protecting citizens from scams and fraud schemes with advocacy and knowledge. Citizens and law enforcement can obtain information on some of the latest scams and also submit new and emerging ones.

www.antiphishing.org—Anti-Phishing Working Group (APWG)
The APWG is an industry association focused on eliminating the identity theft and fraud that result from the growing problem of phishing and e-mail spoofing. Phishing is the act of tricking somebody, usually via e-mail or other electronic means, into providing personal and financial information that is

ultimately used in furtherance of some other crime (i.e., identity theft). Spoofed e-mails are sent by phishers to lead the victim to a Web site where victims are tricked into providing personal and private information. Membership of this site is restricted to qualified financial institutions, online retailers, Internet service providers (ISPs), law enforcement, and solutions providers. Consumers can also report phishing scams and learn about current trends and efforts to combat it.

www.scambusters.org/—Internet Scam Busters
Internet Scam Busters is dedicated to exposing up-to-date Internet scams. First responders and consumers alike can visit this Web site to determine if questionable online content or e-mail is a scam.

Crimes Against Children: Child Pornography, Child Enticement, and Others

Several computer crimes task forces across the country actively search the Internet for child predators and sexual offenders. The U.S. Secret Service (USSS) eInformation site discussed earlier (www.einformation.usss.gov) includes links to some of the electronic crimes task forces throughout the country that can assist with online child predator investigations. First responders need the appropriate training and knowledge to conduct an online investigation of a child predator properly and effectively. Chapter 7 covers this topic in great detail. Coordination with authorities in the offender's city or state, presuming the location is outside the first responder's jurisdiction, is absolutely necessary. A complete listing of states and/or agencies with computer crime task forces is listed in Appendix A. The following Web sites can assist with the investigation of online child sexual predators.

www.icactraining.org/—Internet Crime Against Children (ICAC) Task Force — Training and Technical Assistance Center
Although mentioned earlier in this text, it is worth noting the critical role that the ICAC has played in training the nation's law enforcement officers to respond properly to and investigate Internet crimes against children that are committed by offenders who use the Internet, online communications systems, or other computer technology to sexually exploit children. The ICAC is currently composed of 45 regional task force agencies and is funded by the U.S. Office of Juvenile Justice and Delinquency Prevention. ICAC training programs are free to qualifying law enforcement agents and are offered throughout the country. Some of the course offerings include ICAC Investigative Techniques Training Program (ICAC-IT), ICAC Child Sex Offender Accountability Training Program (ICAC-CSO), ICAC Undercover Chat Investigations Training Program (ICAC-UC), and others. The ICAC is a great resource for any law enforcement agency looking to become well versed in properly investigating Internet crimes against children.

www.ncmec.org/—National Center for Missing and Exploited Children (NCMEC)
The NCMEC is dedicated to protecting children from those who seek to harm them. The NCMEC offers a host of resources dedicated to protecting children, including assistance with preventing and locating missing or exploited children. In addition, the FBI makes full use of all available resources for missing and exploited children investigations by assigning a Supervisory Special Agent to the center. The agent coordinates FBI and NCMEC resources to facilitate the most effective FBI response to child abductions, parental kidnappings, and sexual exploitation of children. The NCMEC provides technical assistance, training, and educational materials to help law enforcement investigate cases of missing and exploited children. In addition, it also offers a toll-free number and a CyberTipline, which handles leads from individuals reporting the sexual exploitation of children.

www.unh.edu/ccrc/—Crimes Against Children Research Center
Located at the University of New Hampshire, the Crimes Against Children Research Center (CCRC) is dedicated to combating crimes against children by providing high-quality research and statistics to the public, policymakers, law enforcement personnel, and other child welfare practitioners. CCRC is concerned with research about the nature of crimes, including child abduction, homicide, rape, assault, and physical and sexual abuse as well as their impact.

Hacking

As mentioned earlier, to combat criminality effectively first responders must "know thy enemy." We do not endorse any of these sites and ask readers when visiting these sites to use caution because they do contain what some might find offensive and disturbing material. At the same time, it is foolish for first responders and criminal justice students to turn a blind eye and pretend these sites do not exist. There is a plethora of them on the Internet, and these are just a few.

www.totse.com—Totse
This Web site was discovered after we arrested three youths for attempted burglary. The youths had visited the Web site and used some of the "advice" on how best to break into a home. Needless to say, it wasn't very good advice and they were arrested. Totse is a Web site devoted to the underground world of hacking, phreaking, and anarchy, to name a few. It's categorized by subject matter, such as "Bad Ideas," "Drugs," "Fringe," and others. This Web site can be viewed by the first responder to learn about recent trends in the hacker, cracker, and criminal underground.

www.2600.com—*2600 Magazine,* the Hacker Quarterly
This Web site is the home of *2600 Magazine,* which has been in existence since 1984 and has stood the test of time. *2600 Magazine* is named after the perfect 2600-hertz tone that was mimicked with a 1971 Cap'n Crunch cereal

box whistle that enable phreakers to make free telephone calls. The *Hacker Quarterly* is produced four times a year and contains articles on a variety of topics related to hacking, cracking, phreaking, and the like. A copy of it can be purchased at major bookstores, and some computer crime units even have their own subscription.

www.jargon.8hz.com/jargon_toc.html—The Jargon File
This Web site is a virtual "Hacker's dictionary," because it contains a wealth of information related to hacker history and meaning. It's a must-read for the first responder and criminal justice student who want to learn more about the history of hacking and get a grasp on the culture.

www.phrack.org—*Phrack Magazine*
This online magazine or ezine (electronic magazine) is free and is made available to the general public at this Web site. Its name comes from two other words in the digital underground: *phreaking* (cracking the phone network), and *hacking*. It is yet another source to keep up-to-date on the latest hacking and phreaking trends. Consistent with its credo, as long as there are computers, there will always be hackers, and this is a great place to learn more about them.

www.wardriving.com—War Driving
This Web site is devoted to the relatively new techno hobby called wardriving. *Wardriving* is the term used to describe the identification and marking of open wireless networks that can then be used to obtain free Internet or even computer network access. Many wardrivers actively communicate with each other via the Internet and share the locations of open wireless networks for their use.

Fake Identification

Many first responders working near or around college campuses have likely been exposed to the fake identification problem that runs rampant in these areas. College students often use fake identification to gain access to night clubs or bars. Some purchase fake IDs on the Internet, make their own, or obtain one from a person who is "of age" and to whom they look similar. However, of greater concern is the very good chance that fake identification cards will and have landed in the hands of terrorists. We are not implying that terrorists have purchased fake identifications from any of the following sites, but it's a very real possibility. First responders throughout the country encounter, seize, and secure as evidence and/or destroy fake identification cards on a daily basis. Many of the following Web sites pass off their products as "souvenir identification" and their templates contain text that states, "For Entertainment Only" or something to that effect. The use of photo editing software can often remove this disclaimer and make the fake identification appear more legitimate.

www.souvenirids.com—Souvenir IDs
This Web site advertises itself as "Your Complete Global Novelty Card Products Solution" and offers identification cards in numerous formats, including Social

Security cards, press passes, driver's license and identification cards, bail enforcement agent identification, and more. Although sold as "novelties," upon first glance these forms of ID can appear authentic, and if not appropriately scrutinized, they could pass as legitimate.

www.driverslicenseguide.com—ID Checking Guides
This Web site offers a very popular I.D. checking guide that can be utilized by first responders to help determine if an identification card is authentic. We have used similar ID checking guides in the field with success.

www.myoids.com—Make Your Own Fake IDs
This site allows users to create their own novelty identifications by printing and downloading templates, images, and logos. Once users have paid for and obtained the templates, they could conceivable run their own fake identification operation. Many first responders throughout the country have encountered such operations.

Cyberterrorism, Terrorism, and Organized Protests

The use of the Internet to carry out cyberterrorism is an ongoing battle in the virtual and physical worlds. Terrorists also use technology to further their agenda, and protestors use it to communicate with members of their cause. The following Web sites contain information on cyberterror, terrorist membership tracking, and scheduled organized protests throughout the United States.

www.cybercrimes.net—University of Dayton Law School Cybercrimes
This Web site (mentioned earlier) was created by University of Dayton Law School Professor Susan Brenner and is dedicated to cybercrimes and law on the "digital frontier." The site includes information on computer security, cybercrimes against persons and property, and cyberterrorism, just to name a few topics. The cyberterrorism page can be viewed at www.cybercrimes.net/Terrorism/ terrorism.html. This page is dedicated to the topic of cyberterrorism and includes articles on cyberterrorism along with other informative links on the topic.

www.protest.net—PROTEST.NET
PROTEST.NET is dedicated to the civil disobedience movement with the primary goal of serving as a media outlet for this group's perspectives. They are determined to create a "better world" free of economic oppression and to oppose the "radical religious right." In addition, the Web site also includes a comprehensive list of cities of protests, including dates, times, and meeting places for various causes. It also offer's a protest handbook for protesters and activists. First responders can visit this site regularly to prepare accordingly for a protest scheduled in their city.

www.trackingthethreat.com/—Tracking the Threat
This Web site is one of the more comprehensive and well-organized ones dedicated to providing a database of open-source information on the Al Qaeda

terrorist network. The names of known terrorists, locations, organizations, and events are all included and displayed in text, photographs, and link analyses that show relationships between terrorists members and organizations. Simply clicking the name of a terrorist member provides information related to whether the person is alive, his or her biographical background, who this person has or had relationships with, and more. This is a fantastic Web site for the first responder and criminal justice student alike.

Imaging and Mapping Web Sites

These Web sites can be utilized to obtain satellite images of locations throughout the world. They are useful for gathering intelligence information on properties or locations that law enforcement may intend to search, travel through or to, or those that are part of an investigation.

www.globexplorer.com/—GlobeXplorer
GlobeXplorer is dedicated to "Delivering the World's Largest Library of Aerial/Satellite Imagery and Maps." All of the images can be searched by completing simple fill-in fields containing the address, city, and state of the location. The response is an aerial/satellite image. Each online print contains a watermark, and high-quality black-and-white or color images can be ordered. However, the aerial views that are provided on the site free of charge are sufficient for most investigative or intelligence gathering purposes.
earth.google.com/—Google Earth
Distributed by Google, the Earth program offers a free software program or viewer of satellite and serial imagery from across the globe. It is great for finding a location or obtaining driving directions. More advanced versions are also available that offer other options such as 3-D map overlays, GPS data importing, higher-resolution printing, data integration, and customer support.
terraserver.microsoft.com/default.aspx—Terra Server, USA
Terra Server is a free service offered by Microsoft and advertises itself as "one of the world's largest online databases, providing free public access to a vast data store of maps and aerial photographs of the United States." Simply typing in an address, city, and state will reveal an aerial or satellite image of the location. All of the images, without watermarks, can be printed from a desktop computer and are above average in quality compared to other free sites offering similar data. The images can be printed and also include lines of latitude and longitude. The images can also be saved to a hard disk drive for later viewing.

ISP Lookup

When conducting investigations of e-mail harassment, cyberstalking, auction fraud, or other cybercrimes, it's often necessary to conduct an IP trace or lookup.

The following sites are great sources to conduct an IP lookup to begin the tracing process.

arin.net/—American Registry for Internet Numbers (ARIN)
ARIN's Web site offers a host of services related to Internet Protocol (IP) addresses and also contains a WHO IS search feature to help determine which server an IP is registered to. This can be used when conducting an e-mail trace to find out the physical location of the server, which may ultimately contain the name of the registered e-mail user.

www.samspade.org—Sam Spade.org
Sam Spade.org contains a very useful IP lookup feature to determine the server to which an IP address is registered. The site also offers a host of online tools, including a trace route function that shows the route an Internet transmission takes from its origin to destination.

www.geektools.com—Geek Tools
Like the previously mentioned sites, Geek Tools also offers a trace route feature and WHOIS lookup.

www.iaf.net/—Internet Address Finder
The Internet Address Finder offers free searches for e-mail addresses, nationwide white pages and yellow pages categorized by state, and a reverse phone lookup. It also offers a public records database search, which is linked to another service that requires the user to pay a fee to view the search results.

Computer Forensics and High-Tech Crimes

Once the first responder and/or criminal justice student masters the basic skills needed to respond properly to and investigate high-tech crimes, the next step in training and skill development is learning how to use computer forensics and other advanced techniques. These Web sites are industry leaders in the field of computer forensics and/or high-tech crimes and are considered reputable.

www.htcia.org—International High-Tech Crime Investigation Association (HTCIA)
The primary goal of the HTCIA is information sharing and exchange of matters associated with high-technology crimes. There are HTCIA chapters throughout the United States and abroad. This organization offers training opportunities for members, and the site also contains a useful link to other computer crime–related sites.

www.cops.org—International Association of Computer Investigative Specialists (IACIS)
IACIS is considered to be the industry leader in the field of computer forensics. It offers a popular basic Certified Forensic Computer Examiner (CFCE) program once a year. The CFCE program is a two-week labor-intensive course on computer forensics followed by a year-long certification process

that involves practical examinations of computer media followed by an extensive written exam. This certification is a must for any first responder or criminal justice student that desires to enter the field of computer forensics. Upon successful completion of the CFCE course, practitioners can also attend the advanced course. A basic course is also available for first responders.

www.nw3c.org—National WhiteCollar Crime Center
NW3C is a federally funded program that is dedicated to providing "a nationwide support system for agencies involved in the prevention, investigation, and prosecution of economic and high-tech crimes and to suppor[ting] and partner[ing] with other appropriate entities in addressing homeland security initiatives, as they relate to economic and high-tech crimes." NW3C also offers several law enforcement–only courses on the topics of computer forensics, cybercrime investigations, economic crimes investigations, and others. The Web site also contains several papers, publications, and reports on economic and high-tech crimes, which would be of interest to the first responder or criminal justice student.

www.e-evidence.info/index.html—Electronic Evidence Information Center
Electronic Evidence Information Center is essentially a one-stop source for information related to digital forensics, high-tech crimes, and other related topics. It is well organized and contains links to books, articles, papers, presentations, and the like. It is an excellent research source for first responders and criminal justice students alike.

Information and Intelligence Gathering and Analysis

Using the Internet for information and intelligence gathering is a must for any law enforcement agency. The Internet is a wealth of free information and potential intelligence that is just waiting to be tapped. The following Web sites contain information related to intelligence-gathering associations, resources, and best practices that are currently used in the industry.

www.ialeia.org/—International Association of Law Enforcement Intelligence Analysts (IALEIA)
The IALEIA is devoted to the role of intelligence gathering in law enforcement. Its membership spans the globe and is restricted to law enforcement and other public and private individuals who play an active role in intelligence gathering and analysis. IALEIA offers a biannual professional journal to its members along with training and networking opportunities.

www.gao.gov/special.pubs/soi.htm—*Investigator's Guide to Sources of Information*
Published by the U.S. General Accounting Office (USGAO), this 1997 guide is still a very useful resource for first responders and criminal justice students.

Although some of the information is outdated, the concepts discussed are still applicable today. The free guide is available in a Portable Document Format (PDF) or as a Web version. Chapter 5 of the guide is devoted to using the Internet for investigations.

www.odci.gov/csi—Center for the Study of Intelligence (CSI)
The primary mission of the CSI is to research, report about, and publish articles and reports on the topic of intelligence. The CSI publishes an unclassified periodical entitled *Studies in Intelligence* and also makes available reports and information on other gathered intelligence that has played a significant role in the country's history, such as information related to the Cold War.

www.intelligence.gov/—United States Intelligence Community
The United States Intelligence Community Web site, funded and supported by the U.S. government, is devoted to the intelligence community, which includes executive branch agencies (i.e., law enforcement) that work separately and together "to conduct *intelligence activities* necessary for the conduct of foreign relations and the protection of the national security of the United States." The Web site also includes a very extensive and useful recommended reading list.

www.odci.gov/cia/publications/facttell—*CIA Factbook on Intelligence*
This Web site contains the *CIA Factbook on Intelligence*. For the reader who wants to learn all about the CIA, from its history and the intelligence cycle, to the CIA Museum, this is the perfect page. You can download a compressed copy of the factbook or view the text-only version on the Web site.

www.assignmenteditor.com—Assignment Editor
The Assignment Editor is a one-stop source for news and research sources from around the globe. It contains links to major local, national, and international newspapers; television stations; useful research sites; law enforcement sites; and much more.

www.fas.org/irp/agency/doj/ncisp.pdf—National Criminal Intelligence Sharing Plan
In response to the September 11, 2001, terrorist attacks, the National Intelligence Sharing Plan was created as a guide for obtaining, identifying, analyzing, and disseminating intelligence information at all levels of law enforcement, including local, state, and federal agencies. A complete copy of the report can be obtained at this link. It's a must-read for all first responders and criminal justice students.

Name, Phone, and Address Lookup Sites

When conducting investigations, oftentimes first responders encounter suspects who they are unable to positively identify because the person is being deceitful or has fled the scene. Sometimes local and national databases do not contain any information that can be used to positively identify the suspect. First responders can turn to the many online databases that are freely available on the Internet to find potential identifying information or leads, such as the name or residence of a suspect's relative, that might help lead to the identification or location of the suspect. Some of these Web sites also offer photographs of convicted criminals or sex offenders who may very well be residing in the first responder's jurisdiction.

www.anywho.com—AT&T AnyWho Online Directory
This is one of the better free online directories and we use it frequently. The AnyWho Online Directory offers yellow pages, white pages, and phone number reverse lookups. Once an address is obtained, another link is available to get a map and directions to the location.

www.crimetime.com—Crimetime Publishing Company
Crimetime is by far the most comprehensive online collection of investigative resources available on the Internet. The Black Book Online portion of the Web site contains an ever-expanding list of free online searches in the areas of Social Security number validation, reverse lookups, phone directories, state criminal and sex offender records, federal records (e.g., aviation records, federal inmate histories, multistate sex offender registries), mail drops, death records, and more. Many of the popular and reliable name lookup and reverse directory sites are listed here. This Web site is a great addition to any first responder's Internet Favorites or Bookmarks list. Crimetime also publishes the popular book, *The Investigator's Little Black Book.*

www.familywatchdog.us/—Family Watchdog
Advertised as "Your Family's Best Friend," this relatively new Web site is the best sex offender locator on the Internet. Dedicated to keeping citizens, children, and the community informed about the locations of sex offenders in the neighborhood in the hopes of preventing yet another tragic story of a child assaulted, abducted, or killed by a registered sex offender. Simply enter an address on the homepage, and within seconds a map is displayed identifying the registered sex offenders that are in the area. Click the icons scattered about the map to display the name, photo (when available), address, crime convicted of, and physical characteristics of each entry. You can also search by offender name as well as search multiple states at once.

■ SUMMARY

This chapter provides the first responder and criminal justice student an introduction to intelligence gathering on the Internet. Open-source databases can provide the first responder with valuable intelligence information that can be used in support of an ongoing investigation or even to prevent a criminal act. Knowing where to search for information is the first step. Then, the key to discovering the information is properly searching for it using Boolean search techniques and keyword searches. Once discovered, the intelligence information needs to be properly scrutinized and ultimately disseminated to the appropriate people within the agency.

The online world is constantly changing, and to keep pace first responders must continually keep track of the latest developments. Some of the Web sites provided in this chapter may not exist in the near future or they will be expanded and become even more useful. The intelligence gathering techniques discussed, however, have stood the test of time and will continue to produce results.

The criminal element also has access to these same resources and criminals, in turn, can also use the Internet to conduct counterintelligence information gathering. Law enforcement should be mindful of what it makes available on the Internet and be wary of the ever-advancing online criminal. Criminals will continue to improve their skills, and it is not acceptable for first responders to remain continuously behind the curve. Ongoing training and personal development must be a priority, and law enforcement agencies should take advantage of the many free training opportunities available.

■ REVIEW QUESTIONS

1. What is the difference between open-source and closed-source data?
2. Explain the three basic concepts that are needed to search the Internet effectively for intelligence information.
3. What are Boolean search techniques? Provide three examples.
4. What are the four steps of the Open Source Intelligence (OSINT) process?
5. Name at least two Web sites that can help law enforcement effectively combat e-mail harassment, threats, and cyberstalking.
6. Name at least two Web sites that can help law enforcement effectively combat auction/online fraud.
7. Name at least two Web sites that can help law enforcement effectively combat identity theft.
8. Name at least two Web sites that can help law enforcement effectively combat credit card fraud and other white-collar crimes.
9. Name at least two Web sites that can help law enforcement effectively combat 4-1-9 scams.
10. Name at least two Web sites that can help law enforcement effectively combat crime against children.
11. Name at least two Web sites that can help law enforcement effectively combat hackers.
12. Name at least two Web sites that can help law enforcement effectively investigate fake identification.
13. Name at least two Web sites that can help law enforcement effectively combat cyberterrorism, terrorism, and learn about organized protests.
14. Name at least two Web sites that can help law enforcement with imaging and mapping.

15. Name at least two Web sites that can help law enforcement conduct ISP lookups.
16. Name at least two Web sites that can help law enforcement with information and intelligence gathering and analysis.
17. Name at least two Web sites that can help law enforcement looks up names, phone numbers, and addresses of individuals.

■ TERMS

Boolean search techniques	information	open source
closed source	Internet Relay	search engine
criminal intelligence	Chat (IRC)	

■ REFERENCES

Carter, David L. 2004. *Law enforcement intelligence: A guide for state, local, and tribal law enforcement agencies*. Washington, DC: U.S. Department of Justice.

Federal Trade Commission. 2005. National and state trends in fraud and identity theft. www.consumer.gov/idtheft/pdf/clearinghouse_2004.pdf (accessed November 19, 2005).

North Atlantic Treaty Organisation. 2001. *NATO open source intelligence handbook*. www.oss.net/dynamaster/file_archive/030201/ca5fb66734f540fbb4f8f6ef759b258c/NATO%20OSINT%20Handbook%20v1.2%20%2d%20Jan%202002.pdf (accessed December 20, 2005).

U.S. Department of Justice. 2003. *The National Criminal Intelligence Sharing Plan, Version 1.0*. www.it.ojp.gov/documents/NCISP_Plan.pdf (accessed July 26, 2006.)

chapter nine

Legal Issues

1. Analyze the Fourth Amendment of the United States Constitution.
2. Explain various applications of the Fourth Amendment related to the search and seizure of computer and digital evidence.
3. Explain the various exceptions to the Fourth Amendment related to the search and seizure of computer and digital evidence.
4. Explain the common format of an affidavit in support of a search warrant.
5. Identify common federal computer crime statutes.
6. Identify various state computer crime statutes.
7. Explain the impact of the USA PATRIOT Act on the investigation of high-tech crimes.
8. Explain the proper execution of a search warrant for digital evidence.
9. Explain the no-knock exception as related to executing a search warrant for digital evidence.

The right of the people to be secure in their persons, houses, papers, and effects, against unreasonable searches and seizures, shall not be violated, and no warrant shall issue, but upon probable cause, supported by oath or affirmation, and particularly describing the place to be searched, and the persons or things to be seized.

Fourth Amendment, U.S. Constitution

The framers of the U.S. Constitution had the foresight to realize that they needed to draft a "living and breathing" document adaptable to change. Never did they think that law enforcement would be collecting virtual, digital, and high-tech evidence, which, in certain cases, cannot be physically seen or touched but is critical to the successful prosecution of a case. The inherent flexibility of the Constitution has allowed it to survive the industrial and technological advancements of the past 200 years. It is imperative that law enforcement and first responders understand how the Fourth Amendment and other laws affect the collection, handling, and processing of high-tech evidence.

This chapter discusses the search and seizure of high-tech evidence and includes an examination of the Fourth Amendment, significant court cases, federal and state legislation, the drafting of search warrants and subpoenas, consent searches and other search warrant exceptions, and special legal issues that have affected both law enforcement and private sector first responders. Voluminous information pertains to the legal issues surrounding computer and high-tech search and seizure. It's important to note that this chapter is limited to those legal issues that most affect first responders. Other legal issues, such as the federal Electronic Communications Privacy Act (ECPA) and the Privacy Protection Act (PPA), have been mentioned elsewhere in this text and are more applicable to forensic examinations and seizures of stored communications normally performed by investigators with the necessary advanced training. However, the USA PATRIOT Act has broadened the powers of federal agents and the processes they use to obtain evidence in high-tech investigations. Implications of the USA PATRIOT Act are also discussed.

9.1 AN EXAMINATION OF THE FOURTH AMENDMENT

The best way to understand and define the Fourth Amendment is to divide it into and discuss it in three separate sections. The first part of the Fourth Amendment is as follows:

The right of the people to be secure in their persons, houses, papers, and effects, against unreasonable searches and seizures, shall not be violated . . .

Everyone (including corporations) subject to United States jurisdiction has the rights of the Fourth Amendment afforded to him or her. Notice that the amendment does not denote "citizens," but uses the word *people* instead, which means that citizens and illegal immigrants alike are afforded these rights. It is quite evident, then, that when law enforcement seeks digital or other high-tech evidence in this country or other U.S. territories, Fourth Amendment restrictions apply. However, the worldwide nature of high-tech crime often takes law enforcement outside of U.S. jurisdiction where Fourth Amendment rules do not apply. For example, if an investigation leads to Japan, with that country's cooperation, investigators could seize evidence consistent with Japanese law and turn over the results to U.S. investigators. The way in which this evidence is obtained wouldn't be subject to the same rules of evidence had it been obtained in U.S. jurisdiction.

In *United States of America v. Rene Martin Verdugo-Urquidez* (1988), the Supreme Court addressed the issue of Fourth Amendment application to the search and seizure of evidence at an overseas location. This was a Drug Enforcement Administration (DEA) case involving the search of two homes (without a warrant) in Mexico for cash proceeds and documents reflecting the defendant's participation in narcotics trafficking as well as evidence of his involvement in the kidnapping and assassination of a DEA agent. The agents had secured the assistance, guidance, and permission of the Mexican government. The district courts had suppressed the evidence seized by the agents. The court of appeals affirmed the suppression of evidence by a divided vote, holding that the Fourth Amendment, and its warrant clause in particular, applied to overseas searches and seizures of property owned by foreign nationals. The court of appeals upheld the suppression of the seized evidence and the United States appealed to the U.S. Supreme Court.

In its reversal, the Supreme Court disagreed with the appeals court analysis in that foreign nationals enjoy Fourth Amendment protection of searches of their overseas residences. In other words, foreign nationals *do not enjoy* Fourth Amendment protections of overseas searches and seizures of property owned by them. The Court's rationale rested on three principles. First, the defendant's territory or location of the search didn't fall under United States jurisdiction. Second, the search had been conducted with the permission and under the supervision of the foreign officials and was thus reasonable. Third, the international nature of criminal activity frequently requires searches overseas with foreign counterparts and imposing the warrant requirement is severely impractical, threatening not only law enforcement efforts, but also ongoing relationships with the hosts.

It can be surmised from the *Verdugo-Urquidez* case, that Fourth Amendment protections related to searches and seizures of evidence overseas do not normally apply. What does matter is the reasonableness of the search, which can be demonstrated by the procedure that was followed when obtaining the evidence. The Court further acknowledged that such cases will likely be decided on a case-by-case basis and that there are provisions of the Constitution that do not necessarily apply in all circumstances in every foreign place.

Using this case as a guide, it is apparent that U.S. law enforcement officials, in conjunction with and/or with the assistance of foreign governments, can seize high-tech evidence without Fourth Amendment implications as long as it is reasonable in light of the circumstances. Reasonableness can be demonstrated by following the laws and legal procedures of the host country, for example.

The Fourth Amendment grants people the right *to be secure* in *their persons, houses, papers, and effects.* This is an inherent right that balances the governments need to investigate criminal activity while preventing unnecessary and unwarranted police intrusions. However, it is a limited right and is not applied to all searches and seizures. Furthermore, it is a personal right and can be claimed only by the person who is the subject of the search. People have the right to be free of a search of their person (i.e., body, personal effects carried with them, intrusion into their pockets, etc.) without a warrant or the existence of a commonly held exception, which is discussed later. Any place people live, including their houses, hotel or motel rooms, apartments, cabins, tents, rented rooms inside a private residence, or any other habitation, falls under Fourth Amendment protection. *Papers* may include writings, check book ledgers, spreadsheets, business records, bank records, and the like. *Effects* is the catchall phrase of the amendment that essentially encompasses everything else. *Effects* could include computers, cars, airplanes, boats, luggage, containers, handbags, or any place where evidence could be concealed. The search and seizure of high-tech evidence falls under the *effects* phrase used in the Fourth Amendment.

. . . against unreasonable searches and seizures, shall not be violated, and no warrant shall issue, but upon probable cause, supported by oath or affirmation . . .

The Fourth Amendment does not prohibit all searches and seizures, but specifically forbids "unreasonable" ones. The standard of reasonableness is viewed in light of the totality of the circumstances. For example, in *Verdugo-Urquidez* (discussed earlier) the justices examined the totality of the circumstances as demonstrated in their ruling (in part) when they highlighted the assistance and cooperation of the foreign agents and the ensuing procedures that were followed when the searches and seizures took place. Reasonableness often is decided on a case-by-case basis in light of prevailing case law and established criteria.

A **search** and a **seizure** are two separate activities and are worth discussing separately. A *search* can be defined as a governmental infringement into a person's reasonable expectation of privacy for the purpose of discovering things, both tangible and intangible, that could be used as evidence in a criminal prosecution (Brandl 2004). Areas where somebody may have a reasonable expectation of privacy include houses, papers, and effects as outlined in the Fourth Amendment. *Seizure* has been defined as the legal act of taking or seizing something that may constitute evidence or controlling (i.e., apprehending or arresting) somebody because that person has violated the law. This definition also extends to things both tangible (e.g., a car) or intangible (e.g., digital text). For example, in *Katz v. United States* (1967), the Court included electronic surveillance within the confines of a search and deemed the interception of words a seizure.

The Fourth Amendment's stance on a person's right to be free of any and all unreasonable searches and seizures is a command written as it *shall not be violated.* This is not an option, and the courts have remedies in place to cure a wrong. One remedy is the **Fruits of the Poisonous Tree** doctrine, which was first established in the case of *Silverthorne Lumber Company Co., Inc. v. United States* (1920). In the *Silverthorne* case, federal agents, without authority, searched the offices of the lumber company and seized all of the books, papers, and documents found there. They then attempted to use the documents as evidence in criminal proceedings. The Supreme Court eloquently chastised the government and said, "The essence of a provision forbidding the acquisition of evidence in a certain way is that not merely evidence so acquired shall not be used before the Court but that it shall not be used at all." Therefore, evidence unlawfully obtained cannot be used against defendants in criminal court proceedings. There is a good faith exception that helps to minimize unintentional illegal searches whereby if police reasonably believed they were acting under proper authority when the search or seizure took place, then the evidence can still be allowed into court (see *United States v. Leon*, 1984). However, intentional or negligent violations can also be remedied through civil or criminal court actions against law enforcement.

All warrants must be issued upon probable cause. *Probable cause* has been defined in several ways with common underpinnings. An acceptable definition includes a reasonable belief that a crime has been, is being, or is about to be committed and the accused committed or was about to commit it. All of the information garnered in accordance with an investigation, observations made by law enforcement, or information reliably reported by a citizen witness can all be used as a basis to establish probable cause. This information must be deemed reliable and ultimately approved by a judge, court commissioner, or magistrate. However, merely telling a judge about it is not enough.

Typically, the probable cause information is spelled out in a written **affidavit.** The affidavit is a chronological and detailed re-creation of the events or facts that tend to establish probable cause. The affidavit is the foundation of the search warrant and is what the judge will base the probable cause determination upon when deciding to grant and/or deny the warrant. Drafting an affidavit is discussed later in this chapter. For now, it's important to understand the role of the affidavit in the search warrant process.

The information provided in the affidavit must be sworn to in the form of an oath or affirmation. Again, it is not enough to merely tell a judge or magistrate about the information that leads to probable cause. The information must be spelled out for him or her. It must also be sworn to in front of somebody who has the power to give oaths or affirmations. Across the country, a judge or magistrate generally has such power. Both oaths and affirmations are formal legal procedures whereby a law enforcement officer swears to the truthfulness of the information contained in the affidavit. The primary difference between the two is that an oath typically invokes "God" as a witness whereas an affirmation does not. In both instances, the oath taker is swearing that the information is true and correct to the best of his or her knowledge.

. . . and particularly describing the place to be searched, and the persons or things to be seized.

The affidavit in support of the search warrant not only contains a detailed chronological explanation of the events, information, or evidence that establishes probable cause; it also establishes the location and/or persons to be searched and/or items to be seized. These descriptions must be done with sufficient "particularity." In other words, when describing a location to be searched the address alone is not sufficient. The full address, including city, state, county, and zip code should be included along with a physical description of the house, business, or property to be searched. The type of structure, whether it's a single story or multiple stories, the color, whether the garage is attached or detached, and the side of the street that it's on (e.g., north or south) help to establish particularity. When describing a person, the person's name alone doesn't suffice. The description should include the full name, date of birth, height, weight, sex, race, hair color, eye color, and any scars, marks, tattoos, or other identifiers—all of the characteristics that make the person unique. The property to be seized should also be particularly described. For example, if searching for a computer, it is inadequate to state, "black laptop computer." A more sufficient description, if available, would include the make, model, size, color, and even the serial number of the evidence. The descriptions should be of such particularity that the warrant could be provided to somebody unfamiliar with the case and that person would be able to properly identify the location, person, or property to be searched or seized. A practical example is provided later in this chapter.

Searching computer files can also pose challenges related to particularity and specificity. For example, drug-related computer files might contain information that is commonly found in text documents or spread sheets, but it is also possible that defendants could hide such data within image files using steganography or by simply changing the file name extension to make a text file, for instance, appear like an image file. This needs to be recognized and explained when drafting search warrants for computers and other digital evidence. Also, during a search, if the scope of the search changes directions because other evidence is located, for example, the search should be stopped and a new warrant obtained for the new criminal offense. These issues are explored further later in this chapter.

9.2 COMMONLY HELD EXCEPTIONS TO THE SEARCH WARRANT REQUIREMENT

There are several commonly held exceptions to the search warrant requirement. Although most prosecutors prefer that warrants are obtained for all arrests, searches, and seizures, it's impractical to obtain one in most instances. Most arrests are made in the field based upon probable cause, and most searches are conducted within one of the commonly held exceptions. Some of these exceptions include consent, plain view, search incident to a lawful arrest, exigent circumstances, private sector searches, and inventory inspections, just to name a few. These exceptions apply directly to the investigation of high-tech crimes and are discussed in the following subsections.

Consent

Law enforcement officers can search somebody or that person's property with the person's **consent.** For somebody to give consent, that person must have the authority to do so and must give it knowingly and voluntarily. Whether consent was properly given is based upon the totality of the circumstances. When determining if consent was given knowingly and voluntarily, the Supreme Court has cited the following factors to be considered: the age, education, intelligence, physical and mental condition of the person giving consent; whether the person was under arrest; and whether the person had been advised of his or her right to refuse consent (see *Scheneckloth v. Bustamonte* 1973). These factors are guidelines and are not absolute. For example, it is not required that a person be told he or she has the right to refuse consent, but it may be a factor when evaluating whether consent was voluntarily given.

Obtaining consent to search a computer can bring up issues related to the scope of consent and whether the party granting consent has the authority to do so. For example, if an officer asks, "Can I search the interior of your car for drugs?" it is quite clear that the scope of consent includes the inside of the car, underneath the seats, inside the center console, and so forth. In contrast, if an officer asks, "Can I search your computer for child pornography?" does this mean all computer files are going to be opened or is consent to search given for only one directory and not another? Experts recommend that computers and computer files themselves be treated as separate locked containers. When obtaining consent to search a computer, it should be expressly stated that the intent is to look into all computer files. The scope of consent can also be expressly stated by having the person granting consent sign a written consent form that outlines the nature or scope of the search (the more explicit the scope of consent, the better). Depending upon what is found during the consent search, the scope of consent can be expanded with additional consent. This is demonstrated in the case of *United States of America v. Shelby Lemmons* (2002), described as follows.

Bloomington, Indiana, police had received a complaint about a camera lens attached to the complainant's trailer home aimed at her bedroom. The camera cable led directly into Lemmons's trailer home. A patrol officer and detective obtained consent from Lemmons to enter his trailer and search for ". . . any recordings of goings-on in his neighbor's bedroom." Lemmons granted consent and also signed a written consent form. During the initial search, Lemmons handed the detective some pictures, saying, "You're going to want to see these too, but they're legal." The pictures were of a female in her late teens; in some of the pictures she was partially nude and could be described as posing in "sexually provocative" manners. Lemmons also pointed out some Polaroid photos of his 17-year-old daughter, one of which showed her wearing a shirt and underwear in a "here I am" type pose. The detective then saw a computer in the room and asked Lemmons if there was anything on it that he needed to be aware of. Lemmons told the detective that he could look if he wanted, and turned the computer on for him.

The detective recognized a program on the computer screen involving photographs. The detective started the program and on the hard disk drive found more than 100 images of child pornography. Lemmons remained either beside or a few feet behind the detective as the images were reviewed and said, "It's not what you think," claiming the images were sent to him by other people. Lemmons was ultimately arrested, charged, and convicted of using a minor to engage in sexually explicit conduct for the purpose of producing a videotape and possessing computer files containing depictions of minors engaged in sexually explicit conduct.

On appeal, Lemmons argued that police had exceeded the scope of his consent while searching his trailer. In evaluating the scope of consent, the court viewed the totality of the circumstances under what a "typical reasonable person" would have understood it to be based upon the exchange between the detective and Lemmons. Although Lemmons had signed a consent form granting consent to search the entire "premises," the court disagreed that this allowed for a blanket search. However, the detective had made it very clear, and the court agreed that he was only there, initially, to search for evidence of a camera or recordings of the neighbor's window. The facts demonstrate that Lemmons's consent was built on shifting sands, and, just as a warrantless search can be authorized by consent, the scope of a search can also be expanded by additional consent. Regarding the search of the computer, Lemmons's consent was demonstrated by him granting consent, turning on the computer, being present during the search of the computer, and never objecting during the search.

In contrast to the *Lemmons* case, in *U.S. v. Turner* (1999), police had obtained written consent to search Turner's residence for evidence of an assault. The written consent form expressly granted consent to search his "premises" and "personal property." However, during the search for the assault evidence in which a knife and bloodstains had already been found, an agent searched Turner's computer and discovered stored images of child pornography. The court determined that the search of the computer expanded the original scope of consent. However, based upon the *Lemmons* case, had additional consent been obtained to search the computer, then it likely would have been deemed appropriate.

Determining if a person has the authority to grant consent is another issue unique to computers. Today, computers can have multiple users, passwords, and logon profiles. For example, typical operating systems allow multiple users on one computer to each have their own accounts, screen names, and passwords to gain access to the computer. Passwords themselves demonstrate that computers are analogous to locked containers that require a key (i.e., password) to be accessed. Therefore, an individual cannot grant consent to search a particular computer or portion of the computer if that person does not have the password. However, can a third party grant consent to search a computer that he or she typically uses but does not own? The case of *U.S. v. Smith* (1999) sheds some light on this issue.

In the *Smith* case, Smith's live-in girlfriend contacted police to report that child pornography was stored on Smith's computer. At trial and upon appeal, Smith argued that his girlfriend didn't have the authority to grant consent to search his computer. In determining that she had authority to grant consent, the Court cited the following factors: she lived with Smith, had free (joint) access to the computer, Smith had encouraged her and others to use the computer, the computer was not password protected, it was located in an open and accessible area, there were other items near the computer (e.g., kids' toys) and other users' software programs were on it, the computer was occasionally used in Smith's absence, and no measures were taken to prevent her (or others) from accessing the computer. All of these factors should be taken into consideration when determining if a third party can give consent to search a particular computer.

When obtaining consent, ideally prosecutors recommend that consent be in writing, although this is not required. Furthermore, individuals have the authority to revoke consent at any time, even though it is not required to expressly tell them that. Again, these factors are viewed under the totality of the circumstances when determining if consent was knowingly and voluntary. Written consent forms can be beneficial in proving that consent was voluntarily given. In addition to information related to searching a person's premises or personal property, including language related to computers or electronic storage devices can help demonstrate consent to search these devices as well (see Figure 9–1).

Because consent forms are not standardized like the Miranda warnings are, they vary widely in wording and content. The consent form shown in Figure 9–1 contains wording that would likely be viewed as clearly understanding the scope

---

I, *(insert full name of person granting consent)*, having been informed of my Constitutional right not to have a search made of the premises hereinafter mentioned without a search warrant and of my right to refuse consent to such a search, hereby authorize Officers *(insert officer's name)* and *(insert second officer's name)* of the City of *(insert name of jurisdiction and/or police department)*, State of *(insert name of state)*, to conduct a complete search of *(insert complete address of location to be searched including city, state, and zip code)*.

These officers are authorized by me to take from this location any property *(a notation regarding specific property, evidence, or contraband, may be beneficial)* that they may desire. This written permission is being given by me to the above-mentioned officers voluntarily and without threats or promises of any kind.

Dated, signed, and witnessed

Figure 9–1   Sample consent to search language.
Source: Thetford, Robert T. (n.d.). Should officers use written consent to search forms? www.icje.org/id57.htm (accessed June 1, 2006).

of consent provided when requesting to search a computer or other electronic devices. Consent to search forms should include sections that allow officers to write in the scope of the consent.

Revoking consent at the time of a search is relatively simple and can be expressed by the grantor any time by merely saying, "Stop." However, sometimes it is necessary to remove a computer or other electronic device from its original location to a forensic laboratory (i.e., police department) to conduct a more thorough search. In these cases, permission or consent would also be needed to remove (i.e., seize) the computer from its original location. In such cases, it is recommended that the person granting consent be provided with written instructions regarding how he or she can revoke consent. Providing the person with 24/7 contact information of whom the person can contact and how to revoke consent would help comply with this standard.

Because there can be multiple users and/or owners of one computer, such as a husband and wife who use the same computer, a case may arise when one party grants consent, but another party objects. The recent U.S. Supreme Court case of *Georgia v. Randolph* (2006) helps address this circumstance. Although this was a case dealing with consent to search a residence for drugs, it has implications in all matters where police wish to obtain consent over property jointly controlled, including computers, and one present party objects while the other present party consents.

In *Randolph,* Randolph's estranged wife gave police permission to search the marital residence for items of drug use after Randolph, who was also present, had unequivocally refused to give consent. The trial courts denied Randolph's motion to suppress the evidence because he objected to the consent. The Georgia court of appeals reversed, and the state supreme court decided that consent given by one occupant is not valid in the face of the refusal of another physically present occupant. In other words, if two people are present and have authority to grant and/or deny consent to search, when one party objects and the other consents, the objection overrules the consent, thereby not allowing police to search. The U.S. Supreme Court supports this position. It is also important to keep in mind that this case only affects the consent exception to the search warrant requirement and none of the other commonly held exceptions discussed in this chapter are affected by it.

In applying the *Randolph* case to computers, if two owners of the same computer are present and officers ask for consent to search, both parties must provide consent. If one objects, then a consent search is not authorized. However, when there are multiple logon names or user profiles, each protected with its own password, the consenting party could consent to a search of only his or her portion (i.e., the locked container) of the computer while other user names/profiles could not be accessed.

In light of the *Randolph* case, had the circumstances been a bit different in the previously mentioned *Smith* case, where Smith's girlfriend granted police consent to search the computer in Smith's absence, had Smith been present to object, then consent would not have been authorized.

> ## Legal Points to Remember Regarding Consent
>
> - Consent must be given knowingly and voluntary.
> - The scope of consent must be understood based upon what a "typical reasonable person" would understand it to be.
> - When obtaining consent to search a computer or other electronic device, the more specific and detailed the request for the consent, the better. Avoid the use of general, broad terms.
> - If necessary to remove the computer from its original location, consent to seize it is also necessary.
> - Although not legally required, it is recommended that consent be in writing, which also includes a statement related to the person's right to refuse and how to revoke, consent.
> - When obtaining consent from people who jointly own a computer and are present, both must consent to the search, but may be able to consent to individual user/logon names unique to only him or her.

Learner Activity

Obtain a copy of the syllabus for the *Georgia v. Randolph* (2006) case at the following address: www.supremecourtus.gov/opinions/05pdf/04-1067.pdf. The syllabus contains a summary of the case and the primary legal issues that were discussed in the case. Read the entire syllabus paying particular attention to the "consent" legal issues at hand. Using the syllabus, your text, the Internet, and other academic sources, explain how the *Randolph* ruling might apply to cases involving computers and/or other devices that contain digital evidence. In the absence of consent, what other exceptions to the search warrant might apply to computers or other high-tech evidence and to what extent? Articulate your answer and provide at least two practical examples.

Plain View

Officers who observe immediately apparent evidence or contraband in **plain view** and who are lawfully in the area where the observation is made can seize the item(s) without a warrant. For example, in the case of *Washington v. Chrisman* (1982), a Washington State University police officer observed an underage student leave a dormitory carrying a bottle of gin. The officer stopped him and requested identification. The student asked to retrieve his identification from the dorm room and the officer followed. The student was not free to go and essentially was under arrest. The dorm was also occupied by Mr. Chrisman. While the officer stood near the threshold of the doorway to the room, he observed, in plain view, what he believed to be marijuana seeds and a pipe. The officer entered the dorm room and seized these items. A further consent search revealed additional marijuana and other drugs. Chrisman objected to the plain view observation and seizure of the evidence and argued that the officer needed **exigent circumstances** to enter the room. The Supreme Court upheld that it was reasonable for the officer to accompany the student to the dorm and monitor him to ensure the officer's safety. Furthermore, the court said that the officer had the right to remain literally at the students "elbow" at all times. Thus, the officer was legally and lawfully present inside the dorm when the observations were made, and the seizure of the evidence was valid.

Using the *Chrisman* case as a guideline, plain view observations can also be applied to computer crime cases. Instances similar to the *Chrisman* case occur on a regular basis during routine police work. If, for example, an officer responds to a loud music complaint, enters the residence in question, and while standing inside speaking with the occupant observes obvious child pornography on a computer screen, that image could be seized and used to establish probable cause in support of a warrant for additional searches and/or seizure. The officer would have to initially seize and preserve the image in question and could do so by merely photographing it or making a read-only copy of the data. This plain view observation, however, does not permit the officer to click and open other files to uncover additional evidence. Computer files that must be manually opened are not considered to be in plain view. It could also be argued in this hypothetical case that exigent circumstances would also permit the officer to seize the image, and this is discussed later.

Observations of potential evidence or contraband that is in public can also be seized under the plain view doctrine. The Internet is an open world of public data. Internet chat rooms, message boards, groups, and the like offer a world of information in the public domain. Items of potential evidence or contraband can be

---

Legal Points to Remember Regarding Plain View

- To seize something in plain view, officers must lawfully be in the area where the observation is made.
- It must be "readily apparent" that the item seized is evidence or contraband.
- Images on a computer screen observed in plain view could be seized and used to establish probable cause in support of a warrant to further search the computer.
- The contents of a file that must be manually opened are not considered to be in plain view.
- Observations of potential evidence or contraband in the Internet public domain can be "seized" without a warrant and used to establish probable cause in support of a search warrant and/or subpoena for additional documents.

discovered in these virtual environments through simple keyword searches, as discussed in Chapter 8. Information gathered in this fashion falls under the plain view doctrine and could be seized and/or used to establish probable cause in support of a search warrant and/or subpoena for additional documents. For example, officers investigating an anonymous tip regarding illegal activity associated with a person's e-mail account who has posted messages to a popular Internet groups site could conduct a keyword search for that particular e-mail account and view all posts made with it. The posts themselves may reveal incriminating information or serve as "digital fingerprints" that could be used to advance the investigation.

Search Incident to a Lawful Arrest

Officers are permitted to conduct a full search of an arrested person and a more limited search of the surrounding area, without a warrant (see *United States v. Robinson* 1973). The limited area is commonly referred to as the "lunge-reach-rule" and extends to the immediate area where one could lunge or reach to obtain a weapon or destroy evidence, otherwise referred to as the area immediately under a person's control (see *Chimel v. California* 1969). In *Chimel*, the court concluded:

> An arresting officer may search the arrestee's person to discover and remove weapons and to seize evidence to prevent its concealment or destruction, and may search the area "within the immediate control" of the person arrested, meaning the area from which he might gain possession of a weapon or destructible evidence.

The *Chimel* decision does not authorize a blanket search of an entire room in which a person is arrested. Rather, it is the reasonableness of a **search incident to a lawful arrest,** and the court will evaluate the totality of the circumstances or the "total atmosphere of the case."

In *Robinson*, Robinson was stopped for operating a vehicle after his license had been revoked. The officer placed Robinson under arrest for the driving offense and conducted a full search of his person. In Robinson's coat pocket, the officer found a cigarette package containing heroin. The district court upheld the seizure, and Robinson was convicted. The appeals court reversed the decision and the state appealed to the U.S. Supreme Court. The Supreme Court held that in the case of a lawful custodial arrest a full search is not only an exception to the warrant requirement of the Fourth Amendment, but is also a "reasonable" search under that amendment.

Using *Robinson* as a guide, it is permissible to search somebody and the person's immediate surroundings incident to a lawful arrest, the search must be contemporaneous (i.e., at about the same time) to the arrest, and the defendant must be present. Although this exception does not apply to typical personal computers, it does apply to electronic pagers, and it's unclear how it applies to other handheld devices; such as personal digital assistants (PDAs), cell phones, digital cameras, and laptop computers. The case law regarding these issues is in its infancy. In any event, handheld devices found incident to a lawful arrest should be removed with care and properly preserved.

Several court decisions, which refer to the *Robinson* case, have permitted the search of an electronic pager contemporaneous to a lawful arrest. For example, in *United States v. Reyes* (1996), the Court upheld the search of the defendant's pager that was found in a bag attached to his wheelchair within 20 minutes of arrest. Also relating to the search of pagers, in *United States v. Ortiz* (1996), the Court said,

> Law enforcement officers have authority to immediately search or retrieve, incident to valid arrest, information from an electronic pager in order to prevent its destruction as evidence; due to the finite nature of a pager's memory, incoming pages may destroy currently stored telephone numbers in a pager's memory. The contents of some pagers also can be destroyed by merely turning off the power or touching a button.

Therefore, because the data stored in pagers are perishable or finite and can easily be lost when the battery dies, it is turned off, a button is pushed, or the battery is removed appears to be the rationale behind permitting the warrantless search. However, because of the ability of other electronic storage devices, such as cell phones, PDAs, and laptop computers, to retain data in memory even when powered off, the rule established in *Robinson* doesn't appear to apply. Furthermore, these other electronic storage devices contain significantly more information than a typical pager does. When applying this exception to digital devices, evaluating whether the search is appropriate will depend upon reasonableness on a case-by-case basis. Technology changes at a much greater rate than case law, and *Robinson* may apply to digital devices that have yet to be commonly encountered by first responders. When in doubt, it is recommended that officers secure a warrant or consent to search the contents of electronic storage devices that are discovered incident to a lawful arrest.

Legal Points to Remember Regarding Search Incident to a Lawful Arrest

- Incident to a lawful arrest, officers are permitted to conduct a full search of a person's person and the area immediately under the person's control.
- The limited area is commonly referred to as the "lunge-reach-rule" and extends to the immediate area where one could lunge or reach to obtain a weapon or destroy evidence.
- The search must be contemporaneous to the lawful arrest.
- The courts have deemed reasonable the search of an electronic pager incident to a lawful arrest.
- To search other electronic storage devices, it is recommended that officers obtain consent and/or seize the device and obtain a warrant to search it.

Exigent Circumstances

The exigent circumstances exception to the search warrant requirement allows officers to search without a warrant if the circumstances "would cause a reasonable person to believe that entry ... was necessary to prevent physical harm to the officers or other persons, the destruction of relevant evidence, the escape of the suspect, or some other consequence improperly frustrating legitimate law enforcement efforts" (U.S. Department of Justice Computer Crime and Intellectual Property Section—Criminal Division 1999). Important factors to consider relevant to the degree of exigency presented include the following:

> (1) The degree of urgency involved and the amount of time necessary to obtain a warrant; (2) the officer's reasonable belief that the contraband (i.e., evidence) is about to be removed or destroyed; (3) the possibility of danger to police guarding the site; (4) information indicating the possessors of the contraband are aware that the police are on their trail; and (5) the ready destructibility of the contraband. (See *United States of America v. Carl M. White*, 1998, citing *United States v. Reed*, 935 F 2d 641, 643, [4th Cir. 1991]).

The exigent circumstances doctrine frequently applies to computer or digital evidence because such evidence is easily perishable. Basic computer commands can easily destroy data in a matter of seconds. Digital media can be altered or damaged by extreme temperature changes or magnetic fields. For example, a criminal could place a powerful magnet on a disk to intentionally damage the data. Exigent circumstances also applies to pagers because the information contained therein can be readily destroyed, as discussed earlier. The basic test to determine whether exigent circumstances exist is an objective one: "Whether a police officer under the circumstances known to the officer at the time reasonably believes that delay in procuring a warrant would gravely endanger life or **risk destruction of evidence** or greatly enhance the likelihood of the suspect's escape" (see *State of Wisconsin v. Rodney F. Volden* 2000).

Legal Points to Remember Regarding Exigent Circumstances

- Exigent circumstances allow a warrantless seizure and potentially a search to prevent physical harm to the officers or other persons, the destruction of relevant evidence, the escape of the suspect, or some other consequence improperly frustrating legitimate law enforcement efforts.
- The doctrine frequently applies to computers or digital evidence because such evidence is easily perishable.
- It is recommended that the exigent circumstances exception be viewed more like a seizure doctrine rather than a search doctrine.
- When in doubt, officers should seize the evidence or contraband and apply for a warrant to search it.

It is prudent to view exigent circumstances more like a seizure doctrine rather than a search doctrine. It essentially allows officers to do what is necessary to stop the destruction of evidence and not necessarily to search. For example, if officers encounter a suspected child pornographer in the process of deleting illegal images on his personal computer, they could take him into custody to prevent further destruction, seize the computer, and apply for a warrant to search it. If the suspect starts some automated process of deleting the images, the officers could then unplug the power supply at the back of the computer to prevent further destruction.

Workplace Searches

The Fourth Amendment applies to agents or officers acting under "color of law" and with governmental authority. It does not apply to private persons who might conduct searches on their own and report criminal activity. The person must have been acting on his or her own and not as an agent of the government.

The best case that addresses private sector searches is *United States v. Jacobsen* (1984). Although a Drug Enforcement Administration (DEA) case involving the discovery of cocaine in a package by a freight employee, it provides clear guidance on how properly to handle evidence discovered by a private person. The *Jacobsen* case also reiterates that Fourth Amendment requirements do not apply to private sector searches, whether intentional or unintentional and/or reasonable or unreasonable. In *Jacobsen*, a freight employee was examining a damaged package consisting of cardboard wrapped in brown paper. He observed a white powdery substance in the innermost series of four plastic bags that had been concealed in a tube inside the package. The employee notified the DEA and replaced the plastic tubes in the bag and put the tube back into the box. When a DEA agent arrived, he removed the tube from the box and the plastic bags from the tube, saw the white powder, opened the bags, removed a trace of the powder, subjected it to a field chemical test, and determined it was cocaine. A warrant was ultimately issued for the place to which the package was addressed, and Jacobsen was arrested, tried, and convicted. The court of appeals reversed and declared the private sector discovery and subsequent DEA discovery unconstitutional without a warrant. The United States appealed to the Supreme Court.

The Supreme Court opined that the freight employee, being a private citizen, is not constrained by the Fourth Amendment and merely reported his discovery to law enforcement. The DEA agent then re-created the search that had been conducted by the freight employee and therefore didn't expand the scope of the private search. The private sector evidence discovery was then properly used to establish probable cause in support of a search warrant.

The *Jacobsen* case provides a basis for computer crime cases where evidence is discovered by a private party. It is not uncommon, for example, for citizens to take their computers to a technician for repair. If contraband is inadvertently discovered during that repair and the technician notifies law enforcement, responding officers could re-create or have the technician re-create the search that led to the discovery and then seize the contraband. However, the officers cannot ask the repair technician to find additional evidence. Making such a request is analogous to deputizing the technician and making him or her an agent of the government. For example, in *United States v. Barth* (1998), a computer technician viewing files on a hard disk drive became a government actor when he contacted a Federal Bureau of Investigation (FBI) agent whom he worked for as a confidential informant and was instructed to copy the files onto disks for delivery to the FBI. It was not the fact that he was already an FBI informant that was problematic, but that the instruction to copy the files violated Barth's (the computer owner) Fourth Amendment rights. A better course of action would have been for the agent to go to the technician's location, view the file that was located, and then use it as evidence in support of a search warrant to search the entire computer.

In these cases, it is recommended that officers clearly document the process by which the private sector discovery was made. The officers should document the types of repairs that were being made; the route, file path, or process that was taken by the private party when the discovery was made; and then properly preserve the contraband (i.e., the illegal file). The discovery can then be used to seize the computer and obtain a search warrant to search it. Officers cannot exceed the scope of the private sector search that led to the initial discovery.

Another unique type of search, consistent with the private sector exception, involves searches at private and governmental businesses/offices. The courts have addressed both of these unique circumstances separately.

It is common for officers to respond to private sector businesses for complaints of fraud or employee theft. Although not as common, employers have also reported inappropriate material, such as images of child pornography, on their employees' computers. The material may have been discovered inadvertently as part of a routine upgrade or repair, or intentionally in conjunction with an internal work-related investigation. Whatever the case, before proceeding, the responding officer must determine to what extent the employer has the authority to search an employee's computer. This can be demonstrated by asking a few questions to help determine the employee's perceived or actual expectation of privacy:

- Is there a signed computer usage policy in place that prohibits unlawful behavior and notifies employees that they have no reasonable expectation of privacy because the computer is the property of the employer?
- Does the policy also notify the employees that all passwords are accessible to the employer and can be revealed to law enforcement for cause in conjunction with an investigation?
- Is there a "splash screen banner" in place that serves as a daily reminder of the computer usage policy in place?

Documenting the answers to these questions will help the officer determine if there is a reasonable employee expectation of privacy. In general, however, law enforcement officers can conduct a warrantless search of a private (i.e., non-government) workplace if the officers obtain the consent of either the employer or another employee with common authority over the area searched (U.S. Department of Justice 1999).

Consent searches of governmental computers pose a different challenge to the first responder. The U.S. Supreme Court case of *O'Connor v. Ortega* (1987) is the common authority on the topic of workplace consent.

Dr. Ortega was a physician and psychiatrist employed at a state hospital, who had primary responsibility for training physicians in the psychiatric residency program. Hospital officials became concerned about possible improprieties in his management of the program, particularly with respect to his acquisition of a computer and charges against him concerning sexual harassment of female hospital employees and inappropriate disciplinary action against a resident. Dr. Ortega was placed on administrative leave and hospital officials, allegedly to inventory and secure state property, searched his office and seized personal items from his desk and file cabinets that were used in administrative proceedings that resulted in his discharge. Dr. Ortega filed an action against his employer alleging that the search of his office violated the Fourth Amendment. The district court disagreed and ruled that the search was proper. However, the 9th Circuit Court of Appeals reversed and concluded that Dr. Ortega had a reasonable expectation of privacy in his office and that the search violated the Fourth Amendment. The U.S. Supreme Court granted certiorari and agreed to review this case on appeal for the 9th Circuit.

The justices applied an extensive analysis in this case, which is summarized here to include a specific application to public sector **workplace searches** of employee offices and, namely, computers.

The bottom line is that the great variety of work environments in the public sector and whether an employee has a reasonable expectation of privacy must be addressed on a case-by-case basis. However, the Court provides law enforcement and other public sector managers with guidelines when determining reasonableness.

First, the area to be searched needs to be considered along with whether a reasonable expectation of privacy exists. In workplaces, those areas and items generally within the employer's control include hallways, cafeteria, offices, desks, and file cabinets. Computers could also be included within this context. However, an employee may bring personal items from home, such as a handbag, briefcase, or closed luggage, and these items are not necessarily subjected to a typical workplace search.

Second, the person conducting the search also needs to be taken into consideration. An employee's expectation of privacy is different when the search is being conducted by a manager for work-related purposes versus a law enforcement official for criminal purposes. In other words, there is a greater expectation of privacy when the search is being conducted for criminal purposes.

Third, the scope of the search needs to be considered as well. The Court recognized that there must be a balance in the invasion of the employee's legitimate expectation of privacy against the employer's need for supervision, control, and efficient operation of the workplace. With that in mind, generally searches of an employee's office for work-related reasons satisfies the Fourth Amendment requirement. Requiring an employer to obtain a warrant whenever the employer wishes to enter an employee's office, desk, or file cabinets for a work-related purpose would seriously disrupt the routine conduct of business and would be unduly burdensome. Therefore, wide latitude is given to public employers in searching an employee's office for work-related, noninvestigatory reasons and work-related employee misconduct.

In summary, a search of an employee's office by a supervisor is "justified at its inception" when there are reasonable grounds for suspecting that the search will turn up evidence that the employee is guilty of work-related misconduct, or that the search is necessary for a noninvestigatory work-related purpose, such as to retrieve a needed file. In this regard, law enforcement officers cannot rely solely on an employer's consent to search a public sector workplace. The existence of a well-written employment policy that notifies employees they do not have a reasonable expectation of privacy in their workplace may help to support a law enforcement government workplace search. Applied to computers, if the initial scope of the search is for a work-related purpose, but during the search contraband (e.g., child pornography) is discovered, this discovery could be turned over to law enforcement and used to obtain a search warrant for additional examination of the computer. The person conducting the search (i.e., a workplace manager versus a law enforcement officer) can also determine the reasonable expectation of privacy that an employee might have.

Legal Points to Remember Regarding Workplace Searches

- The Fourth Amendment does not apply to private persons who might conduct searches on their own and report criminal activity.
- The contraband obtained by the private party can be turned over to law enforcement and be used in support of a search warrant.
- The private party cannot act as an agent of the government and conduct additional searches outside the scope of the initial discovery at the direction of law enforcement.
- Private persons can re-create for law enforcement the search that led to the discovery, but nothing more.
- The extent of a private sector search is determined by the expectation of privacy within the work environment. The extent of perceived privacy can be determined by asking a few simple questions.
- Work-related searches in public sector environments are typically lawful when conducted for work-related misconduct or when necessary for a noninvestigatory work-related purpose.

Inventory Searches

Inventory searches are routinely conducted by law enforcement officers for noninvestigatory purposes, such as to protect a person's property, and within well-established policy. During an inventory search, obvious contraband, such as a marijuana pipe, could be seized. However, an inventory search does not justify additional intrusion into locked containers that may contain evidence. The U.S. Department of Justice guide to searching and seizing computers and obtaining electronic evidence in criminal investigations summarizes the case of *United States v. O'Razvi* (1998), which succinctly addresses the unlawful search of computer media discovered during an inventory search.

In *United States v. O'Razvi*, the defendant moved for a new trial based on ineffective assistance of counsel due, in part, to counsel's failure to seek suppression of evidence obtained from the defendant's briefcase. Reviewing the suppression issue, the Court agreed that the contents of diskettes that were obtained pursuant to an inventory search of the defendant's briefcase were erroneously introduced against him at trial. Proper procedure, absent policy to the contrary, would have been to obtain a follow-up warrant permitting examination of the contents of the diskettes.

With the *O'Razvi* case in mind, if during an inventory search (e.g., when searching an automobile) electronic media or storage devices are found, prior to accessing (i.e., searching) it is recommended that a warrant be secured. If probable cause does not exist to support a warrant, then a search of the device is not warranted.

Legal Points to Remember Regarding Inventory Searches

- The purpose of an inventory search is to protect one's property.
- Inventory searches must be conducted pursuant to written policy and/or guidelines.
- Electronic media or storage devices discovered during an inventory search cannot be accessed without a search warrant.

Federal Laws

Although most first responders will be involved in investigating and/or reporting on high-tech crimes that can be prosecuted in their own state, there are several federal laws that regulate this type of criminal activity. Some of the more common federal statutes associated with criminal offenses that are likely to be encountered by first responders are listed in the following box.

A local law enforcement agency can seek the assistance of federal agencies, especially when investigating criminal offenses that cross state lines and those that are considered to be violations of interstate commerce. For example, a town officer

---

Common Federal Computer Crime Statutes

- Title 15, Chapter 41, Subchapter 1, Part B, § 1644—Fraudulent Use of Credit Cards; Penalties
- Title 18, Part 1, Chapter 47, § 1030—Fraud and Related Activity in Connection with Computers.
- Title 18, Part 1, Chapter 110, § 2251—Sexual Exploitation of Children (including child enticement)
- Title 18, Part 1, Chapter 110, § 2252a—Certain activities related to material constituting or containing child pornography

---

may take a complaint of a missing or runaway female juvenile who the parents suspect left to see a person that she met on the Internet. Subsequent investigation may reveal that she went to see someone she believed was a 16-year-old boy, but who instead is an adult that is now sexually exploiting her in another state. Because the criminal offenses—potential kidnapping, interference with child custody, child sexual assault, and others—have now occurred across state lines, it would be a matter that each state could prosecute and/or the federal authorities could prosecute as well.

State Laws

A local government may enact statutes or local laws that are more restrictive than state statutes. Currently, all 50 states in the United States have some sort of computer and/or high-tech crimes legislation. A listing of these state statutes can be found in Appendix B. The dynamic nature of computer and high-tech crimes in which the suspect and victim can be in different jurisdictions allows for law enforcement to prosecute for essentially the same offense in individual states. This is not considered double jeopardy because the prosecutions are occurring in different jurisdictions. Some computer crime statutes are more punishing than others are. For example, a violation of Wisconsin's Unlawful Use of Computerized Communications System statute (State Statute 947.0125), which addresses electronic (e-mail) harassment, can subject a suspect to a "class B" forfeiture, which is only a fine. In contrast, Arizona's harassment statute 13-2921, which addresses e-mail harassment, makes it a class 1 misdemeanor to "anonymously or otherwise communicate[s] or cause[s] a communication with another person by verbal, electronic, mechanical, telegraphic, telephonic, or written means in a manner that harasses." Conviction for this offense could land the offender in jail and/or subject the person to a fine.

Both state and federal laws are constantly evolving along with advancements in technology and the nature by which criminals use technology. For example, the state of Wisconsin is considering a new bill (2005 Assembly Bill 1010) that will place additional restrictions on computer access and use by offenders convicted of certain serious child sex offenses. The bill, if it becomes law, will prohibit these offenders from using a computer unless it is running software that prevents the person from accessing computerized child pornography or records such access for the agents' review; probationers must consent to a search of their computer by their agent at any time; and probationers shall allow probation officers to install and use software on any computer that the probationer uses for the purposes of preventing the computer from being used in preparation or in conjunction with child enticement or to facilitate a child sex crime.

9.3 IMPACT OF THE USA PATRIOT ACT ON HIGH-TECH INVESTIGATIONS

This section is meant to serve as an introduction to the USA PATRIOT Act. This extensive act greatly enhances the powers of federal law enforcement agents and intelligence officials to effectively combat terrorism and other criminal offenses affecting national security or traversing the country, including computer crime. The following information is summarized from the U.S. Department of Justice (2004) publication titled *Report from the Field: The USA PATRIOT Act at Work*. It is recommended that all students obtain and read a copy of this 30-page report, which can be downloaded at *www.lifeandliberty.gov/docs/071304_ report_from_the_field.pdf*. The report contains several practical examples of the USA PATRIOT Act at work in the field, consistent with other sections of this textbook.

In response to the tragic events of September 11, 2001, the U.S. Congress and the Bush administration reexamined the legal tools available to law enforcement to fight against terrorism effectively. Finding many of these tools inadequate, they set out to update, strengthen, and expand laws governing the investigation and prosecution of terrorism within the parameters of the Constitution while at the same time protecting civil liberties and civil rights. The true challenge within a free nation is finding the balance between becoming more secure and minimizing the government impact and/or intrusion into the civil rights and liberties of its citizens. Congress and the president believe they found this delicate balance within the USA PATRIOT Act. On October 26, 2001, President George W. Bush signed into law the Uniting and Strengthening America by Providing Appropriate Tools Required to Intercept and Obstruct Terrorism Act (USA PATRIOT Act).

The USA PATRIOT Act equips federal law enforcement agents and intelligence officials with the tools they need to mount an effective, coordinated campaign against the nation's terrorist enemies. The primary goal of the act is to prevent terrorist attacks from occurring and thus to disrupt terrorists' plans. The act expands the powers of federal law enforcement agents and intelligence officials, but, more important, breaks down "the wall" of secrecy that once prevented the sharing of intelligence information between intelligence officials and law enforcement agents. Some of the additional expanded powers include facilitating the sharing of federal grand jury and wiretap information obtained during a criminal investigation with intelligence and national defense officials, clearly making it a crime to provide terrorists with expert advice or assistance and/or material support (including all forms of money), making it easier to prosecute those responsible for funneling money to terrorists, strengthening the penalties for smuggling and/or concealing more than $10,000 in currency or other monetary instruments and transporting it out of the United States with the intent to evade reporting requirements, increasing the penalties for intentionally damaging a federally protected computer, and expanding the Internet records law enforcement may seek with a subpoena to include session times and durations, temporarily/dynamically assigned network addresses, and means and sources of Internet service provider (ISP) payments, including credit card and/or bank numbers. How the act has affected high-tech investigations is the primary focus of this section.

It is no secret that terrorists and other cybercriminals use the Internet, cell phones, and other high-tech devices to coordinate and carry out their illegal activities. Utilizing these technologies and common transportation makes the high-tech criminal very mobile; often they travel from one jurisdiction to another. Prior to the passage of the USA PATRIOT Act, federal agents investigating suspects that resided in another jurisdiction required agents to apply for any search warrants within the suspect's jurisdiction. Agents were then forced to forward all the information to the appropriate field office, which required extensive briefing and sharing of information for the other agents to draft the necessary legal documents. The act now allows for agents to apply for search warrants in their own district to be executed anywhere within the United States. This also applies to serving search warrants on Internet service providers and/or voice mail providers. No longer is an intercept order required to obtain voicemail or other stored wire communications. These changes alone save significant time and streamline the process of making out-of-district search warrants available to law enforcement in terrorism or other nationwide criminal investigations.

The act also recognizes that law enforcement is acting at a technological disadvantage in the war against terrorism and other high-tech crimes. The act provides law enforcement with new tools to fight terrorists who use modern technologies to plot attacks; enhances the use of wiretaps, pen register, and trap and trace devices; and helps officials obtain the cooperation of communications providers. The act also extends the jurisdiction of the Secret Service and FBI to investigate computer fraud. It also gives the FBI primary jurisdiction over a number of specific computer fraud offenses, including those involving espionage, foreign counterintelligence, and the unauthorized disclosure of national defense information. The act has also been used effectively to combat the sexual abuse of children facilitated by the Internet and other technologies (see Figure 9-2).

Furthermore, the act allows for the use of administrative and grand jury subpoenas to obtain information about temporarily assigned network addresses and users' billing records from electronic communications service providers. Although recipients of these subpoenas can challenge them in court, the speedy acquisition

In 2003, Indiana state police were informed that child pornography portraying a 13-year-old girl from southern Indiana had been posted to an Internet Web site. The initial investigation revealed that the father of the victim was the offender partially visible in one of the photographs. Using the USA PATRIOT Act, grand jury subpoenas were issued requesting relevant Internet subscriber information. This information confirmed the father's involvement. Ten days after the initial report, using the information obtained by the subpoena, a search warrant was executed at the father's home, and numerous items of child pornography were seized. The girl was interviewed and admitted she was being sexually abused by her father on an ongoing basis and that he was filming and photographing these sexual acts. The father was arrested and later pled guilty to five counts of producing child pornography. He is currently serving out his 10-year prison sentence. Using the USA PATRIOT Act, the investigators were able to significantly speed up their investigation, thus enabling the girl to be removed from her family's house more quickly and preventing further molestations by her father.

Figure 9–2　State and federal police make child porn arrest—prevent further molestation.

of such subpoenas, along with the information received, helps law enforcement effectively combat terrorists and other high-tech criminals, such as child molesters who use the Internet to share contraband, kidnappers who use e-mail to correspond with accomplices, phishers who use e-mail and the Internet to steal credit card information, or hackers who perpetrate denial of service attacks on ISPs.

The USA PATRIOT Act will continue to help authorities properly investigate criminal acts and prevent terrorist attacks. The next section capitalizes on this information and provides first responders with guidelines, legal issues, and practical examples when obtaining search warrants and subpoenas for high-tech evidence.

9.4 SEARCH WARRANTS AND SUBPOENAS FOR HIGH-TECH EVIDENCE

Individual state statutes dictate the proper format for writing a search warrant, but they must all conform to the Fourth Amendment requirements. The search warrant generally contains two parts, the "affidavit of probable cause" and the search warrant itself. The affidavit, consistent with the Fourth Amendment, normally contains the following information: name of the officer requesting the warrant and his/her qualifications to write it, description of the place to be searched and items to be seized, followed by the chronological facts that tend to establish probable cause.

Any experienced investigator or officer knows that drafting the affidavit of probable cause is the most time-consuming and detailed portion of the warrant. However, detail begins with describing the place to be searched with sufficient particularity. An investigator could draft the finest facts that tend to establish probable cause, but failing to sufficiently describe the place to be searched and assuring the judge that the proper location is going to be searched may make the difference between having it signed or completing a second draft. Serving a search warrant at the wrong location is not only embarrassing, but subjects the agency and municipality to civil liability and litigation.

As stated earlier, the items to be seized and where they are located must also be described with sufficient detail to the extent that somebody not familiar with the case could readily locate and identify the property during the search. This can be a daunting challenge when seeking high-tech evidence. Because of the complex nature of high-tech evidence it becomes necessary to define certain terms that are commonly used to describe it. To say that you are going to seize a computer, hardware, or software is not enough. These terms, and others, must be defined. Figure 9–3 provides a list of those terms that are commonly defined in a high-tech affidavit to support the items that are to be seized. It is not an all-inclusive list, and the nature of the computer or digital evidence to be seized will determine the terms that must be defined in the affidavit and ultimately for the court.

Addresses	Cookies	Data compression
Denial of service attack	Domain	Domain name
Encryption	File Transfer Protocol	Firewall
Hacking	Instant messaging (IM)	Internet
Internet Relay Chat (IRC)	Internet service providers (ISPs)	IP address
Dynamic IP address	Static IP address	Joint photographic Experts Group (JPEG)
Log file	Moving Pictures Expert Group 3 (MP3)	Packet sniffing
Peer-to-Peer (P2P) networks	Router	Server
Tracing	User name or User ID	Virus

Figure 9–3 Common terms to define in a high-tech crime search warrant affidavit. *Source:* The definitions for each term can be found in Appendix C and in the most recent U.S. Department of Justice, 2002, *Searching and Seizing Computers and Obtaining Electronic Evidence in Criminal Investigations,* at www.usdoj.gov/criminal/cybercrime/s&smanual2002.pdf.

Seizing high-tech evidence also raises questions about its relationship to the crime in question. For instance, is the computer, pager, or cell phone contraband, an instrument or mechanism by which the crime is committed, or the fruit of a crime? It is important to explain within the affidavit the relationship between the crime that has allegedly been committed and what is going to be seized. For example, a computer used to transmit child pornography is an instrument of the crime, and stolen computers are fruits of a crime. Printers used to print child pornography could also be considered an instrument used to commit the crime. The child pornography on the computer is considered contraband.

The oath or affirmation provision simply means that investigators must either reduce the facts that serve as the basis for probable cause to writing and/or swear to them verbally under oath. Most commonly, the facts are reduced to writing and become part of the affidavit of probable cause in support of the warrant. The reviewing judge or magistrate must be convinced that probable cause exists to sign and authorize the warrant. Prior to signing the warrant, this same judge or magistrate will administer an oath whereby the investigator swears to the facts and circumstances surrounding probable cause. Notice that the responsibility to present accurate and truthful facts upon which probable cause is determined rests completely on the shoulders of the law enforcement officer or investigator who requests the warrant. The judge or magistrate is merely the rubber stamp, and his or her decisions are based upon the information initially presented. These facts can be and often are challenged later during preliminary hearings. Therefore, it is critical that the affidavit of probable cause be truthful and accurate. If it is later discovered otherwise, the evidence obtained will likely be dismissed (e.g., the **Exclusionary Rule**) and the investigator's reputation potentially tarnished. If an officer or investigator has a reputation of being less than truthful, not only will this information be used against him or her on the witness stand, but judges may also become more critical of and even hesitant to sign this investigator's affidavits of probable cause in the future.

The probable cause in support of the warrant, which is articulated within the affidavit and is the basis by which the magistrate authorizes the warrant, is extremely important. Defense attorneys will target the probable cause during motion hearings in an effort to have evidence dismissed. It is often difficult to challenge the integrity of the evidence itself, but if the facts and circumstances that surrounded the discovery of it can be successfully challenged, then the evidence will be discarded. Lacking critical evidence can destroy the prosecutor's case, and as a result charges can be dismissed, unnecessarily reduced, or plead away.

The best way to demonstrate the proper form in which to write a search warrant for computer and digital evidence is to view a warrant that has been successfully in the field. Figure 9–4 contains an affidavit in support of a search warrant for a case that involved online communications between the defendant and an undercover agent posing online as a child. It also contains a definitions section and a chronological description of the events that lead up to the authorization to search the defendant's residence and seize and search his computer. It's also important to know how the investigator demonstrated his qualifications to write the affidavit.

Circuit Court Branch_____   Brown County   State of Wisconsin

State of Wisconsin)

) SS <u>Affidavit in Support of Search Warrant</u>
County of Brown)

Detective William Byte, a law enforcement officer of the Fort Howard Police Department, being duly sworn on oath, says that on this day in Brown County, in and upon certain premises in the City of Fort Howard, in said County, which premises are occupied or owned by **Joe A. Suspect,** and which premises are described as follows:

> **THE RESIDENCE AT 1275 UNIVERSITY AVENUE, UPPER APARTMENT, CITY OF FORT HOWARD, BROWN COUNTY, WISCONSIN. 1275 UNIVERSITY AVENUE IS A TWO-STORY STONE AND WOOD STRUCTURE. "JOE'S ANTIQUES" OCCUPIES THE LOWER LEVEL OF THE BUILDING. THE RESIDENCE AT 1275 UNIVERSITY AVENUE UPPER APARTMENT IS ACCESSIBLE BY A DOOR ON THE SOUTH SIDE OF THE BUILDING WHICH FACES EAST FROM A SMALL ALCOVE.**

There are now located at concealed therein certain things, which are:

1. Computer graphic files, photographs, magazines and printed documents which depict children in a sexually explicit manner contrary to law.

2. Computer hardware, that is, all equipment which can collect, analyze, create, display, convert, store, conceal, or transmit electronic, magnetic, optical or similar computer impulses or data. Hardware includes (but not limited to) any data processing devices (such as central processing units and self-contained "laptop" or "notebook" computers); internal and peripheral storage devices such as computer disks, magnetic media, floppy disks, CD-ROM drives, hard drives, disk drives, tape drives, and other memory storage devices; and any external attachments peripheral input/output devices such as keyboards, printers, scanners, and video display monitors; and related communications devices such as modems, cables and connections, devices used to capture and store electronic images such as digital cameras, scanners, and digital video cameras, as well as any devices, mechanisms, or parts that can be used to restrict access to computer hardware (such as physical keys and locks).

3. Computer software, that is, digital information which can be interpreted by a computer and any of it's related components to direct

(continued)

Figure 9–4 Sample affidavit in support of a search warrant.

the way they work. Software is stored in electronic, magnetic, optical, or other digital form.

4. Electronic media such as, CD-ROM, Digital Video Disk (DVD), Zip disks, and floppy disks.

5. Records and documents that would establish residency of Joe A. Suspect, which things are possessed for the purpose of evading or violating the laws of the State of Wisconsin and contrary to Section 948.12 of the Wisconsin Statutes; and/or; which things were used in the commission of or may constitute the evidence of the crime of POSSESSION OF CHILD PORNOGRAPHY committed in violation of 948.12 of the Wisconsin Statutes.

The facts tending to establish the grounds for issuing the search warrant are as follows:

1. Whereas, affiant, being a 14-year member of the Green Bay police department is currently assigned as a detective. Your affiant is also employed as a computer service technician and has been so employed for 2 1/2 years.

2. Definitions: For the purpose of this affidavit the terms listed are defined as follows:

   a) The term *computer* refers to the box that houses the central processing unit *(CPU),* along with any internal storage devices (such as internal hard drives) and internal communication devices (such as internal modems capable of sending/receiving electronic mail and data) along with any other hardware stored internally.

   b) The term *computer hardware* as used in this affidavit refers to all equipment, which can collect, analyze, create, display, convert, store, conceal, or transmit electronic, magnetic, optical, or similar computer impulses or data. Hardware includes but is not limited to any data processing devices (such as central processing units, and self-contained "laptop" or "notebook" computers); internal and peripheral storage devices, memory storage devices, peripheral input/output devices (such as keyboards, printers, scanners, video display monitors, and optical readers); and related communications devices (such as modems, cables and connections, recording equipment, RAM or ROM units) as well as any devices, mechanisms, or parts that can be used to restrict access to computer hardware (such as physical keys and locks).

   c) The term *computer software* as used in this affidavit refers to digital information, which can be interpreted by a computer

Figure 9–4 *(Continued)*

and any of its related components to direct the way they work. Software is stored in electronic, magnetic, optical, or other digital form. This commonly includes programs to run operating systems, applications (such as word processing, graphics, or spreadsheet programs), and utilities, compilers, interpreters and communications programs.

d) The term *computer graphic* as used in this affidavit refers to such data where photographs have been digitized into computer binary format. Once in this format the graphic file can be viewed, copied, transmitted, and/or printed. Computer graphic files are differentiated by the type of format convention by which they were created. Two common types of computer graphic files encountered are those in JPEG (Joint Photograph Electronics Group) format having the *jpg* file extension, and the GIF (Graphic Interchange Format) having the *gif* file extension. In addition, there are two primary video graphic files, which can display motion picture graphics. The formats encountered are in "AVI" (Audio Visual Interleaved) format having the *AVI* file extension and MPEG (Motion Picture Experts) format having the *mpg* file extension. There are also other formats.

e) The term *Web page* as used in this affidavit refers to an electronic document, which can be viewed on the Internet.

f) The term *URL* as used in this affidavit refers to the Uniform Resource Locator or Web site address.

g) The term *list server* or *listserv* mailing list as used in this affidavit refers to a special e-mail situation where messages are sent from one person to everyone who has subscribed to, or become part of a group. When anyone in the group posts a message to the list server, you can send a message back to just that person or the entire list server.

Internet Service Providers

3. Based on your affiant's knowledge, training, and experience of other law enforcement personnel, your affiant knows that the Internet is a worldwide computer network, which connects computers and allows communications and the transfer of data and information across the country, state, and national boundaries. Individuals that utilize the Internet can communicate by using electronic mail (hereinafter referred to as "e-mail"). E-mail is an electronic form of communication, which can contain letter-type correspondence and computer graphic images. E-mail is similar to conventional paper-type mail in that it is

(continued)

addressed from one individual to another and is usually private. E-mail usually contains a message header, which gives information about the individual that originated a particular message or computer graphic, and importantly, the return address to respond to them. Individuals that have an Internet e-mail address must have a subscription to, membership, or an affiliation with an organization or commercial service, which provides access to the Internet computer network. A provider of Internet access is referred to as an INTERNET SERVICE PROVIDER, or ISP. An example of an ISP is America Online.

4. On May 13, 2000, your affiant was assigned a case of reported child pornography. This case was reported to the Fort Howard Police Department by Detective James Cypher of the Bits Police Department in New Hampshire on June 22, 1999. Detective Cypher is part of a Regional Task Force on Internet Crimes Against Children. Detective Cypher participates in undercover investigations into Internet crimes involving the sexual exploitation of children. Detective Cypher 's report dated June 22, 1999, states that he joined a "listserv" titled "boyz r US." Detective Cypher reports that on May 5, 1999, at 15:35 HRS a subject using the e-mail address of joekid@handspring.com posted the following message to the boyz r us listserv. Note: The owner of the list required new members to fill in a questionnaire listing information about themselves. The subject making this posting gave the following information (shown in bold):

Name (First and Last Initial): **Joe S.**
Age & Birth date: **31 / 10-5-67**
Location (State only): **WI**
Sex & Ethnic Background: **M / White**
Sexuality: **Gay (but prefer yng guyz and chubby dudes)**
Height: **5'7"**
Weight: **228 lbs.**
Hair Color: **Short, red/brown**
Eye Color: **Blue**

****

Detective Cypher reports that attached to the above message was an electronically transmitted computer graphic of a nude prepubertal male child who is posed lying on a bed with his arms behind his head and his genitals displayed. Detective Cypher states that based on his training and experience this boy was under the age of sixteen. A photo of an apparently 31-year-old male was also posted, who is believed to be Joe Suspect.

Figure 9–4 (*Continued*)

5. Detective Cypher reports that on May 13, 1999, he sent a subpoena to Handspring, the Internet service provider from which the e-mail address joekid@handspring.com originates. Handspring replied that the account belongs to:

Joe A. Suspect
1275 University Avenue
Fort Howard, WI 54301

Detective Cypher also reports that the following screen name is associated with the account: joekid, registered to Joe A. Suspect.

Upon receipt of this case in May 2000 your affiant reviewed the records of the Fort Howard Police Department. According to the records, Joe Suspect resides at 1275 University Avenue in Fort Howard as does Joy Suspect, his mother. Upon running a criminal history check on Joe Suspect I learned that he was convicted of receiving child pornography in 1994. Fort Howard Police Department records show that Joe Suspect's birth date is 10-5-67, which matches the birth date given by the subject who posted the photo and message on the boyz r us listserv.

6. On May 24, 2000, your affiant checked the residence at 1275 University Avenue. I observed a tan Mitsubishi truck bearing Wisconsin license AC399999 parked on the West side of the building. Wisconsin D.O.T. records show this vehicle is registered to Joy Suspect, address 1275 University Avenue. I also contacted the U.S. Postal Service and they confirmed that Joe Suspect currently receives mail at this address.

7. On June 1, 2000, I sent a subpoena to Internet service provider Handspring requesting them to identify the account holder of joekid@handspring.com. I also requested the date the account was activated and if the account was still active. The following results were obtained:

   E-mail: Joekid@handspring.com
   Status: Active
   Service dates: 12/28/98–Present
   Name: Joe Suspect
   Address: 1275 University Avenue, Fort Howard, WI
   Phone: 920-555-5555

8. On June 9, 2000, your affiant conducted a search of the Internet in an attempt to locate Internet Web sites linked to the subject, Joe A. Suspect. I located a Web site at the following URL: http://www.handspring.com/~joekid/dbsite

(continued)

Contained within the Web site are computer graphic images of an adult male that I recognize as Joe Suspect. The author of the Web site identifies himself as "Joe." Numerous electronic images on the Web site show Joe wearing only a diaper in a number of sexually suggestive poses. Also contained within the Web site are photographs of an infant, a boy approximately 3 years old, and a boy approximately 12 years old.

9. On July 1, 2000, I contacted Detective James Cypher of the Bits, New Hampshire, Police Department, the Detective who forwarded the original complaint to the Fort Howard Police Department regarding child pornography. I requested Detective Cypher to attempt a new contact with subject Joe Suspect via e-mail to determine if Joe is still involved in child pornography.

10. From July 28, 2000, to the present Detective Cypher has forwarded numerous e-mail messages to me that he has received from Joe (Joekid). For the purpose of this investigation, Detective Cypher purports to be (cory14) Cory Dean, a 14-year-old boy from New Hampshire. I have received the following messages forwarded by Detective Cypher.

August 2, 2000 / 6:58am
Cory14: and do you like boys or girls?
Joekid: I like boys, naked ones in sexual positions.

August 2, 2000 / 8:59am
Joekid: Glad to get your email this morning. I'm at work and I loved your picture. [Detective Cypher had sent Joekid a fictitious picture purporting him to be a 14-year-old boy] You are a cute boy. I have pics of younger dudes too and will send them to you after I scan them.
Cory14: Do you think it is safe to mail them?
Joekid: I can either put them in a thick package or send them to you on a zip disk that I can encrypt. Even if someone got the disk, they could not see them without the password. And yes, I would love to see you naked too. If you want some other pics, I have all kinds of nasty stuff.

11. On August 12, 2000, I conducted a WHO IS name lookup on the Web site http://www.handspring.com/~joekid/dbsite. This query provides the name and address of the person who registers a domain name. The results of the query showed that it is registered to: Joe Suspect, 1275 University Avenue, Fort Howard, WI 54301.

12. On August 25, 2000, I received a report from Community Policy Officer John Cable that he had observed Joe Suspect exit the door leading to the upper apartment of his address, 1275 University Avenue, Fort Howard, WI 54302.

Figure 9–4 (*Continued*)

13. On August 27, 2000, I received an additional e-mail message from Detective Cypher containing the following text (conversation) between him and Joe Suspect:

    TO: Cory14

    Joekid: Okay, I got your disk made and you may choose between the following photos: baby boys, young boys alone, young boys with other boys, young boys with men, and men.

14. Pursuant to my training and experience, I have learned that:

    a) Child pornography is not readily available in retail establishments; accordingly, individuals who wish to obtain child pornography do so by ordering it abroad or by discreet contact with other individuals who have it available.

    b) The use of computers to traffic in, trade, collect child pornography and obscenity has become one of the preferred methods of obtaining obscene and child pornographic materials. An individual familiar with a computer can use it, usually in the privacy of his own home or office, to interact with another individual or a business offering such materials in this country or elsewhere in the world. The use of a computer provides individuals interested in obscenity or child pornography with a sense of privacy and secrecy not attainable by other media. It also permits the individuals to contact and interact with many more individuals than through the use of the mail.

    c) Persons involved in sending or receiving child pornography tend to retain it for long periods of time. The images obtained, traded, and/or sold are prized by those individuals interested in child pornography. In addition to their "emotional" value, the images are intrinsically valuable as trading/selling material and therefore are rarely destroyed or deleted by the individual collector. Graphic image files can be maintained on the computer's built-in hard drive or on storage disks. This tendency is enhanced by the increased sense of security that a computer affords.

    d) Based upon your affiant's knowledge, training, and experience, and the experience of other law enforcement personnel, your affiant knows that to completely and accurately retrieve data maintained in computer hardware or on computer software, all computer equipment, peripherals, related instructions in the form of manuals and notes, as well as the software utilized to operate such a computer, must be seized and subsequently processed by a qualified computer specialist in a controlled environment.

(continued)

Wherefore, William Byte, a law enforcement officer, prays that a search warrant be issued to search such premises for the said property, and if found, to seize the same and take property into custody according to law.

_____
Affiant–William Byte

Subscribed and sworn to before me this
_____ day of _____, 2000
Honorable _____
Judge of the Circuit Court
Brown County, Wisconsin

Figure 9–4 *(Continued)*

The resulting seizure and search of the defendant's computer revealed several hundred images of suspected child pornography, but most of them had been encrypted and couldn't be accessed. However, the defendant failed to encrypt four images of child pornography, which were used to convict him of possession of child pornography and sentenced to nine years in prison followed by two years of extended supervision and registration as a lifetime sexual offender. Some of the facts within the affidavit have been summarized, and the actual names and locations have been changed. However, the overall fact circumstances are accurate.

Within the affidavit there should also be a statement that relates to the need to conduct a forensic examination of the computer off-site after being seized and the necessary time delay that will occur between the seizure and search of it. The Fourth Amendment does not include a time requirement in which a computer may be subjected to a forensic examination. The Fourth Amendment only requires that the subsequent search of a computer be made within a reasonable time. For example, in the case of *United States of America v. Stephen W. Grimmett* (2004), which involved the seizure and subsequent search of the defendant's computer, the court ruled that the subsequent search of the computer within a few weeks of the seizure was reasonable.

Learner Activity

Select a location in your neighborhood or on the college campus. Obtain all of the necessary information about this location to describe it with "sufficient particularity," consistent with the Fourth Amendment. Next, select a piece of potential high-tech evidence (i.e., cell phone, pager, computer, etc.) and obtain all of the necessary information also to describe it with "sufficient particularity." This device will serve as an item to be seized. Using the affidavit that was provided for you in this text as an example, draft your own affidavit that adequately describes the place to be searched and the item(s) to be seized.

Preparing for the Execution of the Search Warrant

Prior to executing the search warrant, it is important to have a proper plan in place. All of the necessary materials needed for the proper search and seizure must be readily accessible. See Chapter 11 for further discussion related to these necessary materials.

Officers should also conduct any necessary surveillance and intelligence gathering regarding the location to be searched. Intelligence gathering must begin early in the investigation. For example, a spouse reports to her husband's probation officer that he is involved in saving and trading child pornography on his computer. The probation officer contacts the police department, and officers respond to the agent's office. Not only would the interview comprise questions related to the child pornography, but it would also be a perfect time to ask certain questions about the high-tech evidence. What kind of computer does he use? Where is it in the house? What is the name of his Internet service provider? What is his user name and password? What is his e-mail address? What software programs does he use? Does he ever talk about what he would do to conceal the images if police come over? Does he save the images to CDs, thumb drives, removable hard drives, or other storage media? Does he allow you to use the computer? Do you know the passwords? These questions, and many others, can reveal valuable information and provide additional leads that would be beneficial to the search team and forensic examiner, saving both time and effort while preserving evidence.

Any information related to the interior of the residence is also helpful, not only at the time of writing the affidavit but especially at time of execution, so the proper tactics can be used when making entry. An exterior sketch of the scene should also be made so a proper approach can be planned. The number of officers needed to properly search the scene also needs to be taken into consideration. If it's going to be a technologically complex search, consideration should also be given to bringing along qualified private sector computer technicians who will act as "agents" for law enforcement. Finally, the necessary tools need to be available to make entry, such as a door ram and/or other prying tools.

Executing the Search Warrant

At the time of executing the search warrant, it is required that law enforcement officers "knock and announce" their presence and wait a "reasonable" amount of time prior to making entry. The courts have not deemed what exact amount of time is reasonable. In our experience, in the execution of several search warrants, the typical "knock and announce" process entails officers knocking on the door using three successive, loud knocks followed by the announcement, "Police, search warrant!" This process is repeated at least three times and on average takes about 20 seconds. This process has been deemed reasonable and is supported by various courts throughout the country. Failing to properly knock and announce can result in the suppression of evidence.

Once appropriate announcement has been made, law enforcement officers are permitted to use any necessary force to gain entry. Upon entry, the search strategy is carried out by first securing the scene and all people inside, and then searching for the evidence and contraband outlined in the warrant.

No-Knock Exception

It is not always necessary for officers to knock and announce their presence when executing a search warrant. There is also a no-knock exception to the search warrant requirement. When there is reasonable suspicion that knocking and announcing police presence, under particular circumstances, would be dangerous or futile, or that it would inhibit the effective investigation of the crime by, for example, allowing the destruction of evidence, then it's not necessary to knock and announce prior to making entry (see *Richards v. Wisconsin* 1997).

The no-knock exception might apply in certain computer crime cases, especially when dealing with a very technically skilled offender who may have special programs set up to destroy data instantaneously with a few keystrokes. This information could be gathered prior to executing the warrant through proper intelligence gathering.

In contrast to the *Richards* case, the U.S. Supreme Court recently ruled in the case of *Hudson v. Michigan* (2006) that failing to properly knock and announce will not necessarily result in the suppression of evidence. The *Hudson* case is viewed by some as a huge victory for law enforcement officers, while others believe that this decision destroys any and all privacy in one's home and essentially erases the knock-and-announce requirement. The true impact of the *Hudson* case remains to be seen.

Postwarrant Considerations

Once the warrant has been served, the scene is secure, and the collection of evidence begins, the proper packaging of the evidence is important along with the transportation of it. Chapter 10 adequately addresses these issues and should be consulted for additional information.

It is also required that a copy of the search warrant itself be left with the homeowner or, if that person is not present, be left on scene. The scene itself must also be properly secured and any subsequent property damage that occurred during the search should be documented (i.e., photographed).

Generally, the written results of the search warrant, including all of the evidence that was seized (i.e., an inventory), must be returned to the court that issued the warrant within 72 hours of the search. This information, along with the probable cause that was used to obtain the warrant, will be made available during the adversarial proceedings to follow and typically during the preliminary hearings.

All of the officers actively involved in the investigation should always be prepared to testify in cases involving the search and seizure of high-tech evidence. It is imperative that officers properly prepare for testimony by reading through the report and knowing the common terminologies associated with the type of evidence that was seized. An officer may also have to educate the prosecutor on some of these matters and assist in providing lay explanation of technical evidence, anticipating defense strategies, making courtroom presentation suggestions for the evidence, explaining proper evidence handling, and assisting in preparing questions. Finally, the ultimate goal of the officer is to provide clear and credible testimony that will help sustain a conviction.

■ SUMMARY

The U.S. Constitution is a "living and breathing document" that has been interpreted time and time again and applied to new criminal trends to maintain the interests of law-abiding citizens, but at the same time, effectively detect and apprehend criminals. Crimes involving the use of technology have posed new challenges to law enforcement, especially in the realm of search and seizure and the Fourth Amendment.

A clear understanding of the Fourth Amendment is necessary to properly comprehend how it is applied to high-tech crimes. Also, regardless of the type of criminal offense and the tools used to commit it, officers must know how to properly apply the probable cause, search warrant, and search warrant exceptions of the Fourth Amendment in all instances. Although there are several exceptions to the search warrant requirement, the ones that normally apply include consent, plain view, search incident to a lawful arrest, exigent circumstances, workplace searches, and inventory searches. These exceptions can also pose unique challenges to the search and/or seizure of computer or other digital evidence.

First responders will sometimes encounter high-tech criminal offenses that may be a violation of federal law and/or applicable state laws. It is not uncommon for crimes involving the use of computers to cross state lines in a virtual sense, which could make the criminal event a federal matter under the idea of violations of interstate commerce. These same offenses could also be prosecuted at the state level, and it would not be considered double jeopardy because of the parallel jurisdiction (i.e., two separate court systems—federal and state—prosecuting for the same offense).

Preparing a search warrant affidavit for computer or other digital evidence all begins with proper intelligence gathering. Within the affidavit, it's critical to particularly describe the area to be searched and the items to be seized. It's also necessary to define certain terms related to the evidence that police are seeking. When executing the search warrant, knocking and announcing is the norm, but the no-knock exception may apply in some cases. However, the recent decision in *Hudson v. Michigan* (2006) may make the knock-and-announce requirement something of the past.

■ REVIEW QUESTIONS

1. What is meant by the "right of the people" provision of the Fourth Amendment?

2. What is the difference between *search* and *seizure*?

3. What is the definition of *probable cause*?

4. Consent must be given _____ and _____ to be considered valid.

5. What is meant by the concept of "scope" of consent when conducting a consent search?

6. What are the pros and cons of getting consent in writing?

7. What is the impact of the U.S. Supreme Court case of *Georgia v. Randolph* (2006) on consent searches?

8. To seize contraband that is in plain view officers must be in the area _____ when the observation is made.

9. How could the plain view exception could be applied to obvious images of child pornography lawfully observed by a law enforcement officer? What would the plain view exception allow law enforcement to do? What would it *not* allow law enforcement to do?

10. How is the "lunge-reach-rule" applied to the search incident to a lawful arrest exception to the search warrant?

11. How does the search incident to a lawful arrest exception apply to pagers and other portable electronic devices?

12. How does the exigent circumstances exception apply to pagers, other portable electronic devices, and computers?

13. What is the private party exception to the search warrant requirement and how has it been applied to computers in the field?

14. What are a few questions that can be asked when determining if an employee has a reasonable expectation of privacy over an area or property to be searched under the workplace searches exception?

15. How has the USA PATRIOT Act changed the way federal agents obtain search warrants for locations outside of their district?

16. Under the USA PATRIOT Act, what legal documents are needed for law enforcement to obtain information regarding temporarily assigned network addresses or billing records from Internet service providers?

17. Used in conjunction with a search warrant, what is the purpose of the affidavit of probable cause? What does the affidavit normally contain?

18. In relation to search warrants, what is meant by the term *knock and announce* and how is it applied in the field? What is the no-knock exception and how is it applied differently from the knock-and-announce requirement?

19. What types of information might a law enforcement officer want to acquire when preparing for the execution of a search warrant for a computer?

■ TERMS

affidavit	inventory search	search
consent	plain view	search incident to a
Exclusionary Rule	Probable cause/	lawful arrest
exigent circumstances	risk of destruction of	seizure
Fruits of the	evidence	workplace search
Poisonous Tree		

■ REFERENCES

Brandl, Steven. 2004. *Criminal investigation.* Upper Saddle River, NJ: Prentice Hall.

Chimel v. California, 395 U.S. 752 (1969). caselaw.lp.findlaw.com/scripts/ getcase.pl?court=US&vol=395&invol=752 (accessed June 9, 2006).

Georgia v. Randolph, No. 04-1067 (2006). www.law.cornell.edu/supct/html/ 04-1067.ZS.html (accessed June 8, 2006).

Hudson v. Michigan, No. 04-1360 (2006). caselaw.lp.findlaw.com/scripts/ getcase. pl?court=US&vol=000&invol=04-1360 (accessed June 15, 2006).

Katz v. United States, 389 U.S. 347 (1967). caselaw.lp.findlaw.com/scripts/ getcase.pl?court=US&vol=389&invol=347 (accessed June 6, 2006).

Lemons, Bryan R. (n.d.). Electronic pagers—May a law enforcement officer access the memory during a search incident to arrest? Citing *United States v. Ortiz,* 84 F.3d 977 (7th Cir.) (1996). www.fletc.gov/legal/qr_articles/ ELECTRONICPAGERS.pdf (accessed June 9, 2006).

O'Connor v. Ortega, 480 U.S. 709 (1987). caselaw.lp.findlaw.com/scripts/ getcase.pl?court=US&vol=480&invol=709 (accessed June 14, 2006).

Richards v. Wisconsin No. 96-5955, (1997). caselaw.lp.findlaw.com/scripts/ getcase.pl?court=us&vol=520&invol=385 (accessed June 14, 2006).

Scheneckloth v. Bustamonte, 412 U.S. 218 (1973). caselaw.lp.findlaw.com/scripts/ getcase.pl?court=us&vol=412&invol=218 (accessed June 7, 2006).

Silverthorne Lumber Company v. U.S., 251 U.S. 385 (1920). caselaw.lp. findlaw.com/cgi-bin/getcase.pl?friend=nytimes&court=us&vol=251 &invol=385 (accessed June 6, 2006).

State of Wisconsin v. Rodney F. Volden, No. 00-1026-CR (2000). Citing *State v. Smith,* 131 Wis.2d 220, 230, 388 N.W.2d 601 (1986). www.law.wisc.edu/ rcid/caselaw/wisconsin/2000opinions/00-1026.htm (accessed June 10, 2006).

Thetford, Robert T. (n.d.). Should officers use written consent to search forms? www.icje.org/id57.htm (accessed June 10, 2006).

United States v. Jacobsen, 466 U.S. 109 (1984). caselaw.lp.findlaw.com/cgi-bin/ getcase.pl?court=US&vol=466&invol=109 (accessed June 10, 2006).

United Staves v. Leon, 468 U.S. 897 (1984). www.oyez.org/oyez/resource/case/ 409/ (accessed October 14, 2006).

United States v. O'Razvi, No. 97-CR1250, 1998 WL 405048 (S.D.N.Y. July 17, 1998). Cited in United States Department of Justice. 2002. Searching and seizing computers and obtaining electronic evidence in criminal investigations. www.usdoj.gov/criminal/cybercrime/s&smanual2002.pdf (accessed May 5, 2005).

United States v. Robinson, 414 U.S. 218 (1973). caselaw.lp.findlaw.com/scripts/getcase.pl?court=US&vol=414&invol=218 (accessed May 9, 2006).

United States of America v. Michael J. Barth, MO-98-CR-33 (W.D. TX. 1998).

United States of America v. Stephen W. Grimmett, 2004 WL 3171788 (D.Kan).

United States of America v. Shelby Lemmons, No. 00-3809 (2002). laws.lp.findlaw.com/scripts/printer_friendly.pl?page=7th/003809.html (accessed May 5, 2005).

United States of America v. Smith, 27 F. Supp. 2d 1111, 1115-16 (C.D. Ill 1998). www.usdoj.gov/criminal/cybercrime/s&smanual2002.pdf (accessed June 7, 2006).

United States of America v. Turner, 169 F. 3d 84 (1st Cir. 1999). www.usdoj.gov/criminal/cybercrime/s&smanual2002.pdf (accessed June 7, 2006).

United States of America v. Rene Martin Verdugo-Urquidez, No. 88-1353 (1988). www.usdoj.gov/osg/briefs/1988/sg880029.txt (accessed June 6, 2006).

United States of America v. Carl M. White, CR-95-32 (4th Cir. 1998). pacer.ca4.uscourts.gov/opinion.pdf/964469.U.pdf (accessed June 10, 2006).

U.S. Department of Justice. 2004. *Report from the field: The USA PATRIOT Act at work.* www.lifeandliberty.gov/docs/071304_report_from_the_field.pdf (accessed August 8, 2006).

U.S. Department of Justice, Computer Crime and Intellectual Property Section—Criminal Division. 1999. Supplement to federal guidelines for searching and seizing computers. www.usdoj.gov/criminal/cybercrime/supplement/s&suppii.htm#oraz (accessed June 9, 2006).

Washington v. Chrisman, 455 U.S. 1 (1982). caselaw.lp.findlaw.com/scripts/getcase.pl?court=us&vol=455&invol=1 (accessed June 8, 2006).

278   Chapter Ten

chapter ten
Handling Digital Evidence

■ LEARNING OBJECTIVES

1. Understand the various types of digital evidence.
2. Identify the proper procedures for securing a crime scene, preserving it, documenting it, and properly packaging and transmitting evidence.
3. Understand the fragility and necessity of the chain of custody.
4. Summarize the concepts of computer forensics.
5. Analyze hurdles to digital evidence recovery such as file deletion and file encryption.
6. Understand the various ways that digital evidence can be destroyed and know how to prevent its destruction.

In the world of criminal law, properly gathering, documenting, and presenting evidence can win or lose a given case. Defense attorneys excel in casting doubt on testimony of prosecution witnesses and go to amazing lengths to discredit or disparage hostile witnesses, particularly when the facts of the case appear to be stacked against the defendant. The Achilles' heel of the defense, however, is well-documented, properly seized, and properly preserved physical evidence. Physical evidence can be difficult to document, preserve, and analyze under the best of conditions, but anyone who has ever tried to preserve and document a muddy crime scene in the rain can tell you that it is a real nightmare. One of the biggest concerns or headaches is the proper chain of custody of evidence and keeping investigators from introducing foreign materials into a pristine crime scene. Nowhere is this more important than in the realm of computer forensics. Digital evidence is very fragile and can be easily destroyed, but of even more concern, is that it can be easily modified.

Defense attorneys in this area of expertise will do everything possible to claim that data was manipulated or that the investigator made changes to a suspect's hard disk drive before the evidence was presented in court. Like the age-old allegation that officers planted dope in someone's pocket and then "discovered it" there, the defense will claim that items of interest were not present on a subject's computer until the computer was manipulated by someone in law enforcement. In the real world, an officer would have to perform some physical act to plant or manipulate evidence. In the digital world, the defense argues, this can be accomplished with a few clicks of the mouse and could be virtually undetectable. At least that is what they will try to convince a jury to believe.

Many of the concerns associated with the handling of physical evidence are still important when dealing with digital evidence, but there are additional pitfalls when dealing with digital evidence. Because this text is not intended to be a beginner's guide to law enforcement, common themes with "regular" physical evidence receive cursory review, while the advanced concepts of digital evidence preservation receive the greatest attention.

10.1 WHAT CONSTITUTES DIGITAL EVIDENCE?

Evidence is data, materials, objects, property, documents, or records that are presented in court to prove or disprove allegations made against an arrestee. That having been said, **digital evidence** performs the same role, but digital evidence takes the form of electronic data, or information stored in bits and bytes on magnetic media. Digital evidence can be photos, videos, text documents, Internet activity logs, phone numbers, or any other data that is stored electronically that has relevance to a criminal case. There are almost countless devices that are capable of storing electronic data and the list of gadgets grows at an amazing pace. Some examples of devices that can potentially hold digital evidence are the following:

- Personal computers
- Computer media, disks, CDs, DVDs, etc.
- Portable storage media such as universal serial bus (USB) memory sticks, compact flash cards, XD media, thumb drives
- Cellular phones or similar all-in-one devices
- Personal digital assistants (PDAs)

- Pagers
- BlackBerry and other wireless devices
- Digital still cameras and digital video cameras
- Digital voice recorders
- MP3 players/portable media players
- Portable video players
- Devices that combine two or more of the preceding functions

This is not an all-inclusive list, but describes the general categories of items that should be considered as possibly holding digital evidence. As one would expect given the wide variety of digital devices, there are a wide variety of formats in which data are written. Personal computers may have standardized file formats such as the ubiquitous .jpg format for pictures or .mpg format for movies. Other devices may have a different format entirely, such as the Palm operating system featured in Palm Pilot PDAs, or even a format that is not compatible with any other computer system.

Some devices are not designed to interface with personal computers and have formats that are specific to their brand name. Data formatted in such a way that it is native only to a certain device or program is often called **proprietary data** or is referred to as a proprietary format. This is often the case with cellular phones and pagers. A recent case in the authors' jurisdiction involved a male who recorded video of himself sexually assaulting a woman using the camera built into his cellular phone. This particular cellular phone did not save the data in a Windows-compatible format, and forensics experts had to obtain specialized software from the phone manufacturer to clone the video files to a computer to preserve the files as evidence and further analyze a copy of that evidence.

One of the biggest challenges facing investigators of high-tech crime is the fast-paced, constantly evolving nature of technology. Companies are coming out with new devices or new versions of old devices almost constantly, and those who gather digital evidence must remain current to be able to locate and preserve all potential evidence. A current example is the new study of iPod forensics. The popularity and marketshare Apple has reached with its iPod personal media player devices has created the need for investigators to be able to properly clone, save, and analyze evidence that could be contained on an iPod. Some models of these devices have 30 gigabytes (GB) in storage on an internal hard drive. As technology evolves, the capacities of these devices will rapidly increase while their form factor grows continually smaller.

The type of digital evidence an investigator seeks is determined by the type of case being investigated. In a child pornography case, digital images or videos of sex acts involving children constitute the digital evidence. In the case of a computer being used by a drug dealer, a simple spreadsheet used to document shipments, pickups, sales, deliveries, and who owes money could be evidence. In the case of online child enticement, it could be a log of all online chat conversations that the computer stores. Even a drug enforcement agent examining a suspect's pager or cell phone and copying down all phone numbers stored in that unit is technically gathering digital evidence, merely evidence that is stored electronically.

The best high-tech crime investigators bear in mind the various types of digital evidence, as well as the various imaginative and crafty ways it can be hidden by a suspect. Thinking like a criminal interested in hiding dope has helped numerous drug agents who are looking for the drug stash, and such a mentality can also help high-tech crime detectives who are looking for the data cache. One example is the suspect who videotapes himself having sex with a minor using the camera built into his cellular phone. The subject was kind enough to provide prima facie evidence of the crime, but this will only help investigators if someone thinks to check the phone for such evidence, and then has the capability to extract the evidence from the phone, or knows where to have it processed by a more qualified forensic specialist.

10.2 INITIAL EVIDENCE PRESERVATION CONCERNS

Similar to doctors' Hippocratic Oath to "do no harm," crime scene investigators must first endeavor never to change a crime scene or alter evidence. In other words, it is the goal of law enforcement to document and preserve the scene exactly as it was when the crime was committed. Extreme caution and care is needed because the mere act of documenting or cataloging a crime scene means that investigators are interacting with the scene. In the physical world, this might be as simple as photographing footprints in the snow before investigators walk in that particular area, or taking photographs and measurements at a fatal accident scene before vehicles are moved or towed. In the digital realm, it means that the first and foremost concern is the preservation of all data on the hard disk drive or other computer media in a pristine, unaltered state—unharmed and unchanged.

The second concern in the physical world is the physical fragility of the evidence. Usually, care must be taken to keep items from getting wet, stepped on, driven over, frozen, and so forth. This can also apply to digital evidence. CDs, floppy disks, USB thumb drives, and other magnetic media can all be fragile and easily wiped out. Anyone who has ever dictated a report onto a cassette tape knows that as soon as the dictation is completed the tape is passed through a large magnet to wipe the tape clean. Cassette tapes are a form of magnetic media, but as old as that technology is, the same technique can be applied to modern media. A floppy disk or hard disk drive exposed to a strong magnetic field can also be wiped, or the data can be damaged at least. CDs and DVDs are not likely to be affected by magnetic fields because the data are physically etched into the surface of the optical disc. They, however, can be easily scratched or damaged in a very basic way that would prevent reading. Other more common threats to digital evidence exist in the form of water, static electricity, physical breakage, or extreme heat. One factor in the investigator's favor, however, is that a sealed hard disk drive unit is very well protected. Forensic examiners have been able to examine hard disk drives that have been through fires because the drives are usually air and water tight and impervious to temperatures into the thousands of degrees. In fact, several hundred hard disk drives were recovered from the World Trade Center after the 9/11 attacks. Some drives were in good enough shape that a German company was able to read data from them using a special blue laser disk reader. There is an ongoing investigation into "unusual" stock transactions that were occurring just before and during the attacks.

A third issue to consider is that digital evidence can be lost simply by turning off or powering down a device. Any computer that is powered on has data written to the random access memory (RAM) and usually has temporary files open. Additionally, the computer may have applications, documents, images, or other data files opened by the user. Investigators need to preserve the open items, if possible, without manipulating any controls. This may mean photographing the screen of the computer to document any open windows or running programs that are visible (see Figure 10-1).

It is a bad idea for an investigator to move the mouse, click anything, use the keyboard, or otherwise to manipulate any input device on a suspect computer system. Even seemingly harmless, minor actions can cause data to be written to the hard disk drive, to temporary files, or into system RAM. Still worse, an advanced user can have special commands built into the operating system that may cause seemingly innocuous actions, such as clicking the Start button, actually to execute a command to repartition, reformat, or otherwise wipe data from a hard disk drive. In any case, a hands-off approach is always preferable.

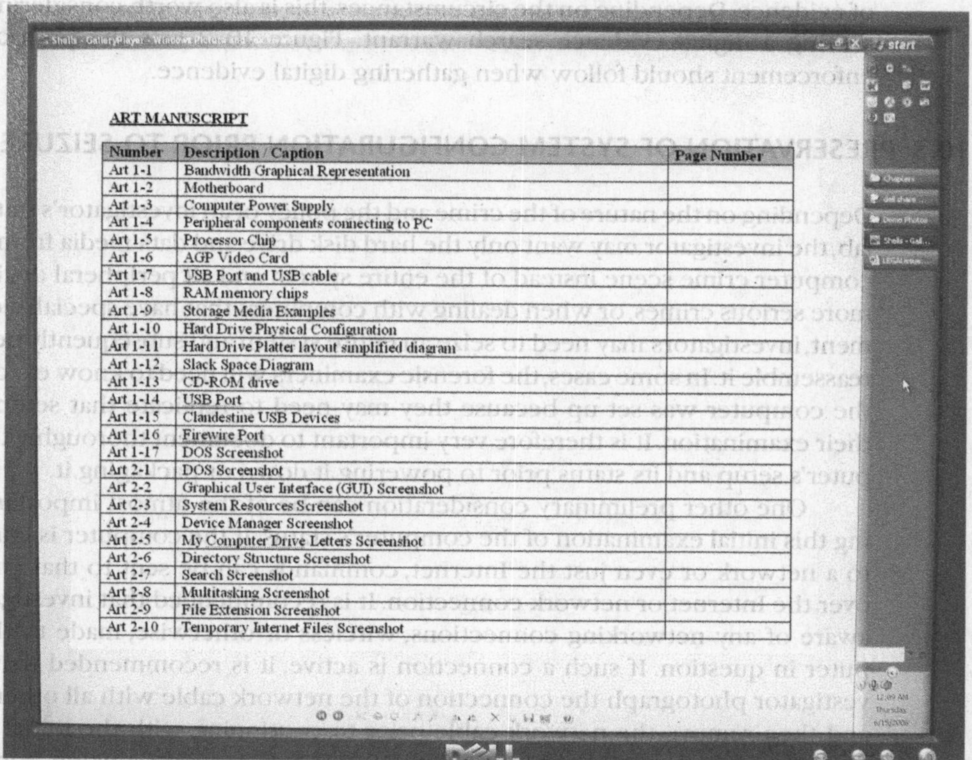
ART MANUSCRIPT

Number	Description / Caption	Page Number
Art 1-1	Bandwidth Graphical Representation	
Art 1-2	Motherboard	
Art 1-3	Computer Power Supply	
Art 1-4	Peripheral components connecting to PC	
Art 1-5	Processor Chip	
Art 1-6	AGP Video Card	
Art 1-7	USB Port and USB cable	
Art 1-8	RAM memory chips	
Art 1-9	Storage Media Examples	
Art 1-10	Hard Drive Physical Configuration	
Art 1-11	Hard Drive Platter layout simplified diagram	
Art 1-12	Slack Space Diagram	
Art 1-13	CD-ROM drive	
Art 1-14	USB Port	
Art 1-15	Clandestine USB Devices	
Art 1-16	Firewire Port	
Art 1-17	DOS Screenshot	
Art 2-1	DOS Screenshot	
Art 2-2	Graphical User Interface (GUI) Screenshot	
Art 2-3	System Resources Screenshot	
Art 2-4	Device Manager Screenshot	
Art 2-5	My Computer Drive Letters Screenshot	
Art 2-6	Directory Structure Screenshot	
Art 2-7	Search Screenshot	
Art 2-8	Multitasking Screenshot	
Art 2-9	File Extension Screenshot	
Art 2-10	Temporary Internet Files Screenshot	

Figure 10–1 A photograph of a computer screen that shows which documents are open.

1. Do no harm to digital evidence; preserve it in a pristine state.

2. Protect digital evidence from physical harm, magnetic fields, and so forth.

3. Preserve the area with photos and document anything that will be lost by powering the system down.

4. Keep the suspect well away from the computer or any potential evidence.

Figure 10–2 Initial digital evidence preservation.

A fourth area of consideration should never be overlooked, and that is the proximity of the suspect. Investigators seizing a computer or serving a search warrant should never let the suspect near the computer(s) to be seized if at all possible. The user may have an electromagnet or erasure protocol built into the system that may only take a second or two to activate. Like a drug dealer trying to swallow crack rocks or throw drugs out the window during a high-speed chase, a computer criminal may make a last-ditch attempt to hide or destroy evidence and, as such, should not be given the opportunity. In the execution of drug-related warrants, no-knock warrants have been issued because of the potential for destruction of evidence. Depending on the circumstances, this is also worth considering when serving a digital evidence search warrant. Figure 10–2 lists the protocols law enforcement should follow when gathering digital evidence.

10.3 PRESERVATION OF SYSTEM CONFIGURATION PRIOR TO SEIZURE

Depending on the nature of the crime and the policy of an investigator's state crime lab, the investigator may want only the hard disk drive and data media from a given computer crime scene instead of the entire system and all peripheral devices. For more serious crimes, or when dealing with computers that have specialized equipment, investigators may need to seize an entire system and subsequently be able to reassemble it. In some cases, the forensic examiners will need to know exactly how the computer was set up because they may need to replicate that setup during their examination. It is therefore very important to document thoroughly the computer's setup and its status prior to powering it down or packaging it.

One other preliminary consideration can be of the utmost importance during this initial examination of the computer's status. If the computer is connected to a network or even just the Internet, commands can be sent to that computer over the Internet or network connection. It is recommended that investigators be aware of any networking connections, wireless or otherwise, made to the computer in question. If such a connection is active, it is recommended that the investigator photograph the connection of the network cable with all other cables, and then remove the network cable prior to continuing with the initial analysis and system documentation. (see Figure 10–3). This prevents anyone from taking

Figure 10–3 Documenting any network connections.

any remote action to destroy evidence. There have been cases in the past in which a suspect's neighbors shared network connections with the suspect computer and were able to dump files off to other computers on the network in an attempt to hide the data in a location where officers were not serving a warrant.

Photographing the system in its entirety is the first step in documenting the computer's setup, but there are actually other photographs that should be taken of a computer crime scene first. Like photographing a traditional crime scene, the investigator should start with the faraway or "wide" view and work his or her way in to the closest, most detailed photos. For example, the photographs might start with the exterior of the house, then move toward the rooms of the house, and finally overall shots of the room where the computer is located. Then once inside that room, the pictures should get progressively closer and more specific, such as the one shown in Figure 10–4.

This process includes taking photos of the front of the tower, the screen, mouse, keyboard, and any attached peripheral devices such as scanners, printers and cameras. A photograph of the screen also might document which program(s) is open at the time, if the computer is powered on. It is also necessary to photograph the rear of the tower where all the connection ports are located to document how items are connected to the computer and where the computer has empty ports. An investigator can also photograph the rear of all peripheral devices where cables connect to those items. (See Figure 10–5.)

An additional technique that will aid a forensic examiner is the use of labels to document cable connections and empty ports. Empty ports should be labeled as empty or not in use. For those ports with connections, one colored label should be placed on the port, and a matching colored label should be attached to the end

Figure 10–4 A photograph of the location of a suspect's computer.

of the cable plugged into that port. For example, a printer port has a red sticker and there is a matching red sticker on the printer cable connected to that port. Several companies sell precoded and labeled stickers for labeling ports and cables, but some investigators opt for making their own.

It is also a good idea to document any network and power connections for a system, especially if the computer is attached to a network router or broadband modem. These connections should also be documented by taking photographs and placing color-coded labels. Remember, the work with the network connections should occur very early in the process because it doesn't take long to transfer several gigabytes of data over a high-bandwidth network. Figure 10–6 lists several protocols law enforcement should follow before seizing a computer.

10.4 POWERING DOWN AND ACTUAL PHYSICAL SEIZURE

Once a computer has been documented, the investigator must prepare the system, peripheral devices, and media for disassembly and transport to a secure location. Part of that process is shutting down the computer. Under normal-use circumstances, this is done by using the mouse or input device to select the shutdown option. Computer

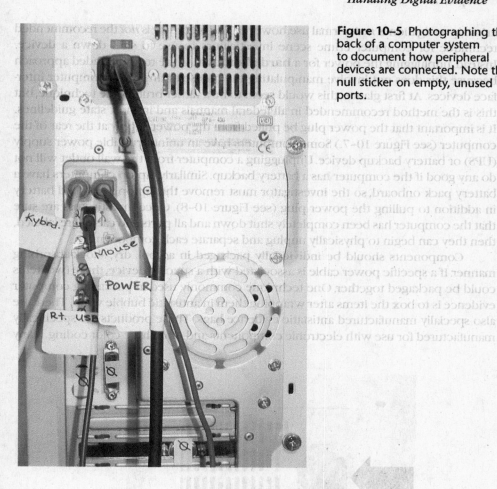

Figure 10–5 Photographing the back of a computer system to document how peripheral devices are connected. Note the null sticker on empty, unused ports.

1. Check to see if the computer is connected to a network or the Internet by either a network cable, or a standard phone wire, or wirelessly. If such a connection exists, photograph it to document it, and then disconnect it.

2. Photograph the crime scene starting with wide-angle generic overview shots and ending with shots documenting specific computer parts, connections, and screen content.

3. Document all connections to the computer using both photographs and labels. Labels should be placed on both the ports and the cables plugged into them. Empty ports should also be labeled "empty" or "open port."

Figure 10–6 Documentation prior to seizing the computer.

crime investigation is *not* normal use, however. The preceding is *not* the recommended technique for computer crime scene investigators to use to shut down a device. Instead, unplugging the power for a **hard shutdown** is the recommended approach because this does not involve manipulating the mouse or any other computer interface devices. At first glance, this would seem to be a rather brute force technique, but this is the method recommended in all federal manuals and in most state guidelines. It is important that the power plug be pulled from the power supply at the rear of the computer (see Figure 10-7.) Some computers have an uninterruptible power supply (UPS) or battery backup device. Unplugging a computer from the wall outlet will not do any good if the computer has a battery backup. Similarly, laptop computers have a battery pack onboard, so the investigator must remove the laptop's onboard battery in addition to pulling the power plug (see Figure 10-8). Once investigators are sure that the computer has been completely shut down and all ports and cables are labeled, then they can begin to physically unplug and separate each component.

Components should be individually packaged in a cool, dry, shock-absorbing manner. If a specific power cable is associated with a specific device, these two items could be packaged together. One technique commonly used in packaging computer evidence is to box the items after wrapping them in antistatic bubble wrap. There are also specially manufactured antistatic evidence bags. These products are specifically manufactured for use with electronic components and often have color coding. Many

Figure 10-7 Shut down a computer by removing the power plug directly from the back of the device.

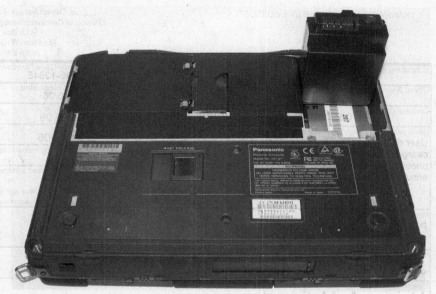

Figure 10–8 Detaching a laptop computer's onboard battery.

types of antistatic plastic films and bags, for example, are pink in color. Standard packing peanuts can generate large amounts of static electricity simply by rubbing against other packing peanuts. Anyone who has ever unpacked a box and watched the peanuts cling to clothing or the item has seen an excellent demonstration of that static electricity, which can damage electronic devices and data.

Serial numbers of all individual components should be recorded for inclusion on evidence inventory forms (see Figure 10–9), and each component should be labeled as a separate evidence exhibit. This is especially important in cases involving multiple computers. It is embarrassing to be asked in court which mouse, keyboard, and monitor belonged to which computer system and not to know the answer. Figure 10–10 lists protocols law enforcement should follow when powering down and seizing evidence.

10.5 TRANSPORT AND EVIDENCE TRANSMITTAL CONSIDERATIONS

Once the computer components and media have been documented, photographed, labeled, and packaged, investigators are ready to transport the items to an evidence locker in the short term, and possibly to a state crime lab for long-term storage and examination. Investigators need to exercise a bit of caution when preparing for transport because they are responsible for the materials seized. Remember, in some cases the items will be returned to the subject. Further, damage can occur to computers or media in transit because they are sensitive electronic devices. It would be

TRANSMITTAL OF COMPUTER EVIDENCE

State Department of Justice
Division of Criminal Investigation
P.O. Box 1234
Madison, WI 54321
(608) 234-1234

Submitting Agency	Anytown Police Department		Agency Case Number 06-12345
City of Agency Anytown, WI		County Brown	Date Transmitted 06/16/06
Criminal Offense Possession of Child Pornography 948.12			Offense Date 05/05/06

Please provide a case summary including the evidence to be extracted

User downloaded numerous images of child porn from a website that charges membership fees for access. There are also several original photographs on the computer showing the suspect engaged in sexual activity with children.

Trial Date
11/10/06

Obtained by consent only?
Yes ✓ No

Search warrant attached?
✓ Yes   No

(Required if evidence was obtained by execution of a search warrant)

Keyword search terms:
Porn, kiddie porn, KP, child porn, kiddie sex, my pictures, Jon, Johnny, Jonathan

Victim(s)
Jonathan P. Victim

Suspect(s)
Marcus A. Malincode

Agency Exhibit Number	Number of Items	Item Description
359-1	1	Off White Compaq Pressario Computer Tower S/N CP105J987
359-2	1	Grey Maxtor External USB hard drive S/N MX193738
359-3	1	Black and Silver LG Brand USB Thumb Drive S/N E-D902-03-5547

Name of Submitting Officer   Officer D. Hasselblad

Name of Case Officer   Officer D. Hasselblad   Phone Number (920) 217-0000

For DCI Use Only Received by:	Date:	Property Receipt Number:
Entered by:	Assigned to:	

Figure 10–9 A sample evidence inventory form that documents device serial numbers.

a shame to lose good evidence of an online child enticement because someone was careless and dropped a box of CDs or allowed a component to get wet or too hot.

Another thing to remember is that electromagnetic fields can wipe or otherwise damage data stored on magnetic media. **Radio frequency radiation** can cause damage to magnetic media, so placement of the items in a squad car trunk or near radio gear should be avoided. In fact, because of the large amount of space a lot of computer components and media take up, a lot of investigators

1. Power down the computer by pulling the plug from the rear. Check to ensure power is lost. In the case of a laptop, ensure the battery is also removed.

2. Package components in protective, padded, and antistatic evidence bags. Special antistatic bubble wrap and packing peanuts are available.

3. Record serial numbers for all items being packaged as evidence.

4. Seal evidence items in their protective containers or pouches with evidence tape, signing the seals to ensure integrity. Some states also require sealing the computer tower, power buttons, and ports with evidence tape. Consult your state's physical evidence handbook for computer seizures to see if this is required.

Figure 10–10 Powering down and system disassembly.

choose to take a minivan or other large transport vehicle along with them when executing a search warrant for a computer.

When a defense attorney cannot attack the facts of the case and is unable to successfully attack the credibility of the investigator or witnesses, the attorney will have no recourse but to attack the "technicalities" such as the chain of evidence custody. Although numerous definitions of **chain of custody** exist, this term is, perhaps, most easily defined as documenting who handled the evidence at each juncture of an investigation. It is called a *chain* because each person who handles the evidence is a link in the chain. Once the evidence is in the custody of law enforcement, the chain of custody should never be broken. A break in that chain is the opportunity a defense attorney dreams about because he or she then can exploit it to cast doubt on the case. If law enforcement did not secure the evidence, some unknown third party could have tampered with the evidence during that break in the chain.

It is of the utmost importance, therefore, to document each person in the chain of custody and what that Person's role was. Actions taken by each person should also be documented. This is especially critical in a digital evidence case, because the forensic specialist will need to state unequivocally that data were not added, modified, deleted, or otherwise manipulated while that computer or digital device was in police custody.

The easiest and safest way to maintain a proper chain of custody is to keep it as short as possible. The fewer people involved in the chain of custody, the better. An example of a basic chain of custody is as follows:

Initial Responding Officer → White Collar Detective → Forensics Specialist → Evidence Locker

It is a safe bet that a defense attorney will cross-examine every single person who had a role in handling evidence. It is in law enforcement's best interest, therefore, to have a short chain of custody, made up of qualified individuals. First responders, with limited training, will likely be the first link in the chain. The prosecution should assist the first responder with preparing for testimony and anticipating cross-examination questions or angles of attack. In the event that the prosecuting attorney is not very knowledgeable in the technology crimes arena, the forensics specialist may need to coach the attorney, as well as the other staff involved in the case, about what to expect.

10.6 STORAGE AND SAFEGUARDING

Once the materials are safely at the police station or agency headquarters, generally they will be completely inventoried before being secured in an evidence locker or other secure holding facility. Remember, investigators need to maintain the chain of custody. Many agencies guarantee evidence security by having a separate evidence locker for digital evidence. Access to this area is limited to a very few key personnel, usually those responsible for performing forensic analysis or those who transmit digital evidence materials to the state crime lab or other forensic analysts. Leaving these materials in an unsecured area, even with notes or evidence tape on them, is like an open invitation to the office scrounger and in direct violation of chain of custody ideals.

As during the transport, care must be taken to ensure the long-term security and stability of these materials. Computer components and media should be kept in a cool, dry place that is free from water pipes or other building utilities that could cause damage to equipment if they fail. They should also be kept well away from magnetic fields or radio frequency interference sources such as communication centers or large electrical boxes and transformers. In warmer climates, these materials should be kept in a climate-controlled or cooler environment.

Learner Activity

This activity includes the search, documentation, and processing of a fake crime scene. You may also want to skip ahead to the Checklist in Section 11.7 in Chapter 11 for this exercise. The instructor will set up a virtual crime scene using old computer equipment (or lab equipment dedicated to that purpose). The instructor will provide a background scenario (possession of child porn, online child enticement, drug trafficking, embezzlement, identity theft, etc.). You will then be responsible for entering the crime scene (as authorized by a search warrant for that particular offense). You will then properly determine which items might contain evidence within that crime scene. Following the checklists provided in Figures 10-2, 10-6, and 10-9, you should document the crime scene along with the setup configuration of the computer and what is on the screen at the time of the search. Ideally, a digital camera will be available so you can photograph the crime scene. Labels, masking tape, or other similar items can be used for documentation of the ports and cable connections. Once the scene is properly documented, you should properly power down the components and disassemble them for packaging and transport. You should also complete an evidence inventory form with available serial numbers for every item. It is the goal of this exercise to give you an idea of processing a high-tech crime scene in as close a setting to reality as possible. This will cement the total procedure concepts and will also give you an opportunity for practice in a controlled environment where any mistakes could be used as a teachable moment, whereas a mistake in the real world could mean losing a case.

10.7 WRITE BLOCKING AND CLONING OF DATA

Once the material has been properly documented, photographed, labeled, seized, and packaged, it will ultimately be analyzed. Many smaller agencies do not have the budget, equipment, or human resources to do their own computer forensics examinations and must instead rely on state or regional crime labs or forensic centers for services. These investigators need to contact their service provider and determine what the lab actually wants them to send. Some labs prefer just the hard disk drive and data media, while others will request every item that was seized by the responding officers or investigators. Officers and investigators working for larger agencies will likely have one or more specially trained and certified computer forensics examiners within their department.

Once the drives and media are in the hands of a forensic examiner, the specialist will attempt to make several copies of the materials to ensure that no evidence is lost during analysis or to any other unforeseen circumstance. Examiners never want to use the original data for fear of altering or destroying evidence. They will therefore install a device on the hard disk drive or other media called a **write blocker.** (see Figure 10–11.). This device completely prevents the forensic examiner from writing any data to the hard disk drive or media. It simply makes it physically impossible by blocking the wires that would communicate the data to be written to the drive. In other words, it is like a one-way valve allowing all traffic from the drive and no traffic to it. Write blockers are available for every type of hard disk drive (including serial ATA) and USB devices such as thumb drives and digital cameras.

Once the write blocker is installed, the forensic specialist will use a drive imaging or cloning utility to make an exact duplicate of the original suspect drive. The accepted forensic practice calls for making an exact **bit-by-bit copy,** also known as a **bitstream** copy. Remember from Chapter 1 that a bit is the smallest possible piece of data represented by a 0 or 1. By making a bit-by-bit copy, the forensic examiner can be sure that the suspect hard disk drive is copied exactly, even blank spaces on the drive. The forensic examiner will then also verify that the drive is an exact copy by computing an MD5 hash value for the original drive and the copy. If the MD5 values are exactly the same, then the copy is an exact copy or clone of the original drive. The standard of certainty as it pertains to MD5 hash values is statistically much greater than the certainty of DNA evidence is. In other words, if two drives have matching MD5 hashes, there is an extremely high

Figure 10–11 A write blocker.
Courtesy of Digital Intelligence, Inc. www.digitalintelligence.com

probability that they are an exact bit-by-bit copy or clone of each other. DNA matching has a somewhat lower probability, but DNA matching has been accepted by courts as a high enough level of certainty, and there is no known rejection of MD5 hash certainty by the courts. As technology advances, new hash algorithms emerge, and some forensic specialists are using the SHA algorithm, which has a certainty level even higher than that of the MD5.

Hashing is a mathematical analysis of the data on the drive that generates a unique string of characters based upon the files and structure of the drive. Individual files can also be hashed to check for identical files. The standard hash utilized by most forensic software utilities is called the Message Digest 5 hash, or MD5 for short. MD5 is an algorithm that generates a 128-bit string of characters. An example of an MD5 value for a single file is included here as an example: b017e028a96ca4fbb536e30f1cb834f8. Another type of hash algorithm is the Secure Hash Algorithm, or SHA-1. A SHA-1 hash is even more exacting than the MD5 is because it is 160 bits. The SHA-1 calculated string for the same file as the preceding MD5 example is F751AB181141EB2BF86769015E3C8666B49C 4BF6. It is 40 characters long as opposed to the 32-character MD5. This grants it a much greater level of certainty than the MD5.

Regardless of which hashing algorithm is used, the string of characters for the suspect drive and the string for the clone drive must match exactly. If they are an exact match, then the original source drive and the clone are an exact bit-by-bit match. The statistical chance of two drives having identical hash values when the drives are not identical is mathematically infinitesimal. The longer the string of text calculated, the less likely it becomes that nonmatching drives will have the same value. In summary, MD5 hashes and SHA-1 hashes are more certain than DNA matching evidence and have been recognized by the courts as the standard way to verify that a cloned drive is exactly the same as the original.

Once the original drive has been successfully cloned, generally it will be secured and will remain in evidence lockup unless or until it is needed at trial. The forensic examiner will then make multiple copies of the clone, using the same exacting procedure described previously and verifying that each cloned drive is an exact duplicate. When this process is complete, the forensic examiner will have several copies. This is necessary because the examiner needs at least one drive to analyze and search using tools from the forensic toolkit and another copy to give to the defense during the discovery phase of any trial. Defense attorneys also generally have an expert or forensic specialist analyze the drive. Plus, having an extra copy might become necessary if a judge orders data returned to the suspect under the Electronic Communications Privacy Act or Privacy Protection Act. A forensic examiner may be ordered to deliver just a portion of the data, in which case the examiner would delete all unneeded material from a clone drive before giving that drive to the suspect. It would be a very rare case for a judge to order the original evidence drive to be returned.

10.8 DISCOVERY AND THE ELECTRONIC COMMUNICATIONS PRIVACY ACT

As with all types of evidence in criminal trials, the defense team has a right of discovery to all evidence held by the prosecution. This is usually the case in high-tech crime investigations as well. Depending on the evidence that is presented, this may consist of an imaged hard disk drive or perhaps just a report of the items found on that hard disk drive made during forensic analysis. Most forensic analysis software has a built-in reporting feature, including capability to log all activities performed with a timestamp of when they were performed. Most of these utilities also enable investigators to flag or bookmark files or items of interest. Reports can include specific information about these items and will generally include thumbnail images of graphics, as well as file locations, dates, times, file sizes, and MD5 data specific to that file. If these reports are to be used in prosecution, they will likely need to be given to the defense as well.

An image of the hard disk drive may need to be given to the defense team, but some caution should be used in doing so. Unless specifically ordered by a judge, investigators should never give a drive that contains contraband such as images of child pornography. In these cases, the investigator may be the most knowledgeable party in the action and may need to impress upon the prosecuting attorney, or the judge, the impropriety of transmitting contraband. A judge may overrule, requiring investigators to transmit contraband, but investigators should never do so without a court order. Investigators can offer the hard copy analysis report as an alternative to transmitting the actual data in the form of illicit files.

10.9 FORENSIC DATA ANALYSIS OVERVIEW

Once evidence has been properly seized, packaged, and transported, it will eventually be turned over to a forensic specialist for a complete **forensic analysis.** Forensic analysis is the process by which a forensic examiner captures, clones, recovers, and analyzes data from a suspect hard disk drive or data device while making absolutely no changes to the data on that drive or device. This either occurs locally, if the agency has a certified forensics specialist and forensics lab, or the evidence is transmitted to a state or regional computer forensics laboratory. Some states handle these materials in their normal state crime labs, others refer the matters to their criminal investigations departments or departments of justice. Federal agencies have the personnel and equipment in-house.

Assuming that all materials have been correctly preserved, documented, protected, and transmitted by the first responders or personnel who handled the initial call, the forensic analyst can begin the process of safeguarding and analyzing all digital evidence. A number of different software utilities are used for forensic analysis and reporting. It is not within the scope of this text to recommend any particular software or approach, but rather to discuss the process generally. Most forensic utilities or utility suites clone or image hard disk drives, find data files, organize files into categories, and perform analysis on the files. Most software also allows analysis of hidden or deleted files, even those that have been partially overwritten. This includes examining the slack space on a given hard disk drive for incomplete fragments of data. Last, some suites offer password-cracking utilities to assist the analyst with unlocking encrypted or password-protected files or file archives.

Most nationally recognized forensic software suites perform core tasks. A suite that offers these functions is essential to anyone interested in setting up a computer forensic laboratory. First, the suite will need to have the ability to acquire digital evidence or data files by reading that information from a variety of media types and formats. Both Guidance Software's Encase™ and AccessData's Forensic Toolkit™ have the ability to read hard drives, CDs, DVDs, USB keys, floppy disks, and a variety of other media types. After reading the data, they acquire it by creating image files of the data (cloning it).

One area in which the higher end utilities distinguish themselves from their competitors is in their ability to analyze the evidence and report on those findings. The two suites listed above both excel in their ability to analyze the data, organize it by category, and flag or mark data of interest for ease of relocating that file and reporting on it later. Both suites, likewise, have utilities that allow the recovery of data that has been marked for deletion but has not yet been overwritten. Finally, some suites offer utilities to crack passwords by supplying random characters and words from a dictionary in an attempt to guess the password used to encrpyt data or e-mails. A summary of forensic software features and functions is shown on page 295.

Functions of Computer Forensics Software

- Acquire digital evidence or data files
- Clone/preserve digital evidence
- Analyze digital evidence files
- Separate and categorize data files by type (graphics, e-mail, videos, etc.)
- Compare evidence files to lists of known contraband files
- Recover deleted or hidden data
- Crack or recover passwords to allow access to encrypted data
- Systematically report findings in a paper report

10.10 ACQUIRING DIGITAL DATA INTO FORENSIC SOFTWARE

The various software utilities approach this topic in slightly different ways and may use slightly different terminology for their respective processes. What remains the same, however, is that the first step in the process is acquiring the digital evidence; in other words, being able to have the device interact with the **forensic workstation.** The forensic workstation is the computer used by the investigator to examine, clone, and analyze the evidence (see Figure 10–12.) This is the computer

Figure 10–12 A forensic workstation. Note the numerous drive bays and interface options.
Courtesy of Digital Intelligence, Inc. www.digitalintelligence.com

that is owned and operated by the law enforcement agency and that contains installed forensic software such as AccessData Forensic Toolkit, Encase, or ILook.

In the case of computer hard disk drives, establishing this interface is relatively easy because hard disk drives are generally connected to computers with an IDE connection, serial ATA, USB 2.0, or FireWire cable. The suspect's hard disk drive is placed on a write-blocking interface, which is then, in turn, connected to the forensic examiner's workstation computer. As mentioned earlier, the write blocker is a specifically designed piece of hardware that physically does not allow any data to be transmitted to or written to the suspect's original hard disk drive. Think of it as a one-way valve similar to a CPR mask. It allows data to travel in one direction only: to the forensic workstation. Data will never travel from the workstation to the suspect's original evidence drive. This concept is extremely important in the forensic examination process and an important element of the forensic process. Investigators will likely be challenged on this part of the process by defense attorneys who claim that the suspect's data were somehow corrupted by the examiner. Once the drive is cloned to another hard disk drive, the forensic examiner will likely seal the original drive and secure it as original evidence. All future work and analysis will be done using the clone. Likely several clones will be made.

Another process, similar in function to the use of a hardware write blocker, is the use of imaging software. This software performs the same two functions as the hardware write blocker: it prevents the writing of any data to the suspect's hard disk drive, and it creates a **disk image**, or exact duplicate, of the suspect hard disk drive. Most software utilities allow the examiner to save the image to a new drive, or load and unload the drive image as a virtual drive. The forensic examiner will then examine the disk image instead of the suspect hard disk drive.

Regardless of whether the examiner has cloned the drive to another drive or has imaged the drive, the forensic software utility will make a bit-by-bit copy, also known as a bitstream copy, of the drive. This ensures that the clone or image will be exactly the same as the original, both in structure and in content. Every sector of the original source drive will be thus duplicated so even snippets of fragmentary data in the slack space of the original drive will exist in matching sectors of the cloned drive.

10.11   ANALYZING DIGITAL EVIDENCE FILES

Once the hard disk drive, CD, Zip disk, DVD, or other media has been successfully cloned and verified as an exact duplicate of the original, the true analysis of the data can begin. Most forensic software utilities begin with an indexing process. This process is extremely time-consuming, particularly because hard disk drives continue to grow larger and larger. Although indexing every file and bit of slack space from a standard 700–megabyte (MB) CD might only take 10 or 15 minutes, it can literally take days to index every bit of a 500-gigabyte hard disk drive. Once the process is begun on a cloned drive, the forensic specialist will usually work on other tasks or other cases using other workstations. The forensic workstation will continue to run the indexing function until the disk is completely indexed, or until it is manually stopped by the specialist. These activities, like most others, are logged automatically by most brands of forensic utility software. The logs have time and date stamps for all activities performed.

The **indexing process** performs a number of functions on every file or file fragment. One thing it does is index every character, letter, number of every file. In the case of text or word processing documents, this means that it indexes every word in every file. This allows the investigator to perform a very exacting word or phrase search on the entire drive. Because the material is indexed during this phase and not when the search is initiated, the investigator will get those search results very quickly. The indexing also checks all file headers so that files can be grouped by file type.

Once the drive image has been completely indexed, the software can easily report on a wide variety of factors. It can tell the specialist how many files are on the drive, what their sizes and locations are, and whether or not they have been deleted. This specialty software can also determine what kind of a file each file is, without referring to the three-letter file name extension. Even if a clever or careless user changes a file name extension, the specialty software can still correctly identify the file type. For example, a user changes a graphic image, photo.jpg to the file name taxes.txt. The forensic utility when indexing the file will record the original file name but will correctly identify the file as a JPG image and will display a thumbnail image of the picture.

Most forensic utilities have numerous preformatted reports. Examples of some reports include reports that sort all deleted files into one section, all graphic images into a report section, all video clips into another section, all e-mail messages into their own section, and so on for virtually every type of file. Files can be sorted by size, file location, date created, or date modified, to name a few ways. By automating these functions, a forensic specialist can quickly generate general summary reports of all files on a given hard disk drive.

Forensic software can also enable the forensic specialist to look at deleted file fragments and other data that are normally hidden from view in the slack space of the drive. This can be very important because the suspect may have tried to delete incriminating files. Files that have not been overwritten or even fragments of the files that have not been completely overwritten can be viewed, potentially yielding clues, passwords, evidence, and more.

Because many computer crime cases seem to involve child pornography, most utilities can generate screens full of miniature images, commonly called thumbnails, of all graphics images on a hard disk drive, enabling an investigator more quickly to search through the hundreds, or more likely thousands, of images on the drive. By using thumbnails, the screen can display numerous images at a time instead of just one. Thus, an investigator can click through pages of thumbnails, visually scanning for potential contraband or other evidence. Because locating and documenting the location of contraband images is part of building the case, investigators must, themselves, necessarily view that content and document it. One word of caution: some investigators have experienced psychological strain related to working on high volumes of child pornography cases.

Another extremely useful feature of most forensic utilities is the capability of highlighting, bookmarking, or otherwise marking files of interest. For example, of an investigator locates an image that appears to be child pornography, and can use the forensic software's tools to select and highlight or bookmark that file for inclusion in a special report. After locating and bookmarking numerous files that are contraband, evidence, or other items of interest, the investigator simply instructs the software to generate a report including information on all highlighted files. This can include printing the graphics images themselves, as well as giving all other relevant data about that particular file, such as file location, file size, date created, date modified, file name, file type, and so forth. This level of exactness in regard to documentation is excellent for prosecuting a child pornography case, and thanks to the design of forensic utilities, it is easy to create, print out, and present in court.

The FBI's Innocent Images National Initiative has made it even easier to locate child pornography images on a suspect hard disk drive. The FBI routinely updates a database of known child pornography files. This database includes the MD5 hash value of files that are known to be child pornography. Most forensic software utilities can compare the FBI database with the files on the hard disk drive, looking for any files that match a file in the FBI listing. If a file with a matching MD5 hash is found, the forensic utility will report that file to the investigator, who can then examine the file to determine if it is, in fact, child pornography. Remember that with the incredibly high level of certainty given by hash values, chances are very good that the file will be an exact copy of the file listed with the FBI. Once the indexing of the drive has been completed, the process of comparing MD5 values to the FBI list does not take a great deal of time.

10.12 RECOVERING DELETED FILES

When a file is deleted on a modern computer, nothing actually happens to the file's data at that time. Executing a delete command simply tells the computer to treat that file space as blank and to allow for programs to write data to that file space if needed later. Unless or until some new data are written to that file space, the original file is still present there. This is the concept that allows for operating systems to have a "recycle bin" or a "trash can." When a user deletes a file, the file is placed in the recycle bin. This means a user can go into that area and retrieve the file after deleting it. When users are sure that they no longer need the file, they can empty the recycle bin or trash can. Doing so supposedly permanently deletes the file. Many criminals believe, to their detriment, that once a file is deleted and then the recycle bin is emptied the file is gone and cannot be recovered by law enforcement. Unless that area of the hard disk drive is overwritten by new data, forensic software can recover deleted files and any potential evidence they contain. In fact, most forensic software products can call the investigator's attention to all recovered deleted files because deleted items are considered "suspicious" and are likely to contain evidence.

In some cases, part of the file space used for the deleted file will have new data written to it, while the rest is still considered blank or writeable. In this case, the fragments of the file that have not been overwritten are still recoverable. Depending on the file type, these file fragments may not be readable under normal conditions. Modern operating systems rely on file headers at the beginning of each computer file to enable the computer to properly view the file. If that portion of the file is missing, damaged, or partially overwritten, then the operating system will not know how to open that file. Forensic software, however, looks at files at a much more fundamental level and can still enable a specialist to view the contents of partially intact deleted files. A hex editor, which can be a standalone application or built into forensic software, enables an investigator to look at files one byte at a time. Thus, even if a file is partially overwritten and even if the file header isn't present, the investigator may still be able to view parts of the file.

The two biggest keys for deleted file recovery are time and the manner in which the hard disk is set up. Time is of the essence because the more time that goes by, the more likely it is that deleted files will be overwritten. If a user inadvertently deletes a file and also empties the recycle bin, there is an excellent chance that the user can recover that file if the person begins working on recovery right away. Simply waiting a few days, restarting the computer, running a virus scan, or defragmenting a drive can cause the file to be overwritten.

As mentioned earlier, hard disk setup is also a major factor in that keeping data files on their own separate partition greatly enhances the chance of successful recovery. Consider a scenario in which a user has partitioned a hard disk into two volumes C and D. The user then installs the Windows operating system to drive C and uses that drive for all system functions such as installing programs and having a swap file. The user then religiously saves all data files such as completed Word documents and JPG images onto the D drive. Windows and other operating systems are constantly reading and writing from temporary files to speed up certain operations and to conserve physical system RAM. These swap files can vary widely in size and change rapidly as needs dictate. If a data file that has been deleted resides on the same drive as a swap file, a momentary enlargement of the swap file could easily overwrite the deleted file. If, however, the user stores data on another drive, as in the described scenario, no amount of changes to the swap file or other system files will affect the deleted file, thus greatly increasing its chances for recovery.

There are many other issued to consider when attempting to recover deleted files. Other supporting items might allow for easy recovery of the file, or if not file recovery, then at least an indication of what the file was. Users might have a system backup device such as a tape drive, CD or DVD burner, or external hard drive where they routinely save their files in an archive. They might have a PDA or iPod device that is set up to autosynchronize with folders on the main computer system. They may also have hard copy printouts of a given file. In the case of graphic images or videos, those items may still remain on a digital camera's media or data cards even though the images may have been deleted from the computer. Last, a file could have been e-mailed or transferred to another user and might still be contained in the e-mail or FTP program.

10.13 RECOVERING/ACCESSING ENCRYPTED FILES

One of the greatest challenges to those who investigate technology-related crimes is the use of encryption or other password-protected security systems. Using freely available software, which can be found on a variety of Internet sites, users can encrypt individual files or entire volumes of information. **Encryption** is the process of encoding regular data into a seemingly random and unintelligible, scrambled form. The program that scrambles the data allows a user to unscramble the information only if the correct user name and password are used. Encryption, then, is the process of scrambling data to protect it from prying eyes, while decryption is the process of decoding it so that it can be viewed again. (see Figure 10–13).

Encryption has been used in various forms for centuries. In eighteenth-century England, for example, members of the British Admiralty wanted a way to send secret messages to their naval captains in foreign ports. They created a series of cutout templates. One example was a cutout of an hourglass. They would then write the secret message within the opening of the hourglass. Then they would take the hourglass off of the paper and continue writing on the page, connecting words to all of the outside edges that had been covered by the hourglass frame. Reading the paper without the cutout in place was like reading gibberish or it seemed like an innocuous letter about fishing or weather conditions. Once the message was received by its intended recipient, who had his own hourglass cutout, the recipient could easily decrypt the relevant part of the message. This was the precursor of the red-tinted decoder ring used to read the secret message on a box of cereal.

Another famous example was the use of an encryption machine by the German Navy in World War II. The Germans had a device that appeared to be similar to a typewriter. It was commonly known as the Enigma machine and was used to encrypt and decrypt secret instructions to Hitler's submarine wolfpacks. At one point, a U. S. naval vessel was able to capture a German submarine before the German crew could throw their Enigma machine overboard. By capturing the key to German secret communications, some historians believe that the Americans shortened the war in Europe by two years.

Examining modern encryption keeping these two examples in mind is quite appropriate because the two historical examples required a device or instrument to be able to decode the encrypted information. Just as the historical encryption depended on the keys of the shaped cutout, modern file encryption also requires a key, or in this case, a password to unlock the information. The more complicated the password, or the greater number of passwords used, the more secure the encryption is.

Figure 10–13 The processes of encryption and decryption.

For example, if a suspect encrypts a file, but only protects it with a password of "dog," this is much less secure than using a password like asd56$#@! Some encryption programs even allow the user to enter multiple passwords for one archive. This increases level of security greatly because not only does the investigator need to know all of the passwords, but the passwords must be entered in the correct order as well.

Encryption, as used by the computer criminal, will likely take the form of an encrypted volume. The criminal will set aside a hard disk drive or a large portion of a hard disk drive to become an encrypted volume. The encryption program will prompt the user to set the level of security and needed passwords. The program will then format that portion of the drive. For example, a criminal may set up an encryption volume for 20 gigabytes of the C drive. When the criminal uses the encryption program to access those 20 GB, the criminal is prompted to supply the proper password(s). Once the criminal has entered the needed key, the computer will mount that 20 GB as a virtual drive. For example, the space might show up as hard drive D with a capacity of 20 GB. With a click of the mouse, the user can then "unmount" drive D, rendering it inaccessible without the proper password credentials. Thus, a pedophile could hide 20 GB worth of child porn pictures or videos, or an embezzler could hide spreadsheets, pin numbers, or other incriminating financial information.

The other form that encryption can take is the encrypting and decrypting of e-mail messages. Software for e-mail encryption is also freely available on the Internet. One example of such software is Pretty Good Privacy, or PGP, for short. To decrypt and read an e-mail message, the recipient needs two keys: the public key and the private key. The public key is shared with the people the user wants to communicate securely with. The private key remains private, staying only on the recipient's computer. The sender encrypts the message using the public key and transmits it to the recipient. Only by putting both keys together can the recipient decode and read the e-mail message.

Encryption is a big challenge to the law enforcement community because it can range from difficult to impossible to defeat. A 1999 report from the Federal Bureau of Investigation states, "The proliferation of secure or encrypted communications and electronically stored information will make it increasingly difficult for law enforcement to obtain and decipher the encrypted content of lawfully intercepted communications and lawfully obtained electronically stored information that is necessary to provide for effective law enforcement, public safety, and national security" (Federal Bureau of Investigation 1999).

A truly savvy computer user, who uses a complex encryption algorithm with complicated passwords who is disciplined in always using it and never writing or recording the key anywhere can thwart an investigator's attempts to access the protected information. The good news is that most street-level computer criminals are not that sophisticated. Even if they have the requisite computer skills, they may not create security-conscious passwords or be organized and disciplined enough always to encrypt all potentially incriminating files. For example, one pedophile and collector of child pornography in Wisconsin was arrested and successfully prosecuted because he forgot to place seven images of child pornography into the encrypted volume. The contraband was located outside of that protected area on his hard disk drive. This particular user demonstrated a great deal of competence and computer skill in creating an encrypted volume, but was defeated by his own sloppiness or an oversight. Although investigators were unable to access materials stored on the encrypted portions of his hard disk drive, he was still convicted on seven counts of possession of child pornography.

Learner Activity

This activity involves writing a brief narrative to answer the presented questions. The goal of this activity is to give you real-world knowledge of available encryption options that might be used by criminals in an attempt to thwart the investigator. Perform an Internet search for encryption programs, both freeware and those available for sale. Compare and contrast these programs in regards to features, strength of encryption, and cost. Does each program encrypt multiple types of files and volumes, or is it very specialized? In other words, does one program allow for encrypted volumes and encrypted e-mail and messaging, or would separate utilities be needed for these functions? Next, research encryption features that are included with operating systems. Does Windows XP offer any encryption? What about the new Windows Vista operating system? Are these features becoming more widespread? What impact will this have on investigators' ability to locate, preserve, and document digital evidence? Last, try to locate articles on biometrics-based encryption such as fingerprint scanner security for laptop computers. What impact will this have on investigators?

■ SUMMARY

This chapter examines the various forms that digital evidence can take and introduces students to the processes of preserving and analyzing that evidence. Although not intended to be an exhaustive manual on computer forensics procedures, it introduces the basic concepts involved with computer forensics and can make an excellent springboard to a forensics certification course. The concepts presented in detail delineate the procedures that are followed by a front-line investigator in properly preserving, documenting, and seizing items from a high-tech crime scene. By following the procedures outlined, investigators can properly perform their role in the chain of custody by transmitting the evidence to the computer forensics specialist for processing and analysis.

■ REVIEW QUESTIONS

1. Define *digital evidence* in your own words.
2. List the seven phases of crime scene processing and describe each phase in your own words.

3. Preservation of a computer system configuration on scene and what the state of the computer was are very important items to document. List several ways you can document how a computer was set up and what it was doing at the time of seizure.
4. Why is it important to know if a computer is attached to a network/the Internet?
5. Why is it important to pull the power cord plug from the back of the computer as opposed to pulling the plug from the wall?
6. How is powering down a laptop different from powering down a desktop system?
7. What is the purpose of a write blocker and why is it important to a computer forensics specialist?
8. When a forensics specialist clones or copies a suspect hard disk drive or other data source, how can the specialist be sure an exact clone or duplicate is made?
9. List several things that could potentially harm digital evidence/computer data.
10. Can a deleted file be recovered? If so, why?
11. Most forensic software applications perform an indexing process on a suspect hard disk drive or data source. What benefits are there to this indexing?
12. Describe the Innocent Images National Initiative in your own words.
13. What is encryption and why does it pose a challenge to investigators?

■ TERMS

bit-by-bit copy	encryption	indexing process
bitstream	forensic analysis	proprietary data
chain of custody	forensic workstation	radio frequency radiation
digital evidence	hard shutdown	write blocker
disk image	hashing	

■ REFERENCES

Federal Bureau of Investigation 1999. Encryption: Impact on law enforcement. www.sion.quickie.net/en60399.pdf (accessed June 6, 2006).

Kessler, Gary C. 2006. An overview of cryptography. www.garykessler.net/library/crypto.html (accessed June 5, 2006).

chapter eleven
Developing a Computer Forensics Unit

1. Identify the current application of computer forensics.
2. Examine the makeup of computer crime units today.
3. Discuss the available training and networking opportunities in the field of computer forensics and investigating high-tech crimes.
4. Discuss available computer forensic software applications.
5. Examine planning considerations for implementing a computer crime unit and forensic laboratory.
6. Explain mobile forensics capabilities and why they are necessary.
7. Explore funding options for computer forensic labs and units.
8. Examine the necessary components of a first responder's high-tech evidence collection field kit.

The nature of computer crime has been highlighted throughout this text. Cybercriminals will continue to exploit technology to their advantage. The cybercriminal is often viewed as an above-average computer user with a unique skill set that makes him or her successful. However, low-level street gang members are now turning to technology to support their illicit organizations. Using a laptop computer and a cell phone to facilitate an identify theft is much safer than perpetrating an armed robbery, and the potential gain is greater, too. This alone forces a law enforcement response.

From simple e-mail harassment or identity theft to sophisticated network system intrusions, local law enforcement agencies often are the first ones notified. In most cases, the patrol officer or first responder is responsible for the preliminary investigation. Many small and medium-sized agencies do not have the in-house resources (trained staff and/or necessary equipment) to completely investigate these high-tech crimes. Knowing the proper protocols and/or the other resources that can be tapped for assistance is critical to the success of the investigation. In addition, understanding how the seized digital or electronic evidence is examined can help the first responder appreciate the value of properly seizing and preserving the evidence, before handing it off to experts. This stage of the investigation begins and ultimately ends in the computer forensics unit.

Once the evidence is collected in the field, whether it is an entire computer system and peripherals or a digital copy of an e-mail message, it must be properly secured as evidence. The evidence is then retrieved and ultimately examined by the forensic examiner. Examiners of digital media or evidence are often referred to as **forensic specialists.** They can be found in both the private and public sectors. Their work is normally performed inside a computer forensic laboratory. These labs must be secure and have the ability to properly maintain the chain of custody.

This chapter explores the history of computer forensics along with an overview of computer forensic units today. The necessary training and role of the computer forensic specialist is discussed along with the most recent industry leaders of forensic examination software. Finally, recommendations and ideas about establishing a computer forensic unit and potential funding sources are given.

11.1 COMPUTER FORENSICS

The idea of computer forensics is relatively new, and, although not referred to as *computer forensics* at the time, this technique was first implemented in 1984 by the Federal Bureau of Investigation in its Magnetic Media Program. In that year, the FBI performed three examinations of computers. The nationwide computer forensics workload has significantly increased since then. Several developments in the world of computer forensics followed, as summarized here:

- *1990*–The International Association of Computer Investigative Specialists (IACIS) was formed to provide training to law enforcement personnel regarding computer forensics and high-technology crime (IACIS 2004).

- *1991*–The FBI's Computer Analysis and Response Team (CART) became operational in the FBI laboratory. CART provides timely and accurate examinations of computers and computer disks as a support to investigations and prosecutions (FBI n.d.).
- *1993*–First International Conference on Computer Evidence is held.
- *1995*–International Organization on Computer Evidence (IOCE) forms. The purpose of the IOCE is "to provide an international forum for law enforcement agencies to exchange information concerning computer investigation and computer forensic issues" (IOCE 2005).
- *2000*–The first FBI **Regional Computer Forensics Lab (RFCL)** becomes operational. These labs are one-stop, full-service forensic laboratories and training centers devoted entirely to the examination of digital evidence in support of criminal investigations. Currently, there are 13 RFCLs throughout the United States (RCFL, n.d.).

The role of the first responder is directly related to the forensic examination of digital media. After the evidence is properly seized and the chain of custody is maintained, to properly examine the media, it is turned over to a forensic specialist. That person may be in-house, especially in larger agencies, or the media might have to be transported to another site at a regional or state forensic lab.

There is no one accepted definition of the term **computer forensics,** and sometimes there is a misconception that this process is analogous to traditional forensic science. Computer forensics is not the use of computers within forensic science, but is better viewed as a "forensic" process. It can be accurately defined as the use of specialized techniques, processes, software, and hardware for the recovery, discovery, analysis, verification, and reporting of electronic data or media to determine if the device contains illegal, inappropriate, or unauthorized text, images, multimedia, or other digital files. The "forensic" aspect of "computer forensics" is the process of copying the media in such a fashion that the original device is not altered in the copying process and the copy itself is an exact duplicate of the original. In other words, the data obtained from the original is a bit-by-bit (i.e., bitstream) copy that is made into the evidence file and that will eventually be examined. Therefore, the original media remains forensically sound and "untouched" and will never be examined or "touched." This is necessary so the original evidence can be provided later in a legal setting in its original state. Making an exact duplicate also helps to defend against allegations of evidence tampering, destruction, or altering. All of the examinations take place on the bitstream copy. If the copied media is ever damaged in the examination process—which is entirely possible—the original media is still intact and can be copied from again.

Similar to the way fingerprints are determined to be an exact match through classification, or the way DNA pattern matching is used to determine that both evidence A and evidence B came from the same source, digital media uses a verification process called the MD5 message digest algorithm to demonstrate that digital media or files exactly "match" one another. Developed by Ron Rivest (1992), the MD5 message digest algorithm is used to produce a 128-bit length "fingerprint" or "message digest" that is unique to a specific volume or file. In other words, the MD5 message digest can be used to demonstrate that the original evidence is untouched by comparing the digest before and after it is copied. If the message digest is unchanged, then the evidence has not been "touched" in the copying process and is therefore said to be forensically sound. This topic is also discussed at length in Chapter 10.

11.2 COMPUTER CRIME UNITS TODAY

Computer crime units or computer forensic units exist at the local, state, and federal levels in the United States. There are also similar units in other regions of the world. For example, the Australian Federal Police (AFP) Computer Forensic Team is the leader in processing electronic evidence stored on computers and other electronic devices in that country.

Local computer forensic units typically exist in larger police agencies. These units can be expensive to implement, staff, train, and maintain. In the day and age of restrictive budgets and doing more with less, many agencies have found themselves consolidating services or depending upon regional or state computer forensic units. The true number of local computer forensic labs is unknown and there is no one-stop directory that lists them all. The cities of Chicago, Milwaukee, Dallas, Los Angeles, and New York are just a few that have their own computer forensic labs within their police departments. These labs typically examine and analyze digital media that have been seized within their jurisdiction. It is not uncommon for them to also assist smaller communities with forensic analysis. However, the demand for computer forensics greatly exceeds the capacity of local labs and all of them experience significant backlogs.

Each state has a state-level computer forensic lab and/or qualified computer forensic examiner. The labs perform the same primary function as their local counterparts and also offer assistance to smaller, more rural communities. They also serve as the primary computer forensic lab for state-led investigations.

Finally, at the federal level, Regional Computer Forensics Labs (RFCLs) are located in regions throughout the United States. As stated earlier, there are currently 13 RFCLs, and they are located in Chicago, Houston, Kansas City, Salt Lake City, Miami, New Jersey, north Texas, Portland, Philadelphia, Centennial (Colorado), San Diego, Silicon Valley, and New York. These RCFLs support local and state law enforcement with examinations of computer and other electronic evidence related to the investigation of terrorism, child pornography, crimes of violence, the theft or destruction of intellectual property, Internet crimes, and fraud.

11.3 TRAINING OPPORTUNITIES AND PROFESSIONAL ORGANIZATIONS

A significant hurdle to overcome when developing and implementing a computer forensic unit is finding and/or training an individual to perform computer forensic examinations. There are several training opportunities and organizations throughout the United States that can assist in this endeavor. Some of the training is costly, while other offerings are free. These organizations also offer great networking opportunities, both in person and online. Some of the best training and networking opportunities in the computer forensics world are listed and summarized in this section. Some of these programs are also discussed in Chapter 8, but are included here as well because of their significance in the training arena.

National White Collar Crime Center (NW3C)—NW3C is a federally funded program that is dedicated to providing "a nationwide support system for agencies involved in the prevention, investigation, and prosecution of economic and high-tech crimes and to support and partner with other appropriate entities in addressing homeland security initiatives, as they relate to economic and high-tech crimes." NW3C also offers several "law enforcement-only" courses on the topics of computer forensics, cybercrime investigations, economic crimes investigations, and others. The Web site also contains several papers, publications, and reports on economic and high-tech crimes, which would be of interest to the first responder or criminal justice student. In addition, member agencies can order numerous free DVD training videos, such as *Cyber Crime Fighting II: Digital Evidence Search, Seizure, and Preservation,* which is a must-see for all first responders. Additional information about NW3C can be found at the Web site: www.nw3c.org/.

International Association of Computer Investigative Specialists (IACIS)— IACIS is considered to be the industry leader in the field of computer forensics. It offers a popular basic Certified Forensic Computer Examiner (CFCE) program that is held once a year. The CFCE is a two-week labor-intensive course on computer forensics followed by a year-long certification process that involves practical examinations of computer media and an extensive written exam. This certification is a must for any first responder or criminal justice student who desires to enter the field of computer forensics. Upon successful completion of the CFCE course, practitioners can also attend the advanced course. Some of the other IACIS course offerings include the Certified Electronic Evidence Collection Specialist Certification (CEECS) and Online Investigations. Additional information about IACIS can be found at the Web site: www.iacis.info/iacisv2/pages/home.php.

High Technology Crime Investigation Association (HTCIA)—The primary goal of the HTCIA is information sharing and exchange of matters associated with high-technology crimes. There are HTCIA chapters throughout the United States and abroad. HTCIA offers an annual educational and training conference. Local HTCIA chapters also offer regional training opportunities on specialized computer and high-tech crime topics. They also have an online e-mail group (an e-group) where members exchange and share information. Additional information about the HTCIA can be found at the Web site: www.htcia.org/.

High Tech Crime Consortium (HTCC)—"Using High Tech Tools to Fight High Tech Crime" is the motto of the HTCC. The mission of the HTCC is to "provide high technology crime investigation education and training in detecting, investigating, and analyzing high technology crime cases where computers are used (1) as a tool to facilitate or enable an illegal activity; (2) as a target of criminal activity; or (3) incidentally to a criminal offense to law enforcement agency personnel." HTCC recognizes that law enforcement have limited budgets and equipment with which to fight high-tech crime, and it offers cost-effective training opportunities in the investigation of computer crime. It also has an online network where members share and exchange information related to the high-tech crime world. Additional information about HTCC can be found at www.hightechcrimecops.org.

Guidance Software—Guidance Software is considered the "world leader in computer investigations." Its popular ENCASE computer forensic software program is an industry standard and is used by local, state, and federal law enforcement agencies. It also offers computer forensic solutions for the private sector. Its law enforcement training offerings include Encase essentials, intermediate analysis and reporting, and advanced computer forensics, to name just a few. The cost of these courses ranges from $1,840 to $2,000, which can be cost-prohibitive for some agencies; however, the quality of the training is well worth the cost. Additional information about Guidance Software can be found at the Web site: www.guidancesoftware.com.

AccessData—AccessData is considered "The Leader in Password Recovery, Electronic Evidence Recovery and Analysis." AccessData works with law enforcement and offers software programs that read, acquire, decrypt, analyze, and report on digital evidence. Some of this company's forensic software utilities include the Ultimate Toolkit (UTK), Forensic Toolkit (FTK), and Registry Viewer (RV). It offers training courses, including AccessData Certified Examiner, AccessData Boot Camp, Applied Decryption, E-mail Forensics, Internet Forensics, Windows Forensics, and others. Additional information about AccessData can be found at the Web site: www.accessdata.com.

New Technologies, Inc. (NTI)—NTI is a company composed of internationally recognized computer experts in the field of computer forensics, computer security, and investigations. NTI has clients throughout the United States and has developed many software programs with the needs of classified government agencies in mind. Some of its software programs include the Stealth Suite, Computer Incident Response Suite, Data Elmination Suite, and Advanced Password Recovery Tool Kit. It also offers courses on computer forensic training, an expert witness course, and a data risk reduction—information leakage course. Additional information about NTI can be found at the Web site: www.forensics-intl.com.

11.4 CONDUCTING A NEEDS ASSESSMENT FOR A COMPUTER CRIMES UNIT

There are four primary considerations to examine when planning the implementation of a computer crimes unit or computer forensic laboratory. The first and foremost is devoting adequate financial resources to the task. The other three considerations flow naturally from the financial issue because staffing, training, and equipping the unit all cost money. Startup costs can seem daunting to police administrators because an initial financial hurdle must be overcome because of the highly technical nature of the training and equipment. Unfortunately, once the initial outlay is made, administrators are also faced with budgeting for upkeep, maintenance, and upgrading of the unit as technology evolves. These are challenges that must be met, however, because computer crimes aren't going away—they are increasing greatly in volume and severity every passing year.

An agency contemplating creating a computer forensic lab or team must understand that the initial investment will be measured in the tens of thousands of dollars. To properly equip the lab with a forensic workstation (Figure 11–1), spare evidence hard disk drives, forensic software, security, and other equipment needs will likely cost at least $20,000.

An industry-standard computer forensic workstation alone can cost $6,000, and that doesn't include the price of the forensic software, such as AccessData Forensic Toolkit, Encase, ILook, or NTI Computer Incident Response Suite. Those suites of forensic software utilities can cost anywhere from $1,000 to $4,000 each. In addition, the lab will need other miscellaneous equipment such as blank hard disk drives for cloning suspect drives, a laser printer, file storage devices, and more. Remember, too, that agencies that have a moderate volume of computer crime cases may want to actually equip two separate computer forensic workstations. To process a large hard disk drive a forensic workstation might be in use for several hours or even days indexing and analyzing. Having a second workstation enables an investigator to continue working on other cases or other evidence within the same case.

In addition to the initial materials and equipment costs, new computer crimes investigators must negotiate a sharp training curve. In an ideal situation, the new computer forensic investigator already has strong computer skills. If someone is chosen for this job who has only basic computer skills, a great deal of time and money will be spent on training that individual. If, however, the person brings a relatively high degree of computer skills to the table, he or she may need to complete only computer forensic training and certification classes. All major forensic software providers offer classes and certification processes for use of their product. Certification classes generally cost about $2,000. In some cases, the cost includes a licensed copy of the forensic software, allowing for some cost savings. Bear in mind that forensic units need a software license for each forensic workstation on which the software is installed.

Figure 11–1 A forensic workstation.
Courtesy of Digital Intelligence, Inc. www.forensicintelligence.com

Because technology is constantly changing, new operating systems are being written, and drive capacities are expanding, computer crime teams must also have the flexibility and the funding to adapt. Starting a computer crimes unit only to neglect its ongoing budget is foolish. The unit should have the necessary equipment and software on hand to clone many types of drives. Unfortunately, this means that the unit must always stay on the leading edge of the technology curve. If a suspect can obtain a 1-terabyte hard disk drive, the computer forensic team will need a 1-terabyte drive to clone the suspect's equipment. Further, the unit will probably need at least two such drives because it may have to give a clone to the defense team during discovery.

Table 11–1 Approximate Costs of Forensics Units Equipment

Item	Cost
Forensic workstation	$5,000 to $7,000 per unit
Spare hard drives for evidence cloning	$3,000 total
Forensic utility software	$3,000/per workstation
Forensic software certification training	$2,500/per investigator
Color laser printer	$600
Miscellaneous cables, adapters, interfaces	$500
Miscellaneous tools, antistatic mat, etc.	$1,000
Uninterruptible power supply unit	$500 per unit

Likewise, the forensic software utilities must constantly evolve to keep pace with new operating systems and the new ways hard disk drives are formatted. One excellent example of this was the change that came when the public transitioned from using the Windows 98 operating system to Windows XP. Up until that time, most of the world had hard disk drives that were set up with file allocation tables (using the FAT32 file system). Windows XP and the business version, Windows NT, both used a new file system format called the NTFS to replace the aging FAT32 standard. Software vendors had to release new versions of their forensic utilities to read and clone the NTFS drives. As a new version of forensic software comes out, the computer forensic specialist must attend the training for it. See Table 11–1 for approximate cost estimates of lab equipment, software, and miscellaneous items.

The other, more basic consideration has to do with the physical layout and configuration of the lab workspace. Ideally, the lab will be a climate-controlled environment. It should also have its own access control door protected by an alarm or biometric-based access. Chain of custody issues are especially prickly in the digital evidence realm. Because of the wide variety and quantity of equipment needed, the lab room should be fairly spacious. For agencies with one forensic specialist, the space should be no smaller than 400 square feet. If the building allows, more space is definitely better.

It is also important to organize that space well, ensuring there is plenty of storage, counter, and desktop space; cable management for the countless cords; and a vast number of electric outlets. Power to the systems should have spike and surge protection and should also be protected with an **uninterruptible power supply (UPS) unit.** That way, no data are damaged or lost in the event of a power outage or surge. An antistatic workbench area equipped with appropriate tools on one wall can serve the unit well because specialists must disassemble computers to remove hard disk drives. Additionally, a large bulletin board or dry erase board should be mounted to allow for organization of multiple cases, tasks, investigators, and so forth. A space for a high-speed laser printer should be available because printing out the very lengthy forensic examination reports might otherwise tie up the department's other printers. Last, an allowance should be made for lots of shelving and filing space. The lab must store numerous technical manuals, case files, software guides, and printed reports for court. An example of a sample forensic lab design is included in Figure 11–2.

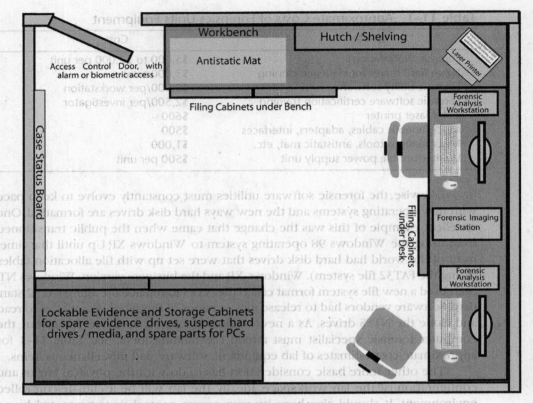

Figure 11–2 Sample layout of a functional forensic lab setup.

11.5 MOBILE FORENSIC CAPABILITIES

Situations may arise from time to time that require forensic specialists to travel and collect evidence in the field. One example is when evidence is contained on a business computer or computer network. Most businesses rely heavily on their computer systems, and they may not want their systems to be offline for the time needed for a full seizure of evidence. Assuming the company is the complainant or victim in the case, investigators may want to accommodate its business interests by collecting the digital evidence on location.

Luckily, there are mobile forensic workstations and applications. A forensic specialist can utilize either a forensic workstation laptop or **briefcase computer** solution, which is a self-contained computer system that can be carried by one person (see Figure 11–3). Unlike a laptop, a briefcase computer still has a number of interfaces and swappable drive bays for easier acquisition of data from a subject's hard disk drive. Laptop forensic workstations generally have to rely on external drive bays that connect to the laptop either via a universal serial bus (USB) connection or a FireWire connection. Laptop forensic systems also require a USB

Figure 11–3 The Freddie mobile briefcase forensic unit.
Courtesy of Digital Intelligence, Inc. www.digitalintelligence.com

or FireWire-based write blocker to prevent any data from being written to that external drive. Lab forensic workstations and the briefcase computers have write blockers built into the swappable drive bays.

Learner Activity

You have been tasked with the responsibility to draft a proposal for a computer forensic laboratory at your agency. Your agency serves a medium-sized city of 120,000 people, and a recent needs assessment predicts that once the laboratory is up and running, it will be processing at least 100 cases per year. Two positions have been approved in the budget for next year. However, the agency head requests that you provide him/her with a proposal that outlines the initial financial outlay necessary to create the unit. The agency already has the space available, but needs all other necessary materials to operate the laboratory. The personnel also need to be trained. Using your text, the Internet, and other academic sources, research and create a list of materials necessary, including their costs and costs to operate the laboratory. Prepare your report.

11.6 FUNDING OPTIONS FOR COMPUTER FORENSIC LABS

Because funding a computer forensic lab and team can be quite expensive at startup and to maintain, it is important to budget carefully for the unit. Further, some smaller agencies may simply lack the financial wherewithal to afford a unit at all. It is important, therefore, to examine funding alternatives and other approaches to make these services accessible to all law enforcement agencies. First, most, if not all, states have a state-run crime laboratory that can perform this work. The problem facing many state crime labs, however, is a high-volume case load and extreme backlog for processing computer evidence. In many cases, the delays are such that agencies must look elsewhere for these services.

If using the state crime lab is not an option, or if an agency has a relatively high rate of these types of crimes, there are several alternatives. First, the agency could partner with another agency or agencies in the same geographic area. This is similar to the concept that many law enforcement agencies use with multijurisdictional drug enforcement units. All of the agencies pool their financial and staffing resources. They can then serve all of the involved agencies, and this setup also makes prosecuting offenders who cross the jurisdictional boundaries easier. Just as drug dealers travel in an out of jurisdictional areas, so too do online offenders.

In an ideal multijurisdictional example, three small municipal police agencies and a county sheriff's department agree to provide support for one computer forensic specialist. The sheriff agrees to provide a large workspace, while one of the municipal agencies supplies a detective who has extensive computer experience. The other two municipal agencies and the sheriff's department each agree to supply one investigator to work with the forensic specialist. All four agencies agree to provide initial funding of $15,000 each and ongoing funding of $10,000 per year to the unit, in addition to the cost of their personnel.

With the sheriff providing the physical location and paying for the utilities, the unit can use the initial $60,000 to set up a well-equipped computer forensic laboratory. This works out well for all four agencies because none of them could justify spending $60,000 for their own in-house forensic lab, nor did they feel they had the forensic case load to devote a full-time staff member to computer forensics. By sharing one forensic specialist and utilizing three additional white-collar crime investigators, however, those agencies all have access to quick and responsive computer forensic services when they do need them and can cooperatively investigate white-collar criminals in their area. A slightly different scenario could be when the sheriff's department builds its own forensic laboratory, staffs it, and sets up contractual agreements with the other agencies. The sheriff's department would provide forensic services in exchange for a yearly contract fee. Again, the local agencies have quick access to services they may need only occasionally, and the sheriff can afford the lab by dispersing the cost over multiple agencies' budgets.

Another option to consider when trying to fund a forensic laboratory is the use of federal and state grants. Every year, the government allocates many millions of dollars in grants to be allocated to those law enforcement agencies that apply. The grants can range from general block grants to grants for a limited, specific purpose. One place to look for grants is the Bureau of Justice Assistance, a branch of the U.S. Department of Justice (www.ojp.usdoj.gov/ BJA/). Many states also have their own Office of Justice Assistance. Another source of grants is www.grants.gov, which bills itself as the interface between those seeking federal grants and the 26 federal agencies that provide grants. Each year, more than $400 million in grant money is awarded. The recent trend has been toward electronic applications and requests for proposals, and even allowing applicants to easily and conveniently apply online. Some law enforcement agencies have even dedicated part-time staff to seeking out and applying for grants, knowing that successful grant applications will more than make up for the salary of the staff involved.

A third option to consider is the use of private, foundation, or community grants. Many businesses, corporations, or citizen action groups provide grant monies for a wide variety of causes. One example is the Mothers Against Drunk Drivers (MADD) dash cam program. In an effort to enhance enforcement of driving under the influence (DUI) laws, MADD provided dashboard video cameras to law enforcement agencies to record intoxicated drivers and field sobriety tests to aid them in the apprehension and prosecution of drunk drivers. A similar approach can be used in funding a computer forensic unit. In regards to online child enticement and child pornography, many organizations want to help law enforcement. They may exist in the form of organizations such as Pedowatch, a group dedicated to fighting pedophiles, or they could simply be local church and citizens' groups such as the Kiwanis Club, Rotary Club, or Knights of Columbus. Almost every city, village, and town in the United States has some form of citizens activism group. Many are looking for ways to help out and need only be presented with a worthwhile cause to support.

11.7 DEVELOPING A FIELD KIT FOR THE FIRST RESPONDER

In addition to assembling a computer forensic laboratory, forensic workstation, and mobile forensic examination capability, it is also important to establish a first responder's field kit. Along those same lines, law enforcement agencies should devote some time and resources to training their first responder staff. Specially trained forensic investigators are few and cannot possibly go to every call where digital evidence might exist. They must, instead, rely on 9-1-1 center operators to screen calls properly and responding patrol officers to identify correctly those calls that might involve digital evidence. Further, once on site, officers must know not to modify the digital evidence, know how to best preserve it, and know when to call out the forensic investigator. The training officers receive in technology crime is, unfortunately, very brief or in many cases nonexistent. Because first responders are the street-level eyes and ears of a law enforcement agency, their lack of training must be addressed.

Once responding officers are trained to properly preserve the scene of a computer crime or other technology crime, it is advisable to assemble a field kit for computer crime response. The kit can help first responders address the basic duties of securing and processing a crime scene. In Figure 11–4, suggested items for the field kit are, therefore, listed next to the phase of crime scene processing to which they relate.

Learner Activity

Your agency head is impressed with the proposal that you provided him/her regarding the overall cost of starting and operating the computer forensic laboratory. You recognized, however, the agency also needs to obtain the materials necessary to create a computer forensic field kit for seizing digital evidence at the scene of a crime. Using the text, the Internet, and other academic research sources, identify the items necessary to create a computer forensic field kit for seizing digital evidence. Provide a comprehensive list of the items and their associated costs. It's anticipated that at least half of the estimated annual case load (50 cases) will require seizing the digital evidence in the field. Submit your report.

■ SUMMARY

It is expensive, time-consuming, and labor- and training-intensive to establish an effective computer crimes response team and/or unit. It is, however, a necessary function of law enforcement in this day and age, and police agencies are already lagging behind the technology curve. Computer crimes are not going away, so it is in every agency's best interest to properly train first responders and forensic

Phase of Crime Scene Processing	Field Kit Items
1. **Secure the crime scene.** This includes physically isolating the crime scene by removing suspects, witnesses, bystanders, etc. It also involves preventing any physical harm or changes to the scene.	• Standard police crime scene items such as **police tape, traffic barricades, handcuffs** for arresting or detaining suspects, etc. • This phase also requires adequate **staffing** to provide for the security of any detainees as well as to prevent anyone else from entering the area.
2. **Evaluate the crime scene.** This is the process that determines the size and scope of the crime scene to be processed. Investigators should always err on the side of making the scene too big because it can always be condensed. Having to enlarge a crime scene at a later date can call the chain of custody into question.	• No equipment is needed; this involves visual observation and prioritization.
3. **Recognize evidence within the scene.** Once the physical outer limits have been set, the first responder must then attempt to identify any potential evidence within that crime scene.	• No equipment is needed; this involves visual observation, recognition, and prioritization.
4. **Document the evidence.** This phase deals with documenting the existence of potential evidence in its original state. It should be photographed and/or videotaped in its original untouched position.	• Agency's **high-resolution digital camera** for photographing the scene and all items in it. Care should be taken to photograph the entire scene, from multiple angles. • **Digital video camera** for documenting large scenes, or scenes where a verbal narrative might need to accompany the image to further explain it. • In the case of computer scenes, **labels** for documenting all cables, ports, and cable connections should be in the kit to document the manner in which equipment is interconnected.

(continued)

Figure 11–4 Field Kit items corresponding to phases of crime scene processing.

5. **Collect the evidence.** Even before the collection can begin, there are a number of things to be done. If the computer has a floppy drive, the disk inside should be removed and an investigator's blank floppy disk should be inserted in its place. Most computers will try to boot from the floppy drive if there is a disk in it, so including a blank disk could prevent damaging or changing data if someone would inadvertently turn the computer on. After all ports and cable connections have been photographed, documented, and labeled, evidence tape should be placed over the ports, power switches, and disk drives.

6. **Transport the evidence.**

7. **Secure the evidence.**

- **Blank floppy diskette.**
- **Bags, boxes, pouches** for storing components, peripheral devices, manuals, paperwork, and media. Antistatic pouches are available for transporting loose computer hardware such as video cards.
- Antistatic **protective wrapping** or antistatic **packing peanuts** to physically protect materials during transport.
- **Tool kit** including a wide variety of screwdrivers, Allen wrenches, Torx bits, etc. to allow for potential disassembly of evidence components for transport.
- Antistatic **wrist band.**
- **Evidence tape** to seal packages, tape off ports, or tape off access to power switches, etc.
- **Evidence sheets** to inventory all items seized, including their serial number, brand, model number, etc.

- Utilize a **vehicle** that has adequate cargo capacity that does not have a radio repeater or other radio frequency device near the evidence. Many squad cars have a radio repeater in the trunk that produces a magnetic field, which could damage or erase digital data.

- Use a cool, dry, **secure place** that is not accessible by other members of the department and not located near any major utilities such as water service, gas lines, etc. Some departments have one **evidence locker** for all evidence; some may have an area specifically dedicated to computer evidence.

Figure 11–4 *(Continued)*

specialists and to give them the equipment and facilities they need to perform effectively.

Computer forensics is a relatively new field that is fluid and evolving. It will continue to change as technology advances and criminal uses of those technologies evolve. It is necessary for the responding front-line officers to understand the role of computer forensics to properly recognize and preserve digital evidence for expert analysis. Although first responders are not expected to perform those tasks, they are the first link in the chain of custody and must be familiar with the proper protocols for preserving and transmitting digital evidence.

There are several training opportunities for first responders who wish to learn more about the front-line duties or to expand their scope into the realm of computer forensics. Furthermore, agencies should explore ways to train every first responder in the proper recognition, collection, and preservation of digital evidence. Organizations such as NW3C, HTCIA, and IACIS are available to provide needed training and support in these areas. For example, the *Cyber Crime Fighting II* DVD referenced earlier is an excellent starting point presentation for annual in-service training, it requires no specialized skills on part of the trainer and it is free.

Because of the technological complexity, the biggest hurdle in creating a computer crime unit is the initial financial outlay. To prepare for this, agencies need to properly budget for and/or seek alternative funding sources, such as grants. Ongoing maintenance and training costs also need to be considered on an annual basis.

Finally, agencies can work toward upgrading their existing evidence collection kits to include the tools necessary for properly processing high-tech crime scenes. Sooner or later, every agency will face crimes of this nature, to one extent or another, and can better serve their communities by preparing in advance.

■ REVIEW QUESTIONS

1. What is meant by the term *computer forensics* and what is the role of the forensic examiner in the forensics process?
2. What is the MD5 message digest algorithm and how is it utilized in the forensic examination of computers?
3. What is the role of the Regional Computer Forensics Labs (RFCL) in the United States?
4. List and discuss three training opportunities for first responders to learn more about investigating high-tech crimes.
5. What are three potential ways to fund a computer forensic lab as discussed in the text?

■ TERMS

briefcase computer	forensic specialist	uninterruptible power
computer forensics	Regional Computer Forensics	supply (UPS) unit
	Lab (RFCL)	

■ REFERENCES

Federal Bureau of Investigation (FBI). FBI history. www.fbi.gov/libref/historic/history/historicdates.htm (accessed June 14, 2006).

International Association of Computer Investigative Specialists (IACIS). 2004. The president. www.iacis.info/iacisv2/pages/thepresident.php (accessed June 14, 2006).

International Organization of Computer Evidence (IOCE). 2005. IOCE board. www.ioce.org/ioce_board.html (accessed June 14, 2006).

Regional Computer Forensics Laboratory (RCFL). RCFL National Program Office. www.rcfl.gov/ (accessed June 14, 2006).

Rivest, Ron. 1992. The MD5 message digest algorithm. www.theory.lcs.mit.edu/~rivest/publications.html (accessed June 14, 2006).

appendix A

State and/or Agency Listing of Computer Crimes Task Forces

Alabama–Alabama Bureau of Investigation
Alaska (*see* Washington)
Arizona–Phoenix Police Department
Arkansas–Arkansas State Police
California, Los Angeles–Los Angeles Police Department
California, Sacramento County–Sacramento County Sheriff's Office
California, San Diego–San Diego Police Department
California, San Jose–San Jose Police Department
Colorado–Colorado Springs Police Department
Connecticut–Connecticut State Police
Florida, Broward County–Broward County Sheriff's Office
Florida, Gainesville–Gainesville Police Department
Georgia–Georgia Bureau of Investigation
Hawaii–Hawaii Department of Attorney General
Idaho (*see* Utah)
Illinois–Illinois Attorney General's Office
Illinois–Cook County State's Attorney's Office
Indiana–Indiana State Police
Iowa–Iowa Division of Criminal Investigation
Kansas–Sedgwick County Sheriff's Office

Kentucky–Kentucky State Police

Louisiana–Louisiana Department of Justice

Maine (*see* New Hampshire for Regional Task Force contact
   information)

Maine–Maine State Police

Maryland–Maryland State Police

Massachusetts–Massachusetts State Police

Michigan–Michigan State Police

Minnesota–St. Paul Police Department

Mississippi–(TBA)

Missouri–Glendale Police Department

Montana (*see* Utah)

Nebraska–Nebraska State Patrol

Nevada–Las Vegas Metropolitan Police Department

New Hampshire–Portsmouth Police Department

New Jersey–New Jersey State Police

New Mexico–New Mexico Attorney General's Office

New York–New York State Police

North Carolina–North Carolina State Bureau of Investigation

North Dakota (*see* Minnesota)

Ohio–Cuyahoga County Prosecutor's Office

Oklahoma–Oklahoma State Bureau of Investigation

Oregon–Oregon Department of Justice

Pennsylvania–Delaware County District Attorney's Office

Rhode Island (*see* Connecticut)

South Carolina–South Carolina Attorney General's Office

South Dakota (*see* Minnesota)

Tennessee–Knoxville Police Department

Texas, Dallas–Dallas Police Department

Texas–Office of the Attorney General of Texas

Utah–Utah Office of Attorney General

Vermont (*see* New Hampshire for Regional Task Force contact
   information)

Vermont–Burlington Police Department

Virginia, Bedford County–Bedford County Sheriff's Office

Virginia, Northern–Virginia State Police

Washington–Seattle Police Department

Washington DC (*see* Virginia)

West Virginia (*see* Virginia)

Wisconsin–Wisconsin Department of Justice

Wyoming–Wyoming Division of Criminal Investigation

appendix B
State Computer Crimes Statutes Citations

This is an abridged version of the computer crime laws found throughout the United States. The statutes cited may contain additional laws related to high-tech crimes, such as unlawful use of computerized communications systems or those laws that prohibit harassing and threatening e-mail messages. Some of the titles have been shortened, but the proper statutes are cited, which will point the first responder in the right direction.

Alabama: § 13A-8-100 Title–Alabama Computer Crime Act
Alaska: § 11.46 Section 740–Criminal Use of a Computer
Arizona: §13-2316–Computer tampering; venue; forfeiture; classification
Arkansas: § 5-41-103–Computer Fraud
California: § 13-5-502–Computer Crimes
Colorado: § 18-5.5-102–Computer Crime
Connecticut: § 53a-251–Computer Crime
Delaware: Title 11 Del. C. § 932 thru 935 - Computer Crime statutes
Florida: § 815.01–Florida Computer Crimes Act
Georgia: § 16-9-90–Georgia Computer Systems Protection Act
Hawaii:§ 708-891–Computer Fraud and § 708-892 Unauthorized
    Computer Use
Idaho: § 18-2202–Computer Crime
Illinois: § 720 ILCS 5/16D-1–Computer Crime Prevention Law

Indiana: § 35-43-1-4–Computer Tampering and § 35-43-2-3 Computer Trespass

Iowa: § 716A.2–Unauthorized Access and § 716A.3–Computer damage defined

Kansas: § 21-3755–Computer Crime; Computer Password Disclosure; Computer Trespass

Kentucky: § 40-434.840–Unlawful Access to a Computer

Louisiana: § 14:73.3–Offenses against Computer Equipment or Supplies

Maine: § 432–Criminal Invasion of Computer Privacy

Maryland: § 146–Unauthorized Access to Computers Prohibited

Massachusetts: § 266-33A–Intent to Defraud Commercial Computer Service; Penalties and § 266-120F–Unauthorized Access to Computers

Michigan: § 28.529(4)–Prohibited Access to Computer Program, Computer, Computer System, or Computer Network and § 28.529(6) Use of Computer Program, Computer, Computer System, or Computer Network to Commit Crime

Minnesota: § 609.87–Computer Crime; Definitions

Mississippi:§ 97-45-3–Computer Fraud and § 97-45-5 Offense against Computer Users

Missouri: § 537.525–Tampering with Computer Data, Computer Equipment, or Computer Users

Montana: § 45-6-311–Unlawful Use of a Computer

Nebraska: § 28-1341–Act and § 28-1343.01 Unauthorized Computer Access

Nevada: § 205.4765–Unlawful Acts Regarding Computer

New Hampshire: § 638:17–Computer Related Offenses

New Jersey: § 2A:38A-1–Definitions, Computer Crime

New Mexico: § 30-45-1–Computer Crimes Act

New York: Penal Code, Title J: § 156.00 Offenses Involving Computers

North Carolina: § 14-454–Accessing Computers

North Dakota: § 12.1-06.1-08–Computer Fraud/Computer Crime

Ohio: § 2901.04–Unauthorized Use of Property; Computer, Cable, or Telecommunication Property or Service

Oklahoma: § 21:1951–Oklahoma Computer Crimes Act

Oregon: § 164.377–Computer Crime

Pennsylvania: § 3933–Unlawful Use of Computer

Rhode Island: § 11-52-2–Access to Computer for Fraudulent Purposes

South Carolina: § 16-16-10–Definitions (computer crime explained within)

South Dakota: § 43-43B-1–Unlawful Uses of Computer

Tennessee: § 39-14-601–Definitions (computer crime explained within)

Texas: § 13.25–Computer Crimes—Venue

Utah: § 76-6-701–Computer Crimes Act—Short title

Vermont: 13 V.S.A. 4102–Unauthorized Access and 13 V.S.A. § 4103
Access to Computer for Fraudulent Purposes
Virginia: § 8.01-40.1–Computer Crimes Act
Washington: § 9A.52.110–Computer Trespass in the First Degree
West Virginia: § 61-3C-1–West Virginia Computer Crime and Abuse Act
Wisconsin: § 943.70–Computer Crimes
Wyoming: § 6-3-503–Crimes against Computer Equipment or Supplies

appendix C

Definitions of Common Terms Used in a High-Tech Crime Search Warrant Affidavit

addresses—Every device on the Internet has an address that allows other devices to locate and communicate with it. An Internet Protocol (IP) address is a unique number that identifies a device on the Internet. Other addresses include Uniform Resource Locator (URL) addresses, such as "http://www.usdoj.gov," which are typically used to access Web sites or other services on remote devices. Domain names, host names, and machine addresses are other types of addresses associated with Internet use.

cookies—A cookie is a file that is generated by a Web site when a user on a remote computer accesses it. The cookie is sent to the user's computer and is placed in a directory on that computer, usually labeled "Internet" or "Temporary Internet Files." The cookie includes information such as user preferences, connection information such as time and date of use, records of user activity including files accessed or services used, or account information. The cookie is then accessed by the Web site on subsequent visits by the user, to better serve the user's needs.

data compression—A process of reducing the number of bits required to represent some information, usually to reduce the time or cost of storing or transmitting it. Some methods can be reversed to reconstruct the original data

Source: U.S. Department of Justice. 2002. Searching & seizing computers and obtaining electronic evidence in criminal investigations. www.usdoj.gov/criminal/cybercrime/s&smanual2002.pdf.

exactly; these are used for faxes, programs, and most computer data. Other methods do not exactly reproduce the original data, but this may be acceptable (for example, for a videoconference).

denial of service (DoS) attack—A hacker attempting a DoS attack will often use multiple IP or e-mail addresses to send a particular server or Web site hundreds or thousands of messages in a short period of time. The server or Web site will devote system resources to each transmission. Due to the limited resources of servers and Web sites, this bombardment will eventually slow the system down or crash it altogether.

domain—A domain is a group of Internet devices that are owned or operated by a specific individual, group, or organization. Devices within a domain have IP addresses within a certain range of numbers and are usually administered according to the same set of rules and procedures.

domain name—A domain name identifies a computer or group of computers on the Internet and corresponds to one or more IP addresses within a particular range. Domain names are typically strings of alphanumeric characters, with each "level" of the domain delimited by a period (e.g., Computer.networklevel1 .networklevel2.com). A domain name can provide information about the organization, ISP, and physical location of a particular network user.

dynamic IP address—When an ISP or other provider uses dynamic IP addresses, the ISP randomly assigns one of the available IP addresses in the range of IP addresses controlled by the ISP each time a user dials into the ISP to connect to the Internet. The customer's computer retains that IP address for the duration of that session (i.e., until the user disconnects), and the IP address cannot be assigned to another user during that period. Once the user disconnects, however, that IP address becomes available to other customers who dial in at a later time. Thus, an individual customer's IP address normally differs each time the customer dials into the ISP.

encryption—Encryption refers to the practice of mathematically scrambling computer data as a communications security measure. The encrypted information is called "ciphertext." "Decryption" is the process of converting the ciphertext back into the original, readable information (known as "plaintext"). The word, number, or other value used to encrypt/decrypt a message is called the "key."

file transfer protocol (FTP)—FTP is a method of communication used to send and receive files such as word processing documents, spreadsheets, pictures, songs, and video files. FTP sites are online "warehouses" of computer files that are available for copying by users on the Internet. Although many sites require users to supply credentials (such as a password or user name) to gain access, the IP address of the FTP site is often all that is required to access the site, and users are often identified only by their IP addresses.

firewall—A firewall is a dedicated computer system or piece of software that monitors the connection between one computer or network and another. The firewall is the gatekeeper that certifies communications, blocks unauthorized or suspect transmissions, and filters content coming into a network. Hackers can sidestep the protections offered by firewalls by acquiring system passwords, "hiding" within authorized IP addresses using specialized software and routines, or placing viruses in seemingly innocuous files such as e-mail attachments.

hacking—Hacking is the deliberate infiltration or sabotaging of a computer or network of computers. Hackers use loopholes in computer security to gain control of a system, steal passwords and sensitive data, and/or incapacitate a computer or group of computers. Hacking is usually done remotely, by sending harmful commands and programs through the Internet to a target system. When they arrive, these commands and programs instruct the target system to operate outside of the parameters specified by the administrator of the system. This often causes general system instability or the loss of data.

instant messaging (IM)—IM is a communications service that allows two users to send messages through the Internet to each other in real time. Users subscribe to a particular messaging service (e.g., AOL Instant Messenger, MSN Messenger) by supplying personal information and choosing a screen name to use in connection with the service. When logged in to the IM service, users can search for other users based on the information that other users have supplied, and they can send those users messages or initiate a chat session. Most IM services also allow files to be transferred between users, including music, video files, and computer software. Due to the structure of the Internet, a transmission may be routed through different states and/or countries before it arrives at its final destination, even if the communicating parties are in the same state.

Internet—The Internet is a global network of computers and other electronic devices that communicate with each other via standard telephone lines, high-speed telecommunications links (e.g., fiber-optic cable), and wireless transmissions. Due to the structure of the Internet, connections between devices on the Internet often cross state and international borders, even when the devices communicating with each other are in the same state.

Internet Relay Chat (IRC)—IRC is a popular Internet service that allows users to communicate with each other in real time. IRC is organized around the "chat room" or "channel," in which users congregate to communicate with each other about a specific topic. A chat room typically connects users from different states and countries, and IRC messages often travel across state and national borders before reaching other users. Within a chat room or channel, every user can see the messages typed by other users. No user identification is required for IRC, allowing users to log in and participate in IRC communication with virtual anonymity, concealing their identities by using fictitious screen names.

Internet service providers (ISPs)—Many individuals and businesses obtain their access to the Internet through businesses known as Internet service providers (ISPs). ISPs provide their customers with access to the Internet using telephone or other telecommunications lines; provide Internet e-mail accounts that allow users to communicate with other Internet users by sending and receiving electronic messages through the ISPs servers; remotely store electronic files on their customers' behalf; and may provide other services unique to each particular ISP.

IP address—The Internet Protocol address (or simply, IP address) is a unique numeric address used by computers on the Internet. An IP address looks like a series of four numbers, each in the range 0–255, separated by periods (e.g., 121.56.97.178). Every computer attached to the Internet must be assigned an IP address so that Internet traffic sent from and directed to that computer may be directed properly from its source to its destination. Most Internet service providers control a range of IP addresses.

Joint Photographs Experts Group (JPEG)— JPEG is the name of a standard for compressing digitized images that can be stored on computers. JPEG is often used to compress photographic images, including pornography. Such files are often identified by the jpg extension (such that a JPEG file might have the name picture.jpg) but can easily be renamed without the .jpg extension.

log file—Log files are computer files that contain records about system events and status, the activities of users, and anomalous or unauthorized computer usage. Names for various log files include, but are not limited to: user logs, access logs, audit logs, transactional logs, and apache logs.

Moving Pictures Expert Group Layer 3 Audio (MP3)—MP3 is the name of a standard for compressing audio recordings (e.g., songs, albums, concert recordings) so that they can be stored on a computer, transmitted through the Internet to other computers, or listened to using a computer. Despite its small size, an MP3 delivers near CD-quality sound. Such files are often identified by the file name extension .mp3, but can easily be renamed without the .mp3 extension.

packet sniffing—On the Internet, information is usually transmitted through many different locations before it reaches its final destination. While in transit, such information is contained within "packets." Both authorized users, such as system security experts, and unauthorized users, such as hackers, use specialized technology—packet sniffers—to "listen" to the flow of information on a network for interesting packets, such as those containing logins or passwords, sensitive or classified data, or harmful communications such as viruses. After locating such data, the packet sniffer can read, copy, redirect, or block the communication.

Peer-to-Peer (P2P) Networks—P2P networks differ from conventional networks in that each computer within the network functions as both a client (using the resources and services of other computers) and a server (providing files and services for use by "peer" computers). There is often no centralized server in such a network. Instead, a search program or database tells users where other computers are located and what files and services they have to offer. Often, P2P networks are used to share and disseminate music, movies, and computer software.

router—A router is a device on the Internet that facilitates communication. Each Internet router maintains a table that states the next step a communication must take on its path to its proper destination. When a router receives a transmission, it checks the transmission's destination IP address against addresses in its table and directs the communication to another router or the destination computer. The log file and memory of a router often contain important information that can help reveal the source and network path of communications.

server—A server is a centralized computer that provides services for other computers connected to it via a network. The other computers attached to a server are sometimes called "clients." In a large company, it is common for individual employees to have client computers at their desks. When the employees access their e-mail, or access files stored on the network itself, those files are pulled electronically from the server, where they are stored, and are sent to the client computer via the network. Notably, server computers can be physically stored in any location: it is common for a network's server to be located hundreds (and even thousands) of miles away from the client computers.

static IP address—A static IP address is an IP address that is assigned permanently to a given user or computer on a network. A customer of an ISP that assigns static IP addresses will have the same IP address every time.

tracing—Trace programs are used to determine the path that a communication takes to arrive at its destination. A trace program requires the user to specify a source and destination IP address. The program then launches a message from the source address, and at each "hop" on the network (signifying a device such as a router), the IP address of that device is displayed on the source user's screen or copied to a log file.

user name or user ID—Most services offered on the Internet assign users a name or ID, which is a pseudonym that computer systems use to keep track of users. User names and IDs are typically associated with additional user information or resources, such as a user account protected by a password, personal or financial information about the user, a directory of files, or an e-mail address.

virus—A virus is a malicious computer program designed by a hacker to (1) incapacitate a target computer system, (2) cause a target system to slow down or become unstable, (3) gain unauthorized access to system files, passwords, and other sensitive data such as financial information, and/or (4) gain control of the target system to use its resources in furtherance of the hacker's agenda. Once inside the target system, a virus may begin making copies of itself, depleting system memory and causing the system to shut down, or it may begin issuing system commands or altering crucial data within the system. Other malicious programs used by hackers are, but are not limited to: "worms" that spawn copies that travel over a network to other systems, "Trojan horses" that are hidden in seemingly innocuous files such as e-mail attachments and are activated by unassuming authorized users, and "bombs" that are programs designed to bombard a target e-mail server or individual user with messages, overloading the target or otherwise preventing the reception of legitimate communications.

Glossary

Account Takeover Occurs when an identity thief gains access to a victim's financial account and makes unauthorized charges.

Active Pedophile A person who performs some physical act against a child or several children. The active pedophile is a person who actually creates or manufactures child pornography by photographing or taking video of sexual acts involving a child.

Affidavit A legal document that is used when applying for subpoenas and/or search warrants that contains chronological and detailed information of events or facts that establish probable cause.

AGP bus Short for Accelerated Graphics Port. This data bus is a 32-bit bus primarily used for sending data to and receiving data from graphics cards. AGP ports on computer motherboards were generally rated by speeds such as 1×, 2×, 4×, 8×, and 16×. AGP has been succeeded by the higher-bandwidth PCI Express port for advanced graphics devices in most current computers. (*See* **PCI Express bus**)

A/S/L Internet slang used in chat rooms to denote "age/sex/location."

Ashcroft v. Free Speech Coalition Landmark case concerning the possession of child pornography. The Pornography Prevention Act of 1996 was later struck down in *Ashcroft* v. *Free Speech Coalition*. The bill would have outlawed computer-generated images of minors engaged in sexual situations to be used as evidence. Because such images do not victimize real children, but are constituted of computerized graphics, the Court reasoned, it does not qualify as child pornography. This case alone provides a defense for defendants arrested for possession of child pornography who can argue that the images are computer-generated images. Whether it would be a successful defense is another matter for the courts' consideration.

ATA-66 (Advanced Technology Attachment 66)   This is a standard for connecting a disk drive to a computer motherboard. The 66 refers to the theoretical top-end data transfer speed of 66 megabytes per second. This standard was common for optical drives such as CD-ROM and DVD-ROM drives. The ATA standard was eventually replaced by the Serial ATA (SATA) standard.

ATA-100   This standard had a theoretical top-end data transfer speed of 100 megabytes per second. (*See* **ATA-66**)

ATA-133   This standard had a theoretical top-end data transfer speed of 133 megabytes per second. (*See* **ATA-66**)

Bandwidth   Term used to measure how much data can travel in a given data path at any given time. A data pathway is often compared to a water pipe: the pipe's diameter (bandwidth) determines how much water (data) can flow through it at one time.

Barely Legal   Pornography Web sites that feature models who may be of legal age (i.e., 18 years old), but who are made to look much younger. This perception of youth is enhanced with youthful outfits, hair-dos, or other props to add to the perception that the model is underage to appeal to the pedophile's compulsions.

Baud   Baud is an older measure of bandwidth used in the infancy of Internet connectivity, when data transfer speeds were very slow. Baud measured how many bits per second of data a modem could send or receive. As technology evolved, modem speeds climbed to 1,200, 2,400, 4,800, 9,600 baud. As modem bandwidth speeds increased, a new speed designation was used called bits per second (bps), and for higher speeds, Kbps and Mbps.

Binary Language   Binary language is so named because there are two possible electrical states for each bit of data, on and off. On is represented by the number one, off is represented as a zero. Think of a light switch in the on or off position. It just means essentially whether an electrical circuit has power or doesn't. Because all computer data are binary in nature the relative sizes are measured in powers of 2 (2, 4, 8, 16, 32, 64, 128, 256, 512, 1,024, etc.). $2^{10} = 1,024$.

Biometrics   Literally means "life measurement" and is the science of using biological properties to identify individuals; for example, fingerprints, retina scans, and voice recognition.

Bit-by-bit Copy   Once a write blocker is installed, the forensic specialist will use a drive-imaging or cloning utility to make an exact duplicate of the original suspect drive. The accepted forensic practice calls for making an exact bit-by-bit copy, also known as a bitstream copy. A bit is the smallest possible piece of data represented by a 0 or 1. By making a bit-by-bit copy, the forensic examiner can be sure that the suspect hard drive was copied exactly, even blank spaces on the drive. The forensic specialist will then also verify that the drive is an exact copy by computing an MD5 hash value for the original drive and the copy. If the MD5 values are exactly the same, then the copy is an exact copy or clone of the original drive.

Bits (b)   The smallest piece of data is called a bit. Binary language is so named because there are two possible electrical states for each bit of data, on and off. On is represented by the number one, off is represented as a zero. A group of bits together can mean different things. One circuit on or off is pretty meaningless, but when eight circuits are grouped together, there are numerous possible combinations. Each potential combination can be assigned a different value, and a character such as a letter or number is made of 8 binary bits. For example, the capital letter *A* is represented by eight bits, 01000001, or in electrical terms off-on-off-off-off-off-off-on. These 8 bits that make up one character are more commonly called a byte of data.

Bitstream   (*See* **bit-by-bit copy**).

Black Hat Hackers   In contrast to white hat hackers, black hat hackers break into systems (e.g., networks, Web sites) with malicious intent to steal, damage, or deface them.

Block of IP Addresses   A group of Internet Protocol addresses that are assigned to and administrated by one owner or Internet service provider (ISP). Most ISPs have more subscribers than they have IP addresses. They have a pool of IP addresses assigned or registered to them. As users go online, their computer talks to a computer at their Internet service provider, which assigns the user a temporary IP address from the block of available addresses.

Boolean Search Techniques   A logic that was developed by George Boole, a nineteenth-century mathematician, which allows an Internet searcher to use three primary commands that will help reduce and/or expand return results. The three standard Boolean search terms are the plus sign (e.g., police + officer) or the *AND* term (e.g., police AND officer), the minus sign (e.g., police – officer) or the *NOT* term (e.g., police NOT officer), and the *OR* term (e.g., police OR officer).

Boot   The process by which a computer starts at a powered-down, inert state, then loads basic instructions, accesses hard drives, and eventually loads an operating system so that it can interact with a user and other computers.

Briefcase Computer   This is a self-contained computer system used by computer forensics specialists that can be carried by one person, but unlike a laptop it still has a number of interfaces and swappable drive bays for easier acquisition of data from a subject's hard drive. Lab forensic workstations and the briefcase computers have write blockers built into the swappable drive bays.

Brief Headers   In regard to e-mail messages, the brief header is what the typical e-mail user sees, which includes the date, time, to, from, carbon copy, and subject line information about a particular message.

Bus Data flows along electrical circuits in many places on a computer system, and each data pathway, called a bus, can move only a certain amount of data at a time.

Bytes (B) One character is a byte. A byte is made of 8 bits of data. For example, the capital letter *A* is represented by eight bits, 01000001, or in electrical terms off-on-off-off-off-off-off-on.

CD Writer or Burner An optical drive that can write data to CDs in addition to reading them. A CD writer is referred to as a burner because it etches data into the optical surface of a blank or rewritable disc such as a CD or DVD.

Chain of Custody Although numerous definitions of *chain of custody* exist, it is, perhaps, most easily defined as documenting who handled the evidence at each juncture of an investigation. It is called a chain because each person who handles the evidence is one link in the chain. Once the evidence is in the custody of law enforcement, the chain of custody should never be broken because the defense will use any break in the chain to cast doubt as to the pristine state of the evidence.

Chat Online communication between two or more Internet users in real time. Chatters type messages that are transmitted across the Internet at near the speed of light to the recipient. This is also commonly referred to as instant messaging.

Child Pornography Collector An avid collector of child pornography for his or her own sexual gratification and for trading illicit images or video with other pedophiles. This person may never physically victimize a child, although possessing a photograph or video or sharing it with others victimizes that child at each viewing, albeit at a somewhat lower level.

Child Pornography Prevention Act A 1996 United States federal act that would have outlawed, among other things, computer-generated images of minors engaged in sexual situations to be used as evidence. This act was struck down in the *Ashcroft* v. *Free Speech Coalition* case (2002).

Clone Fraud This occurs when a legitimate serial number is programmed into an imposter's cell phone. Crooks get the numbers because the numbers are broadcast with every cellular call and can be picked up by ordinary radio scanners.

Cloned Phone A cell phone has two basic ways it identifies itself to the cell phone company it wants to use—its own telephone number, which can be changed, and a special secret number embedded into the silicon chip inside the phone called the ESN. When the phone makes a call, it transmits these numbers, and cell carriers use them to check whether the call is authentic.

Cloning Fraud This occurs when criminals use scanners to obtain legitimate MIN/ESN/PIN combinations and then program them into illegitimate phones.

Closed Source Data that includes the same types of information that can be found in the open sources, but requires authorized access generally controlled by requiring an encrypted user name and password. Closed-source data is highly secured and controlled.

Command Line   The location at which a user can enter commands in an older, text-based operating system such as MS-DOS.

Computer Forensics   The use of specialized techniques, processes, software, and hardware for the recovery, discovery, analysis, verification, and reporting of electronic data or media to determine if the device contains illegal, inappropriate, or unauthorized text, images, multimedia, or other digital files. It is also the process of copying the media in such a fashion that the original device is not altered in the copying process and the copy itself is an exact duplicate of the original. In other words, the data obtained from the original are a bit-by-bit (i.e., bitstream) copy that is copied onto the evidence file and that will eventually be examined.

Consent   One of the most commonly used exceptions to the search warrant requirement. For consent to be valid, the person giving consent must have the authority to grant it, and it must be given knowingly and voluntarily.

Counterfeit "Clone" Phone   With this type of fraud, the criminal puts into a phone a computer chip that can be programmed with both the ESN and MIN of a legitimate user. The criminal obtains valid number combinations, either through the use of illegally used test equipment or through an unscrupulous employee of a retail agent or carrier.

Counterfeit "Lifetime" Phone   This type of fraud enables thieves to reprogram a special wireless phone through its own keypad so that wireless bills are charged to someone else. With the "lifetime" counterfeit phone technology, numerous legitimate MIN/ESN pairs can be stored in each phone.

Counterfeit "Tumbler" Phones   This type of fraud alters a wireless phone so it tumbles through a series of ESNs and makes the caller appear to be another new customer each time a call is made.

Crackers   Another term for *hacker* that was coined by the hacker community to separate themselves from white hat hackers.

Criminal Identity Theft   This occurs when an identity thief is arrested by law enforcement and provides police with a victim's identity, thereby creating a false criminal record.

Criminal Intelligence   Information compiled, analyzed, and/or disseminated in an effort to anticipate, prevent, or monitor criminal activity.

Cyberbullying   Similar to cyberstalking, but always involves a child, preteen, or teenager who uses the Internet, interactive and digital technologies, or mobile phones to torment, threaten, harass, humiliate, embarrass, or otherwise target another minor.

Cyberstalking   The repeated use of the Internet, e-mail, or related digital electronic communication devices to annoy, alarm, or threaten a specific individual or group of individuals.

Cyberterrorism   The term that results from the combination of *cyberspace* (the computer-based world of information) and *terrorism*. Cyberterrorism can be defined as unlawful attacks and threats against computers, networks, and the information stored therein when done to intimidate or coerce a government or its people in furtherance of political and social objectives.

Data Mining The practice of automatically searching large stores of data for patterns. The cellular industry uses data-mining programs to monitor and detect fraud by creating customer profiles that track average call duration, percentage of no-answer calls, percentage of calls to/from a different area code, percentage of weekday calls (Monday–Friday), percentage of daytime calls (9 AM–5 PM), average number of calls received per day, and the average number of calls originated per day.

Denial of Service (DoS) Attack This occurs when hackers attack or flood a server with phony authentication methods preventing legitimate users from accessing it and ultimately shutting it down.

Dictionary Attacks A technique used by hackers to figure out passwords. Software programs are available on the Internet that will randomly apply all letters of the alphabet to a targeted password until the correct password is found.

Digital Evidence Digital evidence is electronic data, materials, objects, property, documents, or records that are presented in court to prove or disprove allegations made against an arrestee. Digital evidence takes the form of electronic data or information stored in bits and bytes on magnetic media. Digital evidence can be photos, videos, text documents, Internet activity logs, phone numbers, or any other data that are stored electronically that have relevance to a criminal case.

Directory A section of a hard disk drive, established to compartmentalize data into an organized structure. Computers organize all of these drives and their directories into a directory structure. The topmost organizational level of a hard disk drive is called the root of the drive. The root can contain a large number of directories. Each directory can contain a large number of subdirectories.

Directory Structure (*See* **directory**)

Disk Image An exact duplicate or clone of a suspect's hard disk drive or data storage device. Disk images are verified using the MD5 hash algorithm. Even a minute difference from one drive to the other will yield a significant difference in MD5 hash values, clearly indicating an imperfect copy.

Disk Operating System (DOS) One of the earliest text-based command-line operating systems for personal computers. DOS was one predecessor to the graphical user interfaces in use today, such as Windows, Linux, or Mac OSX.

Domain Name Server A computer on the Internet that stores routing information for Web site domains. Domain name servers route requests for a Web site (e.g., www.google.com) to the IP address where the Web site exists. They allow users to memorize domain names for the Web sites to which they wish to travel instead of having to remember the IP address for that site (e.g., http:// 72.14.207.99/ for Google).

Domestic Terrorism The unlawful use, or threatened use, of violence by a group or individual that is based and operating entirely within the United States or its territories without foreign direction and which is committed against persons or property with the intent of intimidating or coercing a government or its population in furtherance of political or social objectives.

Drive Cache   A block of RAM found on some high-end hard drives. This temporary memory allows a drive to temporarily store data that are being written to or read from the drive. This can speed up the response time of the drive.

Dumpster Diving   Criminals go through garbage cans, garbage placed on curbs, or even Dumpsters, which are all significant sources of credit card information and other personal information used by the identity thief.

DVD-ROM   This is an optical drive that can read from a DVD disc. This can also refer to the disc media itself, for example, "This software comes written on a DVD-ROM."

Dynamically Allocated IP Address   A term used to describe the allocation of Internet Protocol (IP) addresses by Internet service providers (ISP). Each time a customer connects to the Internet, the ISP assigns the user an available IP address. When the online session is ended, the IP address is released and available to another customer. Each time the customer connects to the Internet, a new IP address is assigned. This is in contrast to static IP address assignment.

Electronic Communications Privacy Act (ECPA)   The Electronic Communications Privacy Act was passed in 1986 and has been amended several times since, including by the USA PATRIOT Act. Although commonly referred to as the ECPA, it is actually part of federal law. It is located in Title 18, Part I, Chapter 119, and is defined in Sections 2510–2522. The ECPA was essentially the modernization of the then-obsolete wiretapping statute. The original code was written to protect the privacy of telephone conversations and simply did not cover the emerging technologies involved with Internet communications. Thus, the ECPA was born to codify when government could and could not intercept Internet and/or stored electronic communications (i.e., those residing on a server). These Internet communications include email that has been sent, is in transmission, has been received at the recipient's server, and/or has been received by the recipient. The ECPA mandates a court order demonstrating probable cause for law enforcement interception of electronic communications.

Electronic Serial Number (ESN)   A unique code programmed into each cellular phone by its manufacturer (e.g. Nokia) in an attempt to reduce the chances of cellular phone fraud. The ESN is transmitted by the phone to the cellular tower. In theory, no two phones have the same ESN. Cellular companies that detect multiple phones with the same ESN are then aware that someone has cloned a phone or otherwise committed cellular fraud.

E-mail Bombs   Hackers flood an e-mail account server with thousands of messages, rendering it unable to accept or send mail.

Encryption   Encryption is the process of encoding regular data into a seemingly random and unintelligible, scrambled form. The program that scrambles the data only allows a user to unscramble the information if the user enters the correct user name and password. Encryption, then, is the process of scrambling data to protect it from prying eyes, while decryption is the process of decoding it so that it can be viewed again.

Entrapment This occurs when a government agent (i.e., police officer) induces a person to commit a crime that he/she wouldn't have ordinarily committed. To be proven, entrapment requires the defense to show that the police induced the unwilling person to commit a crime.

Esoteric Biometrics The lowest level of biometrics, which is still in early development and which includes vein measurement or analysis of body odor.

Exclusionary Rule A legal doctrine that states any evidence obtained in violation of a defendant's constitutional or statutory rights is not admissible at a criminal trial.

Exigent Circumstances An exception to the search warrant requirement that allows officers to search without a warrant if the circumstances would cause a reasonable person to believe that entry was necessary to prevent physical harm to the officers or other persons, the destruction of relevant evidence, the escape of the suspect, or some other consequence improperly frustrating legitimate law enforcement efforts.

Felony The most serious level of criminal acts, which carry a minimum of a 1-year prison sentence for anyone convicted. Substantial fines may also be levied on convicted felons. Some examples of felony crimes include rape, murder, aggravated assault, and many crimes against children.

File Association (File Type Association) A setting of the operating system that defines what software will be used to access a particular type of data file. For example, the operating system might specify a word processor to open a text document.

File Creation Date The date recorded by a computer's operating system of when that particular file first existed on that computer system.

File Extension (File Name Extension) A two- or three-letter naming convention that appears after a file name to indicate what type of data the file contains. For example a file named *picture.jpg* is likely to be a JPEG photo. The three letters after the period—in this case *.jpg*—are the file name extension, while *picture* is the name. Similarly, *document.txt* is likely to be a text item based on the *.txt* file extension. This extension can be changed intentionally by the user to make the file appear, at first glance, to be something it is not.

File Header Binary data coded into the beginning of a data file that directly specifies the type of data file. In a .jpg photo file, for example, the header will list the letters JFIF, which stand for JPEG file image format. Although a file name extension can be changed to make the file appear to be something it is not, the file header will always indicate the true file type.

File Last Accessed Date The date recorded by a computer's operating system of when that particular file was last viewed without being changed or modified in any way.

File Modified Date The date recorded by a computer's operating system of when that particular file was last changed or modified in any way.

File Path The specific location of a data file within the drive and directory it is stored in. For example, C:\Windows\picture.jpg indicates that there is a JPEG file located on the C drive within the Windows directory. File path is used to document where specific data files are found and is particularly important to document when that specific file has evidentiary value or is contraband, as in the case of a file of child pornography.

File Properties Statistics related to a particular data file, including date and time the file was created, date and time the file was last accessed, and date and time the file was last changed or modified. File properties can also include information on whether the file is a read-only or a hidden file.

File Transfer Protocol (FTP) A popular Internet protocol that is the standard method used to upload or download complete data files to a Web server. For example, When a user creates a Web page, the user generally creates the HTML documents that make up the Web page on the home or office computer. To place the Web page on the Internet, that is, to upload the pages to the Web server, the user will generally use an FTP client.

Forensic Analysis Forensic analysis is the process by which a forensic examiner captures, clones, recovers, and analyzes data from a suspect hard drive or data device while making absolutely no changes to the data on that drive or device. Most forensic utilities or utility suites clone or image hard drives, find data files, organize them into categories, and perform analysis on the files. Most software also allows analysis of hidden or deleted files, even those that have been partially overwritten. This includes examining the slack space on a given hard drive for incomplete fragments of data. Last, some suites offer password-cracking utilities to assist the analyst with unlocking encrypted or password-protected files or file archives. Functions of computer forensic software include:

- Acquiring digital evidence or data files
- Clone/preserve digital evidence
- Analyze digital evidence files
- Separate and categorize data files by type (graphics, e-mail, videos, etc.)
- Compare evidence files to lists of known contraband files
- Recover deleted or hidden data
- Crack or recover passwords to allow access to encrypted data
- Systematically report findings in a paper report

Forensic Specialist A computer expert who specializes in the cloning of all digital data on a computer system or other digital device while at the same time verifying that no changes are made to that data. The examiner also performs analysis of the data using a computer forensics software application and forensics workstation.

Forensic Workstation The forensic workstation is the computer used by the investigator to examine, clone, and analyze the evidence. This is the computer that is owned and operated by the law enforcement agency and that contains installed forensic software such as AccessData Forensic Toolkit, Encase, or ILook.

Frauction A slang term, coined by the authors, to describe the intersection of online *auctions* and *fraud*.

Front-Side Bus (FSB) This is the physical data pathway or circuits between the processor and main system memory (RAM). The speed of the FSB is measured in megahertz and the higher the number, the faster the system's performance will be.

Fruits of the Poisonous Tree A legal doctrine that prohibits the introduction of any illegally seized evidence in a criminal trial. It also prohibits the use of any evidence that was obtained as a result of the illegally obtained evidence.

Full Headers In regard to e-mail messages, the full header not only contains the same information found in the brief header, it also displays the various IP addresses along with the date and timestamps from each server that the message passed through to reach its destination. It's necessary to view the full e-mail header when tracing an e-mail message.

Fund Transfer Scam Also known as *4-1-9 scam, advanced fee fraud,* or *Nigerian oil scam,* this scam attempts to convince people to assist with an asset transfer. In most instances, the victims receive an e-mail telling them they can earn a percentage commission by assisting with the transfer of a large sum of money. Sometimes the e-mail author tells the recipient he or she needs to transfer millions of dollars out of his or her own country and needs a foreign bank account to transfer it to. In exchange for using the victim's account, the scammer promises to give the victim a percentage of the fund, for example, 10 percent of a $5 million transfer. If the gullible victim gives the scammer a bank account and routing number, the scammers use that information to siphon money out of the bank accont.

Gigabit (Gb) 1,024 megabits of data. A gigabit is also equivalent to 1,073,741,824 bits of data. A bit is the smallest measure of data and is equivalent to one-eighth of a byte, which equals one printed character. Therefore, a gigabit is equivalent to 134,217,728 characters of text. Although gigabytes are used to measure the size of data files, gigabits are used to measure data transmission speeds such as the download speed of a file from the Internet.

Gigabytes (GB) 2^{30} bytes, or 1,073,741,824 bytes of data. A gigabyte is also 1,024 megabytes. (*See* **bytes, kilobytes,** and **megabytes**)

Gigahertz (GHz) 2^{30} hertz. Hertz is a measure of frequency and is measured in cycles per second. One gigahertz is 1,073,741,824 cycles per second.

Graphical User Interface (GUI) A feature common to modern operating systems, this interface replaced the former command-line-entry structure by allowing a user to see files and directory structures on screen, execute commands, and manipulate files, directories, and programs by using a mouse or other pointer device. Graphical user interfaces feature mouse pointers, icons, and numerous visual cues to make computers user friendly.

Gray Hat Hackers These are those who are on both sides of the hacking fence. A gray hat hacker discovers and supplies information about network security issues and weaknesses to the network administrators and also to black hat hackers to exploit the systems.

Grooming The process of preparing a victim and overcoming a victim's sense of right and wrong and lowering inhibitions about a sexual act.

Hacker A person who gains access to a computer or network of computers to expose weaknesses that need to be addressed or exploit them to gain control of it, steal passwords, or disrupt it with destructive code and/or commands.

Hall v. Earthlink An Electronic Communications Privacy Act case. As the plaintiffs, Hall and the movie company alleged that Earthlink violated the ECPA by "intercepting" his e-mail. He had sent out very large numbers of e-mail messages in an attempt to advertise for a new movie that was set to premier. His sending of mass e-mails was initially interpreted to be spam by an Internet monitoring organization, and his e-mail account was frozen by Earthlink. Hall's service was not reconnected; however, the account still existed on Earthlink servers and received more than 500 e-mails over the course of about a year. Toward the end of that year, Earthlink sent all of those e-mails to Hall. Hall then sued under the ECPA, claiming that Earthlink had illegally intercepted those e-mail messages contrary to his ECPA rights. Earthlink ultimately won, and Hall's appeal was denied because the storage of the e-mail was found to be within the scope of Earthlink's normal business procedures, and therefore not an interception.

Harassment Continued communication or interaction with someone with the goal of intimidating, upsetting, or otherwise emotionally affecting the recipient. It is communication or interaction with no other legitimate purpose but to harass.

Hard Disk Drive A hardware device consisting of magnetic media platters or disks. The disks spin while a read/write arm transfers data to and from the magnetic disks. A hard drive's primary function is the long-term storage of digital data. Hard drives, like RAM, are measured in terms of capacity and seek time. Unlike RAM however, hard drives do not lose data when they are powered down.

Hard Shutdown Once a computer has been documented, the investigator will need to prepare the system for transport to a secure location. Part of that process is shutting down the computer. Unplugging the power for a hard shutdown is the recommended approach because this does not involve manipulating the mouse or any other computer interface devices. At first glance, this would seem to be a rather brute force technique, but this is the recommended method in all federal manuals and in most state guidelines. It is important that the power plug be pulled from the power supply at the rear of the computer because some computers have an uninterruptible power supply (UPS) or battery backup device. Unplugging a computer from the wall will not do any good if it has a battery backup. Similarly, laptop computers have a battery pack on board, so the investigator must remove the laptop's onboard battery in addition to pulling the power plug. A normal or soft shutdown usually involves clicking Start and then Turn Off Computer. This is *not* a good practice for the high-tech investigator to follow.

Hashing The mathematical analysis of the data on the drive that generates a unique string of characters based upon the files and structure of the drive. Individual files can also be hashed to check for identical files. The standard hash utilized by most forensic software utilities is called the Message Digest 5 hash, or MD5 for short. MD5 is an algorithm that generates a 128-bit string of characters. An example of an MD5 value for a single file is included here for your reference: b017e028a96ca4fbb536e30f1cb834f8.

Hertz (Hz) A measure of frequency. One hertz is one cycle per second. One kilohertz is equivalent to 1,024 hertz or 1,024 cycles per second.

High Biometrics The most reliable level of biometrics that measures physical characteristics of high accuracy (e.g., retina, iris, and fingerprints).

Hyperlink A link within a hypertext document that links to another hypertext document. They are often used for navigation between several different Web pages.

Hypertext Markup Language (HTML) Web pages and Internet documents are written in a language called Hypertext Markup Language, or HTML for short.

Hypertext Transfer Protocol (HTTP) This is the language or protocol used on the Internet to transmit and receive hypertext documents such as HTML Web pages. In the address bar or URL section of the Web browser, a full Web address begins with http:// to indicate that this protocol is in use.

ICQ An online chat client that allows for real-time communications. It was originally shorthand for "I seek you." It would allow users to see when their friends and contacts were online and available for chatting. This functionality was then incorporated into most instant messaging applications.

Identity Theft The unlawful use of a person's name, address, Social Security number (SSN), bank or credit card account number, or other identifying information without the person's knowledge and with the intent to commit fraud or other crimes.

IEEE1394 FireWire A high-bandwidth data connection standard that can transmit data at the rate of up to 400 megabits per second (mbps), similar to USB 2.0. FireWire allows for a variety of high-speed devices to be connected to a computer. FireWire connections are often used to connect large external hard drives and video cameras to computers.

Indexing Process The first step of data analysis performed by forensic software after an exact disk image has been obtained and verified. This process is extremely time-consuming, particularly because hard drives continue to grow larger and larger. Although indexing every file and bit of slack space from a standard 700-MB CD might take only 10 or 15 minutes, it can literally take days to index every bit of a 500-megabyte hard drive. The forensic workstation will continue to run the indexing function until the disk is completely indexed, or until it is manually stopped by the specialist. These activities, like most others, are logged automatically by most brands of forensic utility software. The indexing process performs a number of functions on every file or file fragment. One thing it does is index every character, letter, and number of every file. In the case of text or word processing documents, this means that it indexes every word in every file. This allows the investigator to perform a very exacting word or phrase search on the entire drive. Because the material is indexed during this phase and not when the search is initiated, the investigator will get those search results very quickly. The indexing also checks all file headers so that files can be grouped by file type.

Information   Used in the context of intelligence gathering and analysis, information is pieces of raw, unanalyzed data that identifies persons, evidence, events or illustrates processes that include criminal history and driving records, police reports, witness/suspect statements, and license plate information.

Innocent Images National Iniative (IINI)   An initiative run by the Federal Bureau of Investigation that identifies, investigates, and prosecutes sexual predators who use the Internet and other online services to sexually exploit children; identifies and rescues witting and unwitting child victims; and establishes a law enforcement presence on the Internet as a deterrent to subjects that exploit children.

Instant Messaging (IM)   A communications service that allows two users to send messages over the Internet to each other in real time.

Intentional Intercept   To prove a violation of the Electronic Communications Privacy Act, plaintiffs must meet two elements. The first is that electronic communications were intercepted. The second element must prove that there was an intent to intercept them, that is, it was not part of an Internet service provider's standard business operations. See *Hall v. Earthlink*.

International Terrorism   Terrorism that transcends national boundaries and is an act supported by and/or with foreign direction against the population or government of any other country outside the United State or its territories.

Internet Auction Fraud   The use of the Internet in an online transaction between buyer and seller to defraud the seller or buyer through deceptive means, including but not limited to failure to deliver merchandise, intentionally delivering defective merchandise, or delivering merchandise other than what was promised or purchased (of a lesser quality).

Internet Relay Chat (IRC)   Similar to online groups, IRC is a worldwide communications system that contains servers across the globe that host chat rooms or chat channels.

Internet Service Provider (ISP)   A business entity that owns or rents a block of IP addresses and allows its subscribers to connect to the Internet by using one of the addresses. ISPs also typically provide their subscribers with an e-mail account along with their internet access. Examples of Internet service providers include AOL, Earthlink, and NetZero. Reputable ISPs maintain records that can be obtained during criminal investigations by use of a subpoena or search warrant.

Inventory Search An exception to the search warrant requirement that is routinely conducted by law enforcement officers, consistent with written department policy, for noninvestigatory purposes, such as protecting a person's property. For example, officers may conduct an inventory search of an automobile in their possession and make a detailed listing of all property inside to protect themselves from theft accusations. Any contraband found during an inventory search can be seized.

IP address Internet Protocol address. Data are routed along a network or the Internet based on a source address and recipient address. IP addresses are used to properly route the data from place to place. IP addresses are broken into 4 sections called octets. The octets are separated by periods. Each octet has a value between 0 and 255. An example of a valid IP address is 124.210.107.19. Any computer that is online will use an IP address while sending and receiving any data on the Internet, allowing investigators to trace that activity.

IP addressing structure (*See* **IP Address**)

Kilobits (Kb) 1,024 bits. Bits are 1/8 of a byte, and 1,024 bits are equivalent to 128 bytes. (*See* **bits**)

Kilobytes (KB) 1,024 bytes (or characters) of data. (*See* **bytes**)

Logic Bomb ("slag code") A program designed to execute (or "explode") under certain conditions specified in the coding, for example, on a certain date, after a lapse of time, or following some response (or lack of response) by the computer user.

Lolita A term that originated with a Russian novel called *Lolita* by Vladimir Nabokov. Similar to "barely legal," these Web sites feature models who may be of legal age (i.e., 18 years old), but are made to look much younger. This perception of youth is enhanced with youthful outfits, hair-dos, or other props to add to the perception that the model is underage to appeal to the pedophile's compulsions.

Low Biometrics A measure of distinct features that have a reasonable level of accuracy (e.g., hand geometry, face recognition, voice recognition, and signature recognition).

Malware A specific type of computer program that is written with malicious intent to perform bad deeds. There are many different categories of malware, including viruses, browser hijackers, Trojan horses, and spyware. The one thing they all have in common, however, is that they are intended to delete data, damage system software, or allow unauthorized access to a computer for the purposes of stealing data.

Master Boot Record (MBR) Located in the very first sector of the hard drive, the MBR acts as a "table of contents" for the hard drive and stores information such as how the drive is partitioned and which partition the computer should boot from.

MD5 The Message Digest 5 algorithm creates a 128-bit "fingerprint" similar in appearance to an automobile vehicle identification number (VIN), but much longer. It is extremely unique and the possibility of having two data files with the same MD5 value is 1 in 2,^{128} which is a higher degree of certainty than DNA evidence. MD5 algorithms are used to verify that a cloned hard drive is an exact duplicate of the source drive.

Megabits (Mb) 2^{20} bits of data, or 1,048,576 bits. (*See* **bits**).

Megabytes (MB) 2^{20} bytes of data, or 1,048,576 bytes.

Megahertz (MHz) 2^{20} hertz, or 1,048,576 cycles per second. (*See* **hertz**)

Misdemeanor   A criminal act of moderate severity that may result in a jail sentence of up to one year and/or a substantial fine. Many states establish maximum fine limits for misdemeanor convictions.

Mobile Identification Number (MIN)   A unique code assigned or programmed by the vendor or service provider for cellular phone service (for example, Verizon) when the phone is set up for use on their network and is transmitted to the cellular tower. The MIN is different from the ESN, which is programmed by the manufacturer before the phone is shipped to a cellular phone service provider. In theory, no two phones on a provider network have the same MIN. Cellular companies that detect multiple phones with the same MIN are, then, aware that someone has cloned a phone or otherwise committed cellular fraud.

Mortgage fraud   Also known as "account takeover," this type of real estate fraud involves a "customer," real estate broker, straw sellers, and straw buyers who funnel the money into accounts (e.g., home equity loans or lines of credit) that have been established with false or stolen identities.

Motherboard   The main and most important component of any computer is its main circuit board called the motherboard. Every computer has a case or a tower that physically contains the main components of the system. Mounted inside the case are the motherboard, a power supply to power the main board, case cooling fans, and the other installed devices such as hard drives, CD-ROM drives, sound cards, video cards, and modems. The motherboard is the component that ties all of the other components together because they all connect directly or indirectly to the motherboard. The main processor resides on the motherboard in a snap-in processor slot. As data flow to and from the main processor to the other components it travels along circuits on the motherboard, the system's buses.

Multitasking   Performing more than one task at a time. With regard to computer systems, this is the computer's ability to have more than one program running at a time or being able to access many different data files simultaneously. Most operating systems allow a user to multitask easily by allowing the user to easily switch back and forth between multiple programs by clicking an icon on a task bar or by using a keyboard command such as Alt-Tab.

Octet   A byte composed of 8-bit elements, such as 11010010. IP addresses are divided into four octets, and each octet must have a value between 0 and 255.

Online Child Enticement   The use of the Internet to locate, entice, and solicit a child to commit an unlawful sexual act.

Open Source   Information that consists of databases, message boards, media sources/outlets, photographs, tape/video recordings, satellite images, and government and private sector Web sites that are searchable for free or for a fee to anybody with an Internet connection.

Open Wireless Networks   Unprotected or unsecured wireless computer networks. Wireless network connections, commonly referred to as Wi-Fi, can easily be secured by the use of encryption and passwords, yet many users intentionally leave these security features off, allowing anyone with a wireless-capable computer to connect to their network and use their Internet connection.

Operating System (OS)   The software, or instruction set, that enables computer hardware components to interact with each other, with software programs, and with the user. The OS also controls the system's resources such as memory, hard drive space, and processor functions, and prioritizes tasks to allow the computer to run quickly and reliably. Examples of operating systems include Windows XP, Linux, and Mac OSX. Microsoft's Windows operating system has generally dominated the industry with an 80 to 90 percent market share, by most estimates.

Operation Avalanche   An investigation begun in Forth Worth, Texas, in 2001. The operation's name was a play on words, as the company under investigation was Landslide Productions, Inc., an Internet-based company that offered paid subscriptions to over 250 Web sites, many of which contained child pornography. The company amassed more than 300,000 subscribers and, at various times, had monthly earnings in excess of one million dollars a month. It is widely believed to be the largest commercial child pornography site known to law enforcement. Thomas Reedy, the owner, was sentenced to 1,335 years in prison. His wife Janice received a lighter sentence of 14 years because of her secondary involvement.

Operation Hamlet   Announced by the U.S. Customs Service in August of 2002, this operation focused on approximately 20 different families that were molesting their own children and recording the molestations with still photos and video cameras. The members of the group then traded the images and videos with other like-minded individuals. The first detected member of this group was located in Denmark. A citizens action group called Save the Children was alerted to an image of a young girl being molested. Unfortunately for the suspect, a company logo was visible in the picture, which eventually led to his being identified. After searching and analyzing his computer, 10 other Europeans and 12 Americans were identified as participating in molestation and image trading. One member of the group was found to be in possession of over one million images of child pornography. He had approximately 450 CDs containing illicit material. In addition, 37 American children and 8 European children were taken into protective custody.

Operation Snowball   A spinoff of Operation Avalanche that took place in Canada, this investigation centers around approximately 2,300 Canadian citizens who bought subscriptions to the Landslide Productions, Inc., Web site.

Optical Drive   Any drive that reads and/or writes data to optical media such as a CD-ROM or DVD. They are called optical media because lasers are used to visually or optically read data etched into the surface of the media. Similarly, blank CDs can be burned by optical drives with a writing laser, commonly called a "burner."

Ordinance Violation Breaking of a law enacted by a city, local, or municipal government. Because local governments do not have the same legal authority as state or federal governments, the maximum penalty for an ordinance violation is a civil forfeiture (fine) because ordinance violations are not criminal acts. As a result, municipal courts have lower standards of evidence than "beyond a reasonable doubt," and convictions can be had with a "preponderance of evidence."

Paederast An older term commonly used for pedophiles in the eighteenth and nineteenth centuries. *Paederast* (a man who has intercourse with a boy) comes from two Greek words: *pais/paid,* the word for *child,* and *erastes,* the word for *lover.* Most people are probably more familiar with the term *paedophile,* which is an adult who is sexually attracted to children. In modern spelling the *a* is dropped, yielding the word *pedophile.*

PCI Bus The Peripheral Component Interconnect is an older data pathway (bus) that operates at 33 MHz, commonly used for sound cards, modems, and network cards.

PCI Express Bus A modern high-speed bus based on serial technology, Express PCI is usually used for modern high-end graphics cards to provide a responsive, realistic graphics environment.

PEBCAK An acronym that stands for the "Problem Exists Between the Chair And the Keyboard." This term was initially used in help desk circles by computer professionals to describe the person as the problem and not the computer.

Pedophile An adult that is sexually attracted to children.

Pedophilia The psychological disorder of a person at least 16 years old and at least 5 years older than his/her intended preadolescent victim. The pedophile fixates on or fantasizes about sexual activities with the victim, which disrupts the pedophile's life, and the sexual fixation must have lasted at least six months.

Phishing Where thieves use false e-mail return addresses, stolen Web page graphics, stylistic imitation, misleading or disguised hyperlinks, social engineering, and other artifices to trick users into revealing personally identifiable information.

Phone Phreaking The practice of hacking or breaking into a telephone network for the purpose of playing pranks, making free telephone calls, or otherwise fraudulently using the telecommunications network. Phreaking is spelled with the *ph* as in *phone* and is pronounced *freaking*.

Plain View An exception to the search warrant requirement that allows officers who observe immediately apparent evidence or contraband in "plain view" and are lawfully in the area where the observation is made to seize the item(s) without a warrant.

Platters Each individual magnetic data disk within a hard drive is called a platter. Both sides of the platter can contain data, and most hard drives contain multiple platters. A hard drive with 3 platters will be divided into sides 0 thru 5.

Plug and Play (PnP) The term for rapid device initialization without having to reboot the computer. Under older operating systems, the installation of a new piece of hardware meant having to reboot the computer and reload the operating system. Newer operating systems and device interfaces such as USB allow for peripheral devices to be installed and configured on the fly, in a matter of seconds, without rebooting.

Post Office Protocol (POP)　This is the standard language (protocol) used to retrieve incoming e-mail messages from an e-mail server. See also SMTP, which is similar, but used for outgoing e-mail.

Preponderance of Evidence　This is the level of certainty required for a guilty verdict in a municipal ordinance violation case. The standard is met when there is more evidence indicating guilt than indicates innocence. A balancing scales analogy is appropriate in determining preponderance.

Privacy Protection Act (PPA)　A federal law, the Privacy Protection Act (PPA) had many purposes, but the most applicable is the protection of certain materials from government seizure. The PPA is located in Title 42, Chapter 21A, Subchapter 1 of the U.S. Code. The PPA arose because of perceptions that in seizing evidence, government entities were seizing materials that were not evidence and were not directly related to their particular criminal investigations. In the computer age, this became even more problematic because a law enforcement officer might seize a computer that has many multiple uses. A computer's hard drive could, for example, very easily store all of the files needed to run a business in one section and spreadsheets detailing drug trafficking transactions in another. Obviously, the drug transactions are of interest to the investigator, but the accounting files of a real, legal business might not be. Further, holding onto the legitimate business materials could damage or close down that business, which is not within the scope of an investigator's role. The PPA, then, in part, makes it illegal to seize and hold legal or legitimate materials not directly related to the crime being investigated.

Probable Cause　The level of certainty required for law enforcement officers to make an arrest. It is generally defined as the quantum of evidence that would lead a reasonable police officer to believe that the defendant committed a crime. It is more than a hunch or suspicion, but less than the evidence required to convict at trial.

Processor　The microprocessor computes all commands executed by the computer. The rate at which it performs these calculations determines the speed of the processor. Processors are rated by their relative speed using hertz. Hertz, also known as cycles per second, measures the number of calculations a central processor can make within a given time period. The processors of the late 1990s and turn of the twenty-first century commonly had speeds in the 400- to 900-MHz range. Retail personal computers have processor speeds in the billions of hertz, known as gigahertz or GHz. It is not uncommon to see computers running in the 2.5- to 4.0-GHz range, although the speeds are constantly increasing.

Proof Beyond a Reasonable Doubt　This is the level of certainty required for a guilty verdict in a criminal case. A juror voting for a guilty verdict must believe that no reasonable person could doubt the guilt of the accused.

Proprietary Data Data formatted in such a way that thay can be read or written only by a certain device or program. This is also referred to as a proprietary format. This is often the case with cellular phones and pagers, which may store their data in a way different from Windows computers or other standardized devices. Many times, companies will use a native or proprietary format specifically so no other brand can take advantage of their product.

Protocol A common language or set of languages that enables computers to talk to each other on a network or on the Internet even if they have different operating systems or are located in countries whose languages are different.

Radio Frequency Fingerprinting (RFF) The unique pattern of radio frequency transmission that is present in each telephone. This pattern is comparable to the human fingerprint: no two patterns are exactly the same. If a phone has been cloned, it may have the same MIN and ESN as the original, but it will not have the same RFF.

Radio Frequency Radiation Electromagnetic energy that is radiated with the transmission of radio waves from a transmitting antenna. This is sometimes also called radio frequency interference (RFI) or electromagnetic interference (EMI). In sufficient strength, this magnetic field could harm data stored on magnetic media such as a floppy disk or hard drive.

Random Access Memory (RAM) Also called system memory, allows the computer to temporarily store information in its "short-term memory." RAM is very fast and efficient, relying on electrical impulses to read and write small pieces of data. It does not have any moving parts. RAM stores data only temporarily and is cleared whenever a computer is powered down. RAM is measured in terms of how much data it can store (megabytes of RAM) and how fast it can find it (seek time). RAM also functions at a certain rate of speed, measured in MHz. For example, DDR 400 functions at 400 MHz, or roughly twice as fast at DDR 200. Memory chips are also available in a number of physical layouts or formats. The most common format is the DIMM. DIMM stands for Dual Inline Memory Module. It is not uncommon for computer systems to have 512 MB (megabytes), 1 GB (Gigabyte) of RAM, or more. High-end systems used for memory-dependent applications such as digital video editing may have several gigabytes of RAM.

Range of IP Addresses (*See* **block of IP addresses**).

Reasonable Suspicion Commonly referred to as a "Terry Stop" (*Terry* v. *Ohio*, 1968), this is the level of certainty that allows for law enforcement to detain and/or frisk a subject, for the officer's own safety, based on a reasonable belief that the subject is armed or has committed, is committing, or is about to commit a crime.

Records Retention Letter Although many corporations maintain records for years at a time, Internet activity logs maintained by ISPs may be preserved only for a month or two. An investigator can, therefore, write a records retention or data preservation request and send it to the ISP or other record holder, requesting that that organization maintain records for that account for an extended period of time to assist with the investigation. Investigators should recognize that unless this is explicitly stated in and/or in support of a subpoena and/or search warrant, this letter is essentially a request. Most reputable businesses will likely comply with this request, but such a request is not enforceable.

Regional Forensics Computer Lab (RFCL) These labs are one-stop, full-service forensic laboratories and training centers devoted entirely to the examination of digital evidence in support of criminal investigations. Currently, there are 13 RFCLs throughout the United States.

Risk of Destruction of Evidence One type of exigent circumstance that enables officers to take action, even in the absence of a formal search warrant. Exigency in this case means that, unless action is taken, evidence will be lost or destroyed before it can be documented and seized by law enforcement officers. Officers are therefore privileged to take action in the absence of a search warrant to prevent someone from destroying that evidence. For example, if officers encountered a suspected child pornographer in the process of deleting illegal images from his personal computer, they could take him into custody to prevent further destruction, seize the computer, and apply for a warrant to search it. If the suspect had started some automated process of deleting the images, the officers could then unplug the power supply to the computer in order to prevent further destruction. Examples of this type of exigent circumstance are also prevalent in drug cases. For example, police witness people attempting to flush drugs down the toilet. Under normal situations officers would need a search warrant to enter a home and seize the drug materials, but the emergency created by the individuals trying to destroy the evidence means that police could kick in the door and seize the evidence without a warrant.

Roaming Fraud A fraud often committed by the subscriber fraud criminal. With the fraudulently obtained phone in hand, the fraudster takes it to another cell area outside of the provider's network. The phone then enters the roaming mode utilizing cell towers from another provider.

Roaming Verification/Reinstatement (RVR) A technology that provides an added layer of security in an attempt to prevent cellular phone fraud when users are roaming and in higher risk service areas. For example, government agencies and large corporations may require cellular phone users to enter an additional PIN when using the phone in high-risk areas like New York City. The user dials the phone call and then is prompted by the phone system to enter their phone number and their pre-assigned PIN.

Root Computers organize all drives and directories into a directory structure. The top-most organizational level of a hard drive is called the root of the drive. In other words, if a file is not located within any folder or directory, it resides on the root of that drive. The root can contain a large number of directories. Each directory can contain a large number of subdirectories. Subdirectories can have sub-subdirectories, and so on.

Search A governmental infringement into a person's reasonable expectation of privacy for the purpose of discovering things, both tangible and intangible, that could be used as evidence in a criminal prosecution.

Search Engine Web sites that allow users to enter keywords and retrieve related information from the Internet.

Search Incident to a Lawful Arrest An exception to the search warrant requirement that allows officers to conduct a full search of an arrested person and a more limited search of the surrounding area, without a warrant. The limited area is commonly referred to as the "lunge-reach-rule" and extends to the immediate area where one could lunge or reach to obtain a weapon or destroy evidence, otherwise referred to the area immediately under a person's control.

Search Warrant A legal document drafted by a law enforcement agent consistent with Fourth Amendment requirements that enables them to search a location and/or seize a person or contraband and bring the person or the seized items into court.

Secretive Pedophile A person who may appear to be totally normal, might be married, may have children of his or her own, and who might never sexually assault a child. The secretive pedophile still shares the trait of becoming sexually aroused by children, but may never act on it.

Seizure The legal act of taking or seizing something that may constitute evidence, or controlling (i.e., apprehending or arresting) somebody because that person violated the law.

Serial ATA Serial Advanced Technology Attachment is the standard connection bus for modern hard drives and replaces ATA 133. Serial ATA has connection speeds of 150 megabytes per second up to 300 megabytes per second, whereas ATA133 peaked at 133 megabytes per second.

Shoulder Surfing The practice of criminals watching unsuspecting victims enter their PIN numbers into ATM machines or at the checkout line when using a debit or credit card. With the PIN obtained, the thief then tries to "pickpocket" the victim's wallet and walk away with the credit or debit card.

Simple Mail Transfer Protocol (SMTP) The Simple Mail Transfer Protocol is used in handling the addressing and sending of e-mail messages. It is the language or protocol used for the outgoing mailbox used when sending a message from an account to another recipient. (*See* Post Office Protocol [POP]).

Skimming This is the most prevalent form of counterfeit fraud whereby a card's magnetic stripe details, including the account number and PIN, are electronically copied by a small handheld device known as a skimmer, which is used to make a counterfeit card or for online purchases.

Sniffers A program that detects all data traveling through a network, allowing hackers to search for passwords that will allow them account access.

Social Engineering The use of "wetware" or humans to provide the information needed by the hacker to exploit the system. It is the manipulation of people to give out critical information about a computer, network, or phone system. It works well because people are oftentimes the weakest link in a security solution.

Static IP   In contrast to a dynamic Internet Protocol (IP) address, a static IP address is always assigned to the same user. For example, servers normally have a static IP address along with high-speed connections via cable or DSL.

Steganography   The art of hiding messages within messages to conceal and transmit terrorist plans, maps, and photographs.

Steve Jackson Games   This was a landmark case under the Electronic Communications Privacy Act (ECPA) and Privacy Protection Act (PPA) in which the federal government was sued. The company had set up a bulletin board system where employees and game testers could log on and share information, drafts, and other messages about a game they were creating. In 1990, the U.S. Secret Service raided the Steve Jackson Games facility in Austin, Texas, in connection with an investigation of data piracy. Agents seized many items, including the computers that hosted the bulletin board system. One item on the computers was a manuscript for a new role-playing game called "Cyberpunk." This manuscript was not related to the investigation but was held, along with the other materials, by the Secret Service. The Cyberpunk game manual was a work product of a legitimate business entity and was not contraband or evidence of a crime. Steve Jackson Games sued the U.S. Secret Service under provisions of the ECPA and the PPA. They argued that the agents intercepted electronic communications in violation of the ECPA and that in keeping work materials unrelated to any criminal investigation, they also violated the PPA. The Court ruled that although the messages were all seized, they were seized after they had been transmitted and received and were therefore not truly intercepted. The courts found, however, that the Secret Service was liable under the Privacy Protection Act. This was based mostly on the manuscript for "Cyberpunk." This booklet or publication fell under the PPA's "work product materials."

Subdirectory   This is a directory that exists inside of another directory. This is sometimes referred to as a subfolder (a folder within a folder). (*See* **directory**)

Subpoena   From a criminal perspective, it is a written order that is based upon probable cause and signed by a judge that commands a person to appear in court and/or turn over named documents to be used in accordance with a criminal investigation.

Subscriber Fraud   A fraud that occurs when someone signs up for service with fraudulently obtained customer information or false identification.

Sub-subdirectory   This is a subdirectory that exists inside of another subdirectory. This is sometimes referred to as a sub-subfolder (a folder within a folder within a folder). (*See* **directory**).

Terabyte 2^{40} bytes of data or 1,099,511,627,776 bytes. One terabyte is also equivalent to 1,024 gigabytes.

Terrorism   A premeditated, politically motivated violence perpetrated against noncombatant targets by subnational groups or clandestine agents usually intended to influence an audience.

Threats   Communicated warnings in written, verbal, or electronic form of some imminent negative event, injury, or other harm. Often the person communicating the warning implies that he or she will cause the injury or harm.

Timestamps   As electronic mail messages and other data files pass through servers, they are often stamped with the IP addresses of the servers they travel through as well as the date and time they were touched and routed by that server. Timestamps are extremely important in the tracking and tracing of Internet crimes because IP addresses are dynamically assigned, and numerous people could use the IP address in a given day. The timestamp is used, therefore, to isolate who was using that IP address on the exact date and time the crime was committed.

Trojan Horses   A program that appears to be useful or benign but actually conceals another program that is designed to be damaging, annoying, or "humorous."

True Name Fraud   Occurs when the identity thief uses the victim's information to open up new accounts in his/her name.

Uniform Resource Locator (URL)   This is the Internet address associated with a given Web site. To browse to a Web site, a user need only type the URL into the address bar of the Web browser. For example, the URL for the Green Bay, Wisconsin, Police Department is www.gbpolice.org. Similarly, the URL for Prentice Hall is www.prenhall.com.

Uninterruptible Power Supply (UPS)   To prevent catastrophic data loss in the event of a sudden power outage or voltage spike, many users plug their computers into a large battery unit and power filter called an uninterruptible power supply. In the event of a power outage, the battery automatically powers the computer while warning the user to quickly save all open data files and safely shut down the computer before the UPS battery runs down. Battery life will vary by unit, but an average UPS generally gives a user at least 10–15 minutes to save data.

Universal Serial Bus (USB)   A type of bus connection designed by numerous companies working in cooperation to develop a standard way of connecting a wide variety of devices to a computer. USB devices are hot swappable and are plug and play in that they can be connected and removed without having to reboot or reload the operating system. Common examples of USB devices are digital cameras, external hard drives, printers, scanners, and thumb drives. The latest edition of this standard, USB 2.0, features connection speeds up to 480 megabits per second (mbps).

Vicinage   A term used to describe parallel jurisdiction over the same offense when it is not considered double jeopardy. An offender whose cybercrime affects different counties within a state or other states may be tried in any of those locations that are consistent with constitutional limitations.

Viruses   A computer program designed to "infect" a program file that may create annoying screen messages to wipe out an entire hard drive. Like a biological virus, a computer virus infects a "host" and uses the capabilities of its host to replicate. Once executed, a virus can cause damage by erasing or altering data or files, or by simply replicating until no disk space remains and the computer ceases to function. Viruses can be transmitted from one computer to another via e-mail.

Voice Over IP (VoIP) Users with speakers and a microphone attached to their computers can talk to each other over the Internet. This is referred to as Voice over IP, or VoIP, because their voice is routed as a digital file over an Internet connection. The audio signal is converted to digital signals, sent via the IP address connection, and converted back to audio on the receiver's end. Likewise, users with a camera connected to their computer can communicate with video and audio.

War Chalking The process of making marks on the sidewalk or on buildings to tell other wireless computer users there is an open computer network in the area. In a process called wardriving, a user drives around an urban area, say a business district, looking for and noting all open networks in that area. If the wardriver wants to share this information, he or she might engage in war chalking buildings to tell other wireless users there is an open network here. Wardriving and war chalking encourage and facilitate the exploitation of open networks, and the use of open networks is problematic for law enforcement when they are used to commit crimes online.

Wardriving (*See* **war chalking**).

Web-based e-mail An e-mail account that is accessed by logging onto a Web page instead of using an e-mail program that connects using POP and SMTP. Examples of Web-based e-mail providers are Yahoo! Hotmail, and MSN.

Web/IP spoofs When hackers create a false or shadow copy of a legitimate Web site that looks just like the real one, with all the same pages and links. All network traffic between the victim's browser and the spoofed site are funneled through the hackers machine.

White Hat Hacker A person who identifies weaknesses in a computer system or network but, instead of taking advantage of it, exposes the weakness to the system's owners and recommends a fix before the flaw can be taken advantage of by others.

WHOIS Query On the Internet, domain name information and IP address information can be tracked using a WHOIS query. There are many agencies that are responsible for the sale and registration of IP addresses and domain names. The most wide-reaching agency is the American Registry for Internet Numbers (ARIN) and can be accessed by going to www.arin.net. Investigators can type any domain name or IP address into the WHOIS search function, and the databases of registry will provide registration information, including what company owns or maintains a given IP address or range of addresses.

Wi-fi Short for *wireless fidelity*, a wireless local area network that relies on the transmission of high-frequency radio signals instead of transmitting the data along wires or cable. Data is sent and received via a wireless network card's antenna.

Wisconsin* v. *Robins A landmark case debating prosecution of online child enticement when there is no actual victim. Some defendants have attempted to argue that they should not be charged as a result of law enforcement child enticement stings because no actual victim exists. They argue that they had been communicating with an adult (the undercover officer) and therefore there was no ability or intent to harm a child. These defense arguments have been routinely defeated as courts generally determine that, although no actual child victim exists, the defendant did not know that at the time, and therefore the defendant's intent remained the same. This is similar to many cases that are charged as an attempted crime. The mere fact that the defendant is either incompetent or unsuccessful is not a valid defense against charges.

Workplace Search An exception to the search warrant requirement that allows private persons and/or employers to conduct searches on their own during their normal course of duty, or in conjunction with a work-related misconduct investigation, or other noninvestigatory work-related purpose, and any criminal material discovered can be turned over to law enforcement.

Work Product Materials A term commonly used in referencing the Privacy Protection Act, these are items which are seized during an investigation that are not directly related to the crime and are not evidence or contraband, but have a legitimate business purpose. Work products are materials that are legal and legitimate in nature. Depriving a business of legitimate materials can cause the business financial harm, and under the Privacy Protection Act investigators must be careful to return these legitimate items to the business with minimal delay.

Worms Computer programs designed to automatically make copies of themselves. Unlike viruses, a worm is self-executing, largely invisible to computer users, and spread from computer to computer over a network without any user action.

Write Blocker A device installed on the suspect's hard drive or other media that completely prevents the forensic examiner from writing any data to the hard drive or media. It simply makes it physically impossible by blocking the wires that would communicate the data to be written to the drive. In other words, it is like a one-way valve allowing all traffic from the drive and no traffic to it. Write blockers are available for every type of hard drive (including Serial ATA) and USB devices such as thumb drives and digital cameras.

Index

for high-tech evidence, 260–270
for ISP records, 166–177
records retention letter/data preservation request,
168, 174–176
secrecy around, 168
timeliness of, 168, 174
Subscription fraud, 111, 114
Surveillance, for narcotics investigations, 124
Suspect user accounts, gathering records on, 162–164
Suspects, proving guilt of, 177
Swap files, 37, 299
Syntax, 31
System clock, changing, 48–49
System configuration. *See also* Computer systems
preserving, 282–284
System crashes, 34–35
System memory, 10
System resource management, 36–37

T

Technology, evolving nature of, 279
Teens, sexual exploitation of, 203
Temporary files, storage of, 46–47
Terabytes, 2
Terra Server, USA, Web site, 230
Terrorism, 133–137
crime Web sites on, 229–230
versus cyberterrorism, 139
definition of, 133
domestic, 133–135
first responders as front line against, 139–150
international, 133–134
Internet use for, 120, 135–136
steganography and, 136–137
USA PATRIOT Act and, 258–260
Terry stops, 54
Text-based user interfaces, 30–31
Threats, 53–59
crime Web sites on, 221–222
definition of, 54
Three strikes laws, 123
Thumb drives, 16–17
Timestamps on e-mail messages, 159
Totse, 227
Tower, 4–6
Tracing, 333
Tracking a Computer Hacker (U.S. Attorney's Office),
166–167
Tracking the Threat Web site, 230
Trojan horses, 129
True name fraud, 64–65
Truth in Caller ID Act, 104
2600 Magazine Web site, 227–228

U

Ulitmate Toolkit (AccessData), 310
Uniform Resource Locator (URL), 23
Uninterruptible power supply (UPS), 286
for forensics lab, 313
United States Intelligence Community Web site, 233
United States of America v. Rene Martin Verdugo-Urquidez, 239–240
United States of America v. Shelby Lemmons, 243
United States of America v. Stephen W. Grimmett, 270
United States v. Barth, 253
United States v. Jacobsen, 252
United States v. O'Razvi, 256
United States v. Ortiz, 250
United States v. Reyes, 250
United States v. Robinson, 249–250
Universal serial bus (USB), 9
University of Dayton Law School Cybercrimes Web site, 229
University of Dayton Law School Professor Susan Brenner Web site, 222
U.S. Department of Justice Identity Theft and Fraud Web site, 224
U.S. Secret Service eInformation Network Web site, 225
U.S. v. Smith, 244–245
U.S. v. Turner, 244
USA PATRIOT Act, high-tech investigations and, 258–260
USB 2.0, 9
USB keys, 16–17
USB thumb drives, 38
User friendliness, 40
User interfaces, text-based, 30–31
User interfacing, 39–40
User name/user ID, 333
User settings, storage of, 46

V

Vice Lords street gang, 69
Vicinage, 53
Victims' rights legislation, 130
Videoconferencing, criminal use of, 165
Vigilante justice groups, 201
Virtual RAM, 37
Viruses, 21, 129, 333
Virutal child pornography. *See also* Child pornography
definition of, 202
Voice over IP (VoIP), 165
Voice recognition software, 98–99